CAS Paper 2

Volume I

The future of upland Britain

Proceedings of a symposium
held at the University of Reading
in September 1977

Edited by R B Tranter

Centre for Agricultural Strategy
University of Reading
2 Earley Gate
Reading RG6 2AU

November 1978

ISBN 0 7049 0605 8
ISSN   0141 1330

Printed at the College of Estate Management, Reading

The Centre for Agricultural Strategy was established by the Nuffield
Foundation on the campus of the University of Reading in October 1975.

STAFF

Director Professor J C Bowman

Research officers Mr C J Doyle
Mr J L Jollans
Mr C J Robbins
Mr R B Tranter

Information officer Mrs R B Weiss

Secretaries Mrs A Watts
Mrs M Hubbard

LOCAL COMMITTEE

Professor A H Bunting
Professor C W N Miles
Professor C R W Spedding

ADVISORY COMMITTEE

Professor J Ashton
Sir Kenneth Blaxter
Professor D K Britton
Mr B D Hayes
Mr J Maddox
Mr J E Moffitt
Sir Harry Pitt
Professor C R W Spedding

Contents

5

Volume Two:

Abbreviations and metric equivalents

ABBREVIATIONS

COUNTRIES AND ORGANISATIONS

ADAS	Agricultural Development and Advisory Service
BSC	British Steel Corporation
BTA	British Travel Association
CoSIRA	Council for Small Industries in Rural Areas
CSWDB	Central Scotland Water Development Board
DAFS	Department of Agriculture for Scotland
DANI	Department of Agriculture for Northern Ireland
DoE	Department of the Environment
EC	European Community
ERA	Electrical Research Association Limited
GB	Great Britain
HFRO	Hill Farming Research Organisation
HIDB	Highlands and Islands Development Board
ISM	International Symposia on Molinology
ITE	Institute of Terrestrial Ecology
MAFF	Ministry of Agriculture, Fisheries and Food
MLC	Meat and Livestock Commission
NCC	Nature Conservancy Council
NEDO	National Economic Development Office
NFU	National Farmers' Union
NPA	National Park Authority
NPRDB	Northern Pennines Rural Development Board
NRDC	National Research and Development Corporation
OPCS	Office of Population, Censuses and Surveys
RPS	Rural Planning Services Limited
RTZ	Rio Tinto Zinc Corporation Limited
RWA	Regional Water Authority
SPAB	Society for the Preservation of Ancient Buildings
UK	United Kingdom
US	United States of America
WESCO	Wind Energy Supply Company
WNWDA	Welsh National Water Development Authority

OTHER ABBREVIATIONS

AC	Alternating current
AMWS	Annual mean windspeed
BHC	Benzene hexachloride
C	Celsius
CAP	Common Agricultural Policy
d	Day
DC	Direct current
EHF	Experimental Husbandry Farm
F	Fahrenheit
FCGS	Farm Capital Grant Scheme
FHDS	Farm and Horticulture Development Scheme
GMT	Greenwich Mean Time
h	Hour
IDC	Industrial Development Certificate
LASDO	Landscape Areas Special Development Order

8

LCS	Livestock, cattle and sheep	
LEDU	Local Enterprise Development Unit	
LMS	Livestock, mainly sheep	
NFI	Net Farm Income	
p	Pence	
pa	Per annum	
psi	Pounds per square inch	
REP	Regional Employment Premium	
rpm	Revolutions per minute	
rps	Revolutions per second	
s	Second	
SDA	Special Development Area	
SMD	Standard Man Days	
tcmd	Thousands of cubic metres per day	
ua	Units of Account	

WEIGHTS AND MEASURES

g	gramme	$- 10^{-3}\,kg$
kg	kilogramme	
l	litre	$- 10^{-3}\,m^3$
Ml	megalitre	$- 10^6\,l$
mm	millimetre	$- 10^{-3}\,m$
m	metre	
km	kilometre	$- 10^3\,m$
ha	hectare	$- 10^4\,m^2$
W	watt	$- kg\,m^2 s^{-3}$
kW	kilowatt	$- 10^3\,W$
mW	megawatt	$- 10^6\,W$
J	joule	$- kg\,m^2 s^{-2}$
MJ	megajoule	$- 10^6\,J$
GJ	gigajoule	$- 10^9\,J$
TJ	terajoule	$- 10^{12}\,J$

METRIC MEASURES AND EQUIVALENTS

1g	=	0.0353 ounces
1kg	=	2.2046 lbs
1 tonne	=	2204.6 lbs = 0.9842 tons
1 cm^3	=	0.0610 cubic inches
1 l	=	0.21997 gallons = 1.75975 pints
1 m^2	=	10.764 square feet
1 ha	=	2.47105 acres
1 J	=	0.239 calories (thermochemical)
1 mm	=	0.039 inches
1 m	=	3.281 feet
1 km	=	0.621 miles

1 Preface

J C BOWMAN

The "Future of upland Britain" is the title of a working symposium, held at the University of Reading in September 1977 and organised jointly by the Department of Agriculture and Horticulture of the University of Reading and the Centre for Agricultural Strategy. The purpose of the symposium was to arrange a multi-disciplinary discussion about the problems and the future of marginal land areas in the UK. The organisers hoped that some indications of the important long-term objectives for these areas might emerge from the meeting but it was anticipated that coherent strategies would not be formulated in the time available.

There have been several meetings in recent years on aspects of hill farming and other upland problems. Some good ideas have emerged and a great deal of sound action has taken place on the ground. Nonetheless, there are still problems, difficulties and conflicts. In these circumstances a continuing dialogue between all interested and involved parties is desirable and may lead to a better under-standing, if not a resolution, of competing claims. The problems do not affect only the people who live in the uplands but also those who visit the uplands. Indeed, all are affected by what happens there. Water, power, wool and timber are supplied from those areas to the whole population and the uplands are important for recreation, tourism and conservation. Therefore, the uplands are a national, indeed a European, concern.

Though the experience of the symposium organisers is predominantly agricultural, their interests are much broader and they did not wish the agricultural elements of the problem to receive undue emphasis. They wished to consider the "Future of upland Britain" in a national perspective. The UK as a whole is one of the most densely populated areas of the world and yet people in parts of it, the uplands and marginal lands, suffer materially because of under-population. There are competing, and indeed conflicting, demands for the use of the uplands and some uses are at best unhelpful, if not a positive disincentive, to maintaining or providing an acceptable standard of life for those who wish to live there. The major activity in the uplands is usually identified as farming and, for this reason, the main method for injecting national and regional financial support is by means of agricultural grants and loans. It is appreciated that this method of support may be a disincentive both to the existing farmers in the uplands to develop and engage in new productive activities and to others who wish to use the uplands for purposes other than farming. Some forms of farming support may encourage abandonment of farming methods which some organisations are doing their very best to conserve. There are those who believe that the agricultural output of the uplands could easily be obtained with less government support by judicious financial support of lowland farms. Therefore it is argued that hill farming support is provided to achieve social and not agricultural objectives. It then becomes necessary for the social objectives in the uplands to be defined clearly. If government wishes to foster social objectives in these areas are hill farming subsidies the most effective form of support and incentive?

This line of argument broadens the consideration of the "Future of upland Britain" and a whole range of questions seems relevant:

What sort of social structure and population density should be supported?

What activities — forestry, water and power supplies, rural industry, mineral extraction, recreation, tourism and conservation as well as farming — can make use of land in the uplands and to what extent should each and all of them be fostered?

What constraints do these activities place on each other?

Is the infrastructure right for the development of upland areas for a multiplicity of activities?

How can evolution of activities and methods and conservation be fostered simultaneously?

Who should pay for the support of the several activities and how should any support be applied?

It is quite clear from these questions that the problems of upland areas require simultaneous multi-disciplinary consideration. Also the nature of the problems means that it will take many years to solve them. In seeking solutions, and particularly if forestry is an important element in the future, the time-scale of development and change will need to be a long one. As a guide to discusssion the symposium used the period to the year 2000 as the future under study, though for forestry a much longer period of 50 years ahead was taken into account.

The symposium was structured in the following way. Three plenary papers were invited on the history of the uplands, the European Community experience and the Swiss experience of upland development (Papers 53-55). These provided an introduction to nine simultaneous Workshops in which participants discussed the upland problem in specialist groups. As a basis for these Workshops, 51 papers were invited from experienced people and were distributed to participants in advance of the symposium. Papers were discussed and not formally presented. The nine Workshops were Agriculture (Papers 2-7), Forestry (Papers 8-13), Recreation and Tourism (Papers 14-20), Industrial Activities (Papers 21-25), Water Supply (Papers 26-30), Power Supply (Papers 31-34), Conservation and Ecology (Papers 35-40), Social, Economic and Political Structures (Papers 41-46) and Policies (Papers 47-52). After a full day of discussion the chairmen of Workshops I were asked to summarise their impressions. These résumés (Appendix I) were copied so that each participant received a full set the next day. The participants were re-grouped into five multi-disciplinary Workshops II each with members of all nine Workshops I. Workshops II were invited to discuss the uplands according to the format given in Appendix II. At the end of a full day's discussion the five chairmen were asked to summarise their impressions and these (Appendix III) were presented to the closing session of the symposium together with a concluding paper (Appendix IV). It must be emphasised that the résumés given by workshop chairmen are their personal contemporary impressions of the discussions which took place. In no way are they an attempt to summarise the agreed view of participants. Indeed, it is known that some participants would have expressed very different impressions had they been in the chair. However, I consider the résumés are valuable in expressing many of the difficulties of the uplands even if their priorities and their solutions were not agreed. Perhaps of major interest is the view expressed by all Workshop II chairmen that a greater responsibility and the necessary finance for solving local problems should be devolved by central government to local people.

The symposium was a useful exchange of opinions and ideas between those with a common interest in upland problems. It was a surprise to the organisers that some of these people had not previously met or discussed together this subject; long may the dialogue continue.

The organisers would like to take this opportunity of expressing their gratitude to all who participated in the symposium and who have contributed to these volumes. Richard Tranter, who carried the main burden of organisation with a great deal of patience, good humour and careful attention to detail, deserves a special note of gratitude. Thanks are also due to Jane Boddington, Vicky Short and Victoria Withers Green for secretarial assistance, to Sheila Bowman for proof reading and to John Armstrong and his team at the printers.

2 Some agronomic problems and prospects for upland Britain

G J F COPEMAN

INTRODUCTION

Many agronomic problems are basically common to both the lowlands and uplands of Britain. In most cases, however, the causes and effects of these problems are more severe in the uplands. Soil conditions are generally poorer both physically and in terms of available nutrients. The climate is also in general more adverse. Deficiency of rainfall is an exception in that drought is seldom experienced in in the uplands other than for short periods, although excessive precipitation is a problem particularly where drainage is poor.

A major difficulty in discussing the uplands is that using any reasonable definition they are situated from the south west of England to the northernmost point of the Scottish mainland and beyond to the Orkney & Shetland Isles. The climatic, vegetational, physical and other characteristics of the uplands therefore vary enormously. Common to all areas, however, is the relative shortness of the growing season during which fodder must be produced to provide keep for the whole year. Whereas in the most favoured areas of lowland Britain farmers are faced with providing winterkeep for only four months or less, in the worst of the uplands the winter feeding period may last for seven months or more. This has a major impact on the agronomic problems faced.

The alternatives open to upland farmers as to what enterprises they can engage in and crops they can grow are very restricted. Because of the shortness of the growing season and bad harvesting conditions cereal cropping is hazardous. The introduction of earlier maturing varieties and the availability of combine harvesters over the last twenty years have presented some relief particularly as to the increased cost, including transport, of feeding stuffs 'imported' from the lowlands and elsewhere in recent times. Nevertheless, the scope for expansion of cereal growing is very limited. The adoption of new methods of housing such as slatted floors and cubicles has reduced the requirement for straw for bedding and will continue to do so.

While upland farming must continue to be primarily concerned with breeding and rearing livestock, there is considerable scope for carrying through stock thus produced to a finished condition on a wider scale, so keeping more of the potential overall profit from birth to slaughter within upland areas. Brassicaceous crops have a greater role to play in this connection particularly for finishing lambs.

Grassland, interpreted broadly to cover also 'rough grazings', which may in fact consist predominantly of non-graminaceous species, will continue to be by far the most important source of fodder in the uplands. Two further complications arise in any discussion of upland grassland. Firstly, the proportion of rough grazing to fairly easily cultivated land varies greatly. In Scotland, farms classified as 'hill sheep' on average are 97% rough grazings, whereas 'rearing with arable' have only 20% of their acreage as rough. Many upland farms have no access to hill outrun at all. Secondly, the quality of the rough grazings varies enormously. They range from relatively good *Agrostis-Festuca* swards with white clover to blanket bog communities dominated by poor quality *Calluna-Eriophorum-Trichophorum* and *Sphagnum* moss.

If agriculture is to prosper in the uplands it is imperative that the 'grassland' resource must be exploited to the full by managing 'in-bye' grass well and by improving more rough grazings. It is essential that improved pastures should also be managed well because in many instances if the improvement is not maintained the area may revert to a condition from which it is more difficult to reclaim than was the original. Many of the agronomic problems involved are broadly similar on 'in-bye' and other grazings.

THE LENGTH OF GROWING SEASON AND WINTERHARDINESS
The shortness of the growing season is a major problem. Since the war considerable effort has been made at plant breeding stations, in the UK particularly, to produce varieties which will continue to grow when others will not. Two examples of this were the production of Aberystwyth S321 perennial ryegrass and Syn 1 and Syn 2 tall fescues at Cambridge. While S321 has an exceptional capacity for autumn growth it is not winterhardy, a factor of special importance in the uplands. Table 1 shows the percentage winter damage occurring in this variety compared with two Dutch varieties, Talbot and Perma, at the North of Scotland College of Agriculture's farm in the uplands of Banffshire.

Table 1
WINTER DAMAGE TO PERENNIAL RYEGRASS VARIETIES AT
CLASHNOIR FARM, BANFFSHIRE (WINTER 1974-75)

Variety	%damage
Aberystwyth S321	46.33
Talbot	18.42
Perma	12.92
SED	±3.88

Source: North of Scotland College of Agriculture (unpublished data).

The two varieties of tall fescue referred to also had a capacity to grow outwith the normal season but suffered from a lack of winterhardiness. Even among varieties which do not have a particular capacity to grow out-on-season there are marked differences in hardiness. As the use of nitrogen fertiliser tends to predispose swards to winter damage, the importance of using hardy varieties becomes greater as intensification of management proceeds.

While there is also a difference between varieties of Italian ryegrass, this species which otherwise would be useful in the uplands for its potential for spring growth, is relatively susceptible to winter damage and is of little use. Cocksfoot is not normally regarded as lacking in hardiness but in the severe winter of 1976-7 two new varieties from Aberystwyth, Saborto and Cambria, which originate from material collected in the Iberian peninsula, showed a high degree of damage compared with other established varieties. While cocksfoot has become unfashionable in lowland areas because it has an inferior feeding value and is difficult to manage, it has a value in the uplands on three counts. It has a capacity to grow in spring, it has a lower fertility requirement than ryegrass and can be conserved *in situ* as foggage in the autumn.

The importance of hardiness in a variety is now recognised and close co-operation exists between the Welsh Plant Breeding Station and the North of Scotland College of Agriculture. At an early stage in breeding programmes material is grown on in Upper Banffshire and surviving plants are returned for further development. This enterprise is bearing fruit and in future less reliance should have to be put on foreign bred varieties.

THE VALUE AND LIMITATIONS OF WHITE CLOVER
The value of white clover to the uplands will be elaborated later. One of its limitations is that it makes little contribution to the herbage available in spring and autumn. Little effort has been made hitherto to investigate the possibilities

of breeding a variety with a potential to grow earlier in the season. Compared with better grasses it also stops growth earlier in autumn. Overall its season of growth is about 3 weeks less in spring and a fortnight less in autumn. Not only does this limit its potential annual production but it also places clover at a grave disadvantage compared with the grasses against which it has to compete. Large intra-specific variations have been noted to exist for growth at low temperatures in white clover.

Hardiness in white clover is a subject on which information is almost totally lacking, probably because of the difficulty in assessing it. If wide variations exist within other species it is not unreasonable to expect that differences must occur between varieties of white clover. To what extent do these contribute to the variability of its performance in practice?

White clover has two functions. Not only does it contribute directly to grass production and through it to animal production, but it also has the ability to live in a symbiotic relationship with rhizobial bacteria which are able to fix atmospheric nitrogen and convert it into a form useful to the clover and other plants. There is ample evidence that cattle and sheep consuming diets rich in white clover will perform better than they would on grasses alone. In any system which has a relatively low output, it is particularly important to minimise inputs and any saving on nitrogen fertiliser will help in this direction.

Potential dry matter production from grassland is greater where high rates of nitrogen fertiliser are applied. While there is scope for applying greater quantities on 'in-bye' grassland especially to grass for conservation as silage and for increasing grazing at strategic times of the season, reliance must lean towards clover nitrogen in many upland situations. However, farmers frequently rely on white clover which is only present in small quantities and far below the optimum content. The establishment and maintenance of white clover rich pastures is no easy matter and too little is known of the causes for its failure and about how to improve its reliability.

An important factor is the performance of the rhizobial bacteria which fix the nitrogen. There are many gaps in our knowledge here also. The Scottish Agricultural Colleges, Hill Farming Research Organisation, the Agricultural Advisory & Development Service and Welsh Plant Breeding Station currently have an extensive programme to assess the value of innoculating clover seed with appropriate strains of bacteria. While there are preliminary indications that this may be worthwhile under wet, very peaty conditions where improvement may be undesirable for other reasons in any case, there is little to suggest that using present techniques it has value elsewhere.

The highest priority should be given to research and development designed to improve the performance of white clover. The success of such a programme would have an impact in lowland agriculture as well as in the uplands.

SOIL FERTILITY

Hill and upland soils are inherently low in fertility. They are usually very acid and unlike many areas of New Zealand require heavy applications of lime or other neutralising materials in order to bring about and maintain improvement in various categories of grassland. Several tonnes per hectare are required. Transportation costs are high and the use of aircraft is precluded.

Phosphate is almost invariably deficient naturally. Traditionally, basic slag, a byproduct of steel making, has been used for rectifying large deficiencies. Not only does it have a high phosphate content but it also has a neutralising value and contains valuable trace elements. New steel making processes eliminate the production of slag and other forms of phosphate are generally considered to be less effective.

Potash, the other major nutrient normally applied to farm crops, is less often seriously deficient in hill soils. While other elements are seldom limiting in so far as the growth of herbage itself is concerned, deficiencies can have a profound effect on the performance and health of animals eating it. The non-availability of slag, the use of more concentrated fertilisers which are cheaper to transport, greater reliance on on-farm produced feeds with less bought in, and more intensive use of pastures will undoubtedly exacerbate problems associated with trace element deficiencies. The soil/plant/animal relationships are complex and it will take considerable research and development effort to solve the problems increasingly encountered.

Hill and upland soils are generally deficient in available nitrogen. Reference has already been made to the value of white clover in the nitrogen economy of these soils. Many upland farmers are successfully using rates of nitrogen fertiliser on their better grass similar to those used by progressive colleagues in the lowlands. There is scope for increasing nitrogen use. This is not incompatible with other upland interests. No farmer in his right mind wants to apply fertiliser in such quantity or fashion that a high proportion is leached or washed off into drains and watercourses.

WINTERKEEP

Possibilities for lengthening the grazing season by fertiliser treatment or the use of specially adapted grasses are limited. A wiser policy is to concentrate on optimising grass production during the normal growing season and to minimise losses in the processes of conserving it for winter use.

Silage making has many advantages over hay making in the uplands as elsewhere. Most upland areas have a high rainfall which makes the winning of a good quality hay crop unlikely. Silage is less dependent on good weather and is an important tool in intensive grassland management. Production of hay per unit area is limited by comparison with silage because heavily fertilised grass is very difficult to cure into hay. Mouldy hay is a health hazard to humans and animals. Over the past twenty years there has been a steady swing from hay to silage. Figures for England and Wales do not appear to be available, but in Scotland several counties particularly in the north with a high proportion of uplands, now cut more hectares for silage than for hay. In the county of Orkney which is generally classified as all upland this situation now prevails.

Over the British uplands as a whole however, hay is still the main source of winterkeep. For sheep, well made hay is a more satisfactory feed than silage and is certainly more easily handled at the feeding stage. Nevertheless, the making of good hay under upland conditions is extremely difficult. The acreage of hay made on any farm is relatively small and labour scarce. Speeding up of the curing process, essential to securing good hay, is dependent on machinery primarily designed for large scale operation in the drier lowlands. Barn-drying techniques in which hay is partially dried in the field and finished with air blown through it, also presents exceptional problems in the uplands. The initial field curing is difficult and the ambient air used in the second part of the process has a relatively low temperature and high humidity. The only way to overcome these problems is to apply artificial heat and this soon becomes uneconomic. The process is also difficult to mechanise.

The use of chemical additives for preserving hay has developed in recent years. At best they permit the storage of hay at only a very slightly higher moisture content than normal and their value is thus limited. It is fair to say however that the best of them depress mould development and this must be beneficial in terms of health.

If these comments on the chances of improving haymaking techniques in the uplands appear pessimistic, no apology is made. The problems are particularly intractable.

LAND IMPROVEMENT

The value of unimproved hill grazings is very low by any standards. Dry matter production may range from 3 000 to less than 500 kg per hectare per annum as against 15 000 to 5 000 kg from grass elsewhere. Furthermore, quality is poor in terms of digestibility, energy, protein and mineral content and is generally well below the level required for ewe and cow maintenance for long periods of the year.

In the hills, ewe nutrition is the most important factor influencing output. While it is particularly critical at certain times such as mating, late pregnancy and

19

during lactation, there is a need for its general improvement. The key to a better nutritional cycle for the grazing animal lies in pasture improvement. The many beneficial effects on both sheep and cattle are well documented.

The most widely adopted method of improvement has been ploughing and reseeding. Controversy often arises as to whether this is the best technique where it is possible to plough, or whether a cheaper method with minimal cultivation would suffice. No generalisation should be made as circumstances vary very considerably. In many instances, ploughing allows the production of a sward which may eventually be cut for conservation or of land which can later be used for growing an alternative crop to grass once fertility has been built up.

Excessive disruption of the surface as by ploughing or rotovation may, particularly in wet conditions, lead to conditions in which the resown sward may rapidly deteriorate. Many areas are uncultivatable due to wetness, stones, topography and other factors. Here surface treatment can be very effective. Where there is a nucleus of naturally occurring higher quality species, especially of white clover, the use of lime and phosphate alone can produce a marked improvement at low cost. Where the species present are of low quality they may have to be destroyed or checked by chemicals or burning, prior to the sowing of superior species. Under some circumstances surface sowing without previous treatment or cultivation is possible.

While considerable areas of rough grazings have already been improved, there is still much scope for improvement. While constraints on expansion of these areas tend to be other than technical ones, further development of techniques is required in order to reduce costs and to ensure a better establishment of sown grasses and more especially white clover.

The importance of good management and maintaining fertility after initial establishment is frequently overlooked. Often after the first flush of enthusiasm, farmers fail to follow through and swards deteriorate quickly. A much better return from the initial investment would be gained if a policy of regular maintenance dressings of lime and phosphate was adopted. The control of grazing by fencing is also important both from the points of view of the nutrition of stock and the maintenance of the sward in productive condition.

CONCLUSIONS

This paper does not purport to cover all the agronomic problems of the uplands. It highlights some of the most important and indicates certain prospects. As in many sectors of the agricultural industry, the prime need is to get existing knowledge more widely adopted in practice. While research must continue for the future, the most immediate impact would be possible through the development and promotion of better grassland management and conservation techniques and of the wider use of brassicaceous crops.

The reasons for the slower than desirable adoption of the best techniques tend to be non-technical and are more concerned with financial, sociological and psychological considerations and not least with lack of confidence in future prospects.

3 The impact of technical advances on hill and upland sheep production

J EADIE & A D M SMITH

INTRODUCTION

There are 5.43 million ha of 'hill' land in Great Britain; that is land which is included in 'hill sheep' and 'upland' farms in Scotland, and, in the North of England and Wales, farms classified as 'livestock, mainly sheep', and 'livestock, cattle and sheep'. Of the 5.43 million ha, 3.95 million ha are rough grazings and the remainder grass and tillage.

The land supports some 7.8 million breeding ewes of which 5.5 million are on hill farms and 2.3 million on upland farms. Some 16 500 full time holdings employ an estimated 27 500 workers in addition to the farmers and their wives.

The existing pattern of agricultural land use in the hills and uplands of Great Britain has been set by the interplay of many factors. These include soils, climate, topography, remoteness and economic and social history, as well as changing technical possibilities.

The soils and climate of the hills dictate that the growth of plants for agricultural production, including grazing, tends to be depressed by virtue of short and cold growing seasons. Crop harvesting, including grass conservation, is more difficult and less certain than in the lowlands, and winter weather is a more severe constraint on animal production. Topography acts directly on agricultural possibilities by limiting access, and slope constrains land improvement and contributes to increased machinery costs and interacts with climate to increase exposure.

These basic factors combine to determine that hill and upland agriculture is primarily devoted to livestock production from grazing animals, based on the year round maintenance of breeding flocks and herds whose progeny, except for replacements, are disposed of before winter begins.

The basically less favourable physical input/output relationships are exacerbated in their economic effects by remoteness, both from supply points and markets. Remoteness has tended to disadvantage paid labour relative to family labour and to consolidate the effects of modest profitability (and perhaps of a predominantly animal agriculture) in determining that hill and upland farming is typically family farming, and an industry of comparatively small farm businesses.

Inadequate size of operation is the fundamental source of the economic problems of the hills and uplands and, as Allen (1973) points out, if the difference in land values does not reflect the disadvantages of location, the explanation lies in the number of hill and upland farmers competing with each other for holdings which are commonly too small. At the levels of Government support of the last decade or so farm level input/output relationships are not significantly different from those of other types of farming. The net income disadvantage of the hill and upland farmers is accounted for, in the main, by the generally smaller size of farm business.

Farm business size can be increased by amalgamation and by intensification. Structural change will continue, but on past experience its pace will be comparatively slow. Intensification would appear to offer a more hopeful line of approach and one which is in line with the aspirations for the hills and uplands expressed in *Food from our own resources* (MAFF, 1975).

Government interventions have been, and continue to be, crucial to the modest profitability of hill and upland farming. They help to sustain the stratification system by which hill and upland sheep farming are inter-linked to each other and to lowground sheep production. From time to time the maintenance of the stratified structure of the sheep industry is called into question, usually on the basis of arguments to do with the magnitude of Government payments to hill sheep production or to do with the expansion of forestry in the hills. It has however been calculated (MLC, 1972) that the replacement of the sheep output of the hills by means of a self-sufficient lowland sheep population would require an additional 3 million lowland ewes. In the light of the size of the lowland area which would have to be diverted from other forms of agricultural production it is reasonably safe to assume a continuation well into the future of the present stratification system.

It is important to recognise that home production of mutton and lamb has never even remotely matched the demand. Decreasing imports from New Zealand, together with a growing export of fresh lamb carcasses to EC countries promise to maintain for the sheep industry its almost unique freedom from demand problems. The long term prospects for sheep seem as secure as anything can be in a rapidly changing world, whose few predictable elements include the high value to be attached to indigenous sources of food.

TECHNICAL ADVANCES

There seems little prospect that technical advances will significantly alter the dominant influence of climate on the length of the growing season or on the difficulty of harvesting crops in the hills and uplands. These quite basic constraints will remain to determine that the framework within which the impact of technical advance has to be examined will remain that of livestock rearing.

The sheep will continue to benefit from its ability to select for itself, from grazed pasture, a winter diet which makes a much greater contribution to its requirements than the beef cow is able to do, particularly in periods of snow cover. The economic value of this attribute will continue to give the sheep a competitive edge over the beef cow on hill farms in particular.

The range of sheep production systems in the hills and uplands varies from those based entirely on rough grazings to systems which largely utilise upland sown pasture. Between these extremes, circumstances are found in which hill ewes spend varying amounts of time between October and June on enclosed pasture at lower elevation. Likewise rough grazings play a widely varying role in upland systems.

Most hill sheep farms utilise self-replenishing stocks of one or other of the pure hill breeds. On some hill sheep farms an attempt is made to utilise hybrid vigour through the periodic use of rams of another hill breed, whilst on some of the better hills another breed may be used to produce a proportion of cross-bred lambs. Upland farms typically use a half-bred such as the Greyface, one of the Mules or the Welsh half-bred. Others may use draft hill ewes either to produce store/fat lambs, or cross-bred females for further breeding. On some upland farms purebreds such as the Clun find favour.

For the purpose of this discussion it is convenient to consider hill sheep and upland sheep systems separately even though such a discrete sub-division over-simplifies what is in fact a continuum, and ignores the variations which take place around these two major themes.

HILL SHEEP SYSTEMS

Very great advances have been made in the last two decades or so in our understanding of hill sheep, the indigenous pastures which provide the major part of their food supply and the interactions between them.

It is now well recognised that the major determinant of sheep performance in the hills is nutrition. The significance of improving nutrition in pregnancy to lamb mortality and subsequent lamb growth (Russel, 1967); the importance of better quality ingested pasture feed to improving milk yield (Peart, 1970) and lamb growth (Armstrong & Eadie, 1973); and the role of previous and contemporary nutrition on reproductive performance (Doney & Gunn, 1973) are all now well understood and documented. Current research is consolidating this understanding and contributing to a quantification of response and improved predictability.

Major advances have also been made in the evaluation of the productivity and nutritive value of the economically important indigenous pasture types and in understanding their ecology. An analysis of the biology of the hill sheep problem and a synthesis of the available knowledge leading to improved systems of hill sheep production has been made (Eadie, 1970). These improved systems are currently being evaluated in practical-scale tests in the Hill Farming Research Organisation (HFRO) and elsewhere (eg Redesdale EHF).

A central feature of these improved systems is hill land improvement. The various constraints on land improvement arising out of topography — access and slope — and out of economic considerations which have to do with the short-term cash flow consequences of capital expenditures, (Maxwell, Eadie & Sibbald, 1973) dictate that the improved pasture component of any development scheme is comparatively small. The management strategy of these two-component systems aims to maximise the impact on individual sheep performance of the comparatively small amount of improved land.

Very substantial improvements both in total output and animal performance have been demonstrated in widely contrasting hill environments. Table 1 summarises the output and performance changes which have followed from the minimal improvement of some 190 ha of indigenous *Agrostis-Festuca* pasture by fencing in a unit of 283 ha in the Eastern Cheviots. A second phase of improvement involving the addition of 7.2 ha sown pasture and further upgrading of one of the indigenous pasture enclosures began in 1974 (Eadie, Armstrong & Maxwell, 1976).

Table 1

PRODUCTION DATA FROM A TWO-PASTURE YEAR-ROUND GRAZING SYSTEM AT SOURHOPE FARM (283 ha)

	Pre-development	1969	1970	1971	1972	1973	1974	1975
Ewe numbers	387	398	451	518	528	573	600	601
Weaning proportion (per cent)	90.6	84.7	86.5	103.3	104.7	99.5	91.5	102.7
Weight of weaned lambs (kg)	7 924	7 785	9 189	14 178	14 046	14 193	14 329	16 042
Weight of wool (kg)	869	850	1 017	1 253	1 369	1 561	1 454	1 535
Increase in lambs (per cent)	—	− 1.8	16.0	78.9	77.3	79.1	80.8	102.4
Increase in ewes (per cent)	—	2.8	16.5	33.9	36.4	48.1	55.0	55.0
Lamb ha^{-1}	28.0	27.5	32.5	50.1	49.6	50.2	50.6	56.7

A similar study is being carried out on blanket peat in Argyll, where the improved pasture component comprises surface seeding both in wholly fenced areas and in a mosaic of improved patches throughout large enclosures of indigenous pasture. A 405 ha unit whose traditional stock carry was some 200 ewes, weaning some 60% of lambs, now carries around 450 ewes weaning around 95% (Eadie, Maxwell & Currie, 1976).

Existing knowledge provides a wide range of techniques for the replacement of indigenous hill vegetation by sown grass and clover (Newbould, 1976). Current and projected work will almost certainly lead to a more accurate definition of the chemical and physical characteristics of soils which limit herbage growth and production. This information, together with advances in plant nutrition, may well lead to better criteria for the selection of sites for improvement and to a reduction in the costs of, and a greater degree of predictability and effectiveness in, land improvement procedures.

Improved varieties of grass may well result from the inclusion of hill and upland sites in herbage evaluation trials, and current attempts to breed clover varieties for hill conditions may result in plants better adapted to the late springs and colder summers of the hills. It seems likely too that current work on clover nitrogen fixation and rhizobia, some of which takes account of hill environments, will also contribute to pasture productivity and nutritive value.

Continuing work on sheep nutrition will contribute to a more precise understanding of the role of both energy and protein nutrition in reproduction, lactation and lamb growth. Active programmes are being pursued in studies of the digestion and supplementation of poor quality hill herbages in winter, and this work together with studies aimed at a more precise knowledge of requirements throughout pregnancy will provide the basis for a more precise use of feed inputs. Advances are also being made in the trace element nutrition of sheep and fundamental work is increasingly being backed by field studies in the hills and uplands (eg Whitelaw et al, 1977).

The potential significance of genetic improvement has to be seen in the context of the known large responses to nutritional improvement. A largely unresolved question is the extent to which there is a useful amount of heterosis in crosses between the hill breeds. Recent work suggests that it does exist, but at a rather low level (King, 1976). Perhaps the most significant current trend is the attempt being made to introduce the concept of group breeding schemes. But the rate of development is likely to be slow, not least because it involves a degree of breeder co-operation not previously attempted in the UK.

The increasing attention being given to land improvement, together with the substantial differences between store and fat lamb prices in many areas may well further stimulate the trend towards more lamb fattening on greencrop on hill farms. To the extent to which pioneer cropping is encouraged in the process, so land improvement will benefit from a reduction in costs, as the returns from lamb fattening can be set against these costs.

There appear to be good grounds for believing that whilst these various areas of investigation will contribute to the future of sheep production in the hills there is little to suggest a major departure from the development framework now being tested at HFRO and elsewhere with some success. The ideas upon which this is based seem capable of application in a wide range of hill environments and of accommodating many of the regional variations in practice, as well as providing for hill cattle stocks across the possible range of sheep/cattle ratios.

UPLAND SHEEP SYSTEMS

Upland sheep production systems are based importantly, and sometimes exclusively, on enclosed sown pasture. The role of hill land resources in such systems is extremely variable; it is often limited to providing grazing for ewes after lambs are weaned, and in the winter.

The sheep are often crossbreds derived from one or other of the hill breeds, though draft ewes from the hills are also widely used.

A considerable amount of research has been carried out in recent years in increasing litter size and/or lambing frequency in sheep. The application of this knowledge to commercial sheep production in the uplands is unlikely in the near future for a variety of reasons. In particular the nutritional implications of such highly productive systems require substantial increases in the use of feeds of higher energy concentration than grass can provide. It seems very unlikely that the relativities of grass and concentrate costs and lamb prices will conspire to make such systems sufficiently attractive to supplant grass based systems of sheep production on any scale especially in the uplands. It seems much more likely that, for the foreseeable future, developments in sheep production in the uplands will continue to depend on the more efficient use of grass and forage crops.

Although care has to be exercised in interpreting the data, because there is no way of knowing the extent to which the recorded farms are typical or otherwise of the whole population, Meat and Livestock Commission figures confirm other survey evidence that outputs of weaned lamb/ha are substantially lower than outputs obtained in the lowlands (eg 427 cf 636 kg/ha). Stocking rates are much lower in the uplands than in the lowlands (9.1 cf 11.4 ewes/ha) (MLC, 1976 b). Part of the reason for this is undoubtedly poorer levels of pasture production. Apart from the effect of higher altitudes and shorter and colder growing seasons, much upland pasture is renewed much less frequently, and drainage is often poor. Management also tends to be more difficult. Topography constrains the integration of conservation and grazing much more than in the lowlands. Weather conditions often interfere with the all-important timeliness of operations especially for sheep, where hay continues to offer advantages over silage.

Much upland pasture is however capable of improvement given present day techniques. It is noteworthy that the most profitable third of MLC's recorded upland flocks are stocked at an average of 10.4 ewes/ha as compared to the overall mean of 9.1 ewes/ha (MLC, 1976 b). The range of stocking rates observed in recorded flocks suggests that there is a great deal of scope for improvement in pasture production and management in the uplands.

Individual sheep performance in the uplands falls well short of the known potential of the various breeds and crosses commonly used. The number of lambs reared per 100 ewes is on average well below reasonable expectation. MLC data suggests rearing percentages in the region of 125% over a run of years. (MLC, 1977). Data from the same organisation reveals that over 20% of their recorded upland flocks rear fewer than 100 lambs per 100 ewes mated, and 130 lambs reared per 100 ewes mated is exceeded in only 20% of their recorded flocks (MLC, 1976 a). The number of lambs born per 100 ewes mated is the biggest single source of variation in reproductive performance. While recent work with upland Greyface ewes suggests that post-conception nutrition may be a much more important factor in lambing performance than had hitherto been thought (Gunn & Maxwell, personal communication), the application of current information on the effect of body condition on conception rates could considerably improve farm production figures.

Surveys tend to reveal high levels of lamb mortality in upland flocks. Some MLC data indicate that over 34% of their recorded upland flocks lose more than 15% of the live lambs born, and over 16% of them lose more than 20%. Whilst weather conditions in the uplands undoubtedly contribute to these losses, proper attention to nutrition and disease control could do a great deal to improve matters.

Data on lamb growth rates on upland farms are much less readily available. The importance of lamb growth rate varies with the system and marking objectives. It is less crucial to success where lambs are retained on the farm to be fattened on forage crop, as lambs or hoggets, but it is of great importance where lambs are sold off grass either fat or as stores. Lamb growth rate is probably the most satisfactory aspect of upland sheep performance but this is so partly because of the relatively low stocking rates found in practice.

The problem of maintaining high rates of lamb growth at high stocking rates is not yet completely resolved. Despite advances, prophylaxis parasites remain a problem in this context. The work of Rutter (1975) has demonstrated convincingly the value of systems in which sheep and cattle alternate on a year-to-year basis. Better lamb growth rates at higher stocking rates than under conventional management have been achieved and the practice seems likely to become more widely adopted.

Current work on the factors affecting the grazing intake of the sheep, lactation performance in grazing sheep and the relative importance of milk and pasture feed to lamb growth will all contribute to a better understanding of aspects of this major question. Other ongoing research at various centres will continue to provide better quantitative information on relations between nutrition and the other components of upland sheep performance. But, perhaps more importantly, current work at HFRO and elsewhere promises to provide greater insight into what is arguably the central problem of upland sheep production. The selection of a stocking rate for any given set of land resources which will optimise the balance between output per hectare and output per ewe remains a matter of not-too-enlightened guesswork and trial and error. The optimisation in the last analysis has to be judged on economic criteria, but its more objective attainment will only be possible when there is a much fuller understanding of the impact of stocking rate on the pattern of the relationship between feed requirement and feed provision from pasture. Choice of lambing date similarly affects the pattern of that relationship. This understanding is especially important in the short growing seasons of the uplands.

Only in the light of this understanding will it be possible more effectively to utilise the increasing body of information on the various aspects of upland sheep performance, pasture production, and utilisation, to develop improved management strategies aimed at superior, economically worthwhile output.

The multiplicity of breeds and crosses used and the range of upland environments encountered make it unlikely that the rate of genetic improvement in existing upland sheep will be very great in the foreseeable future. The difficulties which face genetic improvement in the hill breeds have already been referred to. The introduction of criteria related to the performance of hill sheep as parents of crossbred ewes for use in the uplands would only further complicate an already difficult matter. Genetic improvement in the ram breeds, eg the Border Leicester is more likely, but work is currently confined to pure-bred flocks.

A more likely development is the use of ram breeds other than the traditional ones, such as the Texel and the Animal Breeding Research Organisation's Dam line as sires of crossbred ewes, and current work on slaughter lamb sire breeds, including the Texel, is likely to lead to a more objective selection of appropriate sire breeds in the future.

An important development in recent years has been the accumulation of data by MLC from recorded flocks in the uplands. The value of the contribution of this body of information to improved management can be expected to increase.

CONCLUSIONS

The existence of technical opportunities does not by any means guarantee that they will be taken up at any speed, or even at all. The time lag in the uptake of research is at best in the region of a decade, and there are many factors in the hills and uplands which combine to suggest that the rate of application of technical advances will be slow.

More extensive agricultures tend to be more conservative and to change more slowly than more intensive systems of farming. Traditional lore and experience play a much larger part in extensive systems, and resistance to change where, historically, change has been limited in extent and slow, is to be expected.

Smaller units tend to be less well-endowed with the know-how and capital on which innovation depends so much. The family nature of hill and upland farming may also tend to slow the pace of change, partly because insufficient capital from family resources is often allied to a very cautious approach to borrowing. It is in the hills where these factors might be thought to operate with greatest force that technical advance requires a deliberate and conscious decision to invest capital in what is to many hill farmers a substantial departure from traditional practice.

Raeburn (1972) points out that the supply prices of family owned capital are comparatively low, and low rates of return tend to be accepted if they are regarded as properly related to the farming system and the family's way of life. But the capital requirements of hill sheep system development are considerable at £5-£15/ewe net cost to the farmer. The wide range of costs depends on the nature of the land to be improved, the means by which it is improved and the degree and extent of the improvement. Although such investment can be shown to be profitable at present costs and prices the longer term nature of the investment requires a judgment by the farmer about the future. Here it must be said that recent changes in capital taxation, the collapse of the cattle market in 1973 and 1974, the problems of the CAP and general economic uncertainty all detract from the confidence so necessary to longer term investment.

The nature of the upland sheep problem is different from that of the hills in a variety of respects. The various factors operating against change probably do so with less force in the uplands. But the major difference lies in the fact that technical advance in the uplands can and does take place in an evolutionary fashion. There is much less of a 'once and for all' major decision to be made, and we can look forward to a steady improvement in the quality of the land resources used, and in the efficiency with which these and other resources are employed in upland sheep production.

Finally, mention must be made of one or two other constraints placed on agricultural development in the hills.

Hill sheep farming's major competitor in the land use sense has been, and will continue to be, forestry. For many years land transfers to forestry did not lead to a reduction in hill sheep stocks, but since 1968 hill sheep numbers in Scotland have declined significantly. This trend is most marked in those counties where afforestation has been most evident.

It has been argued recently (Cunningham *et al*, 1977) that the continuation of afforestation along present lines will be increasingly at the expense of meat ouput, and that the problem of conflict between the future development of hill farming and forestry is more urgent than is generally appreciated. There is both an urgent need, and a new opportunity arising out of the technical advances which have been made in hill farming, to reassess the whole question of agriculture/forestry integration in the hills.

A substantial proportion of the common land in the country is rough grazings. In Scotland the common land is largely in crofting tenure and the special problems of crofting agriculture lie outwith the scope of this paper. In England and Wales the traditional arrangements for the management and regulation of use of common land have in many cases broken down. Registration is proceeding under the Commons Registration Act, 1965, but its pace is slow and because of this and the difficulty of identifying ownership in many cases and the legal complexities surrounding the whole matter, it seems likely that the constraints on agricultural advance on much of the common land will remain for the foreseeable future.

Many of the operations essential to agricultural development in the hills, eg scrub clearance, fencing, etc. affect the texture and the character of the land-scape, create systems of production more sensitive to interference and generally heighten the potential conflict between more intensive land use on the one hand, and recreational opportunities and, to some eyes, visual amenity on the other. The issue is more sharply focussed in the National Parks and Regional Parks than else-where. In the future much will depend on the view which Government takes of the proposals of the National Parks Policies Review Committee (1974) with respect to constraints on agricultural development.

It seems possible that what is decided for the National Parks will set the scene for future pressures to constrain hill land development generally. It is to be hoped that adequate regard will be paid to the prospects for meat referred to in the Introduction, and the likely future value of systems of production whose output of food per unit of energy 'subsidy' is low relative to that of meat from intensive systems. If the real long-term contribution that the hills can make to the vital matter of home-produced food is to be realised, the industry must have a frame-work within which advantage can be taken of economically worthwhile technical advance. It cannot prosper and develop if it is to be constrained within the bounds of an outworn technology.

REFERENCES

Allen, G R (1973) The economic background to scientific and technical research for hill and uplands. In: *Colloquium Proceedings No. 3.* Henley-on-Thames: The Potassium Institute Ltd.

Armstrong, R H & Eadie, J (1973) Some aspects of the growth of hill lambs. *6th Report, Hill Farming Research Organisation.* Edinburgh: HFRO.

Cunningham, J M M, Eadie, J, Maxwell, T J & Sibbald, A R (1977) Inter-relations between agriculture and forestry: an agricultural view. Paper presented to a symposium of the Royal Society of Edinburgh, May 1977.

Doney, J M & Gunn, R G (1973) Progress in studies on the reproductive performance of hill sheep. *6th Report, Hill Farming Research Organisation.* Edinburgh: HFRO.

Eadie, J (1970) Hill sheep production systems development. *5th Report, Hill Farming Research Organisation.* Edinburgh: HFRO.

Eadie, J, Armstrong, R H & Maxwell, T J (1976) Responses in output achieved in improved systems of sheep production in two hill environments. Part I: In the Eastern Cheviots. In: *Proceedings of the international hill land symposium.* Morgantown: West Virginia University.

Eadie, J, Maxwell, T J & Currie, D C (1976) Responses in output achieved in improved systems of sheep production in two hill environments. Part II: On blanket peat in the West of Scotland. In: *Proceedings of the international hill land symposium.* Morgantown: West Virginia University. .

King, J W B (1976) National sheep breeding programmes – Great Britain. In: *Proceedings of the 1976 international congress on sheep breeding.* Muresk and Perth: Western Australia Institute of Technology.

MAFF (1975) *Food from our own resources.* London: HMSO.

Maxwell, T J, Eadie, J & Sibbald, A R (1973) Economic appraisal of investments in hill sheep production. *6th Report, Hill Farming Research Organisation.* Edinburgh: HFRO.

MLC (1972) *Sheep improvement.* Scientific Study Group Report. Bletchley: MLC.

MLC (1976 a) *Sheep production data sheet.* February 1976, Bletchley: MLC.

MLC (1976 b) *Sheep notes, No. 10.* November 1976, Bletchley: MLC.

MLC (1977) *Sheep data sheet, 77/1.* May 1977, Bletchley: MLC.

National Parks Policies Review Committee (1974) *Report.* London: HMSO.

Newbould, P (1974) The improvement of hill pastures for agriculture. *Journal of the British Grassland Society,* **29,** 241 & **30,** 41.

Peart, J N (1970) Factors influencing lactation of hill ewes. *5th Report, Hill Farming Research Organisation.* Edinburgh: HFRO.

Raeburn, J R (1972)   The economics of upland farming. In: *The remoter rural areas of Britain.*   Eds. Ashton, J & Harwood Long, W.   London: Oliver and Boyd.

Russel, A J F (1967)   Nutrition of the pregnant ewe.   *4th Report, Hill Farming Research Organisation.*   Edinburgh: HFRO.

Rutter, W (1975)   *Sheep from grass.*   Bulletin No. 13.   Edinburgh: East of Scotland College of Agriculture.

Whitelaw, A, Armstrong, R H, Evans, C C & Fawcett, A R (1977)   An investigation into copper deficiency in young lambs on an improved hill pasture. *Veterinary Record,* **101,** 229-230.

4 The impact of technical advances on hill and upland cattle systems

J M M CUNNINGHAM & A D M SMITH

INTRODUCTION

In upland and hill areas cattle systems are based primarily on the beef suckler cow. The main output is the weaned calf, varying from 5-6 months to one year old at sale, when a large percentage are transferred to lowland farms. Sales are held in autumn and there is a substantial premium on size, or weight, so that lightweight calves of less than 200 kg liveweight derived mainly from hill farms are at a disadvantage.

By exploiting the ability of the suckler cow to utilise relatively poor quality and lower cost feeds, generally unsuitable for the dairy cow, and some of the byproducts of the arable farm in the finishing of store calves, an efficient integration of resources is achieved.

Around 85% of the total energy input in weaned calf systems is utilised by the cow while 45-65% is similarly utilised, depending on breed and finishing system, when the slaughter animal is included.

Beef production is frequently criticised as being inefficient, based largely on the calculation that the beef cow/suckled calf converts protein into meat at a conversion ratio of 20:1 (Baker, 1975) and additionally because of a dependence on cereals. The total quantity of protein used in supplementary feeds is about 4.5 kg per kg of saleable meat from the suckled calf and if lowland grass used in the finishing system is excluded the figure is 2.9 kg (Baker, 1975). Comparable figures for calves from the dairy herd vary from 4-8 kg depending on the intensity of the system. The additional protein is derived from poor quality grass and arable by-products which have limited use. The production of two-year old beef from the suckler herd requires around 1.5-1.8 kg cereal per kg liveweight gain, including the input to the cow. This competes favourably with systems based on calves from the dairy herd. Beef derived from the suckler herd contributes almost 30% of our domestic production and the expansion of the beef herd has undoubtedly contributed to the increase in self-sufficiency which is currently 83%.

Table 1
CONCENTRATE USAGE IN DIFFERENT BEEF SYSTEMS

	Lifetime concentrates		Slaughter weight		Concentrates per kg gain	
	Average	Top third	Average	Top third	Average	Top third
	(tonnes)		(kg)		(kg)	
Dairy calves to slaughter:						
Cereal beef	1.8	1.7	391	394	5.4	4.9
15 month grass/cereal	1.2	1.1	431	428	3.3	3.0
18 month grass/cereal	1.1	0.8	470	489	2.7	1.9
24 month grass/cereal	1.0	0.8	483	498	2.3	1.8
Beef calves to slaughter:						
15 month Autumn suckler	0.9	0.7	416	420	2.5	1.9
24 month Spring suckler	0.7	0.6	442	461	1.8	1.5

Source: Baker (1975)

The dramatic increase in beef cow numbers since the early post-war years can be attributed to a number of factors. The introduction of the hill cow subsidy and the manipulation of the levels of payment stimulated an increase in hill areas as also did the marginal production assistance paid during the 1950's and early 1960's. The deficiency payment support system which maintained end product prices was also of importance. The prospect of an expanded market within the EC was an additional reason for the increase in numbers in the early 1970's.

Compared with England and Wales, a high proportion of cows in Scotland (around 80-85%), receive the hill cow subsidy now known as the Hill Livestock Compensatory Allowance, the cost of which has been increasing. However, a detailed examination of the Scottish figures indicated that only 19% of all cows (22.4% of those granted hill subsidy), are on true hill farms. The majority are kept on 'upland' farms and numbers appear to be broadly related to the area and probably quality of the 'inbye' land.

Table 2

SOURCES OF HOME PRODUCED BEEF

	Per cent	
From the dairy herd:		
Pure-bred calves	21	
Beef-cross calves	20	
Cull dairy cows	17	
	58	58
From suckler cows:		
Beef calves	25	
Cull beef cows	6	
	31	31
Cattle imported from Ireland		11
		100

Source: Baker (1975)

USE OF RESOURCES

The majority of calf production systems are based predominantly on the utilisation of grassland, grazed in summer and conserved as silage or hay for winter
fodder with either home grown cereals or purchased concentrates used as supplements. However, some of the expansion which occurred in the 1950's and 1960's
was based on the purchase of hay and straw, mainly from lowland farms, and
compounded concentrates and/or block feeds and liquid supplements. As a
consequence of joining the EC the price of cereals has increased substantially (eg
barley cost £22/ton in 1968 and £70/ton in 1976) with a consequent increase in
all feed prices without a commensurate increase in end product prices.

This is currently causing a decline in cow numbers which it is predicted will
continue. It is probable that farms keeping beef cows will have to become largely
self-sufficient in bulky food supplies. The national herd may be constrained by
the ability of farms to achieve this objective, unless beef prices increase substantially, which is improbable. Since no information is available on the extent to
which hill and upland farms are dependent on purchased fodder, it is not possible
to predict more precisely the likely trends in the national herds, but it is certain

Table 3

NUMBERS OF ALL BEEF COWS IN GREAT BRITAIN AND THOSE RECEIVING HILL COW SUBSIDY, 1962-1976

	1962	1964	1966	1968	1970	1972	1974	1975	1976
Scotland	304 (73)	304 (80)	343 (84)	368 (85)	417 (86)	456 (87)	551 (84)	566 (81)	542 (84)
England & Wales	562 (21)	553 (32)	597 (37)	606 (40)	667 (43)	746 (36)	1015 (36)	1020 (35)	944 (39)
Great Britain	866 (39)	857 (49)	940 (54)	974 (57)	1054 (59)	1202 (55)	1566 (53)	1586 (52)	1486 (56)

Note: Proportion of cows receiving hill cow subsidy in brackets (%).

Source: DAFS & MAFF.

Table 4

SOURCES OF SUPPLY OF CARCASS BEEF AND VEAL CONSUMED IN THE UK, 1962-1976 (thousand tons)

	1962	1964	1966	1968	1970	1972	1974	1975	1976
Domestic	865 (71.1)	903 (73.3)	803 (70.1)	891 (77.6)	932 (72.0)	903 (70.0)	1055 (77.0)	1197 (84.0)	1033 (83.0)
Imported	343	329	310	257	261	273	245	193	210

Note: Proportion of total supply domestically produced in brackets (%)

Source: MLC Quarterly Review.

Table 5

COST OF SUPPORT FOR BEEF COWS AND OF DIRECT SUPPORT TO HILL AND UPLAND FARMS FOR HILL COWS, 1967-1975

| | Beef cows | | Hill cows | | |
	Subsidy rate per cow (£)	Total (£m) subsidy	Subsidy rate per cow (£)	Total (£m) subsidy	Winter keep scheme (£m)
1967/1968	7.50	2.9	14.25	8.7	2.5[1]
1969/1970	10.00	5.0	17.25	11.8	3.0[1]
1971/1972	11.00	6.7	18.75	14.7	3.5[1]
1973/1974	11.00	9.2	24.50	16.9	7.0[2]
1974/1975	11.00	22.1	24.50	35.4	12.3[2]

1 Payments made on a headage basis.
2 Payments on an area basis which includes hill sheep.
Source: MAFF (1977)

Table 6

DISTRIBUTION OF HILL COWS BY FARM TYPE IN SCOTLAND AND THE LAND RESOURCES PER COW IN 1974

| | Type of full-time farms[1] | | | |
	Grade A	Grade B	Grade C	All farms
No of farms	480	922	2 041	3 443
No of beef cows	41 281	67 561	103 776	212 618
Average herd size	86	73	51	62
Average area of 'inbye' land (ha)	124.6	83.0	42.9	55.3
Average area of grass-mowing (ha)	24.4	19.1	10.9	15.0
Area (ha) per cow of:				
Rough grazing	2.6	6.3	22.2	
'Inbye' land	1.4	1.1	0.8	
Mowing grass	0.3	0.3	0.2	
Ratio of Rough grazing to 'Inbye' land	1.8	5.5	26.4	
Rough grazing as proportion of total area (%)	3.5	13.7	74.6	

1 Farm types as in the Winter Keep (Scotland) Scheme, 1975
Source: DAFS

that it will be the herds on the true hill farms purchasing fodder which are most vulnerable. However, the reduction or disposal of herds may substantially reduce farm gross output while not achieving a reduction in fixed costs, eg labour, machinery etc. Also, enterprise substitution on the hill farm is limited and replacement of cows with additional sheep may not be acceptable for a variety of reasons. In recent years systems of suckled calf production have become more precisely defined (MAFF, 1973) being classified on time of calving, with there being four main periods:

(i)   Autumn: September — mid-October
(ii) Spring: February — March
(iii) Summer: July — August
(iv) Hill: April

Table 7

NUMBERS OF COWS AND AREA OF ROUGH GRAZING, CROPS AND GRASS, AND MOWING GRASS PER COW IN SCOTTISH REGIONS[1] IN 1974

Region	No. of cows	Area per cow (ha)		
		Rough grazing	Crops and grass	Mown grass
Highland	30 095	37.7	1.0	0.2
Grampian	17 217	5.4	1.4	0.3
Tayside	22 814	16.5	1.2	0.2
Central	8 553	14.9	0.7	0.1
Fife	701	2.6	2.3	0.2
Strathclyde	59 312	10.7	0.9	0.2
Lothians	3 459	8.4	2.0	0.3
Border	19 483	9.0	1.3	0.3
Dumfries and Galloway	44 423	4.9	0.9	0.2
ALL SCOTLAND	212 618	13.4	0.9	0.2

[1] Not including Orkney, Shetland and Western Isles Islands Areas

Source: DAFS

It is the food supply which should broadly determine the appropriate system even though Howie and Broadbent (1967) did not find any relationship between time of calving and winter food inputs. However, work at Trawscoed EHF

(MAFF, 1973) clearly indicates the substantial difference in these inputs as between spring and autumn calving systems, the former requiring 0.92 tonnes of hay plus 165-216 kg concentrate compared with 7.1 tonnes of silage (2.0 tonnes hay) and 76 kg concentrates to autumn calvers.

Research is currently in progress at HFRO and the Grassland Research Institute to quantify the relationship between food inputs to the cow at different physiological phases, ie pregnancy, lactation, etc, and animal performance as related to the use of body reserves of varying magnitude. In addition, the complex relationship between milk yield and performance of the calf as influenced by birth weight, rate of growth, genotype and the quantity and quality of solid food ingested are also being investigated.

Although maximum biological efficiency implies no use of body reserves, this is not realistic in practice and maximum economic efficiency is more important but will change as input/output costs and prices vary. However, more comprehensive biological data is needed to permit systems models to be produced.

HILL FARMS

Farms of this type may have less than 10% 'inbye' land so that utilisation of rough grazing is important and winter fodder is either purchased or limited amounts are home produced so that calving in spring or early summer is general.

Opinions on the place of cattle on the hills vary. Meiklejohn (1976) stated, "without doubt cattle are excellent improvers of rough hill pasture by keeping the rougher parts in check and improving the grazings for sheep" and this reflects much of the accepted conventional wisdom. On the other hand McCreath (1963) says, "Many farmers strongly hold the view that adding appreciably to cattle numbers must eventually lead to a reduction in sheep output".

In an *ad hoc* experiment (Peart, 1962) in which sheep only and sheep plus cattle were compared, an increase of 18-37% in lamb output was obtained but this left unresolved the consequences of a comparable increase in livestock units with sheep and the changes in herbage composition, notably the dead to green ratio which would have assisted extrapolation. Nothing is known about the nutritive value and intake of the wide range of indigenous vegetation which is utilised in practical systems nor the effects of grazing pressures. Obtaining the necessary knowledge and understanding for more objective structuring of cattle/sheep systems has only started recently (Hodgson, 1977) and will take some time and will require to be related to the systems described by Eadie (1973) as well as the set-stocked system used by Peart (1962). McClelland (1977) has suggested that currently cattle are relatively uneconomic compared with the 'two-pasture' system for sheep and additional investment for several years ahead on hill farms will be best directed to an expansion of the sheep enterprise. Also, cattle enterprises dependent on purchased fodder will probably be eliminated if present cost/ price relationships continue.

Sheep systems as traditionally practised utilise only around 15-20% of the dry matter produced (Eadie, 1973) and agistment of cattle from lowland farms, eg dairy heifers, or the integration of arable and hill farms is advocated and indeed practised, the former providing housing and winter fodder, mainly straw, and the latter summer grazing. That dual farm systems of this type have not developed, depending as it does on co-operation, may be partly attributable to the streak of independence characteristic of the hill farmer, the lack of promotion to encourage it and a suitable structure for its development as well as the increasing marginal economics due to ever increasing transport costs. A modern version of the old shieling system (Symon, 1959) is probably a pious hope.

UPLAND FARMS

This category includes farms ranging from those with no access to rough grazings, to farms with substantial areas of hill land, but the cattle enterprise normally being based on the enclosed pastures which provide most of the winter fodder and a high percentage of summer grazing and where autumn or spring calving is more general.

Mudd and Meadowcroft (1964) showed the potential of upland permanent pasture and Cunningham and Harkins (1966) demonstrated that intensification using moderately high inputs of nitrogen and controlled grazing were technically possible. Work at Liscombe EHF (MAFF, 1968) suggested that one acre (0.405 ha) per cow/calf unit could meet grazing requirements and produce a substantial part of winter feed requirements. Meiklejohn (1976) observed that on farms in South East Scotland, intensively managed grass involving paddock grazing increased stocking rate by 25% compared with set-stocking and the aim should be half an acre per cow/calf unit for grazing requirements.

Mixed grazing, usually co-grazing, is very widely practised and experimental evidence suggests that animal output from intensive grazing systems can be improved by grazing cattle and sheep together (Nolan, 1977) or in sequence (Rutter, 1975). The weight of evidence indicates (Nolan, 1977) that mixed grazing generally improves sheep performance while the benefit to cattle is more variable.

There is, as yet, inadequate information about the factors contributing to this improvement so there is no objective basis for deciding on the appropriate cattle/ sheep ratio or the best overall stocking rate for particular circumstances. It is understandable therefore, that controversy exists about the merits of incorporating cattle into hill sheep grazing systems as well as grazing cattle and sheep together, as opposed to grazing each species alone in enclosed grazings.

If informed decisions are to be made about the best balance of cattle and sheep for particular circumstances, it will be essential to understand more about the place of different animal species in the soil-plant-animal complex and the degree to which they complement or compete with each other.

Hodgson (1977 & private communication) suggests that this basically consists of a consideration of species differences in diet selection and herbage intake and of the impact of mixed grazing on the control of worm parasites, although other factors may well be important (eg Monteath et al, 1977). On the farm the efficient use of pastoral resources will be dependent upon the effective integration of sheep and cattle enterprises when the optimum balance becomes not only an issue of biological efficiency but also of economic efficiency which can be dependent on circumstances of individual farms. This demands a much wider spectrum of information such as nutrition/production response data for both species (eg the seasonal changes in nutrition and the species response) as well as information on the biology of grazing systems.

Table 8
THE EFFECT OF SIRE BREED ON CALF 200-day WEIGHTS (kg)

| | Weight at 200 days: | | |
	Lowland	Upland	Hill
Charolais	241	227	205
Simmental	232	222	198
South Devon	232	221	200
Devon	226	215	191
Lincoln Red	222	214	189
Limousin	215	204	187
Sussex	215	204	187
Hereford	208	194	184
Aberdeen-Angus	194	183	176
Overall	221	211	191

Source: Kilkenny (1977)

GENOTYPES
The unique system of 'stratification' whereby the so-called hardy breeds, eg Galloway, are kept on the poorest land and are used for the provision of breeding

replacements, eg Bluegrey (Shorthorn x Galloway) traditionally has been an efficient means of resource use. However, much of the expansion in beef cow numbers has been obtained using a variety of dairy-type crossbreds of which the Hereford x Friesian has been the most popular. This has been associated with the introduction of exotic breeds amongst which the Charolais, Simmental and Limousin predominate and an increasing use of native breeds, eg Lincoln Red and South Devon with high growth potential. Although the effects of the larger breeds are less apparent in the hill situation, sire breed effects become evident and are reflected in slaughter weights in finishing systems. However, widespread use of such sires is constrained because of a greater incidence of calving difficulties (Kilkenny, 1977) which may be an important disadvantage when close supervision at calving is difficult.

FIXED EQUIPMENT
Considerable advances have been made in the design, layout and fittings (eg cubicles) of buildings to house cows and calves (North of Scotland College of Agriculture, 1975) and also in systems of feeding, eg self and easy feeding, with the aim of reducing labour inputs in feed handling and in the disposal of waste which is still nonetheless a problem of some importance. There is little evidence which would suggest that investment in buildings can be justified on the basis of improved animal performance but labour inputs can be significantly reduced and the management of large herds of 100 to 400 cows become logistically feasible.

OTHER ASPECTS
Reproductive performance both in regard to calving rate and the spread and pattern of calving have a major influence on the economic and biological efficiency of suckled calf production (McCreath, 1970 and Bailie *et al*, 1977). For example, McFarlane *et al* (1977) have clearly shown the importance of nutrition during early lactation on conception rate and fertility. Research on the synchronisation of oestrus to reduce the spread of calving is being actively pursued (Wishart, 1974).

For example, (Kilkenny, 1977) showed that a seven day increase in calving spread reduced profit per cow by £3.40 and £3.80 for spring and autumn calving respectively.

CONCLUSION
Beef cattle have a valuable role in that the movement of stock from hill to upland and/or lowlands, exploits the range of farm environments (MLC, 1976) since cattle utilise rough grazings which otherwise might not be used, and produce high quality and acceptable protein from land which cannot grow food for direct

human consumption. As Wilson (1977) has recently observed, competition between animal and human feed is now a cause for socio-political concern. He suggests that it is likely there will be a return to the situation in which the animal feed industry utilises materials surplus to, or non-competitive with human food.

The National Economic Development Office (1973) stated, "from the data available on production costs and returns it was not feasible to measure the relative economic advantages to the nation of expanding cattle and sheep production in the hills, uplands and lowlands".

An expansion of cattle in the hills is improbable in the near future and the current retrenchment may continue unless policies are implemented to contain numbers at their present level. This is due to: the collapse of the beef market in 1974; the current adverse relationship of costs and prices for beef production compared with the situation for lamb; and an EC surplus of beef compared with a deficiency of lamb.

REFERENCES

Baker, H K (1975)   Competitive meat from British farms. Paper presented to the MLC National Meat Conference at Stratford-upon-Avon on Meat in Tomorrow's World.

Bailie, J H, Dury, N S & Norman, J A (1977)   The significance of herd conception rate in the economics of beef suckler cow management. *Animal Production*, **24**, 130. (Abstract).

Cunningham, M M, & Harkins, J (1966)   Intensive production from suckler cows on marginal land. *Scottish Agriculture*, **46**, 106-110.

Eadie, J (1973)   Sheep production systems development on the hills.   In: *Colloquium Proceedings No. 3.*   Henley-on-Thames: The Potassium Institute Limited.

Hodgson, J (1977)   Factors limiting herbage intake by the grazing animal. Paper presented in Dublin to an international meeting on animal production from temporary grassland.

Howie, A & Broadbent, P J (1967)   Factors affecting single-suckled calf production in the North-East of Scotland. *Animal Production*, **9**, 285 (Abstract).

Kilkenny, J B (1977)   Economic evaluation of breeds. Paper presented to a National Agricultural Centre Conference, Stoneleigh.

MAFF (1973)   *Liscombe E H F; report and guide to experiments.*   London: MAFF.

MAFF (1973)   *Trawsgoed, E H F; report and farm guide.*   London: MAFF.

MAFF (1977)   *Annual review of agriculture.*   London: HMSO.

MLC (1976)   *Beef from the hills and uplands.*   MLC Leaflet. Milton Keynes: MLC.

Meiklejohn, A K M (1976)   *The agriculture of South East Scotland.*   Bulletin No. 15. Edinburgh: East of Scotland College of Agriculture.

McClelland, H (1977)   Hill cattle — not on.   *Scottish Farmer,* 13 August 1977.

McCreath, J B (1963)   Hill cattle in the West of Scotland.   *Journal of the Chartered Land Agents Society,* **62**, 130-139.

McCreath, J B (1970)   *Calves from the hills.*   Report No. 130. Auchencruive: West of Scotland College of Agriculture.

McFarlane, J S, Somerville, S H, Lowman, B G & Deas, D W (1977)   Effect of nutrition and other factors on the reproductive performance of beef cows.   *Animal Production,* **24**, 131 (Abstract).

Monteath, M A, Johnstone, P D & Boswell, C C (1977)   Effects of animals on pasture production.   *New Zealand Journal of Agricultural Research,* **20**, 23-29.

Mudd, C H & Meadowcroft, S C (1964)   Comparison of the improvement of pastures by the use of fertilisers and by reseeding.   *Experimental Husbandry,* No. 10, 66-84.

National Economic Development Office (1973)   *Evaluation of the economic significance of the hills and uplands of Great Britain.*   London: NEDO.

Nolan, T (1977)   An ecological appraisal of mixed grazing. Paper presented to the 28th Annual Meeting of the European Association for Animal Production.

North of Scotland College of Agriculture (1975)   *Housing of the single suckled cow.*   Farm Buildings Division Advisory Leaflet.   Aberdeen: North of Scotland College of Agriculture.

Peart, J N (1962)   Increased production from hill pastures.   *Scottish Agriculture,* **41**, 147-151.

Rutter, W (1975)   *Sheep from grass.*   Bulletin No. 13. Edinburgh: East of Scotland College of Agriculture.

Symon, J A (1959)   *Scottish farming: past and present.*   Edinburgh: Oliver and Boyd.

Wilson, P N (1977)   The composition of animal feeds.   *Journal of the science of food and agriculture,* **28**, 717-727.

Wishart, D F & Young, I M (1974)   Artificial insemination of progestin (Sç21009) treated cattle at predetermined times.   *Veterinary Record,* **95**, 503-508.

5 The future of upland farming

J R THOMPSON

INTRODUCTION

It is generally accepted that the hills and uplands extend to approximately
6.6 million hectares and from an agricultural point of view, use is limited to
sheep and the production of store cattle.

Out of the 12 million breeding sheep in the UK about 7¼ million or 61% are
maintained in the hills and uplands.

According to an MLC (1972) sheep breeding survey of the 1972 lamb crop,
76% of the total lamb carcass meat produced annually in the UK is derived from
cross-bred lambs, and pure bred hill lambs contribute only 18%. Despite this
very low contribution of lamb carcass meat from the hills, hill sheep have a very
vital part to play and form the basis of the whole sheep industry.

Attempts have been made, and are being made, to breed a self-perpetuating
lowland breed of sheep which combines all the virtues of cross-breds bred from
hill ewes. It is right that this work should continue, but at the moment it appears
as though the sheep industry will continue to be based upon the present system
of stratification, with each section having a very definite and vital role to play.

EEC PROSPECTS

According to the report on 'Sheep and Wool' by the National Economic
Development Office (1974) the total breeding sheep population within the EC
is only about 29 million, and this must place sheep farmers in the UK in a very
strong position. If there is a future for the sheep industry within the Common
Market then a future for sheep in the hills and uplands is assured.

To be economically viable though there will have to be changes in management and certainly greatly increased output from those areas amenable to land improvement and favourable for sheep production.

SHEEP

The 7¼ million breeding sheep maintained on the 6½ million hectares of hill and uplands represents overall an extremely low stocking rate. Within this figure are concealed very wide variations. It is difficult to find an accurate lambing percentage figure for the whole flock. If we assume that including those ewes which are crossed there is a 100% lamb crop, and that these lambs have a mean weaning weight of 25 kg this only represents a production of aroung 28 kg of weaned lamb per hectare, which is abysmally low.

It has been demonstrated on many individual commercial farms, as well as by HFRO and MAFF experimental husbandry farms (EHF), that this figure can be doubled and even trebled. While climate conditions do influence output from the hills it is the management imposed by the farmer that finally decides the level of productions.

Work at HFRO has demonstrated the influence of body condition of ewes pre-mating on fertility, and the importance of post-mating nutrition upon subsequent lamb percentage. It has also identified the critical periods for nutrition, and how these can be controlled following land improvement and the adoption of a two-pasture system of management.

These findings have not been widely adopted and put into practice. Apart from the natural caution and resistance of hill farmers to change, there are very good reasons why they have not been taken up. Hill farming had been very much the poor relation in British Agriculture struggling along with very meagre returns and with no confidence that it had any real long term future.

In order to obtain any worthwhile increase in lamb production there had to be land improvement. This required inputs of capital, and there was little, or no capital available out of income to finance it. In fact during the 1960's, returns were low and the future looked so uncertain that you could hardly advise any hill farmer that it was prudent to invest capital in long term improvement.

In the early 1970's returns improved and there were indications that hill farmers were beginning to make long term investments, with improvements to fencing, drainage, and land reclamation. This investment came to an abrupt halt after the disastrous slump in livestock returns in 1974. It will be difficult to persuade hill farmers to make much capital investment without long term assurances about the future.

CATTLE

With increasing costs of feeding stuffs there is likely to be a reduction of breeding

47

cattle in the hills. Where bulk fodder can be produced numbers will probably remain but are unlikely to expand. With spring-calving herds, breeding cows may be reduced to enable all calves to be over-wintered.

On many hill areas summer grazing with cattle is necessary to maintain a satisfactory sheep sward. There may be more co-operation between hill and lowland stock farms. In exchange for summer grazing for cattle which would release quality land for grass conservation or cereals lowland farms could over-winter flock replacements from the hills.

DECLINING RURAL POPULATION

Another major factor in the lack of expansion from the hills has been the declining rural population and the subsequent difficulty in attracting and retaining high calibre stockmen. Active steps must be taken to attract people back into the countryside. I cannot see this happening in the very remote and inaccessible areas, and these may well have to be given over to deer, forestry and sporting interests. They could be taken for recreation purposes but when these areas are no longer actively farmed they are not as attractive to tourists.

There has been a tendency for the age of shepherds to increase with only a limited number of young people taking up the profession. To be successful in the future stockmen must be technically trained, as well as practically sound. Some of the agricultural colleges now run specialist courses for hill shepherds and this work should be extended. To date every student so trained at Kirkley Hall has found acceptable employment which indicates the value farmers now place upon technical training.

LAND AVAILABILITY

There will be increasing pressures from interests other than agriculture for the limited and dwindling land available. Numerous authorities will also wish to have a say in how land is used. Farmers must accept this and learn to live with it. People from cities will come to the countryside in increasing numbers and must be educated how to behave. Farm walks and demonstrations specially for these people can be very valuable.

In some of the national parks and more popular beauty spots pressures will become so severe that normal commercial farming operations become impossible. This has already occurred in some areas, notably the Lake District, parts of Wales, and the south west. On many farms in these areas agriculture is now secondary to tourists. There are restrictions upon the farming systems, upon the class of stock which may be kept, and far more seriously from an agricultural point of view, controversy as to whether land should be reclaimed at all. Work at HFRO, at Pwllpeiran EHF in Wales, and at Redesdale EHF in Northumberland shows that without land improvement output from the hills is very limited.

Following a programme of land improvement on only 10-15% of the total hill area, with integration into the farming system, output of weaned lamb can increase from 28 kg to over 65 kg per hectare.

If for amenity, scenic, or conservation reasons farmers are prevented from reclaiming and improving hill land then they must receive adequate financial compensation. Hill farming in the past has been based upon a system of low costs and low output. Low costs are now a thing of the past and those farmers who do not increase production to cover these rises will suffer financial hardship. For a time large units can be 'ranched' but this will lead to further deterioration of the hills. With most systems of land improvement in the hills there are no sudden and drastic changes. There are new and improved techniques of land improvement available and these must be allowed to develop.

Following land improvement grazing control is necessary and this entails fencing, which will be opposed in many areas. Co-operation between forestry and agriculture as happened at Pwllpeiran EHF can often reduce the amount of fencing required and may also provide valuable access into the hills.

With so many competing interests, and attempts by many organisations to control the hills and uplands, it will be necessary to make a proper land survey and classify the land. This could fairly rapidly be accomplished using aerial photography as was demonstrated in the Hill Project area in Northumberland. Such a survey should at least ensure that land with a comparatively high agricultural potential is not taken for afforestation and so sterilised. With full consultation and adequate planning there is a place for all the various interests in the hills. Some may have to modify their very extreme views though, and accept that a degree of change is inevitable. Farmers must be more tolerant and not think they have a divine right to be the sole occupants and users of the hills.

REFERENCES

Meat and Livestock Commission (1972) *Sheep Improvement — report of a scientific study group.*   Oct 1972.   Milton Keynes: MLC.

National Economic Development Office (1974)   *UK Farming and the Common Market: sheep and wool* — a report by the Economic Development Committee for Agriculture, London: NEDO.

6 A review of some economic aspects of hill and upland farming

W DYFRI JONES

INTRODUCTION

Just over one quarter of the agricultural area of Britain is occupied by rough grazing, practically all of which is within our hill and upland areas, where extensive livestock rearing systems of farming are predominant. Not all the land in these areas is under rough grazing; a substantial proportion is cultivated and provides better quality forage and/or is ploughed for cereals and roots.

For convenience of analysing and presenting certain of the data it has been assumed that hill and upland farms are broadly represented by the following type classification of holdings used by the MAFF and the DAFS:

Region	Hill farms	Upland farms
England (Northern Region) and Wales	Livestock rearing and fattening (mostly sheep)	Livestock rearing and fattening (cattle and sheep)
Scotland	Hill farms	Upland farms Rearing with arable

It is not suggested that such an allocation of hill and upland farms is foolproof. For instance, it is highly likely that some farms in these types are situated outside the accepted hill and upland areas and farms in other categories eg dairying, will be situated in these areas. Furthermore, there are other, smaller, hill and upland areas in England eg the South West and Shropshire. Hill farms are, generally, situated at the higher altitudes, on steeper slopes, have a higher proportion of their land under rough grazings, and a higher ratio of sheep to cattle. Upland farms, on the other hand, have gentler sloping land, a lesser proportion of rough grazings, and carry more livestock per unit area.

It is estimated that hill and upland holdings of less than 275 SMD account for just over 40% of all hill and upland holdings in Great Britain. Although these are regarded as being part-time, to a substantial number of their operators they are their only source of income. Part-time holdings are more important in Wales than in Scotland and the North of England. Part-time hill and upland farms, although numerically significant, occupy only 23% of the total agricultural area in Great Britain, compared with 33% occupied by full-time hill and upland farms (see Table 1).

Of the 21 000 or so full-time hill and upland farms in Great Britain, only one in six are in the hill category. Hill farms are more predominant in Wales, where there is one for every three upland farms compared with one in five and one in ten in the North of England and Scotland respectively. The smallest full-time farms, in this instance those of 275-599 SMD, number nearly half the total. Again it is worth noting that Wales has a higher proportion of these 'small' farms than has Scotland and the North of England.

Being situated on the poorer land, hill farms, on average, have an appreciably larger land area than the upland farms, and those in Scotland are very much larger than those in the North of England and Wales.

THE OUTPUT OF THE HILLS AND UPLANDS

Since they occupy such a substantial (albeit the poorer) proportion of the agricultural area, and engage about 10% of all people employed in farming, it is of interest to assess the economic significance of the hills and uplands, measured in terms of their contribution to the gross output and the net income of British agriculture. Table 2 presents estimates of the situation in 1974-75, arrived at by applying average gross outputs and net incomes per farm (Farm Management Survey data) weighted by the number of farms in each SMD size group, to the number of holdings in each, the hill and upland, category.

Table 1   DISTRIBUTION OF HILL AND UPLAND HOLDINGS BY SMD SIZE GROUPS, 1974-75

Farm size by SMD	275 - 599[1]		600 - 1199		1200 +		All full-time holdings		Part-time holdings[2]		Total all holdings[3]		Average size full-time farms
	No	%	No	%	No	%	No	%	No	%	No	%	Acres
NORTH OF ENGLAND													
Mostly sheep	227	36.7	271	43.8	121	19.5	619						720
Cattle & sheep	1233	39.2	1244	39.6	667	21.2	3144						407
Total	1460	38.8	1515	40.3	788	20.9	3763	100	2519	40.1	6282	100	459
% of all holdings	23.2		24.1		12.6		59.9						
WALES													
Mostly sheep	858	49.9	633	36.8	229	13.3	1720						384
Cattle & sheep	2711	52.3	1942	37.4	534	10.3	5187						222
Total	3569	51.7	2575	37.3	763	11.0	6907	100	6350	47.9	13257	100	263
% of all holdings	26.9		19.4		5.8		52.1						
SCOTLAND													
Hill sheep	459	44.0	362	34.7	222	21.3	1043						
Upland	2758	46.3	2112	35.5	1085	18.2	5955						
Rearing with arable	1609	47.4	1140	33.6	648	19.0	3397						
Total	4826	46.4	3614	34.8	1955	18.8	10395	100	6131	37.1	16526	100	971
% of all holdings	29.2		21.9		11.8		62.9						
GREAT BRITAIN[4]													
Mainly hill	1544	45.7	1266	37.4	572	16.9	3382						1727
Mainly upland	8311	47.0	6438	36.4	2934	16.6	17683						441
Total	9855	46.8	7704	36.6	3506	16.6	21065	100	14960	41.5	36025	100	647
% of all holdings	27.4		21.4		9.7		58.5						

1   % of full-time farms
    250-599 SMD for Scotland

3   All holdings over 1 acre
4   Scotland, Wales and North of England

Sources: Annual Digest of Welsh Agriculture Statistics;
           Agricultural Statistics, 1974, Scotland;

Table 2

ESTIMATED GROSS OUTPUTS AND NET FARM INCOME FROM FULL- AND PART-TIME HILL AND UPLAND HOLDINGS, 1974-75 (£ million)

	Hill and Upland Holdings							
	Full-time				Part-time	Total Hill & Upland	Total Agriculture	Hills & Upland % Total Agriculture
	Hill	Upland	Rearing & Arable	Total				
				Gross Output				
North of England	6.94	52.0	–	58.94	4.63	63.57	–	–
Wales	12.55	53.47	–	66.02	9.02	75.04	290.00	25.86
Scotland	14.02	111.04	76.0	201.05	13.34	214.39	607.30	35.30
Great Britain	33.51	216.51	76.0	326.01	26.99	353.00	4610.20	7.67
				Net Farm Income				
Great Britain						96.25	1199.20	8.02

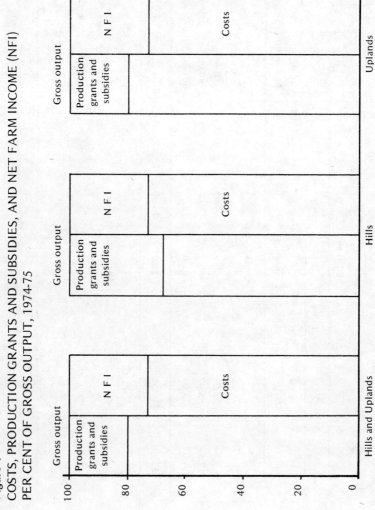

Figure 1
COSTS, PRODUCTION GRANTS AND SUBSIDIES, AND NET FARM INCOME (NFI)
PER CENT OF GROSS OUTPUT, 1974-75

The figures for Great Britain in the last column of Table 2 agree closely with those calculated on a similar basis by the National Economic Development Office (1973) for 1971-72, except that the latter exclude part-time holdings. The contribution of the hills and uplands to the total gross output and net income of British agriculture is rather small, at only 7.7% and 8% respectively. Within the hill and upland sector, part-time holdings account for only about 7 or 8% of the gross output. The contribution of the hills and uplands to the total output of agriculture in each of the countries varies appreciably (Table 2). Hill farms alone account for only about 10% of the total hill and upland output for Great Britain, but for Wales, North of England and Scotland the corresponding figures are 19, 13, and 7% respectively.

Since physical and climatic factors dictate that almost three-quarters of the output of the hills and uplands consists of cattle and 'sheep and wool', it is more meaningful to express their contribution in these categories. In 1974-75, hill and upland farms contributed a quarter of the value of the total output of cattle and nearly half that of 'sheep and wool' produced in Great Britain; they therefore play a far more significant role in our agricultural economy than is at first realized. They provide a very substantial proportion of the breeding and store stock for, and thereby play a most important complementary role with, our lowland farms.

It is well known that production grants and subsidies (hill cow and hill sheep subsidies, ploughing grants etc) contribute substantially to the gross outputs and the net incomes of hill and upland farms. For instance, in 1974-75, a bad year for these farms, grants and subsidies accounted for 20% of their total gross output and for 74% of their total net farm income (Figure 1). However in 1975-76, a much better year, their contribution was about 40% (still a very substantial proportion) of the overall net farm income.

ECONOMIC PROBLEMS AT FARM LEVEL
The classification of Welsh Farm Management Survey farms into the hill and upland categories in the following tables and in the appendices has been done on a somewhat different basis to that used for presenting data for the individual countries. The main difference is that hill farms, as classified at Aberystwyth, include those with a rather lower proportion of rough grazings and narrower ratio of sheep to cattle, than do those in the MAFF's 'Mainly sheep' category. However, sheep production is still the predominant enterprise. The actual net income achieved by individual farmers depends on the size of business, which varies with the acreage and quality of land, and upon the operator's aspirations, and technical and managerial skill.

Figure 2
INDICES OF NET FARM INCOME ON WELSH, ENGLISH AND SCOTTISH
HILL AND UPLAND FARMS, 1965-75 (1965 = 100)

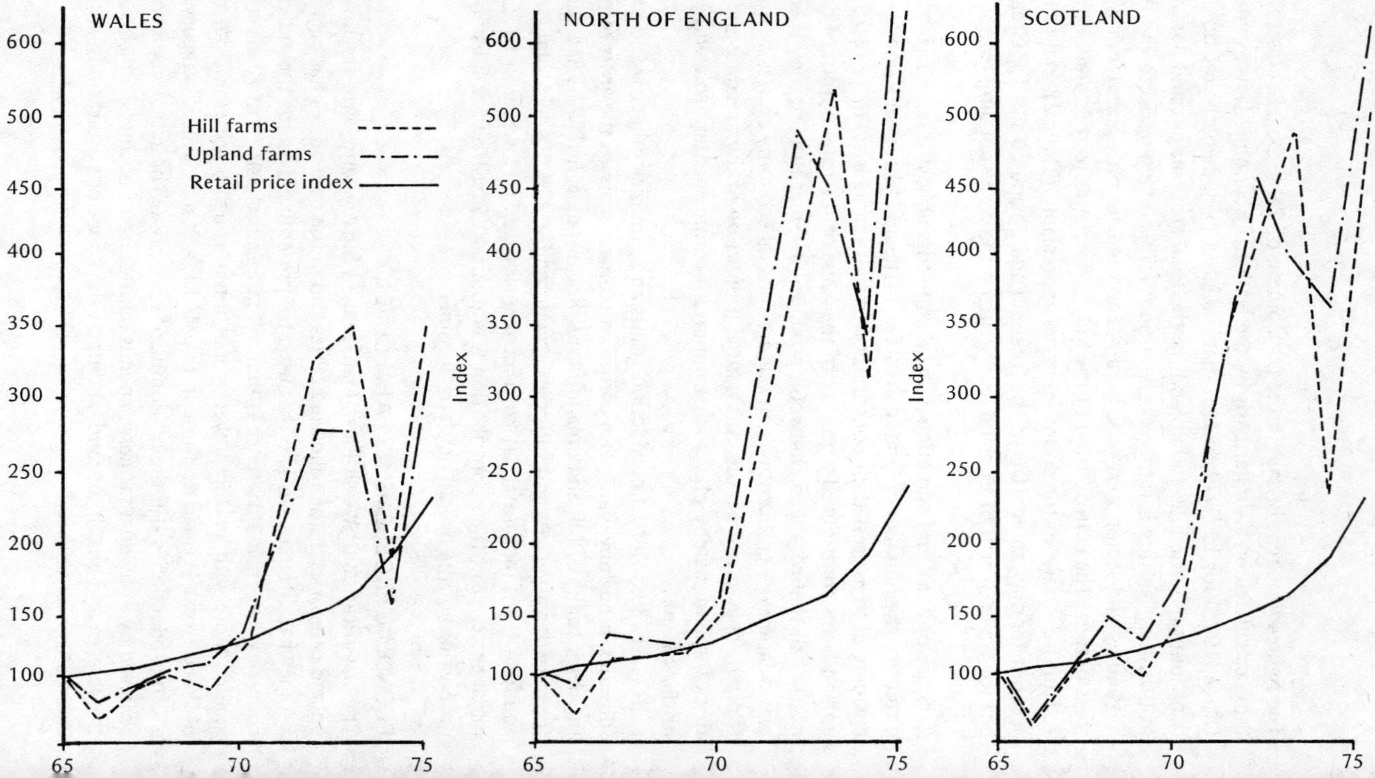

56

Figure 3
AVERAGE NET INCOMES ON WELSH FARM MANAGEMENT SURVEY FARMS, 1965-75 (£'s per farm)

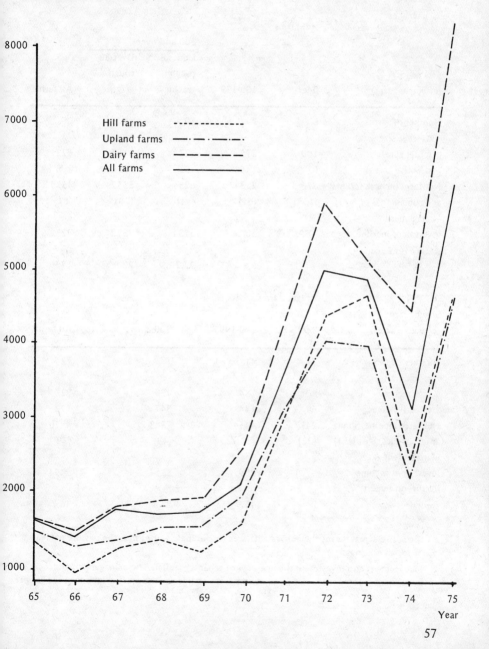

Table 3

AVERAGE NET FARM INCOME (PER FARM) AND RETURN ON TENANTS' CAPITAL FOR SAMPLES OF WELSH HILL AND UPLAND FARMS, 1975-76

Size of farm (effective acres)[1]	Hill farms		200 and over		
	0-99	100-199	Under 80% rough grazing	Over 80% rough grazing	All farms
Number of farms	8	29	30	29	96
Average size —					
actual acres	100	275	577	1162	622
effective acres	61	145	353	485	306
Net farm income (grants and subsidies % of NFI)	576 (133)	2834 (61)	6254 (51)	5552 (70)	4535 (61)
Management & investment income	−795	508	3734	3372	2272
Return on tenants' capital[2]	−19.2	5.8	22.2	22.8	17.9

Size of farm (effective acres)	Upland farms			
	0-99	100-199	200 & over	All farms
Number of farms	14	41	17	72
Average size —				
actual acres	80	184	450	226
effective acres	69	144	347	177
Net farm income (grants and subsidies % of NFI)	2477 (32)	4454 (38)	7843 (43)	4870 (39)
Management & investment income	0	2097	5517	2494
Return on tenants' capital[2]	0	15.9	22.6	16.7

1 'Effective acres' means the cultivatable area (including pasture) plus the pasture equivalent of rough grazings.

2 Management and investment income as % of tenants' capital. The management and investment income is the net farm income less a charge for the manual labour of the farmer and wife.

Figures 2 and 3 indicate that net incomes per farm for livestock rearing and dairy farms fluctuate to varying degrees, more or less annually. In the late 1960's in Wales the fluctuations were somewhat sharper for hill and upland than for dairy farms. Moreover, the actual levels of net incomes were appreciably lower for the former categories than for the latter.

Table 3 shows clearly that there is an income problem on small farms of both the hill and upland type, notably the former. In 1975-76, the average net income per hill farm of less than 100 effective acres was far below the level necessary to provide the farmer with a farm worker's wage before even considering any return for his management and his tenant's capital, and provision for possible future development. This low net income is partly explained by the relatively high proportion of occupiers in this group who were pensioners but still regarded as the 'farmers' (see section on 'Economies of Scale'). The average, even for the medium sized hill farms and the small upland farms, was also much lower than the average annual earnings (about £3 100) of adult male manual workers in other industries at that time. Moreover, if it were not for annual Exchequer support, the situation would be very much worse than depicted by these figures. Both small and medium sized hill farms and small upland farms provide either a negative or a very poor return on tenants' capital.

The most significant economic characteristic of hill and upland farming is the relatively low output per unit area provided by the extensive systems of cattle and sheep rearing enforced by natural conditions. There is a very considerable difference in output per unit area even between hill and upland farms, but it is very much less than that between these and dairy and general cropping farms.

Table 4

GROSS OUTPUT FOR VARIOUS FARM TYPES IN GREAT BRITAIN, 1974-75 (£ per acre)

Type of farming	Hill	Upland	Rearing with arable	All hill & upland farms	Dairy farms	Cropping farms
North of England	11.9	46.5	—	37.6	141	145
Wales	13.0	39.7	—	30.0	131	n.a.
Scotland	4.5	20.6	83.7	18.7	126	126
Great Britain	6.0	28.6	83.7	22.6	146[1]	n.a.

1 From the figure for England rather than those for the North of England.

Sources: MAFF *Farm Incomes in England and Wales, 1974-75;*
    Scottish Agricultural Economics, 1976.

Detailed financial data are given for various sizes of Welsh hill and upland farms for 1975-76 in Appendices 1 and 2. The total enterprise output per effective unit area declines with increases in farm size, largely because of the higher proportion of rough grazings, a higher proportion of sheep to cattle and a lower stocking density, measured in livestock units per unit area. The enterprise output of a livestock enterprise is its gross output adjusted for the value of animals transferred out to and in from another enterprise, plus any part of its production used on the farm. The enterprise output of crops is the total value produced, regardless of disposal. Pig and poultry enterprises also contributed towards a higher output for small upland farms. The increasing proportion of sheep is revealed as a higher contribution of sheep to total output.

To maintain or raise their net incomes in the face of a gradually deteriorating input:output price relationship, hill farmers are fattening an increasing proportion of their lambs. According to Dummer (1962) in the late 1950's only about 15% of lambs reared in hill flocks were sold fat, compared with between

Table 5

LAMBING RATES AND DISPOSAL OF LAMBS ON WELSH FARM MANAGEMENT SURVEY FARMS, 1975-76

Size of farm (effective acres)	Hill farms			Upland farms	
	0-199	200 and over		0-199	200 and over
		Under 80% rough grazing	Over 80% rough grazing		
Number of farms	13	13	13	11	6
Per 100 ewes tupped:					
Lambs born	91.2	93.8	88.2	99.3	110.1
Lambs reared	86.3	90.4	83.2	97.9	108.7
% lambs reared:					
Lambs sold — fat	57.0	46.9	43.6	78.5	73.7
— store	14.0	16.4	19.2	4.7	7.5
— breeding	1.2	2.3	—	1.4	—
Lambs retained for breeding	27.8	34.4	37.2	15.4	18.8
Price(£)—per fat lamb	10.9	10.9	10.3	12.7	13.3
—per store lamb	6.4	8.7	5.8	7.3	11.4

40 and 50% in 1975-76, (Table 5). There is a substantial margin for fat lambs, which can be earned with little or no additional costs because lambs are fattened on rape grown annually in the process of maintaining or improving the quality of hill pastures. The lambing rate (governing the number of lambs available for sale and the gross output per ewe and per unit area) is of paramount economic importance on both hill and upland farms. Because it is a function of both physical and climatic conditions, and of the quality of management, the rate varies from farm to farm and within farms from year to year. The effective lambing rate (lambs reared per 100 ewes tupped) is considerably higher under the more favourable conditions of the uplands. The quality of management is as good, often better, for the smaller flocks because of the greater attention paid to them, especially at lambing.

The kinder conditions of the uplands also permit relatively more cattle to be kept and a higher proportion to be sold fat rather than in store condition. Better prices for beef in more recent years, and the inclusion of breeding stock only for the assessment of compensatory allowances for livestock in less favoured areas, may discourage expansion in numbers of breeding stock, and encourage keeping more store cattle to an older age (18-20 months).

The stocking density, and the ratio of sheep to cattle, both play important roles in determining the output per unit area (Table 6). Broadly, as the farm area increases, the ratio of sheep to cattle widens, stocking density, subsidies, and levels of cost, output and net farm income per unit area, decline. Obviously, the poorer the land, the larger the area necessary to provide adequate levels of output and net income.

ECONOMIES OF SCALE

The reduction in costs per effective unit area associated with increasing farm area (see Appendices 1 and 2), are even more striking than those in the output per effective area. For both hill and upland farms, total costs for the largest size group are less than half what they are for the smallest. On average, the fixed costs, namely labour (including that of farmer and wife), rent, machinery and power costs, etc, account for two thirds of the total costs for both hill and upland farms.

A few interesting facts emerge from the relationships between the costs per effective acre and the increasing area of the farm:

(i) The reduction in variable costs is almost as much as that in fixed costs for upland, but very much less for hill farms. One reason for this is that pigs and poultry, heavy consumers of concentrated feed, are quite prominent enterprises on small upland farms.

(ii) The reduction in fixed costs is greater for upland than for hill farms.

(iii) Labour is the main source of 'economy' in fixed costs on both types of farm

Table 6

OUTPUT, COSTS AND NET FARM INCOME PER EFFECTIVE ACRE BY STOCKING DENSITY ON WELSH FARMS, 1975-76.

Forage acres per grazing livestock unit	No. of farms	Average size of farm (effective acres)	Forage acreage per grazing livestock unit	Number of breeding sheep per cow	£'s per effective acre					
					Subsidies	Enterprise output (including subsidies)	Cost (including farmer & wife)	Management & investment income	Labour of farmer & wife	Net farm income
HILL FARMS										
Under 2.5	3	86.2	1.8	10.9	16.6	99.4	92.5	6.9	23.0	29.9
2.5 & under 3.5	15	181.8	3.1	17.7	13.4	68.8	51.0	17.8	12.6	30.6
3.5 & under 4.5	17	284.3	4.1	28.4	11.1	40.9	35.3	5.6	7.4	12.3
4.5 & under 5.5	11	271.3	4.9	28.4	9.5	44.0	31.9	12.2	9.7	21.9
5.5 & under 6.5	11	400.8	6.1	26.8	8.9	35.8	28.2	7.6	4.7	12.3
6.5 & under 7.5	13	382.2	6.9	35.4	8.7	35.0	27.3	7.7	6.2	13.9
7.5 & under 8.5	10	214.9	8.0	38.0	7.9	32.5	33.2	-0.8	11.3	10.6
8.5 & over	16	438.5	13.2	56.4	6.2	22.7	18.0	4.7	4.9	9.6
UPLAND FARMS										
Under 2.5	34	137.6	2.0	11.3	12.6	98.0	85.5	12.6	17.2	29.8
2.5 & under 3.5	27	220.0	3.6	19.8	8.8	51.9	38.3	13.6	9.6	23.2
3.5 & over	11	194.7	4.3	18.4	8.5	51.0	40.5	10.5	10.4	21.4

because of the 'family' nature of most small and many medium sized farms. The lesser cost of farmer and wife labour for small hill than for small upland farms was because a high proportion (five of the eight) small hill farmers in our sample were semi-retired or farming part-time and their sons were regarded as 'hired' workers. The upland farmers were younger, could farm more intensively and be more fully occupied on their own farms. Associated with the more intensive farming in the upland sector were, a heavier cost of machinery and a greater economy of scale in this item and, on the small farms, a very much heavier reliance on purchased feed. The cost reductions per effective acre do not wholly reflect economies of scale, since the output per acre also declines with increasing unit area. However, the total inputs per £100 of output, although very high for small farms of both the hill and upland type, also decline appreciably with increasing farm size. These reflect the economies of scale to be reaped by farmers with larger areas, although the larger area has usually a lesser overall productivity per unit area.

Table 7
INPUTS[1] PER £100 OUTPUT FOR WELSH FARM MANAGEMENT SURVEY FARMS, 1975-76.

Size of farm (effective acres)		0-99	100-199	200 and over		All farms
				Under 80% rough grazing	Over 80% rough grazing	
	No. of farms	£	£	£	£	£
Hill farms	96	123.8	95.1	75.5	76.2	84.2
Upland farms	72	100.0	82.4	74.5		81.6
Lowland dairy farms	95	87.5	76.7	75.9		79.3

1   Total costs, including labour of farmer and wife.

It is the hill farms which appear to offer the greater scope for economies of scale; the greatest economies appear to be achieved between the smallest and the middle sized group, although substantial economies are also achieved by the largest compared with the middle sized farms.

POST-WAR DEVELOPMENTS

Much has been attempted in post-war years to overcome income and other problems associated with hill and upland farming. Amalgamation of holdings has taken place to a very considerable degree, forced by economic pressure and, more recently, encouraged by government sponsored financial incentives. For instance between 1966 and 1974 the total number of full-time hill and upland farms in Wales was reduced by about 1 290 or 15%. The need for and the actual occurrence of restructuring has been greater amongst the hill farms, the number which were reduced, during this period, by about 1 560 or 45%. The 'upland' sector showed a net increase of 270, a situation probably due to a movement of some farms from other sectors to the 'upland' sector.

Whilst the government has assisted financially to rehabilitate many hill and upland farms, technological improvements have been few in comparison with lowland farms, because of the lesser scope for development in hill farming systems and a lesser incentive to invest as a result of low net incomes and a shortage of capital.

About a quarter of the 11 or 12 million acres (4.5 or 4.9 million ha) of rough grazings in Great Britain are probably improveable, about half by ploughing and reseeding. In Wales about one quarter of a million acres (100 000 ha), or 20% of the hills and uplands have been improved by ploughing and reseeding alone over the last 25 years.

The cost of hill land improvement is high and the higher the cost, the greater the increase in stocking and/or in livestock performance necessary to justify, economically, the improvement. Estimates made by the author (Dyfri Jones, et al, 1973) showed that ploughing and reseeding the better hills justified itself (in terms of return on capital) more than did the low-cost surface-treatment of the poorer soils. However, because most of the better hills have by now been improved and because of the shortage and the high cost of capital, surface-treatment is now more commonly practised.

Supplementary feeding with feed blocks, although rather expensive, is economically justified by the saving in costs of agistment and labour, and by the better performance of both ewes and lambs. The adoption of mechnical shearing has resulted in much labour saving, especially on large farms. Some farmers have tried winter housing but it has proved very expensive and has not yet become common practice. However, because of rapidly rising costs of away-wintering, it may well be more widely adopted in future.

Various sheep-breeding societies and marketing groups, by conveying consumer needs to farmers, have done much to improve performance and quality of hill sheep and cattle.

An examination of all hill and upland farms in the Welsh Farm Management

Table 8

ESTIMATED PRODUCTIVITY OF LAND AND LABOUR ON SAMPLES OF WELSH HILL AND UPLAND FARMS, 1955/56 to 1971/72

	Hill farms						Upland farms					
	1955-56	Index	1965-66	Index	1971-72	Index	1955-56	Index	1965-66	Index	1971-72	Index
Number of farms	65		82		113		58		76		67	
Average size of farm (actual acres)	470		485		541		189		200		211	
Per 100 acres:												
Density of stocking (livestock units)	15.1	100	22.4	149	26.2	174	29.4	100	40.3	137	41.9	142
Man units	0.51	100	0.41	80	0.35	69	1.58	100	1.05	66	0.95	60
Gross output[1] £	601	100	753	125	689	115	2063	100	2360	114	2356	114
Net output[1] £	496	100	613	124	539	109	1719	100	1984	115	1910	111
Gross output[1] per man unit £	1178	100	1837	156	1969	167	1306	100	2248	172	2480	190
Net output[1] per man unit £	973	100	1495	154	1540	158	1088	100	1890	174	2011	185
Purchased feeds and seeds as % of gross output	17.4		18.5		21.7		16.7		15.9		18.9	

1 Excluding grants and subsidies and at constant 1969-70 prices

Survey reveals some very interesting, although not statistically highly conclusive, information about the broad changes in productivity of inputs of land and labour in post-war years.

The general impression gained from Table 8 is that the gross output (excluding production grants and subsidies), measured at constant 1969-70 prices, and on a per 100 acre basis, fluctuated but increased generally between 1955-56 and 1971-72, the increases, however, being far less than proportionate to increases in the stocking rate. This suggests that the productivity of the livestock on a per head basis must have declined, especially in the later 1960's. Owing to reductions of about 30% and 40% in the number of man-units employed on hill and upland farms respectively, the gross output per man unit increased substantially, especially in the upland category.

A better measure of the productivity of the farm resources is the net output since it excludes from gross output the cost of purchased feeds and seeds ie it excludes the produce of 'bought in' areas. The net output (excluding grants and subsidies), at constant 1969-70 prices, and expressed per 100 acres, showed similar increases to the gross output between the mid-1950's and mid-1960's, but thereafter lesser increases. After the mid-1960's a rising proportion of the gross outputs was eroded by increased purchases of feed — as concentrates, hay, and away-wintering.

Since the samples of farms used were not identical over the whole period, the results must be viewed with caution. Nevertheless, they suggest that many Welsh hill and, to a lesser extent, upland farms are overstocked to an extent that has a deleterious effect on the performance of ewes and lambs. Possibly the payment of the hill sheep subsidy on a per head basis since about 1965 has accentuated the situation and, whilst the main aim of the subsidy is to supplement farm incomes, it may well have contributed to some inefficiency in the use of some resources in the hill and upland sector. This situation poses the question of whether the areas of hill land improved in post-war years has been used to best advantage. Have many of our hill farms been too concerned with using their improved land for carrying more stock in summer and too little with providing more winter keep? It is imperative to strike a proper balance between the number of stock carried in summer and the farm's capacity to support them in winter, especially now that all purchased feeds have become so expensive. Although increasing use over recent years of protein-rich feed blocks for hill ewes has eased the situation, the stocking density on many hill and upland farms needs nevertheless to be reviewed.

PROBLEMS AT NATIONAL LEVEL
In view of the relatively high cost of production on our hill and upland farms, in

terms of both actual costs and government support, it is logical to inquire whether or not we could replace the output of the hills and uplands by stepping up the intensity of our lowland farms, or by importing its equivalent either as store animals to be finished on our lowland farms, or as finished products? What other uses can these areas be put to? They cannot wholly be allowed to become a wilderness, or kept in trim for tourists, or even put under forestry. At least one previous estimate, that made by the National Economic Development Office (1973) has suggested that even if it were possible to make up for the loss in output by increasing beef and sheep output from lowland farms, the additional costs would be greater than the saving in subsidies for hill sheep and cattle. Nevertheless, some economies may be achieved by transferring some of the inputs from hill and upland farming to the more productive, lower cost, lowlands.

If the present area under timber (4½ million acres (1.8 million ha) providing about 8% of our requirements) were extended to cover the whole of our hills and uplands we would be about 25-30% self sufficient. However, as the Treasury report on Forestry (HM Treasury, 1972) points out, "new planting compares unfavourably with the hill farming it replaces in economic resources and in Exchequer costs per acre". Although it provides higher employment per unit of land, the cost of job creation is much higher in forestry than in farming in hill and upland areas. Therefore, whilst further expansion of forestry may be desirable, it should be carefully planned so as to occupy those areas where it has least effect on the viability of farming units, and can play a complementary role with farming by providing access roads, shelter belts, and part-time employment for farmers and farm workers.

Returning to the question of cost saving, the alternative to maintaining the present level of hill and upland output (other than to relocate a portion on lowland farms) is to import more store cattle or beef carcases and mutton and lamb. Increasing our imports of these products, although it may result in a saving in over-all costs, will, inevitably widen the trade gap (Houston, 1975) which would not be welcomed under the present unsatisfactory balance of payments conditions. This situation, along with the growing shortage of world food supplies causing the price of imported food to rise, suggests that we should be producing as much as possible from our own resources (House of Commons, 1975).

The factors determining the role that our hills and uplands should play in our agricultural and national economies are diverse and intricate. Most of the present day evidence seems to point towards the need to at least maintain our hill and upland output, but to achieve this at a reduced cost per unit of output.

How can such a situation be achieved? Firstly it is obvious that the structure of our hill and upland farming is still very much out of line with present-day economic circumstances. From a purely economic point of view there are still far too many small units, even small 'full-time' units, which cannot possibly survive without substantial government support and which cannot achieve much by cost economies. Hence the deliberate policy of restructuring is essential and must be continued. However, such a policy leads to rural depopulation and a reduction in the amenity and recreational value of the countryside at a time when urban people are becoming more appreciative of such values and can contribute to small-farm incomes. This argument is gaining momentum and is taken account of in the EC farm policies for Less Favoured Areas. Whilst the extent of the recreational facilities required and farmers' desire to provide such facilities on their farms is as yet not known, these considerations are now taken into account in formulating restructuring policies. Restructuring should not be carried to such an extent that the rural scene is drastically changed by the removal of most of the family farms. A properly planned restructuring policy must lead to the creation of more fully-viable farm units eg a minimum in Wales, of about 250 acres (100 ha) for upland farms (about 450 ewes and 30 beef cows) and of about 500 acres (200 ha) for hill farms (about 1000 ewes or about 30 breeding cows and 800 ewes), (see Appendices 1 and 2). Smaller farms can exist alongside these, provided some additional part-time employment is available (in a nearby village or town, or in forestry) or even on other farms, or a tourist activity is introduced. Bearing in mind the relatively small contribution of hill farms to total output, the high cost per unit of output of small farms of this type, and their remoteness, it is not unreasonable to think that restructuring policy should, perhaps, be applied more vigorously in hill than in upland areas. Appreciably increasing the size and reducing the number of hill farms will not seriously affect the total output. The large hill and lowland farms can provide part-time or seasonal employment for some of the small least viable upland farmers.

CO-OPERATION

Full co-operation, especially between small farms, in the production processes, is often cited as a means of achieving cost economies, especially in the use of machinery and labour, and higher productivity of labour through specialization; possibilities which otherwise would not be open to them. However, there are many problems associated with such ventures and, because of the already specialized nature of hill farming and the relatively low investment in machinery, the economic benefits which can accrue on hill farms are relatively small compared with those achieved from complete amalgamation, with the associated saving in farmer's labour. Co-operation between upland rearers and lowland dairy farmers in the rearing of dairy replacements is also cited as providing economic benefits for both. However, bearing in mind the somewhat longer rearing period for dairy heifers than for beef cattle, whether sold store or fat, there can be little financial advantage in the former for the upland farmer, except that the system ties up less capital. The system is more beneficial to the dairy farmer in that it sets free land which can be used to carry more dairy cows or for some other enterprise.

One venture which many hill and upland farmers may consider in future is the setting-up of co-operative feed-lots for finishing their store cattle. In view of the high capital costs involved, and the high quality management required, these must be large-scale units. This is a system which may catch on if maize becomes a popular crop in Britain. Alternatively, maize-growers may well set up their own feed-lots and contract with hill and upland farmers to provide them with regular supplies of store cattle.

CONCLUSIONS

(i) The hills and uplands make a very substantial contribution to the output of sheep, wool, and cattle produced in the UK. At present, and in the world economic climate of the foreseeable future, the hills and uplands can and must continue to play an important role in our agricultural and national economies.

(ii) The main economic problems in hill and upland farming, more than in other farming systems, is that too many people are still seeking a livelihood on small farm units on land whose quality dictates that it should be farmed in relatively large units. Consequently the small units are operating at high costs and providing low outputs and low returns to capital and labour. In post-war years productivity per unit area has risen less than expected, but considerable reductions in numbers employed have resulted in appreciable improvements in productivity per man. It is likely that the payment of hill subsidies on a headage basis has encouraged some inefficiency and the system needs to be reviewed with a view to payment in relation to livestock performance.

Despite heavy subsidy and capital grant payments, and very considerable farm amalgamation, the 'small farm — low income' problem is still acute.

(iii) There can be no question of government assistance being discontinued, since the output from the hills and uplands must at least be maintained and even the larger hill farmers are so dependent upon this assistance. However, national policies must be directed at speeding up amalgamation of non-viable holdings, and ensuring that capital grants for farm improvements are paid only to those farmers who can make use of them to make their farms fully viable. In this respect the EC Farm and Horticultural Development Scheme is clearly a step in the right direction.

Those small farmers whose farms cannot become viable will be forced out of business, unless they can find means of supplementing their farm income.

Appendix 1
WELSH HILL FARMS 1975/76

Size of farm (effective acres)	0 - 99	100 - 199
Number of farms	8	29
Average size — actual acres	99.8	275.1
Average size — effective acres	60.7	145.4
% Rough grazing	52	70

Enterprise output:	per Farm	per effective acre	per Farm	per effective acre
Cattle	1143	18.8	2486	17.1
Sheep	1109	18.3	2842	19.5
Grants & subsidies	768	12.6	1740	12.0
Other output	346	5.7	350	2.4
Total enterprise output	3366	55.4	7418	51.0
Variable costs:				
Foods	746	12.3	1490	10.3
Fertilisers	148	2.4	371	2.5
Other	201	3.3	330	2.3
Total variable costs	1096	18.0	2191	15.1
Fixed costs:				
Labour (incl. farmer & wife)	1910	31.5	2809	19.3
Machinery & power	498	8.2	833	5.7
Other	657	10.8	1077	7.4
Total fixed costs	3065	50.5	4719	32.4
Total all costs	4161	68.5	6910	47.5
Management & investment income	−795	−13.1	508	3.5
Labour of farmer & wife	1371	22.6	2326	16.0
Net Farm Income	576	9.5	2834	19.5
Grants and subsidies as % of Net Farm Income	133		16	

Tenants capital:	£	Per effective acre	£
Livestock	46.1		44.1
Machinery	17.5		12.0
Crops and deadstock	4.5		3.7
Total	68.1		59.8
Return on tenants capital (%)	−19.2		5.8
Net output per effective acre	£ 42.6		£ 40.6

WELSH HILL FARMS 1975/76

	200 and over		
Size of farm (effective acres)	Under 80% Rough grazing	Over 80% Rough grazing	All farms
Number of farms	30	29	96
Average size — actual acres	576.6	1162.4	622.8
Average size — effective acres	352.6	484.9	305.7
% Rough grazing	60	89	77

Enterprise output:	per Farm	per effective acre	per Farm	per effective acre	per Farm	per effective acre
Cattle	4697	13.3	3496	7.2	3370	11.0
Sheep	6719	19.1	6397	13.2	4983	16.3
Grants & subsidies	3220	9.1	3884	8.0	2769	9.1
Other output	666	1.9	296	0.6	432	1.4
Total enterprise output	15302	43.4	14073	29.0	11554	37.8
Variable costs:						
Foods	2371	6.7	2771	5.7	2090	6.8
Fertilizers	806	2.3	563	1.2	547	1.8
Other	782	2.2	494	1.0	510	1.7
Total variable costs	3959	11.2	3828	7.9	3147	10.3
Fixed costs:						
Labour (incl. farmer & wife)	3960	11.2	3552	7.3	3318	10.9
Machinery & power	1696	4.8	1485	3.1	1272	4.1
Other	1953	5.6	1836	3.8	1545	5.1
Total fixed costs	7609	21.6	6873	14.2	6135	20.1
Total all costs	11568	32.8	10701	22.1	9282	30.4
Management & investment income	3734	10.6	3372	6.9	2272	7.4
Labour of farmer & wife	2520	7.1	2180	4.5	2263	7.4
Net Farm Income	6254	17.7	5552	11.4	4535	14.8
Grants and subsidies as % of Net Farm Income	51		70		61	

Tenants capital:	£		£ Per effective acre		£	
Livestock	34.2		22.9		30.5	
Machinery	9.9		5.9		8.4	
Crops and deadstock	3.5		1.6		2.6	
Total	47.6		30.4		41.5	
Return on tenants capital (%)	22.2		22.8		17.9	
Net output per effective acre	£ 36.3		£ 23.2		£ 30.7	

Appendix 2
WELSH UPLAND FARMS 1975/76

Size of farm (effective acres)	0 - 99		100 - 199	
Number of farms	14		41	
Average size — actual acres	79.7		183.3	
Average size — effective acres	68.7		143.8	
% Rough grazing	13		29	
Enterprise output:	per farm	per effective acre	per farm	per effective acre
Cattle	2529	37.0	4851	33.8
Sheep	2296	33.6	4256	29.6
Grants & subsidies	794	11.2	1672	11.6
Other output	3548	51.6	1039	7.2
Total enterprise output	9167	133.4	11818	82.2
Variable costs:				
Foods	3173	46.2	1893	13.2
Fertilizers	328	4.8	609	4.2
Other	473	6.9	644	4.5
Total variable costs	3974	57.9	3146	21.9
Fixed costs:				
Labour (incl. farmer & wife)	2777	40.4	3410	23.7
Machinery & power	1048	15.2	1440	10.0
Other	1368	19.9	1730	12.1
Total fixed costs	5193	75.5	6580	45.8
Total all costs	9167	133.4	9726	67.7
Management & investment income	0	0	2092	14.5
Labour of farmer & wife	2477	36.1	2362	16.4
Net Farm Income	2477	36.1	4454	30.9
Grants and subsidies as % of Net Farm Income	32	38	38	

Tenants capital:	Per effective acre	
	£	£
Livestock	86.4	62.8
Machinery	27.0	20.0
Crops and deadstock	12.6	8.8
Total	126.0	91.6
Return on tenants capital (%)	0	15.9
Net output per effective acre	£ 86.0	£ 68.1

Appendix 2 (continued)
WELSH UPLAND FARMS 1975/76

Size of farm (effective acres)	200 & over		All farms	
Number of farms	17		72	
Average size — actual acres	450.3		226.3	
Average size — effective acres	347.1		177.2	
% Rough grazing	31		29	
Enterprise output:	per farm	per effective acre	per farm	per effective acre
Cattle	8357	24.1	5227	29.5
Sheep	8483	24.5	4873	27.5
Grants & subsidies	3379	9.7	1904	10.7
Other output	1411	4.0	1615	9.1
Total enterprise output	21630	62.3	13619	76.8
Variable costs:				
Foods	3326	9.6	2480	14.0
Fertilizers	949	2.7	634	3.6
Other	1033	3.0	703	3.9
Total variable costs	5308	15.3	3817	21.5
Fixed costs:				
Labour (incl. farmer & wife)	5361	15.4	3747	21.2
Machinery & power	2372	6.8	1584	8.9
Other	3072	8.9	1977	11.1
Total fixed costs	10805	31.1	7308	41.2
Total all costs	16113	46.4	11125	62.7
Management & investment income	5517	15.9	2494	14.1
Labour of farmer & wife	2326	6.7	2376	13.4
Net Farm Income	7843	22.6	4870	27.5
Grants and subsidies as % of Net Farm Income	43		39	

Tenants capital:	Per effective acre	
	£	£
Livestock	50.8	59.0
Machinery	13.8	17.7
Crops and deadstock	5.9	7.7
Total	70.5	84.4
Return on tenants capital (%)	22.6	16.7
Net output per effective acre	£ 51.9	£ 54.3

ACKNOWLEDGEMENTS
The author gratefully acknowledges the assistance given by his research officers, Messrs A Bell, A Lloyd, and J Robinson, in the preparation of much of the data used in this paper.

REFERENCES
Dummer, M H (1962)   *Economic studies in sheep farming in Wales, No. 4.* Aberystwyth: Department of Agricultural Economics, University College of Wales.

Dyfri Jones, W et al (1973)   *The economics of hill sheep farming.* Aberystwyth: Department of Agricultural Economics, University College of Wales.

H M Treasury (1972)   *Forestry in Great Britain: an interdepartmental cost/ benefit study.*   London: HMSO.

House of Commons (1975)   *Food from our own resources.*   Cmnd 6020. London: HMSO.

Houston, A M (1975)   Agricultural expansion, import substitutions and the balance of payments: a comparative study. *Journal of Agricultural Economics,* **26**, 351-365.

National Economic Development Office (1973)   *Evaluation of the economic significance of the hills and uplands of Great Britain.*   London: NEDO.

7 The contribution of hill sheep to the production of sheep meat in the United Kingdom

F ARGENTESI, L OLIVI & J G W JONES

INTRODUCTION

The complex system of UK sheep production has been described by a suitable compartmental schematisation and then by a mathematical model in order to designate the characteristic parameters, the values of which have been estimated on the basis of the past history of the system, and to determine what population changes may be required to achieve desired objectives. The model that has been constructed takes into account the geographical stratification of the sheep population into hill, marginal and lowland stocks and makes a distinction between ewes and lambs in the populations.

MODEL FORMULATION

The present population of sheep in the UK can be represented by a compartmental model which simulates the three main levels of stratification — hill, marginal and lowland. In order to maintain the population structure, the levels interact with one another through transfers of ewes from the hill to the marginal and lowland levels and through the transfer of female lambs produced at the marginal level to the lowlands.

A flow diagram of the UK sheep population is shown in Figure 1 in which the mechanics of production are also represented. Mortality is expressed as a fraction (DM) of the ewe population at each level of stratification. The output of sheep for slaughter is the sum of the fractions (S[k]) of the ewe populations, the male lambs produced (DN[k]$\frac{X[k]}{2}$) and the fractions (C[k]) of the female lambs sent for slaughter. The various transfers of ewes (TR [k] .X[1]) from the hill populations, the development of female lambs to maturity and the lambs born are also shown.

76

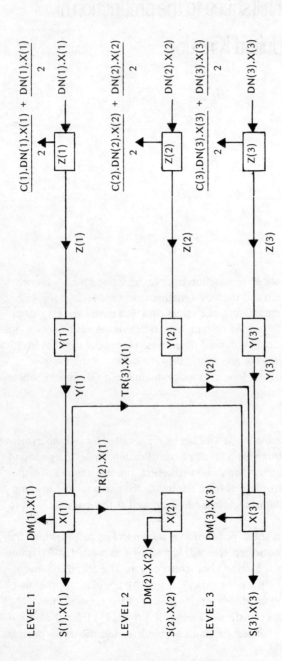

Figure 1   FLOW DIAGRAM OF UK SHEEP POPULATION

Where: Level 1   represents hill land;
        Level 2   represents marginal land;
        Level 3   represents lowland sheep population.

$X(k)$ = population of ewes at level k
$Y(k)$ = population of yearling ewes at level k
$Z(k)$ = population of ewe lambs under 1 year old retained for rearing at level k
$S(k)$ = proportion of ewes sold for slaughter from level k
$C(k)$ = proportion of ewe lambs sold for slaughter from level k
$DN(k)$ = relative reproductive rate of the ewe population at level k
$DM(k)$ = relative mortality rate of the ewe population at level k
$TR(k)$ = proportion of ewes which are transferred from level 1 to level k

From this flow diagram, a mathematical model has been formulated as a system of difference equations representing the rates of change in the populations:

$(\dfrac{dX[k]}{dt}, \dfrac{dY[k]}{dt}$ and $\dfrac{dZ[k]}{dt})$. The values of DN[k], DM[k], S[k], C[k] and TR[k] were taken from Department of Agriculture, University of Reading and Grassland Research Institute (1973). The difference equations were:

$$\frac{dX[1]}{dt} = Y[1] - (DM[1] + TR[2] + TR[3] + S[1]).X[1]$$

$$\frac{dX[2]}{dt} = TR[2].X[1] - (DM[2] + S[2]).X[2]$$

$$\frac{dX[3]}{dt} = Y[2] + Y[3] + TR[3].X[1] - (DM[3] + S[3]).X[3]$$

$$\frac{dZ[k]}{dt} = \frac{DN[k].X[k]}{2} - (C[k].\frac{DN[k].X[k]}{2}) - Z[k]$$

$$\frac{dY[k]}{dt} = Z[k] - Y[k]$$

In the equilibrium situation the rates of changes are zero and this was found to be the case, as expected, when the 1971-72 population data for ewe stocks were taken as initial values.

CHANGING THE SIZES OF EWE POPULATIONS

Changes in the supplies of sheep meat were related to the changes required in the ewe populations. The sheep meat consumption of the UK was taken as 547 000 tonnes in 1972. Of this, 230 000 tonnes were produced in the UK, 38 000 tonnes as ewe meat and 192 000 tonnes as lamb meat, and the remainder was imported. The breeding sheep populations which supplied the UK-produced meat were:

Hill ewes: 4 488 000
Marginal land ewes: 1 267 000
Lowland ewes: 6 530 000

The model was run to determine the ewe populations required to achieve the output of sheep meat envisaged in different scenarios. The major changes of scenario from the present one were:
(i) all sheep meat was produced from hill ewe populations or from lowland ewe populations;
(ii) all sheep meat produced was in the form of lamb;
(iii) all sheep meat consumed was produced in the UK.

Table 1
THE EFFECT ON EWE POPULATIONS OF CHANGES OF SCENARIO FOR SHEEP MEAT PRODUCTION (millions)

Scenario	Hill ewes	Marginal land ewes	Lowland ewes	Total
1 Sheep meat from hill, marginal and lowland ewe populations:				
(a) 230 000 tonnes produced				
(i) meat in form of mutton and lamb (current situation)	4.49	1.27	6.53	12.29
(ii) meat as lamb only	5.39	1.52	7.85	14.76
(b) 547 500 tonnes produced				
(i) meat in form of mutton and lamb	10.69	3.02	15.56	29.27
(ii) meat as lamb only	12.82	3.62	18.66	35.10
2 Sheep meat from hill ewe population only:				
(a) 230 000 tonnes produced				
(i) meat in form of mutton and lamb	19.53	–	–	19.53
(ii) meat as lamb only	23.46	–	–	23.46
(b) 547 500 tonnes produced				
(i) meat in form of mutton and lamb	46.50	–	–	46.50
(ii) meat as lamb only	55.77	–	–	55.77
3 Sheep meat from lowland ewe population only:				
(a) 230 000 tonnes produced				
(i) meat in form of mutton and lamb	–	–	9.61	9.61
(ii) meat as lamb only	–	–	11.55	11.55
(b) 547 500 tonnes produced				
(i) meat in form of mutton and lamb	–	–	22.89	22.89
(ii) meat as lamb only	–	–	27.45	27.45

Table 2
THE NUMBERS OF EWES AND LAMBS SLAUGHTERED (millions)

Scenario	Hill		Marginal land		Lowland		Total	
	Ewes	Lambs	Ewes	Lambs	Ewes	Lambs	Ewes	Lambs
1 (a) (i) (current situation)	0.04	2.22	0.38	0.92	0.96	7.49	1.38	10.63
(ii)	0.05	2.66	0.46	1.10	1.16	9.00	1.67	12.76
(b) (i)	0.10	5.28	0.91	2.18	2.29	17.84	3.30	25.30
(ii)	0.12	6.34	1.09	2.62	2.75	21.39	3.96	30.35
2 (a) (i)	1.21	12.27	—	—	—	—	1.21	12.27
(ii)	1.45	14.74	—	—	—	—	1.45	14.74
(b) (i)	2.87	29.22	—	—	—	—	2.87	29.22
(ii)	3.44	35.04	—	—	—	—	3.44	35.04
3 (a) (i)	—	—	—	—	1.11	10.27	1.11	10.27
(ii)	—	—	—	—	1.34	12.33	1.34	12.33
(b) (i)	—	—	—	—	2.65	24.45	2.65	24.45
(ii)	—	—	—	—	3.18	29.33	3.18	29.33

Table 3
MEAT PRODUCED FROM EWES AND LAMBS (thousand tonnes)

Scenario	Hill		Marginal land		Lowland		Total	
	Ewes	Lambs	Ewes	Lambs	Ewes	Lambs	Ewes	Lambs
1 (a) (i) (current situation)	0.91	34.67	9.00	17.20	28.63	139.85	38.54	191.72
(ii)	1.09	41.64	10.82	20.66	34.38	167.97	46.29	230.27
(b) (i)	2.16	82.54	21.44	40.96	68.17	332.99	91.77	456.49
(ii)	2.59	99.00	25.72	49.13	81.76	399.37	110.07	547.50
2 (a) (i)	25.85	191.72	—	—	—	—	25.85	191.72
(ii)	31.04	230.26	—	—	—	—	31.04	230.26
(b) (i)	61.54	456.50	—	—	—	—	61.54	456.50
(ii)	73.81	547.50	—	—	—	—	73.81	547.50
3 (a) (i)	—	—	—	—	33.08	191.72	33.08	191.72
(ii)	—	—	—	—	39.73	230.26	39.73	230.26
(b) (i)	—	—	—	—	78.77	456.50	78.77	456.50
(ii)	—	—	—	—	94.47	547.50	94.47	547.50

Tables 1, 2 and 3 show the outputs of the model at equilibrium for each of these changes of scenario together with interactions between the changes.

THE EFFECT OF PRODUCING CURRENT UK SHEEP MEAT PRODUCTION AS LAMB

The effect of this is relatively minor overall requiring a 20% increase in total ewe population, the numbers of ewes and lambs slaughtered and in the amount of meat produced from lambs, with similar increases for the hill sector.

THE EFFECT OF PRODUCING IN THE UK ALL SHEEP MEAT CONSUMED IN THE UK

Again the effect is what might have been expected but of much greater magnitude. Nearly 2.5 times as many ewes as are currently carried would be required in all sectors and, if this effect is combined with that of producing current UK sheep meat consumed as lamb, the figure becomes 2.8 times the present population.

THE EFFECT OF PRODUCING ALL SHEEP MEAT FROM LOWLAND EWE POPULATION

On the basis of present production the increase required in the lowland ewe population would amount to about 47%. This would only involve increases of 15% in the number of lowland ewes slaughtered and of 37% in the number of lowland lambs slaughtered; these figures are matched by those for the increases in the meat produced from lowland ewes and lambs. If the current UK sheep meat production were to be produced from lambs, the increases would be 77% for the lowland ewe population, 38% for the number of lowland ewes slaughtered and 65% for the number of lowland lambs slaughtered. In the event of all UK consumption of sheep meat being produced at home in the form of lamb the corresponding figures would be 320, 231 and 291%.

THE EFFECT OF PRODUCING ALL SHEEP MEAT FROM HILL EWE POPULATION

On the basis of present production the increase required in the hill ewe population would amount to about 335%. This would involve an increase of 2925% in the number of ewes slaughtered and of 453% in the number of lambs slaughtered. The corresponding increases in meat produced from ewes and lambs were similar. If the current UK sheep meat production were to be produced from lamb the figures would become 422, 3525 and 564%. If all UK consumption of sheep meat were produced at home in the form of lamb, the corresponding figures would be 1142, 8500 and 1478%.

CONCLUSION

It is clear that the greatest effect of ewe stocks would be produced by attempting to concentrate the production of sheep meat in the hill areas. The implications in terms of stocking rates, land and pasture improvement, capital investment, subsidies and other inducements which might be required to bring about such a change are discussed elsewhere.

REFERENCE

Department of Agriculture, University of Reading and Grassland Research Institute (1973)   *An assessment of continuous lamb production in the United Kingdom. Report of a Working Party.*   Reading: Department of Agriculture, University of Reading.

8 Mechanization or husbandry?
An economist's speculation

C PRICE

INTRODUCTION

Enterprises, like men, find difficulty in serving two masters. I once heard, on successive days, two officials of an organization measuring its success, one by the large number of men it employed, the other by the reduction in the man-hours required for a given output.

This conflict between the apparent imperatives of increased efficiency and provision of rural employment may be endemic to forestry, but that does not mean that no rational solutions are available. It is my contention, firstly that there is a curious misalignment on this point, both in practice and in theory, between overt national forest policy, and the implementation of that policy; secondly that, in a condition of rapid resource depletion, even national policy does not go far enough in encouraging labour-intensive husbandry. The paper concludes with a sketch of possible changes indicated by the viewpoint.

SHADOW COST AND MANAGERIAL DECISIONS

The economist interprets the need to provide rural employment by assigning to labour a shadow cost lower than its market price (ie wage plus labour overheads); and by using this in calculations of net social benefit. The cost-benefit study of forestry (HM Treasury, 1972) based a shadow cost on the assumption that a man employed in forestry would otherwise find employment locally, or migrate to other employment, or remain unemployed. On this basis the shadow cost in upland Britain was given as 44% of financial cost; and, after allowing for savings of social capital, a figure of 40% was used. But even costing labour this way, the cost-benefit study considered that a rate of return of no

more than 4% would be made on afforestation. It was left to the 1972 forestry policy document (HM Government, 1972) to justify forestry's low rate of return by the further benefits conferred by forest employment on the rural community in general. In areas where forestry is a major employer, the survival of a vital community may hinge on continuing afforestation. Whether the objective of maintaining rural communities is worth pursuing is a matter for debate; but while the policy is pursued by one means or another, forestry contributes something to the upkeep of services which would in any case have to be run, and thus reduces the direct subsidy required. To the extent that this is true, the saved direct subsidy or cost of providing alternative employment could be deducted from the shadow cost of forest labour.

It is of course arguable that if other enterprises were offered a labour force at around 50% of normal price, there would be no difficulty in attracting sufficient industrial investment to maintain a thriving rural community. Nevertheless, lacking this dispensation, and given that forestry at the national level is frequently justified by employment generated and communities maintained, it would be appropriate for local decisions to reflect a low social cost of labour.

The natural way for the Forestry Commission to achieve this would be to use the same shadow costs of labour in its managerial decisions as were thought appropriate to making the case for forestry in general. In practice, decisions on the amount of labour used in silvicultural operations, as with other silvicultural investments, are increasingly being taken by reference to a test rate of return of 5%. It can be argued that, as this is lower than the Treasury's test discount rate (10%), the criterion not only encourages planting of a larger area than would otherwise be undertaken, but also a greater investment in the cultural operations on a given area.

Three counter-arguments should be noted here. Firstly, that the 10% rate is in any case suspect, and that even the 5% rate can be regarded as too high (Price, 1973; Helliwell, 1974). Secondly, that manipulations of the discount rate are unsatisfactory as a means of allowing for social benefit (Price, 1976), since discounting provides not only a means of rationing capital, but of giving weight to values at different points in time.

Thirdly, the lower discount rate does nothing to distinguish the labour input from other inputs. In purposely favouring copious use of labour, the 5% criterion also favours, unintentionally, copious use of machinery, fuel and materials. Now it is current Commission practice to cost machinery at 10% interest, and it may appear that, rates of return from silviculture being what they are, this will be a powerful disincentive to mechanized investment. In fact, it is 5% and not 10% that is used as a test rate of return for the investment. 10% is used only in dividing the machine's cost over its lifetime's output; the cost then being compared with the value of the resultant revenue discounted at 5%. Over a working period of a few years, this causes some, but relatively little, increase in machine cost, and for an item with a short life, such as a saw chain, it hardly makes any difference at all. Why the Commission should thus wish to favour capital with rapid depreciation is unclear.

To sum up: in the state sector the use of labour is officially encouraged in:
(i) extending the estate largely by pursuit of afforestation targets set politically in relation to social criteria (limited, apparently, by a 3% target rate of return (Forestry Commission, 1975));
(ii) intensifying silviculture by use of a low discount rate for investments: which, while normally more lenient than allowing a c.50% shadow cost of labour, is arguably still too stringent a criterion;
(iii) choice of technique by somewhat penalizing long-lived capital with a 10% interest charge.

The private sector, apart from any tendency to follow Commission norms, is likewise encouraged to make investment indifferently in capital- or labour-intensive silviculture. The system of switching income tax schedules (Hart, 1975) generally means that expenditures are relieved under schedule D, so that more extensive planting and more intensive silviculture are profitable than would otherwise be justified. Planting grants, however, favour extension rather than intensification.

The case can be made that in the phase where the cost of labour is currently least correctly emphasized — that is in choice of technique — a correct mode of assessment would anyway make little difference to choice. Some operations, such as furrow ploughing, are so time-consuming and arduous when replaced by manual work that even major reductions in the shadow cost of labour would not affect method. What can still be urged is that in the search for productivity, future developments of machinery are related to the correct price of labour, and not to some notion that increased capital intensity is a mark of progress and that all opportunities to mechanize should be seized, independently of the scarcity of capital and of labour.

THE DEPLETABLE RESOURCE DIMENSION

Some rethinking along these lines would be indicated, even if present relative costs and values were likely to be maintained, and the use of high discount rates shown to be justified. It is, however, arguable that present social accounting procedures give insufficient attention to the future, and in so doing tend to undercost capital and undervalue timber production. The use of depletable resources in the forestry production process diminishes the stocks available for future use. And, while economists such as Beckerman (1974) have argued that improving technology will more than compensate for depletion of stocks, the uncertainty of the prediction justifies a less sanguine approach.

If use of a resource now means less consumption in future, and if the rationale of heavily discounting future benefit is rejected, shadow cost is no longer properly regarded as the value of the resource in present alternative uses, but its value if reserved for future use. Technological developments could lead to the future value of fossil fuels falling; but against this must be set the possibility of very high values emerging, should the advance of technology falter through internal weakness or constrained by reasonable public fears of its possible effects. On balance, in a state of uncertainty it is rational to regard fossil fuels and the fertilizers based on them as underpriced. Machinery too and many raw materials have high energy content, and their employment can equally be given a high shadow cost. This basis for rationing use of resources is more realistic than, for example, Feldstein's (1964) social opportunity cost of capital, and vastly more satisfactory than the current 10% test discount rate criterion, which is applied equally to resources, whether they are depletable or not.

There is no parallel sense in which forestry's labour force could be reserved for the future. The small extra energy input required as a result of manual labour is at least theoretically renewable. Moreover, if a portion of the rural labour force is diverted from industrial employment, a deduction from shadow cost can be awarded on the grounds that resource-extravagant production elsewhere in the economy is thereby obstructed: though a certain element of opportunity cost might be attributed if alternative uses of some labour promoted long-term investments.

These suggestions may appear fanciful, but they seem the logical conclusion of ideas on stock depletion (Georgescu-Roegen, 1971) that have not been satisfactorily refuted. They are further discussed in Price (1977).

The philosophy embodied in such a system of costs for forestry inputs should also be reflected in the value attributed to increased production. Doubt is increasingly being cast (Wood, 1975) on predictions of abundant imports of (Richardson, 1970) or substitutes for (Dawkins, 1969) timber. If Britain were to be thrown more heavily onto its own timber resources, a rise in the value of timber would certainly ensue, on top of what is implied by the historic 1½% per annum real price rise: and, unlike food production, it is necessary to take account of values 50 years hence in present managerial decisions. Furthermore, a belief in sustained or rising values of future crops puts emphasis on measures of husbandry which will maintain the productivity of sites. The adoption of a 5% discount rate in place of 10% is obviously an improvement in giving more weight to the future. Even at this 'low' rate, however, the discounted value of all future production if the land is kept under forest is only 10% greater than the value of the first rotation taken alone. This is hardly a stimulus to put emphasis on long-term site quality, and the Forestry Commission tends to treat site maintenance as a constraint. Alternatively, an analytical approach can be made which both abandons the suspect reasoning underlying discounting, and adopts a system of shadow pricing.

CONSEQUENCES FOR FOREST MANAGEMENT

If all these ideas are taken in conjunction, what kind of balance is suggested in silviculture? Choice of technique is obviously affected. For example, cleaning and weeding by bill-hook, reap-hook or hand-held power saw would be favoured against energy-intensive tractor-mounted devices. But a shift to labour-intensive processes, or rather a retardation of the rush to mechanize given operations, is not the only indicated change. A more comprehensive picture emerges if the increased shadow cost of materials and machinery is treated separately from the reduced shadow cost of labour. Several general effects can be distinguished.

The advance of mechanization should be concentrated into those fields where economy in energy and raw materials can be achieved. What is needed is not for example tractors that economize on man-days to fulfill a task, but tractors which achieve a good fuel economy, and are constructed for long life. The preferred machine should be that whose total output for unit creation and lifetime fuel costs is high, no matter how long the period over which output is spread. The predilection of high discount rates for short-life capital should be rejected. Energy economics is a developing field, and foresters might well orientate their notions of efficiency towards energy-productivity rather than towards man-productivity.

Secondly, those operations which are necessarily intensive in capital should be avoided where feasible. If furrow ploughing is put in this category, perhaps a somewhat wider spacing of furrows should be contemplated, with closer spacing in rows, more hand-pruning of excessive side-branches, and selective thinning within rows replacing the normal line-thinning of rows.

This already gives some impression of the proper effect of 'cheap' labour. The cultural operations just mentioned that have been abandoned with rising market costs of labour might well be reintroduced. Emphasis shifts away from treatments that can be applied rapidly to an entire crop towards those that require examination of the condition of the individual tree. For example, the aerial fertilization of areas where check in growth occurs patchily might be replaced by more selective application where microsite conditions require it.

Over large areas of moorland, Sitka spruce will no doubt remain the most profitable species, but in heterogeneous country a closer-than-current attention to matching species to site would be indicated. This could be directed not only to increasing overall productivity in the medium term, but to species selection and mixture for site quality maintenance. Several species seem to have a growth potential equalling or exceeding Sitka spruce on appropriate sites (Forestry Commission, 1974), and the lack of favour shown them is at least partly attributable to their lengthier maturation period, of which high discount rates give such a jaundiced view. The other argument, of high management costs for mixed forests and stands, is largely related to high financial costs of labour and supervision.

It is in the harvesting phase that the most dramatic feats of mechanization may be expected. Again, this is a field where the case for heavy machinery seems emphatic, especially where, as in Britain, there is yet little sustained evidence of damaging soil compaction and erosion following mechanical exploitation. Nonetheless, there are choices to be made between the labour-intensive horse, and the capital and fuel intensive timber harvesters. Within the latter category are monster 'combine harvesters' which, even at market labour rates in Britain, are more costly than a sequence of simpler processes. Less starkly, there is the choice between winch-and-cable systems and tractor skidding (that is, drawing out logs behind a moving tractor). Normally this is made according to terrain, cable systems being preferred only on steep slopes. Yet the cost advantage of skidding, particularly with large units, stems mainly from a faster rate of output, with consequent saving in labour cost and interest charges, compared with a cable system, which requires two men to work it and frequent delays in setting up a winching position. By contrast, both fuel costs and physical depreciation of machinery can be expected to be much higher when, in addition to hauling out logs, a tractor has itself to travel into and out of the stand.

Naturally, an ascribed increase in the real value of timber has in itself an impact on the extent of cultural operations justified. My general feeling is that, taken in conjunction with revised shadow costs, no increase from the present level of capital-intensive investment would be warranted, but that considerable advances in selective manual or lightly mechanized operations — what would properly be termed husbandry — are in order. At the end of the growth period, a more thorough utilization of the wood is indicated. Whole-tree utilization is a concept more usually associated with mechanization; but labour-intensive methods could be worked out, involving processing with simple machines within the forest, and return to the site of the leaves, twigs and bark which contain the elements central to fertility maintenance.

After the harvest, replanting is normally accomplished without resort to ploughing — a factor favouring reforestation over afforestation. Natural regeneration — normally frowned on partly because of high tending cost — might be more readily tolerated, provided that long delay of establishment was not entailed.

A consequence of these changes, might be a switch in the type of planting land acquired, away from large uniform areas amenable to mechanized treatment, towards heterogeneous country where mixture of species is called for, and hand cultural operations are necessitated by difficult terrain. Often these are areas where the value of alternative material production is low. A closer relation to location of existing settlements would be desirable to reduce fuel-extravagant commuting by the labour force, assist the creation of a stable coherent community, and eventually facilitate transport to small-scale processing industries which would themselves be better able to fulfill rural policies.

The changes suggested are proposed in consideration only of shadow costs and of benefits of timber production, without regard to environmental effects. It is nonetheless obvious that many of them are amenable to recreation, landscape and wildlife conservation, at least in so far as they refer to the qualitative impact on areas presently under commercial forest management. Where areas of semi-natural woodland on rough terrain are considered economically workable as a result of low labour costings, some detriment may be expected, as will arguably be the case if the forest estate is greatly extended onto moorlands. These values provide a separate element in the overall argument.

Even one who accepts the viewpoint outlined (and it is admittedly a rather extreme one by the standards of the day) must be aware that substantial difficulties lie in the way of implementation. In terms of economic theory, it is not difficult to translate shadow costings into operable criteria for the state forest service or fiscal arrangements that could produce an appropriate response from the private sector. The real difficulty lies in the practicality of 'putting the clock back' to an era of greater husbandry and less assistance from the machine. The increase in productivity wrought by machines is of course associated with an increased individual pay packet. However appropriate to circumstances a reduction in some aspects of living standard may appear, it is unlikely to be embraced avidly by any one sector of the population, especially when perhaps the majority of economists would argue that it is unnecessary.

When the question arises of how far these major (and some would say retrogressive) changes should go, the honest answer must be that it is hard to say. The derivation of systems of shadow prices is still in its infancy (Little & Mirrlees, 1974) and has hardly been touched on in relation to zero discount economics (Price, 1977). However, the urgency of change, if the above perspective is as much as plausible, is such that any degree of change that is acceptable to the existing institutions is bound to be a step in the right direction.

ACKNOWLEDGEMENTS

Thanks are due to Jim Dewar and Eric Huggard for their comments on the subject matter of this paper.

REFERENCES

Beckerman, W (1974) *In defence of economic growth.* London: Jonathan Cape.

Dawkins, H C (1969) The future of industrial cellulose: unlimited or end in sight? *Forestry Supplement,* **42,** 89-92.

Feldstein, M S (1964) Net social benefit calculation and the public investment decision. *Oxford Economic Papers,* **16,** 114-31.

Forestry Commission (1974) *The potential of Western hemlock, Western red cedar, grand fir and noble fir in Britain.* Forestry Commission Bulletin 49. London: HMSO

Forestry Commission (1975) *Investment appraisal.* Forestry Commission Planning and Economics Papers, 4. Farnham: Forestry Commission.

Georgescu-Roegen, N (1971) *The entropy law and the economic process.* Boston: Harvard University Press.

HM Government (1972) White paper on *Forestry policy.* London: HMSO.

HM Treasury (1972) *Forestry in Great Britain — an interdepartmental cost/benefit study.* London: HMSO.

Hart, C E (1975) *Taxation of woodlands.* C E Hart: Chenies, Coleford, Glos.

Helliwell, D R (1974) Discount rates in land use planning. *Forestry,* **47,** 147-52.

Little, I M D & Mirrlees, J M (1974) *Project appraisal and planning for developing countries.* London: Heinemann.

Price, C (1973) To the future: with indifference or concern? *Journal of Agricultural Economics,* **24,** 393-8.

Price, C (1976) Blind alleys and open prospects in forest economics. *Forestry,* **49,** 99-107.

Price, C (1977) *Project appraisal and planning for over-developed countries.* Unpublished.

Richardson, S D (1970) The end of forestry in Britain. *Commonwealth Forestry Review,* **49,** 324-35.

Wood, P J (1975) The world situation as it will affect the United Kingdom. *Scottish Forestry,* **29,** 25-38.

9 The hidden input: water and forestry

D M HARDING

INTRODUCTION

The interaction between land use and watershed processes is a topic which has received recent attention in the UK. Watershed management as a research field in the USA dates back some fifty years and much has been written on the policy implications of research results. No such debate has properly developed in the UK partly because the information on which a thorough debate of the issue might be launched is incomplete or unavailable. Steps have been undertaken to provide research results of substance, however, through the establishment of a programme of watershed research by the Institute of Hydrology at Wallingford and an interesting stage has been reached where data are emerging from their catchment experiments.

The implications of land use changes in terms of water yields have not been known in any detail in the past, but substantive results should now become available to supplement those results which have been produced from limited or short-period investigations. That forestry, in particular, has a significant impact on the hydrologic regime of catchments is well-known from many studies in other parts of the world and in this paper, the relationship between forestry and water yield and other hydrologic processes is discussed with an evaluation of the policy implications of such results for land use planning in the uplands.

WATERSHED RESEARCH

The effect of land use on the hydrology of catchments was first studied in a scientific manner in the early part of the present century. The research was based on the catchment (or watershed) as an integration of the hydrological processes operating in any area, and despite the development of laboratory and research plot investigations, this approach has persisted as representing the ultimate proof of hydrological conclusions derived from other techniques (Reynolds & Leyton, 1967). Two early studies of considerable interest and importance were those conducted by Engler (1919) and Bates & Henry (1928). Engler studied two catchments in the Emmenthal Mountains in Switzerland, one completely forested and the other mainly pasture, without reaching any firm conclusions as to the effect of land use cover on the water yields from the catchments. Bates & Henry, in an early pioneering study, however, produced some results from an investigation of two small forested catchments at Wagon Wheel Gap in Southern Colorado. Both catchments were instrumented and monitored for eight years. After this period, one catchment was deforested and the measurements of the hydrological parameters were continued for a further seven years. The analysis of the data for the two periods showed that while both catchments had very similar average run off in the first eight year period, the run off from the deforested catchment was some 25 mm or 15% higher than on the 'control' catchment in the following seven year period. This early experiment, using a 'paired' catchment approach was the forerunner of a large number of subsequent investigations which indicated that a forest land use produces a reduction in water yield — in effect, a hidden input in terms of the resources available from the watershed system.

A substantial increase in watershed management research occurred in the 1930's, particularly through the work of the United States Forest Service. The establishment of the Intermountain Forest and Range Experimental Station, the Sierra Ancha Experiment Station, The Soil and Water Conservation Research Station at Coshocton, Ohio and the Coweeta Hydrologic Laboratory in this period were significant developments as was the formation of the Tennessee Valley Authority. Research at Coweeta in particular, was ambitious with the development of an outdoor laboratory consisting of a series of small catchments with varying degrees of forest cover and subject to different treatments over a long period of time. Early results (Hoover, 1944) confirmed that clearcutting increased run off, but effects on flood peaks and other parameters were related to the precise nature of forest operations. Other experiments were undertaken in the United States including some important work by the Tennessee Valley Authority and catchment research was also initiated in other countries.

Some catchment research was undertaken in the UK in the late 1940's and 1950's although in some cases, no change of land use was involved (Penman, 1950; Rodda, 1961). However, in an important and controversial experiment on the Hodder catchment in West Yorkshire, Law (1956, 1957) studied the water balance of a small (0.045 ha) natural lysimeter in a Sitka Spruce plantation set in a rather larger block of woodland (0.24 ha). He concluded that losses from the forest area were substantially higher (711 mm) than for the Hodder catchment as a whole (421 mm), an increased loss of some 290 mm. He therefore suggested that there should be a moratorium on planting in water catchment areas until further results could be obtained. His research thus represented one of the first studies in the United Kingdom from which land use implications were derived, and although the proposals caused some controversy largely because of the small size of the plantation used in the study and hence were by no means generally accepted, the results attracted considerable attention at a time when water supply undertakings were being encouraged to afforest their catchments (Clarke & McCulloch, 1975).

Research in the United States continued and during the 1960's some important results were published (Tennessee Valley Authority, 1961; North Carolina State College, 1963). In particular, Hibbert (1967) published a valuable comparative study of some 39 catchments relating to the effects of forest treatment on water yields. While he illustrated that there were significant differences between results from the various catchments studied, a reduction in forest cover generally led to increased water yields while the reverse occurred, with lower yields, if forests were established from previously bare land. Such results have generally been supported in the other research that has been undertaken in the USA and several authors have reported on the large number of forested experimental catchments which have been studied (Lull & Reinhart, 1972). Indicative of progress in the USA is that recent studies have been concerned not merely with the grassland/forest relationship, but with the effects of different forest species on streamflow and Swank & Minor (1968) and Swank & Douglass (1974) have indicated that managers now have documentation that substantial changes in streamflow will occur when hardwoods are converted to pine.

RECENT RESEARCH IN THE UK
Research in the UK has developed much more slowly. After Law's work in the mid-1950's, there was little progress until the mid-1960's when the Hydrological Research Unit, which became the Institute of Hydrology in 1968, set up a series of catchment studies in various parts of the country with the study of land use effects as a major concern. Two of these projects are of particular relevance here. At Coal Burn, a tributary of the River Irthing in Northumberland a small catchment (152 ha) was instrumented and studied for five years from 1967 to 1972. The catchment was ploughed in 1972 following standard forestry practice and the effects of this treatment on the volume and other characteristics of streamflow in subsequent years are being investigated. The other study is at Plynlimon in Mid-Wales, where an experiment was set up to compare the hydrology

of the upper Wye (1055 ha) which is almost entirely upland pasture, with that of the upper Severn (870 ha) which has a coniferous forest cover of Sitka Spruce, Norway Spruce with some Japanese Larch over rather more than two thirds of its area (Newson, M D, 1976). The study is designed to answer the following questions:

(i) is the mean annual loss (precipitation minus streamflow) greater for the forested Severn than for the hill pasture of the Wye, and if so, how far is the difference explicable in terms of different land-use?

(ii) does the rapidity and magnitude of response to unit depth of precipitation differ for the two catchments, and if so, how far are the differences explicable in terms of different land use (Institute of Hydrology, 1976)?

This project is now producing some most valuable data and reports have been published on rainfall (Newson, A J, 1976), physiography, deposits and vegetation (Newson, M D, 1976), aspects of erosion processes and sediment yield (Painter, Blyth, Mosedale & Kelly 1974) and, importantly, on the water balance of the catchments for the period 1970 to 1974 (Institute of Hydrology, 1976). The key results in the context of this paper are shown in Tables 1 and 2 which show the annual values of rainfall (P), streamflow (Q) and loss (P-Q) for the Wye and Severn catchments between 1970 and 1975 (Table 1) and the adjusted values of these factors when only the forested area of the Severn is taken into account (Table 2).

Table 1

ANNUAL VALUES OF P, Q AND P-Q: WYE AND SEVERN CATCHMENTS, YEARS 1970-75

	P:		Q:		P-Q:		Ps-Qs-Pw+Qw:
Year	Wye : mm	Severn mm	Wye : mm	Severn mm	Wye : mm	Severn mm	mm
1970	2869	2690	2415	1963 (1991)*	454	727 (699)*	+273 (+245)*
1971	1993	1948	1562	1196 (1328)*	431	722 (620)*	+321 (+189)*
1972	2131	2221	1804	1567	328	654	+326
1973	2606	2504	2164	1823	442	681	+239
1974	2794	2848	2320	2074	474	774	+300
1975	2099	2121	1643	1406	456	715	+258
Mean	2415	2388	1985	1672 (1698)*	431	717 (690)*	286

*Values shown in brackets are those derived from estimated streamflows on the Severn catchment for the years 1970-71. Source: Institute of Hydrology (1976).

94

Table 2

ANNUAL VALUES OF P, Q AND P-Q: WYE AND FORESTED AREA OF THE SEVERN CATCHMENT ONLY, YEARS 1970-75

Year	P: Wye mm	P: Severn mm	Q: Wye mm	Q: Severn mm	P-Q: Wye mm	P-Q: Severn mm	Ps-Qs-Pw+Qw: mm
1970	2869	2485	2415	1636	454	849	+395
1971	1993	1762	1562	797	431	965	+534
1972	2131	2124	1804	1342	328	782	+454
1973	2606	2380	2164	1581	442	799	+357
1974	2794	2703	2320	1785	474	918	+444
1975	2099	2035	1643	1213	456	822	+366
Mean	2415	2248	1985	1392	431	856	425

Source: Institute of Hydrology (1976)

The factor $Ps - Qs - Pw + Qw$ is of major interest because this measures the differences between the annual losses between the two catchments. It is clear that the annual loss for the Wye catchment is 18% of the precipitation input compared with 30% as the unadjusted value for the annual loss for the Severn. Allowing for the adjustment for the unforested part of the Severn catchment, however, produces a figure for mean annual loss for the forested part of the catchment of 38% of the mean annual precipitation input (Institute of Hydrology, 1976).

It is clear, therefore, that as Clark & McCulloch (1975) state, "there is increasing evidence that the water lost from a forested catchment is greater than that lost from a catchment of similar geology, soil and climate, used as pasture". It follows that if maximisation of water yield is the prime objective within water supply gathering grounds then grassland is the more appropriate form of land use.

FORESTS, FLOOD CONTROL AND SEDIMENTATION

While in hydrological terms, maximisation of water yield is likely to be the priority objective in terms of land management in water storage areas, there are, of course, other considerations which must be taken into account concerning the hydrological effects of different land uses. It has long been appreciated that forests have a substantial effect in reducing flood run off rates and flood peaks (Burger, 1943; Rutter, 1958; Pereira, 1973) and for this reason, land use change to forest from grassland is a component of multi-element flood loss reduction programmes (Tennessee Valley Authority, 1964). However, such a land use adjustment may well take some time to be effective and controversy surrounds the effects of drainage and forestry operations associated with the establishment of forests in upland areas. Howe, Slaymaker & Harding (1967) tentatively suggested that such drainage for forestry and agricultural purposes might have been a factor in increasing flood peak discharges in the Severn catchment in Mid-Wales and recent work by Jones (1975) suggests that such drainage, which can greatly increase the effective drainage density of a catchment, produces higher flood peaks as a result of more rapid response to rainfall input. Thus while the establishment of forests can be a useful flood control measure, it may be some time before the effects on flood peaks will be seen (Rutter, 1958).

There is also evidence that forest land use can reduce erosion and sedimentation in catchments (Pereira, 1973), but again the situation is complicated by the effects of forest operations. Both Painter, Blyth, Mosedale & Kelly (1975) and Jones (1975) have demonstrated the effects of ditching on erosion and sediment transport at Coal Burn in northwest England and the Upper Tywi valley in Mid-Wales respectively. Logging activity can also severely affect sedimentation although much can be achieved through careful practice and many papers have been written on the subject (Bethlahmy, 1960; Kidd, 1963; Haupt & Kidd, 1965). The role of forestry in the rehabilitation of watersheds combining flood control objectives with erosion control has also been demonstrated (Tennessee Valley Authority, 1962) and therefore while attention has been concentrated, not unnaturally, on yields from catchment systems, it is important that other hydrological effects of land use changes are appreciated.

CONCLUSION
Substantial areas of the uplands of Britain are now used as water supply gathering grounds. Additional reservoir projects are planned and will be developed in the future. Further, many upland catchments contain flood-prone settlements and are the headwater regions of major rivers which cause flood problems in lowland Britain. Because watershed management as a research field has been very well developed in the USA, it has been possible to discuss in some depth the policy implications of land use changes and effects. A multiresource approach to the use of both forests and watersheds has developed (Hewlett & Douglass, 1968) and the need for land managers to consider the importance of the hydrological consequences of land use decisions has been strongly emphasized (Nelson, 1974).

While it is difficult to imagine that water management in the uplands of Britain could ever become such an important issue in land use terms as it is in parts of the USA (Hewlett, 1966) any debate on the use of the upland areas of Britain should include consideration not only of the primary resource responses, but of the interaction of land use and other environmental factors. It is to be hoped that this debate will move from the often superficial consideration of conflicts in land use to a more thorough evaluation of impacts and effects through a more objective multiresource analysis.

The information necessary to develop a proper appraisal of the relationship between land use and hydrologic processes in the UK is now becoming available. As the demand for water rises and as water resources become increasingly expensive to develop, it is important that 'hidden inputs' are considered in policy formulation and that hydrological considerations are included in a thorough evaluation of the resources of the uplands.

ACKNOWLEDGEMENTS
The author would like to thank Dr. Malcolm Newson of the Institute of Hydrology at Plynlimon, Mid-Wales for supplying material for this paper.

REFERENCES
Bates, C G & Henry, A J (1928) Forest and stream flow at Wagon Wheel Gap, Colorado. Final Report. *Monthly Weather Review Supplement*, **30**, 1-79.

Bethlahmy, N (1960) Surface runoff and erosion — related problems of timber harvesting. *Journal of Soil and Water Conservation*, **15**, 158-161.

Burger, H (1943) The water economy in the Sperbel and Rappen watersheds from 1927-28 to 1941-42. *Mitteilungen der Schweizerischen Zentralanstalt fur das forstliche Versuchswesen, 23*. Translation (Johnson, C W): Paper No. 368, US Forest Services, Division of Forest Influences, Washington, DC (1945).

Clarke, R T & McCulloch, J S G (1975) *Recent work in the comparison of the effects of alternative uses (Coniferous Forest, Upland Pasture) on water catchment behaviour.* Conservation and Land Drainage Conference, Water Space Amenity Commission.

Curtis, W R (1966) Forest zone helps minimize flooding in the Driftless area. *Journal of Soil and Water Conservation*, **21**, 101-102.

Engler, A (1919) Untersuchungen uber den Einfluss des Waldes auf den Stand der Gewasser. *Mitteilungen der Schweizerischen Zentralanstalt fur das forstliche Versuchswesen, 12.*

Haupt, H F & Kidd, W J (1965) Good logging practices reduce sedimentation in Central Ohio. *Journal of Forestry*, **63**, 664-70.

Hewlett, J D (1966) Will water demand dominate forest management in the East? *Proceedings of the Society of American Foresters, 154-159.*

Hewlett, J D & Douglass, J E (1968) *Blending forest uses.* United States Department of Agriculture Forest Service Research Paper SE-37.

Hibbert, A R (1967) Forest treatment effects on water yield. In: Sopper, W E & Lull, H W (eds.) *Forest Hydrology:* Proceedings of the International

Symposium on Forest Hydrology, Pennsylvania State University: Pergamon.

Hoover, M D (1944) Effect of removal of forest vegetation upon water-yields. *Transactions of the American Geophysical Union*, **27**, 969-977.

Howe, G M, Slaymaker, H O & Harding, D M (1967) Some aspects of the flood hydrology of the upper catchments of the Severn and Wye. *Transactions of the Institute of British Geographers*, **41**, 33-58.

Institute of Hydrology (1976) *Water balance of the headwater catchments of the Wye and Severn 1970-74.* Wallingford, Oxon: Institute of Hydrology Report No. 33.

Jones, A D (1975) *Rainfall, runoff and erosion in the Upper Tywi catchment.* Unpublished PhD thesis, University of Wales.

Kidd, W J (1963) *Soil erosion structures on skidtrails.* United States Department of Agriculture Forest Service Research Paper 1NT — 1.

Law, F (1956) The effect of afforestation upon the yield of water catchment areas. *Journal of the British Waterworks Association* **38**, 489-494.

Law, F (1957) *Measurement of rainfall, interception and evaporation losses in a plantation of Sitka spruce trees.* International Union of Geology and Geophysics, General Assembly of Toronto, International Association of Scientific Hydrology, II, 397-411.

Lull, H W & Reinhart, K G (1972) *Forests and floods in the Eastern United States.* United States Department of Agriculture Forest Service Research Paper NE-226.

Nelson, R E (1974). Water for Hawaii — mountain watersheds. In: *Water for Hawaii.* Summary of proceedings, Honolulu, H.I., 31 Jan-1 Feb 1974, 1-12.

Newson, A J (1976) *Some aspects of the rainfall of Plynlimon, Mid-Wales.* Wallingford, Oxon: Institute of Hydrology Report No. 34.

Newson, M D (1976) *The physiography, deposits and vegetation of the Plynlimon Catchments.* Wallingford, Oxon: Institute of Hydrology Report No. 30.

North Carolina State College (1963) *Parker Branch Research Watershed Project Report 1953-1962.* North Carolina State College in co-operation with Tennessee Valley Authority, Knoxville.

Painter, R B; Blyth, K; Mosedale, J C & Kelly, M (1974). *The effect of afforestation on erosion processes and sediment yield.* Proceedings of the International Association of Scientific Hydrology Symposium on Effects of Man on the Interface of the Hydrological Cycle with the Physical Environment, 62-67.

Penman, H L (1950) The water balance of the Stour catchment area. *Journal of the Institution of Water Engineers*, **4**, 457-469.

Pereira, H C (1973) *Land use and water resources.* Cambridge: Cambridge University Press.

Reynolds, E R C & Leyton, L (1967) *Research data for forest policy: The purpose, methods and progress of forest hydrology.* Proceedings of the Ninth British Commonwealth Forestry Conference, Commonwealth Forestry Institute, University of Oxford.

Rodda, J C (1961) *An investigation of the hydrological cycle in the catchment area of the river Ystwyth.* Unpublished PhD thesis. University of Wales.

Rutter, A J (1958) Effect of afforestation on rainfall and runoff. *Water and Water Engineering, 62,* 99-102.

Swank, W T & Douglass, J E (1974) Streamflow greatly reduced by converting deciduous hardwood stands to pine. *Science, 185,* 857-859.

Swank, W T & Miner, N H (1968) Conversion of hardwood – covered watersheds to white pine reduces water yield. *Water Resources Research, 4,* 947-954.

Tennessee Valley Authority (1961) *Forest cover improvement influences upon hydrologic characteristics of White Hollow Watershed 1935-58.* Division of Water Control Planning, Tennessee Valley Authority, Knoxville.

Tennessee Valley Authority (1962) *Reforestation and erosion control influences upon the hydrology of Pine Tree Branch Watershed 1941-60.* Division of Water Control Planning, Tennessee Valley Authority, Knoxville.

Tennessee Valley Authority (1964) *Flood damage prevention: an indexed bibliography.* Tennessee Valley Authority, Knoxville.

10 Comparative advantage in wood production

J J MacGREGOR

INTRODUCTION

In this symposium we are looking at one aspect of national land-use policy and it could be argued that if the national need is synonymous with policy objectives under existing institutions it should be possible to construct an 'optimum' allocation of land resources. Current consumer preferences, demonstrated by willingness to pay, will give greater weight to the desires of those with larger incomes and, incidentally, ignore some preferences of the next generation. However, the price mechanism in these circumstances could be a very efficient allocator of resources without being equitable and it is a feature of the uplands that some of its benefits do not attract payment. These points are made as introductory generalisations but they also have a bearing on comparative advantage in the narrower commercial or technical sense because they bring up the notion of comparative desirability, for, to a large extent, we are dealing with populations and regions which are currently underprivileged in many respects.

The major forestry and afforestation activities in the uplands are likely to lie with the Forestry Commission — an institution which sets fairly precise objectives about the areas of its annual operations. On the other hand the Agricultural Ministers hope to achieve their aims by the responses of many individuals and enterprises and it is thus difficult to know in advance how far the expectations will be realised; in other words there is less central control in agriculture and there have been criticisms of the levels expected in the MAFF's (1975) *Food from our own resources*. It is for examination, therefore, that forestry production would be more dependable and this would in some ways represent a form of comparative advantage for long-term planning.

On *a priori* grounds, as wood and food products imports represent about 90 and 40% respectively of requirements, there would appear to be more scope for forestry expansion — particularly in upland areas which provide a relatively small proportion (about 4%) of total food needs — and the EC experience would support this view of afforestation expansion.

Over the post-war years in Britain there have been several intensive enquiries, each adopting different emphases or approaches, on the problems of upland or 'marginal' land uses and these have attempted to measure the comparative advantages of forestry and of agriculture after sifting the available evidence. The issues are complex but a brief review of the assumptions in one or two of these studies can set the stage for looking at the main causal factors affecting comparative advantage although these can broadly be described as falling under the general economic environment, the national policies for agriculture and forestry, their technological and structural changes and their relative dependence on imports.

SOME RECENT STUDIES ON THE UPLAND ECONOMY

In any comparison with agriculture the long term of the forest rotation made it necessary, in several studies, to calculate over correspondingly long periods; and fifty years has frequently been used for such purposes. By discounting the income and expenditure items to the initial year of the investment the net present worth or net discounted revenue is obtained. At the lower rates of discount the more competitive is forestry investment in commercial terms — the reason being that the heavy initial establishment cost is scarcely reduced by discounting whereas the intermediate and final incomes are heavily affected and increasingly so if higher discount rates are used. Agriculture has a different balance or incidence of income and expenditure and discounting levels make less impact on the net result. At the extremes there are identifiable types of land which are suitable to agriculture only or to forestry only at almost any rate of discount; in between — and this is the area where considerations of competition between agriculture and forestry are most justified — forestry would be more competitive in the lower range of rate. There is also the position where neither forestry nor agriculture could make a financial profit although having the potential to provide some social benefits. The relative merits of extensive systems of agriculture and of forestry for providing such benefits has frequently been argued.

There is probably less argument about the prospect that the bulk of any expanded tree planting in the upland areas will be undertaken by the Forestry Commission and the forest companies rather than by the private estate owners. An approximate distribution of the Forestry Commission forests by site types (Wardle, 1966) revealed that upland heaths, moors and bogs were 70% of the total; the remainder being lowland heaths (13%); chalk downland (4%);

heavy clay (6%); other sites, with high growth potential (7%). According to the Government's Consultative Document (HM Government White Paper, 1972) in future the Forestry Commission expected a net rate of return in real terms from about 1% on poor sites distant from markets to about 3% on good sites within reasonable distances; these were levels of return as high as forestry was likely to earn anywhere in the temperate parts of the northern hemisphere.

A most comprehensive and penetrating analysis of the competition for marginal farming land by the Forestry Commission was pioneered in a study in economic policy for a doctorial thesis (Walker, 1958) later to be summarised in the Scottish Journal of Political Economy (Walker, 1960). Although his views about the competitive ability of forestry were more optimistic than those of later investigations by others, the value of his study lay in its methods of approach and the fact that his realistic statistical and other evidence was derived from intensive field studies in upland areas of Wales, North England and Scotland. At the time of his enquiries, even when some of the assumptions were weighted heavily in favour of agriculture, forestry investment came out at a distinct advantage at the lower rates of discount around 4%. Any reckoning of the relative movements of prices, costs or of 'terms of trade' between agriculture and forestry in, say, 50 years is bound to be speculative but the merit of the above analyses is that they demonstrate some of the significant variables that have to be weighed and measured when attempting to unravel a whole host of complex influences which frequently change with kaleidoscopic speed and shape. It is perhaps worth mentioning here that Walker's assumptions for forest products were based on levels obtained in remote areas containing little or no large-scale forest industries. Yet, any evaluation of forestry's contribution to the national economy would need to consider the value added in the harvesting, marketing and processing stages. A national study from the US Department of Forestry (Hair, 1963) on the importance of timber in USA assessed the substantial added values — of about 25 times of the growers' prices — by the time the product was in the hands of the consumer. In Britain similar estimates of the scale of processing additions and also of the general benefits of forestry production and its industrial integration were made by the founder of the Economic Forestry Group (Rankin, 1973).

Problems of hill-farmers and the causes of their low incomes were widely explored in a survey emanating from the East of Scotland Agricultural College (Martin, 1970); rises in land prices have tempted many owners to sell, especially where they have low ground or separate farms, in order to raise capital for their better development and sometimes as a basis for their retirement. Isolation also creates problems for the farmer and his family as well as making it difficult to recruit and retain farm labour. Among Martin's general conclusions are that the expansion of forestry in Britain would seem to be logical on the supposition that the world's traditional suppliers of timber do not become more efficient and that timber prices remain competitive enough to prevent greater use of timber substitutes.

In a case study of combined land uses at Fassfern in Inverness-shire (Mutch, 1972) the advantages of integration were very clearly stated. Although the precise extent to which external subsidisation, whether government or private, was involved in this development, is not so evident, the claim is made that Fassfern was relevant to the review of forestry policy because it demonstrated that "impoverished soils can be restored in such a way that a fraction of the area can yield an increased animal production, and commercial forestry can occupy most of the ground".

The indiscriminate transfer of whole farms to forestry by blanket planting is wasteful and unnecessary. Fassfern shows the financial advantages of integrated land use: the shared labour force; the shared specialised machinery; the shared roads and fences; the winter grazing in plantations; the farming use of dry hill-tops that are unattractive for forestry, etc.

The developments at Fassfern also showed the power of integrated land rehabilitation to provide employment. Earlier the Land-use Study Group (Department of Education and Science, 1966) drew attention to the integration possibilities of the kind associated with multiple use in a crowded Britain.

The contributions of the Interdepartmental Cost/Benefit Study (HM Treasury, 1972) have been extensively reviewed and evaluated; it has provided much controversy and some of its assumptions have been called in question. The test discount rate of 10% on which the calculations were made was widely regarded as being inappropriate for judging the several distinct benefits derived from forestry. Price (1973) and Helliwell (1974) have developed arguments on this issue.

General arguments, postulated in the first chapter of the Treasury study, should be highly relevant for the objectives of this symposium and to partake of their flavour a few of the introductory observations are summarised here. On the opportunity costs for forestry or hill-farming the view was "it could be suggested that the sum total of production grants and price supports to hill-farming has been precisely tailored to reflect the non-commercial benefits accruing from hill-farming to society as a whole" and similarly for private forestry. The land market it could be inferred "was being manipulated by the authorities in such a way as to take precise account of the relevant non-commercial considerations in forestry and agriculture and that the market mechanism was therefore adequately performing its traditional allocative role between alternative land users".

One of the main objectives for the study was to clarify and quantify the non-commercial factors which in a broad sense were thought to justify support for public and private forestry and it was recognised that the economics of hill-farming should be examined in a complementary way. It would thus be possible to establish the opportunity costs of land for forestry and agriculture represented by the true value of land in the other use. "It is of course possible that, on examination, the values of land in both forestry and agriculture could turn out to be negative, when measured against the test rate of discount now applied in public sector investment. This conclusion would suggest that the present margin of cultivation (defined to include trees as well as sheep) happens to have been pushed slightly too far into the uplands in the light of present and expected price relationships between home produced and imported products." It was recognised that while unemployment was socially an evil it was not clear how far society was willing to expend real resources in order to reduce it, after allowing for the net output of those employed. For that reason it was thought relevant to calculate the 'implied cost per job' of maintaining employment in agriculture and forestry for comparison with current standards in other fields. The width of the analyses in the study can be inferred from titles of some of its chapters: shadow cost of labour in areas of high long-term unemployment; balance of payments considerations; strategic considerations; recreation and amenity; water, climate and wild-life; future timber prices; agricultural revenues and costs; forestry revenues and costs; new planting; the re-stocking decision; management of forests up to time of clear felling; local employment provided and exchequer cost in forestry and agriculture; and the new planting and restocking decisions: resources, jobs and exchequer cost.

TIMBER SUPPLIES FROM OVERSEAS

My particular task leads me to consider some other aspects of competitiveness. Existing competitive ability by itself does not ensure adequacy of supplies and thus the export potential of other countries becomes highly relevant. The main exporters of sawn softwood — one product most directly in competition with that from our upland areas — are in current order of importance Sweden, Finland, Canada and USSR.

In a well-documented article (Sutton, 1975) the ability of the USSR to boost future world supplies was called in question and it was concluded that it would be unlikely to remain as a major exporter to Britain and that its products would not be cheap. Quoting other sources Sutton suggested that the expected surplus production of Canada by the year 2000 would be about equal to the estimated deficiency of the USA where it is the supply of sawn timber that is likely to be the most critical. In the EEC it has been claimed by others (Palmer & Tabb, 1974) that while pulpwood could still be imported from Canada , USSR and some European countries it was hinted that this might not last very long; similar conditions applied to pulp. Industrialised exporting countries will tend to process their own raw material, including pulp, to a greater extent. Conifers from temperate regions remained the most suitable for pulp but these tended to grow relatively slowly and supplies from warmer areas will become more significant. These were influences which would tend to improve the comparative advantages of production from the upland areas which in north Scotland already had the scale-economy advantage of containing a large pulp mill.

THE INFLUENCE OF MAN-MADE PLANTATIONS

Although spectacular production is obtained from the pine plantations in Australasia, South Africa and South-Eastern USA and of eucalyptus, teak and other tropical broadleaved species in many parts of the world, these supplies, on the whole, are not directly competitive for Britain, with the coniferous species from the Northern Hemisphere. This is especially true where the countries producing the quick-growing species are trying to achieve greater self-sufficiency. In New Zealand where very high yields are obtained from *P. radiata* it is quite clear that the output is likely to find its best markets in Japan — a country which, since the war and for some time to come, is likely to attract an important part of the available international trade in wood products and particularly so in the Pacific region.

Hopes of meeting shortages of conifers have often been pinned on the expansion, mainly in the tropical or semi-tropical countries, of broadleaved man-made plantations. These have the competitive advantages of a homogeneous product, short rotations, rapid growth — poles, pulpwood and saw timber have been achieved in as little as 8, 10 and 15 years respectively — the ability to be sited close to ports, other services and to relatively cheap labour. However, these advantages tend to be offset by the limited areas of sufficiently fertile land and by the usual position of being at some distance from the main consuming centres. It is arguable, too, that the quality may preclude it from a wide international trade. Another point for consideration is that coniferous wood for many purposes is much easier to work or process than broadleaved and this is a telling criterion when wages have risen significantly and in industries where labour cost is often a major item.

As more and more of the world's timber supplies are derived from man-made plantations, world prices will be more influenced by the cost of growing timber whereas previously it was likely to be affected more by the costs of felling and harvesting in accessible virgin forests. As the margin or accessibility is stretched further away from the demand centres the cost effect would be apparent in general world prices. For the cost of growing timber to be, and to remain, competitive methods of handling, exploiting and processing must be efficient and this implies that the latest technology must be applied wherever possible throughout the industry.

COMPETITIVENESS WITH WORLD PRICES AND SUBSTITUTES
In the present world situation where the price trends of wood products of internationa trade have been rising the competitive enhancement of the home production achieved through a heavy devaluation of sterling in recent years must not be overlooked. In the same general environment consideration has to be given to the impact of substitutes. Until recently the development of plastics in common uses appeared to gain at the expense of wood but with the surge in the price of oil this competition is less effective. Price alone is not the only determinant of substitution because quality, convenience and fashion — apart from technological changes — may bring about changes in use but this is perhaps too large an issue to explore on this occasion.

POTENTIAL FOR INTEGRATION
Perhaps it is fitting to end with another aspect of the upland problem where the comparative advantages of individual forestry or agricultural sites could be enhanced by integrating them, say, on the lines of a Rural Development Board. Such an arrangement would ensure that where there are distinct comparative advantages in a region they could be complementary without being competitive; additionally where there are widely different pressures from a number of distinct interests these could be handled in an interdisciplinary or multiple-use way and thus avoid some of the friction which arises from group pressures often motivated by rather single-purpose objectives. A comprehensive integration of the several commerical and social resources would also provide a milieu for the development of local forest industries. Possibilities of such development is highly significant for the welfare of the upland inhabitants because it is from the industries dependent on the home-produced raw-material — much of which is likely to come from the upland and remote regions — that they are most likely to benefit directly; and the benefits would go far beyond the mere commerical, value-added and linkage effects.

REFERENCES

Department of Education and Science (1966) *Forestry, agriculture and the multiple use of rural land.* Report of Land Use Study Group. London: HMSO.

HM Government White Paper (1972) *Forestry Policy.* London: HMSO.

Hair, D (1963) *The economic importance of timber in the United States.* USDA Forest Service, Misc. Publ No 941.

Helliwell, D R (1974) Discount rates in land-use planning. *Forestry*, 47, 147-152.

Martin, P C (1970) *The hills — farming or forestry?* Economics Department, East of Scotland College of Agriculture.

MAFF (1975) *Food from our own resources.* Cmnd 6020 London: HMSO.

Mutch, W E S (1972) *Study of combined land uses, Fassfern — Inverness-shire* Edinburgh University.

Palmer, E R & Tabb, C B (1974) *Pulpwood production prospects.* Tenth Commonwealth Forestry Conference.

Price, C (1973) To the future: with indifference or concern? The social discount rate and its implications in land use. *Journal of Agricultural Economics*, 24, 393-397.

Rankin, K N (1973) Forestry in Britain — the pattern of industry: plans for integration and efficiency. *Commonwealth Forestry Review*, 52, 31-54.

Sutton, W R J (1975) The forest resources of the USSR; their exploitation and their potential. *Commonwealth Forestry Review*, 54, 110-138.

HM Treasury (1972) *Forestry in Great Britain: an interdepartmental cost/benefit study.* London: HMSO.

Walker, K R (1958) *The competition for land between the Forestry Commission and the agricultural industry in Great Britain — a study in economic policy.* D Phil. Thesis. Oxford University.

Walker, K R (1960) The Forestry Commission and the use of hill land. *Scottish Journal of Political Economy*, 7, 14-35.

Wardle, P A (1966) Land-use policy: the claims of forestry on resources and its contributions. *Timber Grower*, 19, 18-25.

11 Forestry's long-term environmental role

D R HELLIWELL

INTRODUCTION
The main topics of relevance to forestry's long-term environmental role appear to be:

(i)   Discount rates
(ii) Timber as a renewable resource
(iii) Amenity and recreation
(iv) Wildlife conservation
(v)   Genetic reserves of tree species
(vi) Soil fertility
(vii) Effects on climate

DISCOUNT RATES
Discount rates are central to all calculations of long-term costs or benefits. Current economic orthodoxy, as embodied in the HM Treasury (1972) cost/benefit study of forestry, adopts a uniformly high rate of discounting for all investments, which implies that anything which will be of value, in say, 100 years' time is more or less completely discounted by the economist, and tends, therefore, to be disregarded.

Other economists have proposed the use of lower rates of discounting for calculating the costs and benefits of future actions in as much as they affect the public at large, rather than any one particular individual (eg Baumol, 1968), but in the author's opinion the use of any standard discount rate is inappropriate (Helliwell, 1977). Actions with a low degree of risk in their outcome should be discounted at a lower rate than more risky actions, and some operations, such as growing timber on reasonably fertile soils, should be discounted at rates of about 1% or less, and some, such as conserving wildlife or stocks of fossil fuels, should be discounted at rates approaching zero. In fact, Price (1973) has suggested that it may be realistic to use zero or even negative discount rates in some instances, but this implies that the capitalised value of a stream of benefits in such a case will be infinite, which does not seem realistic.

Using fairly low discount rates, as proposed, the situation shown in Table 1 emerges:

Table 1
SOME HYPOTHETICAL CAPITALISED VALUES OF VARIOUS RESOURCES
USING DIFFERING DISCOUNT RATES

	Estimated annual returns (Market values or 'shadow prices', as appropriate)	Capitalised value using standard 10% discount rate	Appropriate discount rate	Capitalised value using appropriate discount rate
Timber	£3000	£30000	1.0%	£300000
Ice-cream kiosk	£1000	£10000	5.0%	£20000
Wildlife conservation	£500	£5000	0.2%	£250000
Genetic reserve	£50	£500	0.2%	£25000

Using current methods of calculation, the importance of timber production appears to be twice as great as everything else combined, both in the short term and the long term, but, using the suggested alternative approach, it is placed on a more or less equal footing with the other benefits, in the long term.

TIMBER AS A RENEWABLE RESOURCE
Timber is one of our most important renewable resources, and its production is, on the whole, non-polluting and not very energy-intensive. Trends towards whole-tree logging, and the use of shorter rotations and more fertilizers may change this, but it is expected that these trends will be halted or reversed at some fairly early stage, due to the increasing shortage of cheap sources of energy.

The growing of timber as carried out in Scandinavia some 20 years ago typified many aspects of timber production using a low input of energy, and being capable of continual production indefinitely. Trees were felled by hand-saw, trimmed by axe, and de-barked on the spot with a barking spade. The logs were then left for several months, by which time they had lost some of their moisture and were easier to transport, by horse, winch, or light tractor. Most of the branches and bark, which contain about 75% of the nutrients in the tree (Rennie,

1956) were left on site, and the stands were open enough and contained a sufficient mixture of broadleaved trees to prevent undue detriment to the soil, the flora, or the fauna (Helliwell, in preparation). The forest was also fairly natural in appearance and was easy and pleasant to walk in.

The coming of the chain-saw did little to alter this situation, but the recent advent of the 'feller-buncher', clearing a hundred hectares or so at a time, and the large increase in aerial applications of fertilizer are changing the situation in as yet unpredictable ways.

However, some form of forestry is likely to be regarded as profitable (if appropriate discount rates are used) under any foreseeable energy/resource situation, giving Man a steady supply of raw materials and easing the pressure on other, more damaging, methods of obtaining the necessities of life.

AMENITY AND RECREATION
Forestry has a considerable potential for recreational use, being capable of absorbing large numbers of people without the area appearing to be crowded. Caravans, tents, chalets, etc. can be hidden from view, and any which are visible will be less obtrusive if they are in a forest setting than on a bare hillside.

Amenity is a slightly different question. Many people prefer open hillsides to dense forest, and it is likely that, in the long term, a mixture of open land and afforested land will be preferred (Dürk, 1965); although sudden change may be resented, if afforestation proceeds too rapidly, for example. Much has been written, and more will be written, about the size and shape of plantations, size and shape of felling coupes, location of rides, mixtures of species, silvicultural systems, etc. However, it should be sufficient to say that, for greatest amenity value, the forest should not disrupt the overall unity of the landscape, yet it should contain sufficient variation within it to avoid monotony, and should appear to be more 'natural' than artificial (Helliwell, in preparation-b). If these criteria are met, forestry should be able to contribute both to the quality and quantity of recreation that the uplands can provide.

WILDLIFE CONSERVATION
A mixture of forested and non-forested land in our uplands can support a wider range of wildlife than a completely non-forested landscape (Helliwell, 1971), as a large proportion of our wild plants and animals are inhabitants of forests. Appropriately managed forest can, therefore, contribute to the conservation of our wild fauna and flora.

This contribution will be enhanced if the forest is diversified within itself, and if conditions within it are relatively stable. The adoption of even-aged monocultures throughout the forest area (which is the present trend) will be less useful in this respect than would a more varied range of forest management. The use of selection systems or group selection systems in some places could provide more stable conditions for the development of a more diverse woodland flora than is presently found in most commercially-managed timber-producing forests, and an admixture of broadleaved trees such as birch would be beneficial in this respect also (Helliwell, in preparation — a).

GENETIC RESERVES
I have no pretence of possessing any expert knowledge on the maintenance of gene pools in forest trees but it is evident that some areas of forest should be maintained for this purpose, in relative isolation from other forest areas of the same species, in order to maintain a resource of material for breeding trees which are resistant to particular pests or diseases, or for producing better yields of turpentine, timber, or other products. This is, in some respects, merely an extension of wildlife conservation in one particular direction.

The area of forest required for this particular purpose is probably less than 1% of the total forest area, and is not a major consideration in the overall picture.

SOIL FERTILITY
The question of soil fertility is a difficult one. It is known that our main coniferous species (spruces and pines) have certain effects on many soils, resulting in a tendency towards acidification of the surface horizons of the soil and a leaching of soluble material from these horizons, giving a tendency towards podzolisation. However, this effect may be less strong than under such non-forest cover as *Calluna*, and it has not been demonstrated that this podzolisation causes any reduction in the rate of growth of the pines and spruces grown on these soils (Laatsch, 1963). It does reduce the diversity of plant species in the forest (Helliwell, in preparation — a) and may make it more difficult to plant other tree species, but it is possible that the changes in the soil could be reversed by ploughing, fertilizing, or growing a species such as birch for one rotation (Dimbleby, 1962).

In general, therefore, it would be dangerous to place too much emphasis on the question of maintenance of soil fertility. On the other hand, claims by some foresters (eg Chard, 1972) that conifers 'build up' the fertility of the soil should be treated with equal or greater scepticism.

EFFECTS ON CLIMATE
In rough, hilly areas forests will add little to the general reduction in windspeed caused by the terrain, although they can supply local shelter for buildings and livestock; but in areas of less rugged terrain, forests can decrease the general windspeed as well as providing local shelter (Caborn, 1976).

111

The effects of forests on humidity, rainfall and temperature at a regional or global scale could also be important (Protopopov, 1975). Gay and Stewart (1974) report that a "Douglas-fir forest transformed 60% of its net radiation into latent energy as opposed to 36% for Scots pine". Such differences, or the differences between these figures and those for *Nardus* grassland or *Sphagnum* bog, could possibly affect climatic patterns if extensive areas are de-forested, forested, or planted with different species.

Nor is forestry completely neutral in the question of the concentration of CO_2 in the atmosphere, for, although during the life of a tree as much CO_2 will be produced in respiration and decay as has been used in photosynthesis, the destruction and burning of large areas of forest will release large amounts of CO_2 that would otherwise be held in the forest ecosystem. The concentration of CO_2 in the atmosphere is reported to have risen by about 15% in the last 100 years (Lewin, 1976), due mainly to the increased use of coal, oil, and natural gas. This increase represents only about half of the total estimated amount of CO_2 that has been emitted during this period (Gates, 1972). Much of the rest has been dissolved in the oceans, which currently contain about 60 times as much CO_2 as there is in the atmosphere. It is possible, however, that the oceans may become less effective as a 'sink' for CO_2 as they become more saturated.

Destruction of forests, for agricultural use, will add to any increase in CO_2 in the atmosphere, as the biomass of the agricultural system will be less than that in the forest; and, conversely, afforestation of bare land will decrease the CO_2 in most cases. Wood which is used for structural purposes, and which is not burned or allowed to rot, will also help to decrease the CO_2 level.

Increases in CO_2 are likely to increase the overall temperature of the earth's surface (although it is possible that the increase in CO_2 is the result of atmospheric warming rather than the cause). However, increased amounts of vapour trails from aeroplanes may be reflecting sunlight and causing a reduction of temperature in recent years, and as Gates (1972) says, we really do not know what is going on. It is possible, however, that the amount of forest and unburned wood in the world could be a significant factor in affecting global climate.

SUMMARY
I would stress the long-term value of forestry for timber production, wildlife conservation, and recreation; and, possibly, for influencing the climate. In the case of wildlife conservation and recreation, the distribution and type of forestry will be as important as its total extent. In all cases, calculations of costs and benefits should be carried out on a realistic basis and not on the basis of outmoded and irrelevant economic dogma.

REFERENCES

Baumol, W J (1968)   On the social rate of discount.   *American Economic Review*, **58**, 788-802.

Caborn, J M (1976) Shelter, In: *The future of the small woodland.* Castleton: Peak District National Park Study Centre.

Chard, J S R (1972)   Forestry and wildlife.   *Quarterly Journal of Forestry*, **66**, 113-122.

Dimbleby, G W (1962)   *The development of British heathlands and their soils.* Oxford: Clarendon Press.

Dürk, P (1965)   [The importance of the forest for the health of the population.] *Forst- und Holzwirt*, **20**, 209-211.

Gates, D M (1972)   *Man and his environment: Climate.*   New York: Harper & Row.

Gay, L W & Stewart, J B (1974)   *Energy balance studies in coniferous forests.* Institute of Hydrology, Report No 23.   Wallingford: Institute of Hydrology.

Helliwell, D R (1971)   *Changes in flora and fauna associated with the afforestation of a Scottish moor: an evaluation.*   Merlewood R & D Paper No 29.   Grange-over-Sands: ITE.

Helliwell, D R (1977)   The end of the bank rate?   *Environmental Conservation*, **4**   (in press).

Helliwell, D R (in preparation – a).   *Floristic diversity in some central Swedish forests.*

Helliwell, D R (in preparation – b).   *Perception of landscapes: a preliminary investigation.*

H M Treasury (1972)   *Forestry in Great Britain: an inter-departmental cost/ benefit study.*   London: HMSO.

Laatsch, W (1963)   [Soil fertility and the planting of conifers.]   Verlagsqesellschaft: Munich.

Lewin, R (1976)   Why the Yule logs must not burn.   *New Scientist*, **72**, 750-751.

Price, C (1973)   To the future: with indifference or concern? The social discount rate and its implications in land use.   *Journal of Agricultural Economics*, **24**, 393-397.

Protopopov, V V (1975)   [The role of dark-coniferous forest in the formation of the environment.]   Institut Lesa i Drevesing, Novosibirsk.

Rennie, P J (1956)   The uptake of nutrients by mature forest growth. *Plant and Soil*, **7**, 49-95.

12 Farming and forestry in the hills and uplands: competition or partnership

J P NEWTON

INTRODUCTION

Is there a case for attempting to use the uplands and hills of Britain for productive purposes, that is, for farming and forestry, or should the land be allowed to revert to wilderness used only for the sport, recreation, and other leisure activities of a largely urban population?

The hills and uplands are used for two other productive purposes, namely water supply and mineral extraction, but these although essential, are limited to specific areas. Barely productive but covering very large areas are the deer forests (estimated at 1.1 million ha (2.5 million acres) Darling, 1969) and grouse moors (extending to about 303 000 ha (750 000 acres)) but these are minor competitors with farming and forestry because of their elevation.

The Centre for Agricultural Strategy (1976) suggests a net earning ability of Welsh and English sheep farms of 2.5% without grants and up to 4.0% with grants. The Inter-departmental Cost-Benefit Study (HM Treasury, 1972) found that forest plantations were capable of earning between 1 and 3% on the capital invested in them.

If there is to be investment in either farm or forest enterprises in the hills and uplands further justification than that of interest on capital must be found. A number of these appear to exist:

(i) Much of the land if no longer used for grazing, would gradually become scrub covered and difficult or impossible to use for recreation (Fairbrother, 1970). The land having the greatest productive capacity for farming or forestry would become the most impenetrable.

(ii) If in future there was no employment in farming or forestry large areas of the

114

uplands and hills would become virtually uninhabited. Areas lacking population would also lack the infrastructure of accommodation, maintained roads, services and shops needed by holidaymakers. This would frustrate the aim of making the countryside accessible to urban dwellers unless special holiday villages were created and maintained.

(iii) Large areas of land capable of adding to the nation's home-produced food supplies or of producing timber as a raw material for manufacturing would remain idle. Increasing world population may make food supplies more difficult to obtain because of intensifying international competition. This will cause the price of food to rise and demonstrate the immorality of leaving land unused which is capable of producing food. The EC countries as a group may become self-sufficient in basic foodstuffs but Britain scarcely can, and must continue to import. Likewise there is no possibility of Britain and no likelihood of the EC countries becoming self-sufficient in timber (Hummel, 1977). Land in Britain capable of producing timber for our own use or that of our EC neighbours cannot remain unused.

(iv) Hill farming and forestry are two industries effective in using sunlight for power through photosynthesis and thrift in their use of power derived from fossil fuels.

Thus the case for using the hills and uplands for farming and forestry is based not only on the rate of interest earned on capital but on the production of renewable resources in systems which are frugal in their use of power derived from non-renewable resources. It is also based on the need to keep the remoter rural areas open for health-giving recreation by those who wish to have it. This will follow from the creation of employment and associated infrastructure. Thriving farms and forests will create a more varied landscape, an added attraction for tourists and holiday makers (Bain, 1969).

If agriculture and forestry are to be the primary users of the hills and uplands what claim can each industry make to use land for its own particular purpose? Must they compete for the land or is a partnership possible and desirable? In the discussion which follows some additional benefits gained from a complementary structure of farming and forestry are rehearsed.

POINTS OF COMPETITION
The price of land
Figure 1 shows the trends of Scottish hill and upland farm purchase prices and Forestry Commission UK land purchase prices from 1956 to 1976.

The classification of farms used by the North of Scotland College of Agriculture is:

(i) Hill Farms: high lying farms with 95% or more of their land classed as rough grazing and which depend mainly for their income on a breeding ewe flock.

Figure 1
LAND PURCHASE PRICES

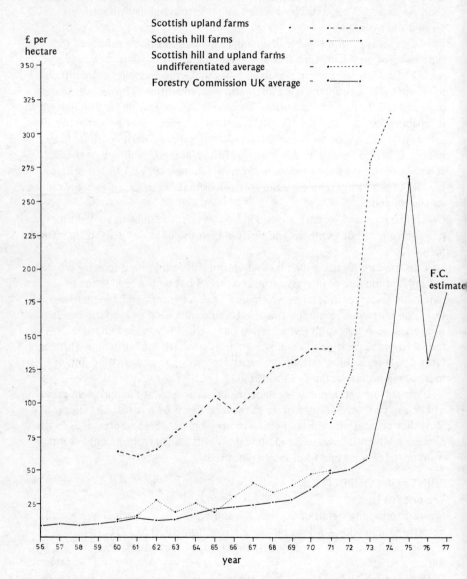

Sources: Scottish Agricultural Economics and Forestry Commission Annual Reports (1956-76)

Breeding cows may also be carried but these tend to be of secondary importance. All hill farms are eligible to receive the hill sheep and hill cattle subsidies.

(ii) Upland Rearing Farms: tend to occupy land at lower elevations than hill farms but extensive rough grazings are still important amounting to not less than 30% of the total farm area. These farms are also eligible to receive the hill sheep and hill cattle subsidies. Cattle tend to occupy the dominant position in their economy and sheep are of subsidiary importance (Isaacs, 1976).

Figure 2 shows the purchase of hill and upland in Scotland from 1954 to 1974 by farmers and from 1955 to 1976 by the Forestry Commission.

There are no reliable statistics for hill and upland or indeed any land purchased privately for forestry but Figure 3 shows the annual total of planting in the UK done by the Forestry Commission and private woodland owners between 1954 and 1976 and also compares total planting and bare land planting by the Forestry Commission in Scotland. Table 1 displays the percentage of private planting on bare land in the UK between 1970 and 1974 and from this the approximate areas of bare land planted annually.

Table 1
PRIVATE PLANTING IN THE UK, 1970-1974 (hectares)

Planting year	Total Planting	% on bare land	Bare land planting (approx.)
1970	19 304	52	10 038
1971	23 070	83	19 148
1972	24 496	82	20 087
1973	24 545	84	20 618
1974	23 658	83	19 635

Source: Forestry Commission Annual Reports (1970-1974)

It is also clear from Figure 1 that upland farm prices are substantially higher per unit area than those paid for forest land. Competition in the purchase of land is likely to occur only for land of hill farm capability.

Figure 2 shows that before 1963 a very much larger area of hill and upland changed hands annually than has been the case since 1963. This latter situation is likely to have increased competition. Price increases for upland farms were generally steep after 1962 (Figure 1) while prices paid by the Forestry Commission and hill farmers rose more steadily.

Until the early 1960's there was scarcely any demand from the private sector of forestry for the purchase of hill and upland land. Previously almost all planting

Figure 2
LAND PURCHASES IN SCOTLAND

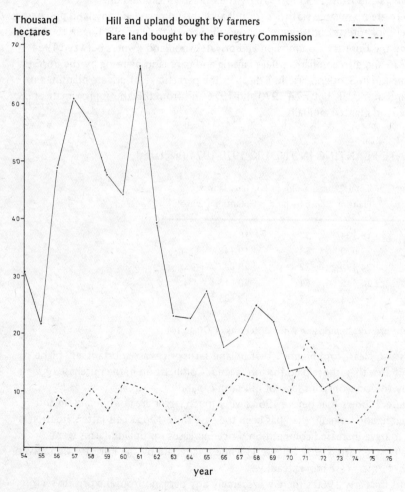

Thousand hectares

Hill and upland bought by farmers

Bare land bought by the Forestry Commission

year

Sources: Scottish Agricultural Economics and Forestry Commission Annual Reports (1954-76)

Figure 3
FORESTRY PLANTING

Thousand
hectares

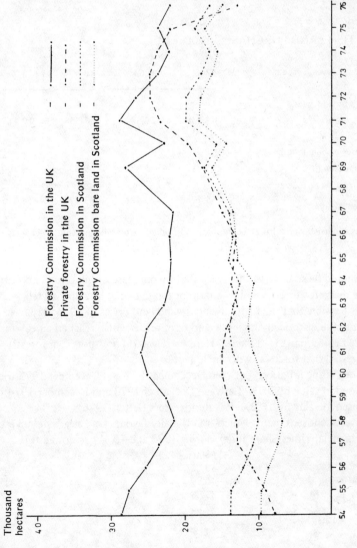

Forestry Commission in the UK
Private forestry in the UK
Forestry Commission in Scotland
Forestry Commission bare land in Scotland

year

Source: Forestry Commission Annual Reports (1954-76)

done by private woodland owners was on old woodland sites, that is, on sites from which timber crops had been felled. (Forestry Commission, 1971).

Figure 3 and Table 1 indicate that the entry of a third potential purchaser may have caused land prices to rise but up to 1974 when combined hill and upland farm prices reached an average level in Scotland of £315/ha (£127.5/acre) there was no indication that the rising prices had encouraged any more land onto the market (Table 2).

Table 2
SCOTTISH LAND PURCHASES (hectares)

	1960	1964	1970	1974
Hill and upland sales, farmers to farmers	44 289	22 542	13 538	10 115
Purchases of bare land by Forestry Commission	11 419	5 986	9 632	4 500
Totals	55 708	28 528	23 170	14 615

Sources: Scottish Agricultural Economics and Forestry Commission Annual Reports.

It should be stressed at this point that no purchase of hill or upland farm land can be made for forestry unless a farm or estate owner is willing to sell.

It is possible that the high hill and upland land prices of 1974 may have reflected the historically high lowland farm prices which reached a peak in 1973 at over £3 459/ha (£1 400/acre). Here there was no pressure from forestry and it is suggested that forces at work included:

(i) Accelerating inflation: between December 1972 and December 1973 the pound decreased in value by 9.7%. Between December 1973 and December 1974 it decreased in value by 16.2% (Private Investors Letter, 1976).

(ii) Investment sentiment: which traditionally favours land as a 'safe' investment. The Financial Times Share Index during 1973 and 1974 performed thus:

Date	Points
January 12 1973	507.2
June 1 1973	462.9
January 12 1974	337.8
June 1 1974	273.3
December 12 1974	150.4

(iii) The 'roll over' tax provisions: effectively brought to an end in the Finance Act 1974 by the introduction of Development Gains Tax, had formerly allowed freedom from Capital Gains Tax for sales of agricultural land provided that the capital was reinvested in further agricultural land within twelve months. This had particularly favoured the owner of farm land who sold it for building development and thus made a large capital gain.

(iv) Very large capital sums had accumulated during the commercial property boom of the late-1960's and up to 1972. Some property companies began investing in agriculture where interest on capital at 4% was comparable with the interest they could earn if they reinvested in commercial property. Large capital sums also accumulated in the hands of private individuals when during the period 1970 to 1972 many private companies were bought by public companies or became public companies on their own account. These individuals wished to protect their capital against the effects of inflation and estate duty. Investment in agriculture seemed to offer such protection.

It is suggested that these new sources of capital for investment in agriculture caused the rise in farm prices, investment pressure being increased by the declining value of the pound and by the declining capital value of Stock Market investment.

Production of meat, wool and timber

For many years Government and Treasury have been ambivalent in their attitudes to farming and forestry in the hills and uplands of Britain. It appears that the 'drift from the land' since the beginning of the Industrial Revolution has had sufficient emotive power to influence Government thinking and decisions.

One reason for making afforestation plans for Great Britain stated sixty years ago in the Acland Report of 1917 was the need to bring social benefits to sparsely populated districts. "The districts which would benefit most from afforestation are those which are now poorest and most backward such as the hilly regions of Northern Ireland, Wales, the Border Country and most of all the Highlands of Scotland. No-one disputes that large areas in those districts now devoted to sheep or deer ought if possible to be put to more productive use. In those tracts, now almost uninhabited . . .". (Ministry of Reconstruction, 1918). The Acland Report followed the Royal Commission on Coast Erosion and Afforestation (1909). This stated: "Your Commissioners concur in the view that it is difficult to over-estimate the probable benefits which should result from a scheme of afforestation in retaining in the country districts the percentage of the rural population which now commonly migrates to the urban areas there to increase the congestion of the labour market."

Much has changed during the past sixty years but in 1917 farming alone could apparently not offer sufficient employment. The Government of the day, which acted on the recommendations of the Acland Report and in 1919 created the Forestry Commission, believed it had to stem rural depopulation. This same attitude of Government could still be seen in the Forest Policy statement of 1972. "In one important respect, however, the approach used makes less than complete allowance for social benefits: account is taken of the additional output provided by the creation of new employment but no allowance is made for the social cost of depopulation of whole areas and the value of job creation as a means of preventing this" (HM Government, 1972).

Although emphasis has been placed on the ability of forestry to help stem rural depopulation the Ministerial Statement of July 5th 1974 says, "The main general objective of the Forestry Enterprise remains that of producing wood as economically as possible." Some contradiction of this is shown by the apparently grudging attitude of the Treasury which emphasises the 'Exchequer Cost' of maintaining a rural population in the hills and uplands but appears to attach little value to the products of the hills.

Table 3
CAPITALISED EXCHEQUER COSTS IN AGRICULTURE AND FORESTRY

| | Costs per ha (£) | | Costs per job (£) | |
	New Planting	Hill Farming	New Planting	Hill Farming
North Wales	270.57	63.26	16 400	9 500
South Scotland	158.14	25.57	23 000	7 400
North Scotland	159.38	6.08	17 400	8 200
South Scotland (private forestry)	74.13	—	10 800	—

"Hill farming in the areas now being afforested in North Wales, South Scotland and North Scotland produces a negligible or even negative social return (at the 10% cost discount rate.)"

"New planting in the three conservancies studied fails to produce a 10% social rate of return on present forestry practice, and would fail to do so even if regimes were modified so as to maximise the rate of return."

"The above conclusions about both forestry and agriculture would be somewhat modified if import saving as such was considered desirable. With a 20% import saving factor, new planting based on present forestry practices would still fail to produce a 10% social rate of return" (HM Treasury, 1972).

"We entirely accept that there are very strong social grounds for a continuing programme. At the same time we do not regard investment in forestry as a very good way of spending public money from a commercial point of view." (Parliamentary Civil Estimates Committee, 1964).

Table 3 shows that the Exchequer cost per job for hill farming is only about half that of new planting in forestry. The inference drawn is that in the Treasury view, hill farming is only half as undesirable as forestry. Thus, before there is any likelihood of competition between the two main hill using industries both must convince the Treasury of their need and their merit relative to other forms of public sector investment, ie, water resources, recreation, national parks, nationalised industries, aid to private industry.

Competition between farming and forestry may arise in terms of their 'Value to the Nation' in three ways:
(i)   The amount of renewable raw material each can produce;
(ii)   The import saving or export generating ability of each;
(iii) Their social value, that is, the number of rural jobs each can produce.

Smith (1970) estimates that the hills and uplands carry 60% of the breeding ewes, produce 50% of the lambs and 33% of the sheep meat, not allowing for lowland fattening. It seems correct to credit the lowland fattening to the hills and 50% of Britain's sheep meat production is then considered to have its origin in the hills.

Cunningham (1976) estimates that Britain is 57% self-sufficient in her production of lamb and mutton and that British production is 258 064 tonnes per year. If half of this does originate in the hills and uplands the 129 032 tonnes so produced would, at 113.4 g (4 ozs) per meal per person, provide 21 meat meals each year for each of Britain's 55 million people.

The target production set for the Experimental husbandry farm at Pwllpeiran, Blaenmyherin Unit, is three weaned lambs/ha. Assuming a quarter of these return to the flock as breeding ewes an average of 2.25 fat lambs/ha will be slaughtered. This will yield 32 kg dead weight/ha (Pwllpeiran Annual Review, 1976) and provide an import saving of some £35/ha (Fountain Farming Ltd., 1977). In comparison with this target for production the actual 1974/75 production at Blaenmyherin would give an import saving performance of £19.6/ha.

Smith (1970) estimated that half of Britain's annual wool clip comes from hill sheep. The Wool Marketing Board Annual Report (1976) records the wool clip for 1975 at 34 770 000 kg and the raw wool exported by Britain as 26 000 000 kg for a price of £17.5 million. The clip from hill sheep, 17 385 000 kg, thus has an approximate value of £11.7 million.

Rankin (1973) calculates that Britain's 1.6 million ha managed forest estate will sustain a yield of 12.7 million m^3 of timber a year, 7.93 m^3 per year per ha. Forestry Commission standing sales in 1976 gave an average value in Scotland of £5.994 per m^3 indicating a sustained yield value of £47.5/ha per annum. These are standing sales in Scotland where the Forestry Commission has a high proportion of its plantations on land which was formerly bare hill land (Figure 3).

Very large areas of hill farm land still remain unimproved but when improvements have been done substantial increases in stocking and yield will be possible. Future timber production capacity/ha is perhaps more certain and it is clear that the value of the yield/ha in pounds (£) is greater now for forestry than for hill farming.

Employment in forestry and hill farming

Some data on employment serves to set the scene. The labour requirement on hill farms in the North of Scotland during 1974/75 was estimated by the North of Scotland College of Agriculture from a sample of 17 farms covering 55 753 ha.

The figures are:

Average farm area	3 280 ha
Average farm labour cost including husband and wife	£3 540

During 1974/75 the average farm labour cost/ha was thus estimated to be £1.07. The same calculations for the two previous years gave in 1973/74 £0.90/ha and in 1972/73 £0.69/ha.

Employment in private forestry in Scotland during 1974 was estimated by the Economic Surveys of Private Forestry from a sample of woodlands on 61 estates covering 33 997 hectares of plantations. The figures are;

Forest Managers	9	earning	£21 000
Foresters	16	"	£25 517
Foremen	23	"	£35 640
Drivers	37	"	£55 719
Sawmillers	6	"	£8 399
General Workers plus contractors	205	"	£273 109
Total	296 people earning		£419 384

The average cost of wages and salaries/ha are therefore estimated to be £12.33.

In the case of both farm and forest all employees work within the farms or estates including sawmillers. No allowance has been made for external employment in slaughterhouses, dairies, sawmills, pulpmills etc.

These calculations appear to show a labour requirement ratio between forestry and hill farming of 12:1 but it must be noted that the two figures are not truly comparable for several reasons. The farm sample covers only hill farms in the North of Scotland which are very extensive and where substantial areas may be above the tree line. The forest sample covers private woodlands throughout Scotland and some of these are on land at elevations where upland farms are plentiful.

A further comparison may however be based on data in the Interdepartmental Cost/Benefit Survey (HM Treasury, 1972). These data refer to an average of hectares per person employed by forestry and hill farming:

Region	Forestry	Hill Farming	Ratio
North Wales	61	150	2.5:1
South Scotland	146	289	2:1
North Scotland	109	1335	12.2:1

There is probably no direct competition for labour between farming and forestry but since forestry in general employs more men per managed hectare it would seem to give a greater social benefit.

Government encouragement for hill and upland farming and forestry
Methods of encouragement or assistance to farming and forestry include the following:
(i) Direct grants to reduce current expenditure, increase current income and offset part of capital expenditure.
(ii) Income tax relief for excess annual expenditure and for capital expenditure.
(iii) A choice of taxation schedule and a cash accounting basis for annual trading.
(iv) Relief from certain forms of capital taxation.
Grant Aid to Forestry: The grants which will come into force for new planting and forest management on October 1st, 1977 will apply to bare land as follows:
(i) Accepted by the Forestry Commission to be managed according to the terms of a Dedication Basis III Agreement (areas of 10 ha or above.) To be eligible a forest owner must sign a deed of covenant with the Forestry Commissioners as

the other party, in which he agrees to maintain adequate standards of management. He must draw up and revise every five years a forest management plan which, when it has been approved by the Forestry Commission, he must adhere to within narrow limits.

For planting (per hectare)

Conifers	£100
Supplementary grant for hardwoods	£125
Caledonian Pine on areas approved by the Nature Conservancy	£225

For management, payable 5 years in arrears of planting, annual grant of £3 per hectare.

(ii) Small woods planting grant (per hectare)

¼ ha to 3 ha	£300
3 ha to 10 ha	£250

Seventy-five % of the grant will be paid on completion of planting and 25% following inspection five years later.

(iii) Hill and upland farmers are eligible for 50% grants for shelter belt planting under the UK Farm Capital Grant Scheme or EC Farming and Horticulture Development Scheme.

(iv) There are no grants towards the cost of capital schemes in forestry.

Grant aid to agriculture: The annual grants for hill and upland farmers are as follows:

Hill Cattle Subsidy	£29 per head
Brucellosis eradication incentive	£5 per head
Calf subsidy, male	£8.50 per head
Calf subsidy, female	£6.50 per head
Sheep subsidy on hill farms	£3.60 per ewe
Sheep subsidy on upland farms	£2.85 per ewe

The Capital Grants are available under the UK Farm Capital Grant Scheme or the EC Farming and Horticulture Development Scheme. Grants are paid on a percentage of cost basis. Table 4 gives the details.

The EC scheme is not available to smallholders with farms below 7 ha. Moreover small farmers often feel unable to undertake the complicated forecasting over five years and the complicated record keeping required by the EC scheme.

A third factor which limits the ability of farmers to use the EC scheme is that forecast and achievable profit after interest on capital and improvements must be £3300 per labour unit, 2200 man hours.

One valuable feature of the EC scheme is the advance payment of Guidance Premium which gives a welcome injection of capital, half in the first year, one-third in the second year and one-sixth in the third year. The amount of the

Table 4

FARM CAPITAL GRANT RATES, HILL AND UPLAND FARMS

	FHDS (%)	FCGS (%)
General Farm Buildings	30	20
Cattle Buildings	40	30
Dairy Buildings and Services	40	30
Milking Equipment, bulk tanks	25	20
Grass silos	40	30
Barn hay-drying fans, etc.	25	20
Hay and silage machinery	25	—
Other agricultural machinery	15	—
Field drainage	70	70
Water supply	50	50
Pens, dips, stells, etc.	50	50
Roads, paths, bridges, etc.	50	50
Fences, hedges, walls, gates	50	50
Clearance and reclamation	50	50
Regeneration of grassland etc.	50	50
Shelter belts	50	50
Purchase of livestock	15	—
Preparation of development plans	25	—

guidance premium is the product of the livestock units forecast for the end of the five year improvement plan and the farm area in hectares up to a maximum of 100 ha. The weight given to each animal as a part of a livestock unit is:

Cow or Bull	1.0
Other Cattle, 2 years+	0.8
Other Cattle, 1 year +	0.6
Other cattle, 1 year —	0.4
Ewe or Ram	0.15
Lamb with ewe	0.15
Lamb, 8 months +	0.08

Annual Taxation: Hill and upland farmers are taxed on a normal profit or loss basis. Annual variations in livestock values are taken into account unless the farmer has elected to be taxed on a 'herd basis'. In such cases changes in value of a herd of constant size are not brought in to the annual accounts. The Inland Revenue normally expects farms to be profitable but will accept losses for several years if a programme of farm improvement is being undertaken. Losses can be carried forward and set off against future profits or can be set off against profits from other sources during the same year.

A privately owned forest can either be taxed under Schedule B, in which case an annual tax is levied at a rate which is one-third of the annual value of the land in its natural unimproved state, or the forest owner can elect to be taxed in whole or part under Schedule D. In the latter case profits will be taxed or losses can be set off against income from other sources, on an annual cash basis, no account being taken of standing crop values. Tree crop rotations are very long and there normally is no limit to the number of successive loss-making years which the Inland Revenue authorities will accept.

Both farms and private forests can set off net expenditure on capital improvement works one-tenth of the expediture in each of the ten years following the year in which it took place.

Because most hill and upland farmers have little capital other than that invested in their farms and little income other than that earned by their farms grant aid is in general more valuable to them than taxation relief (Table 5).

Table 5
HILL FARM INCOMES IN THE NORTH OF SCOTLAND

	1972	1973	1974	1975
Net Income per farm (£)*	3 114	4 946	6 834	1 545
Grant support per farm (£)*	1 795	1 969	2 034	3 566
Grants as % of net farm income	58	40	30	231

*Net farm incomes do not include interest on capital borrowed or end of year stock valuations and are calculated before any drawings by the farmer or his wife.

Source: North of Scotland College of Agriculture.

Many forest owners have incomes from other sources against which they can set net Schedule D forestry expenditures before they are assessed for tax. For these forest owners annual income tax relief is more important than annual grant payments. These latter are however very valuable to augment annual cash flow. Capital taxation: Farm land and forest land are equally treated for Capital Gains Tax. On sale or on gift the increase in value since acquisition or since 1964 if appropriate is taxable, allowance being made for the cost of new capital works. Capital Gains Tax is not applied to farm or forest crops. If it were, foresters in particular would be unable to grow and sell timber because their selling prices are largely governed by timber import prices and could not be raised to cover the required tax payment.

Capital Transfer Tax: A full time working farmer and many hill and upland farmers are such, is apparently more generously treated in comparison with owners other types of taxable asset. The value of farm land and buildings, up to 2 428 ha (hill and upland) or £250 000 is halved before being assessed for tax. In addition the Business Assets Relief means that the value of the other farm assets is reduced to 70% of true value before tax is assessed. These arrangements were required because the recipient, often an inheriting son or daughter, even with the benefit of eight years in which to pay the tax, would have been unable to do so without selling part of the farm. Farm profits during the eight years following inheritance, themselves subject to annual income tax, would have been insufficient to cover both taxes and living expenses.

A forest owner has the benefit of the Business Assets Relief on both land and tree crops which are taxed as though worth 70% of their true value. The tax payable by the recipient of the property can be paid by instalments during a period of eight years. By making an election under Schedule 9 of the Finance Act 1975, payment of tax on the value of growing plantations can be deferred until the trees are felled, sold or given away. This deferment is of debatable benefit because tax will be assessed on the value at the date of sale or gift and not on the value at the date of death of the previous owner.

Since the introduction of Capital Transfer Tax private forestry planting in Scotland has fallen to one-third of that planted in 1974. Capital Transfer Tax is thought to be mainly responsible for this widespread decision by Scottish forest owners.

Conclusions

(i) There is competition between farming and forestry for the use and therefore the purchase of land of hill farm capability. In general neither industry has any advantage in the price it can afford to pay for suitable land.

(ii) While in the long term forestry seems capable of producing crops of greater value per unit area of land than hill farming and timber production capabilities are known, production from agriculture is more immediate and may be very greatly increased above present levels by means of proved techniques for the improvement of land and farm management.

(iii) Forestry has a greater employment capacity per unit area of land than hill farming and would seem to be capable of maintaining a higher level of rural employment.

(iv) Treatment by Government through grant and taxation structures has a different effect on each industry and tends to keep them separate. New investment in forestry is encouraged more than it is in hill farming but the final section of this paper seeks to demonstrate that hill farming and forestry are complementary and not competitive industries, that land of varying capabilities can be used by each industry in close association with and often giving aid to the other.

REDUCTION OF COMPETITION OR DEVELOPMENT OF A PARTNERSHIP

Traditionally, large private estates in hill and upland areas have managed their land for several diverse purposes, notably agriculture, forestry, deer stalking, grouse shooting and fishing. The actual mix often is guided by the owner's interests and the fashions of the time but also by sound economic sense and a desire to 'do well' by the countryside. Many landowners have as a major incentive the well-being of their tenants and employees. It is easy to understand that human well-being is promoted by so managing the resources of an estate that a balanced production is achieved suited to the economic circumstances of the time.

The most fortunate estates appear to be those having land of varied capabilities, the best, at the lower elevations, being sheltered, well watered and drained, which typically makes good grassland for over-wintering stock.

The surrounding higher land often rises to high tops exposed to fierce winds, subject to much rain and snow and carrying nourishing grass growth during the summer months only (Cunningham, 1976). Sheep at these elevations may share the short grazing season with Red deer and on the lower heather moors grouse shooting can provide a share of the total estate income, but on most larger estates the major uses for rough grazing land are for sheep with some cattle and commercial forestry. The balance differs on each estate. The area kept in hill grazing is determined by the number of animals that the owner wishes to overwinter on low ground, purchasing additional feed if it pays to do so. The techniques of land improvement sponsored by the Hill Farming Research Organisation enable higher numbers of animals to be maintained on the best hill land for three or even four weeks longer each year than was formerly possible, thus relieving pressure on the low ground. Even so, many estates and hill farms have an excess of rough grazing on which the nourishing summer growth is wasted, since it is of little grazing value after it has withered (Cunningham, 1971).

An example of an estate where a previous imbalance has been corrected is Fassfern, near Fort William. In 1968, 2 023 ha (5 000 acres) of hill land produced only 325 lambs from 500 breeding ewes and 20 calves from 30 cows. The lambing percentage was 65%. By 1975, 364 ha (900 acres) of much improved low ground carried 450 breeding ewes and 90 cows. Eighty-eight calves were born and the lambing percentage had risen to 125%, giving 562 lambs.

The target is for 500 breeding ewes to lamb at 150% to yield 750 lambs and for 120 cows to produce 100 calves. Of the 1 659 ha (4 100 acres) not now used for farming, 1 012 ha (2 500 acres) now supports a very healthy growth of trees while the high tops remain wild and grazed by Red deer. The farm still employs two men who do their work with greater ease and efficiency and in addition the forestry labour force numbers eighteen (Mutch, 1972; Dulverton, 1975).

The tree planting and farm improvement demanded substantial investment. Mutch (1972) estimated that capital amounting to £50 000 for farming, £80 000 for forestry and £36 000 for road building had been injected. As noted earlier many hill farmers have no capital other than the value of their land but in the long term such farms could be much more profitable if the best land were improved for agriculture and land more suited for forestry were to be planted with trees.

One approach to the problem of increasing the growth and out-turn of meat, wool and timber from the hills and uplands is further to encourage committed farmers who already occupy the land. At present, "The hill ewe subsidy merely sustains farm incomes at a minimum acceptable level. Indeed subsidies may be to some extent a distincentive to the attainment of increased production and economic viability" (Cunningham, 1976). Such farm subsidies which act as a support for personal income must be replaced by capital grants to enable real income to be earned from the land. During a transition period income support subsidies should be based on the production of lambs and calves rather than on numbers of ewes and cows.

Land suitable for afforestation and not required for improvement of farm productivity should be planted with the aid of grants set at a high rate expressed as a percentage of cost. This was proposed in the EC Draft Council Directive 1131/75.

Receipts from grants will fall short of total costs both in farming and forestry. Since commercial borrowing rates are generally too high the gap should be bridged by cheaper loans repayable as the invested capital begins to yield income. In the case of forestry this will be 25 to 30 years after the date of planting when the plantations begin to yield thinnings.

Past experience shows how traditional landowners have gained financial stability through the possession of capital reserves in the form of timber. Modest areas of planting could bring the same benefits to hill and upland farmers who have excess rough grazing land.

The advantages to hill farming integrated with forestry by conversion into farm-forest production units are:
(i) Creation of new roads initially for protection of the plantations and later for timber extraction. These roads can be aligned and constructed to give access to

hill farm land so that it can be improved.

(ii) Access for machines will permit cultivation of the land, fertiliser and lime can be applied and reseeding done. Stock can be moved quickly and easily and be supplied with additional feed.

(iii) Correctly placed forest fences can become the basis for dividing land to control grazing. Additional fences are easily erected from the improved access.

(iv) Forestry plantations provide shelter for stock and improved grass growth through a longer period of the year. Soil temperatures are higher and windspeeds lower because of the increased roughness of the terrain (Caborn, 1976).

Recent examples of integration leading to increased farm production are:

(i) Blaenmyherin Unit of Pwllpeiran EHF, Dyfed.

The improvement work began in 1971.

Total area of land in 1971	647.5 ha	
Sold to Forestry Commission	160.5 ha	
Farm area now	487.0 ha	

	1967-71	1974-75	Production Target
Stocking (ewes)	1 300	1 600	1 800
Ewe liveweight Oct. (kg)	31.75	34.88	38.56
Lamb weaning (%)	92.8	93.6	110.0
Lamb weaning weight (kg)	22.23	23.77	26.31
Output (Kg weaned lamb/per ha)	31.94	53.8	78.5
Additionally the cow stocking is	85+ followers	85+ followers	120+ followers

(ii) Hendrewallog Farm-Forest Unit, Gwynedd, farmed as tenant by Fountain Farming Ltd.

Total area in 1972 (ha)	485.6
Selected for forestry use, 1973 (ha)	208.0
Rocky area (ha)	14.5
Farmed since 1972 (ha)	263.0

Forest roads were built during 1973, 1974, and 1975. Improvement of the farm began in 1973.

	1974	1976
Ewes per hectare	1.63	4.45
Ewe numbers	792 (on 485.6 ha)	1170 (on 263.0 ha)
Lambing percentage	60	94
Return on tenants capital (%)	−27.1	+6.9 (excluding herd increment)

Improvement work continues on both these farms and results are confidently expect to improve further.

The target levels of stocking on the better hill farm land in Wales, without incurring loss of output, is 12.3 ewes/ha (5 ewes/acre) for limited periods of summer grazing or 7.4 ewes/ha (3 ewes/acre) throughout the year. This includes cattle at a ewe equivalent of 1:5. This does assume purchase of some additional winter feed, especially for the cattle.

Some firm guarantees are needed to ensure that the grant aid given will result in benefit to the nation.

The first stage of entry to the proposed scheme should be a land capability survey made by the farmer in association with MAFF or DAFS. The survey would be used to determine a desirable balance of winter and rough hill grazing and the possibilities for farm improvement. On many hill and upland farms there would remain a substantial further balance of land suitable for forestry.

Forest owners are used to drawing up and working from long term management plans and indeed farmers wishing to benefit from the EC Farming and Horticulture Development Scheme must prepare a five year plan and budget for the planned improvements. The next stage therefore is for the farmer to prepare an improvement plan for his property in consultation with the Agriculture Departments and the Forestry Commission to cover five and possibly ten years.

The third stage is implementation of the agreed plan. Each phase will be supported by grants in aid and cheap loan instalments. The sanction exercisable by the Agricultural Departments and the Forestry Commission would be judgement of the farmer's will and capability to undertake the work, withholding further loan and grant payments if the improvement work at each year end was not satisfactory and raising the nominal loan interest to a commercial rate.

The improvement grants for agricultural and forestry work would be capital grants not subject to income tax. Interim support subsidies so far as they were part of farm profit would be taxable but interest on loans would qualify for tax relief.

If during the period of the improvement plan or within, say, five years thereafter the property were to be sold (but not if there was a transfer of ownership by gift or death provided that the new owner retained and managed the farm for a minimum of five years), the vendor would be obliged to repay all grants to the grant aiding authority.

As the improvement work proceeded so the value of farm and forest land, farm stock and forest plantations would be likely to increase. Since the purpose of the scheme is to encourage land improvement and productivity, Farm-Forest Production Units should be liable only for income tax assessment on an annual cash basis during the period of the improvement plan. At the end of the plan period there would be a new opening stock valuation and thereafter the owner could elect whether to be taxed on a 'herd basis' or not. The forestry section would continue to be taxed according to the existing tax rules.

While the main benefits to be gained from the creation of farm-forest units are the increase in productivity of meat, wool and timber per hectare of hill and upland, there are four other benefits:

(i) Forestry on average provides more employment than hill farming and the two run together will maintain a higher year round rural population with greater capability to provide accommodation at holiday times.

(ii) Labour requirements in farm and forest can be smoothed out and dovetailed to take account of slack and busy seasons.

(iii) The appearance of the countryside will be more varied; less bleak than extensive hill farming and more interesting than large tracts of forest. It will also support larger and more varied populations of plants and animals.

(iv) Farmers sometimes complain that forests harbour foxes and crows. Control of these pests will be in the farmer's own hands. Increased sport from game birds will be available on the farmer's own property.

REFERENCES

Bain, S (1969) *Royal Grampian Country* Report prepared for Scottish Tourist Board. Geography Department, University of Aberdeen.

British Wool Marketing Board (1976) *Annual Report, 1976.*

Caborn, J M (1976) Personal Communication.

Centre for Agricultural Strategy (1976) *Land for agriculture.* CAS Report 1.

Cunningham, J M M (1971) Hill Sheep Farming. *Scottish Forestry,* **25,** 175-180.

Cunningham, J M M (1976) *Constraints on the expansion of sheep production in Scotland.* Colloquium on Highland Agriculture and Land Use. Inverness, Oct. 1976.

Darling, F F (1969) *The Highlands and Islands.* London: Fontana.

Dulverton, Lord (1975) *Co-ordination of forestry with other land uses.* Conference on Forestry Management. The Royal Society of Arts, Nov. 1975.

Economic Surveys of Private Forestry (1976) *Employment in Private Forestry in Scotland during 1974.* Forestry Department, University of Aberdeen.

Fairbrother, N (1970) *New lives, new landscapes.* London: Architectural Press.

Forestry Commission (1954-1976) *Annual Report.* Edinburgh: Forestry Commission.

Fountain Farming Ltd (1977) Personal Communication.

HM Government (1972) *Forestry Policy.* London: HMSO.

HM Treasury (1972) *Forestry in Great Britain: an interdepartmental cost/benefit study.* London: HMSO.

Hummel, F O (1977) *Common Market forest policy.* Lecture to Royal Scottish Forestry Society, March 1977.

Isaacs, R J (1976) *Farm incomes in the North of Scotland.* Farm Management Review, North of Scotland College of Agriculture.

Mutch, W E S (1972) *Study of combined land uses — Fassfern-Inverness-shire.* University of Edinburgh.

Ministry of Reconstruction (1918) *Forestry Sub-Committee, Final Report.* London: HMSO.

Parliamentary Civil Estimates Committee (1964) *Seventh Report* from the Estimates Committee HC 272, 1963-64. London: HMSO.

Private Investors Letter (1976) No 23. Published at 13 Golden Square, London W1.

Pwllpeiran Annual Review (1976) Ministry of Agriculture Fisheries and Food. Agricultural Development and Advisory Service.

Rankin, K N (1973) Forestry in Great Britain, The Pattern of Industry. *Commonwealth Forestry Review,* **52,** 31-54.

Royal Commission on Coast Erosion and Afforestation (1909) *Final Report 2 (1)* Cd 4460, Vol XIV. London: HMSO.

Scottish Agricultural Economics. *Annual Reports 1954-1974.*

Smith, W (1970) *Hill and upland farming.* National Technical Conference, Peebles.

13 The location of forest-based industries

A W DENBY

INTRODUCTION

This paper is not intended as a statistical report on Britain's forest output nor a detailed survey of industries based upon it. These subjects are amply covered by Forestry Commission publications and reports on the forest industries carried out by various independent companies on behalf of the Commission. Data from these sources are the basis of any figures or projections used.

Upland Britain is unlikely to contain large quantities of commercial hardwood and so the paper refers throughout to softwoods.

The objective of the paper is to identify the broad trends and possible changes that may effect the locating of forest-based industry during the next quarter century. The conclusions are mainly drawn from twenty five years of service within the industry.

THE BRITISH TIMBER INDUSTRY ENVIRONMENT

The market place

Consumers of forest produce in Britain draw over 90% of their softwood material from overseas sources. Converters of British grown trees therefore operate in a market subjected to world supply and demand patterns and dominated by a relatively few large, well organised and profitable importing companies. Most users are familiar with imported timber and sheet materials, accustomed to the quality grades and stock list service provided by its professional management and the convenience of dealing with its army of well trained salesmen. User industries (building, packaging, furniture, etc) are prepared to pay a premium price for a known product conveniently and reliably delivered from shipping dry stock, as they see it the most beneficial to their needs.

The performance of British grown timber converters in the market place has been abysmal. There are hundreds of relatively small firms mixing a wide variety of species with no common grading system, selling mainly wet offsaw, often with poor dimensional tolerance and late delivery with an almost total absence of stock lists or salesmen. Changes are taking place, most significantly:

(i) The increasing volume of a more limited range of British softwood species grown under managed forest conditions are coming into the market place.

(ii) The realisation by the industry, particularly the growers (in particular the Forestry Commission) that the British timber industry must improve its performance and image and the sponsoring of research and development with this end in view.

(iii) The appearance in the industry of a few large national companies with massive capital resources, professional management and a large sales force, attracted by diversification and the obvious potential.

Materials supply pattern

Importers enjoy the benefit of supplies from countries and companies with the economic advantage of an enormous scale of production plus the integration of activities to utilise the maximum of woody tissue. Some of these sources work on a sustained yield basis. A few, notably Canada and Russia have vast reserves of forests which given an upward change in the relative value of timber could and probably would be tapped. It should also be noted that bulk transportation cost

Table 1
BRITISH TIMBER OUTPUT IN COMPARISON WITH CONSUMPTION
(million m^3)

Date	British output (1)	Roundwood Equivalent Total British consumption (2)
1970	2.5	39.21
1975	2.86	46.01
1980	3.43	53.43
1985	4.21	61.22
1990	5.36	–
2000	6.78	–

(1) Forestry Commission Production Forecast. (2) Total consumption average of a number of forecasts.

by water from distant forests is often at a far lower unit cost than for a relative short land haul.

Availability of British grown timber in quantity is a relatively new event and increasing rapidly (see Table 1). Roughly half of British output is sawlog, the rest pulp, fibre, chip or mining material.

Distribution of British timber is over a large number of relatively small holdings: the 252 holdings of the Forestry Commission average 3 143 ha; the 45 000 private holdings average 25.2 ha. An advantage of upland areas is, or could be, that holdings are larger, but accessibility with steep or rough terrain may make for more difficult and expensive extraction. The cost of harvesting on a small scale from scattered plantations is, and will probably always be, an economic disadvantage for British grown timber.

Harvesting resources

Some 500 harvesting contractors (gangs 80% of which employ 5 or less workers) operate either for the grower or consumer and handle about half the total. Some 500 of the growers and 400 of the users make good the shortfall by the use of directly employed labour. The proportion of grower/user own harvesting is likely to increase. The problem is in parts the difficulty contractors have in obtaining labour; in supervision over scattered sites; obtaining and justifying capital for expensive harvesting machines (a feller buncher might cost £30 000, a delimber £50 000, a whole tree processor £80 000 or more); inadequate training; difficulty in obtaining long term contracts (or unwillingness to); and problems in obtaining profitable work from organisations who employ some direct labour harveste

Methods vary but the most prevalent system is one tree length harvesting (75% of total) and skidding to a loading point for tree length delivery. Shortwood systems account for much of the non saw log harvesting, the advantage of these modern methods of handling with forwarders and grapples is introducing this system to an increasing proportion of saw log harvesting. The increasing supply of logs and the difficulty in attracting labour to the harvesting operation will encourage the development of more mechanised and costly systems — processors, whole tree chippers, rough terrain cable crane systems etc.

Grower co-operatives, management companies and round timber merchants are expected to become increasingly involved in harvesting; the location of these units is likely to be within the forest area.

LOCATION PROSPECTS OF MAIN BRITISH ROUNDWOOD USERS
Paper products, including fibre board
Consumption is expected to rise slowly from 8 million tonnes in 1975, to 11 million tonnes by 1985. British grown timber will contribute around 10% of

this total from relatively good quality pulp logs delivered to already established plants. Water and/or port facilities are vital to the location of this industry.

Particle products, including wood wool

The demand for particle sheet materials is an accelerating post war phenomenon, speeded by advancing technology and successful substitution for other materials on both technical and commercial grounds. Consumption is likely to reach 5 million m^3 by 1985 from under 1 million m^3 in 1970. Using a relatively low grade roundwood, mill offcuts, hardwood and possibly whole tree chips, this is a growth sector for British timber and one in which it can be competitive. Although the input of chip material (50% round, 50% waste offcut) will rise from under a quarter of a million m^3 to over 1 million, the home produced percentage of the total consumption will fall.

Location of particle based industries close to the bulk material resource has economic advantages, particularly if integrated with a sawmill. This may be an upland region growth industry.

Roundwood products, excluding pulpwood etc.

Pitwood and fencing cut from thinnings and where applicable peeled and treated, together with transmission poles, ladder poles, hop poles etc. are relatively small (under half a million m^3) but are generally a profitable forest based industry.

Location of this type of operation is within the forest area at a suitably located processing depot. It is frequently associated with a merchant or harvesting activity.

Sawn timber

Of maybe 600 sawmills in Britain, 400 cut some softwood (10% or more of input) but only 151 are principally or exclusively softwood (85% or more of log input). Of these: 89 are in Scotland; 11 are in Wales; and 51 are in England. The majority of Scottish and Welsh mills are located in or on the periphery of upland areas whilst perhaps half the English softwood mills are on the periphery of upland regions. Of the softwood mills only 4 are large (25 000 m^3 log input per annum and over) and a further 20 moderately large (10 000/25 000 m^3 log input). Some of these are integrated with particle board production and some manufacture products such as pallets etc.

The consumption of sawn softwood is expected to remain fairly static at around 10 million m^3 per year but home production will rise from under 5% currently to over 15% of this total by the year 2000.

Few of the existing mills were 'custom built' for softwood conversion. They tend to be under-capitalised, use relatively labour intensive methods and sell to the lower priced markets. (Pallet/fencing as opposed to construction/building.)

With increased log availability, the probability is that the larger mills will get much bigger, more efficient and go up market. (Building timber, mostly stress graded.) Some medium sized mills will continue to compete by adding value with manufacturing or specialisation. Small mills will continue on a semi-retail basis serving local markets.

The saw log market is and is likely to continue to be the most lucrative for British grown softwood.

Other minor users
Fuel, chemicals (charcoal), residues (bark fibre), foliage, rustics etc. Very small in total volume, for softwood production of only limited local significance.

SOME FACTORS INFLUENCING LOCATION
The entrepreneur
Behind every private business venture is to be found a person or persons of vision, with the courage to risk their own money and future prospects backing this vision with all the skills they have available. Amongst the more desirable attributes are: marketing/selling ability; man management/motivation capability; financial acumen; production/product knowledge; engineering flair; common sense; plus the health to exercise these attributes with diligence. A rare individual, but one to be cherished for the risks he will take, the jobs he may create, the service he may provide and the product he can enrich the nation with. He is more easily found in a corporate body, provided it does not suffer from multiple vision.

Incentive
Creating the forest environment for visions of forest based business ventures to occur is admirable; unfortunately these visions are increasingly being obscured by high levels of taxation, restrictive planning conditions, bye laws, factory vehicle and employment regulations of increasing complexity and expensive to comply with.

Circumstances again are more readily contended with by the large corporate body rather than the individual or small business.

Capital
Individual entrepreneurs tend to follow their vision of a money-making opportunity in the hope that sufficient capital will accrue *en route* from retained profits. They tend to underestimate the probable total requirement and frequently

have no planned reserve; one of the most serious of debilities in times of high inflation and recurring financial crisis.

Corporate bodies are usually good at financial planning and only a major crisis or error will upset the plan. However, they do not as a rule see opportunities on a small scale or in high risk operations, both of which may well exist in upland areas with potential spin-off benefits for the area.

Site

The need for adequate space to start and for growth: the road, power, water and drainage requirements; materials supply *vis-a-vis* the market location are all factors affecting the choice of location. Many individual entrepreneurs will see this on a 'parochial' basis; are more likely to be successful if they are able to operate within the community and environment with which they are familiar. In many cases this will greatly benefit the chosen locality.

Corporate bodies tend to plan more on a regional or national basis and are probably able to acquire the requisite services if not available at a chosen position. The location is less likely to be in a remote or upland area but the benefits may well be greater from a national point of view.

Labour and skills

Critical to many ventures is the availability of suitable labour. This means that the proposed business can afford the 'going wage rate' of the chosen area, and that the selected location is in an area containing the type of worker and training facilities appropriate to the enterprise.

Other back-up facilities

Many timber based businesses will require supplies of minor materials of a specialised type and will operate with plant and equipment unique to their trade. The ready availability of supply and maintenance facilities will affect both their cost and the productive time loss in the event of a breakdown.

The location of these services is often associated with large urban populations, ports associated with timber importing or areas traditionally associated with a particular timber based industry, eg furniture and High Wycombe. Training facilities and skilled labour will also concentrate in the same areas.

CONCLUSIONS
Upland afforestation

With such a high dependency on imports of timber based products, many of which are subject to all manner of economic and political vagaries, the continued use, maintenance and extension of land use for forestry in upland Britain should be a matter of national importance. Today's plantings are the pulp crop of 2000 and the saw log of 2030; by which time man's dependence on this 'solar energy capturing' renewable material may well have risen world wide to make it one of the most scarce and valuable of crops.

Volume production
The rapidly increasing log harvest, doubling again by the turn of the century, will enable the British timber based industries to rationalise and become more competitive with imported timber by:
(i)   The economies of bigger scale production;
(ii)   Development of better techniques in harvesting and utilisation;
(iii)   Providing the opportunity to offer a more consistent quality with the guarantee of continuity of supply;
(iv)   Justifying the capital cost of the necessary management and marketing effort that needs to be made.

Harvesting
Harvesting on a large scale is a relatively new experience for Britain's forest industry. New methods and greater mechanisation will need to be introduced to cope with the increase, particularly in view of the difficulty in obtaining labour. This may well mean more direct involvement of the grower/user in harvesting. The location of the harvesting unit and the back-up facilities could well be in upland areas with the added benefit of helping to maintain or establish economically viable communities.

Pulp, fibre and chip
This sector consumes half the forest output, either as small roundwood or chipped waste. Production of pulp (paper) and fibre from selected roundwood will increase steadily, mainly from existing estuary located plants.

The rapid increase in consumption of particle type sheet materials is expected to continue, aided by advancing technology which will enable more of the tree to be used and semi-finished products to be made.

Future development will be for larger scale plants probably integrated with sawmilling to make the best use of available materials. Although capital intensive, these plants are consumers of relatively low grade bulky material and could well be located in the upland forest regions.

Roundwood
Small scale consumers of under half a million m^3, processors of roundwood

products for mining support, transmission poles and fencing use the structural strength of timber in the most economical manner.

A steady rather than a growth sector but one easily located within the forest area, often combined with roundwood harvesting and/or merchanting.

Large sawmills (25 000 m^3 log input and over)

The need for a big investment of capital, for professional team management, for a major marketing effort to overcome past prejudices in order to enter the large, more lucrative construction and building industry market, will probably be met by large public companies. The economic utilisation of waste will, in most cases, mean they are located with a particle board plant. The pattern of future development in this sector is probably already set in outline plans if not in substance.

Medium sawmills (5 000 to 24 000 m^3 log input)

This size of mill will find it hard to pay the price for sawlogs if selling without the benefit of mass-production and/or up-market prices. Added value from further manufacturing into packaging, fencing and building components etc will enable some to thrive; probably using a selected grade of log or serving a special market.

Location of many of this type of mill will lie between the forest area and the chosen market. Manufacturing sawmills create more direct employment and a bigger cash return/m^3 of log input.

Small sawmills (4 000 m^3 or less log input)

Where orientated towards a local market — such as agriculture — or integrated with another activity — such as round timber merchanting — this type of business will often succeed. What is lost in small scale production and lack of professional approach may be compensated for by low overheads, the ability to survive on small (often cheap) parcels of timber and retail rather than bulk selling. Many upland areas would benefit from the services and employment they provide, given the entrepreneur with the will and skill to run such a unit.

14 The development and role of interpretation in upland Britain

T R STEVENS

PREFACE

This paper attempts to outline the conceptual base of countryside interpretation together with the development and application of this methodology in areas of upland Britain. Those points considered to be of particular importance are pursued, illustrating the problems and potentials for translating this adequate theory into practical, effective interpretation. Each situation is unique, requiring an individual approach, although experiences gained elsewhere can prove valuable for interpreters. The empirical examples which are cited in the text are drawn from the author's experience; however the reader's attention is drawn to the excellent, comprehensive coverage of interpretation facilities and media development in Britain available in the Countryside Commission's *Guide to Countryside Interpretation Vol. 2* (Pennyfather, 1975), which should be read in conjunction with this text.

INTRODUCTION

The increasing pressures for recreational and educational opportunities in the uplands of Britain, arising from the new demands spawned during the mid-1960's and early-1970's, has intensified the burden of responsibility upon those managing rural land. It also required the development of a new machinery designed to cater specifically for this demand and its resultant problems: over visitation; degredation and despoliation of the actual resource and the character which makes it attractive; and the inevitable conflict of interests. The traditional, almost exclusive, reliance upon land management techniques to solve these visitor pressures, often neglecting any regard of a human response to the environment

144

is being slowly eroded as the role of visitor or social management is given greater consideration (White, 1973). The use of interpretation and applied interpretive planning is the key to meeting this environmental challenge.

DEFINITION

What is environmental interpretation? Let's take a moment to define it. The concept of the art of interpretation presented by Tilden (1957) in his classic thesis has been generally received without demur. It is not surprising, however, to find that individual interpreters have moulded this basic definition to suit their own particular requirements. Despite these many adaptations and refinements the original remains the most useful starting point: "Interpretation is an educational activity which aims to reveal meanings and relationships through the use of first hand experience, original objects and by illustrative media, rather than to communicate simply factual information." (See also: Jenkins, 1975; Aldridge, 1972; Society for the Interpretation of Britain's Heritage, 1975; Snowdonia National Park Authority, 1976; United Nations, 1976).

PURPOSE

The main concern of interpretation is to impart an understanding of the significance of a site, area, or object, common-place or unique, to casual visitors conditioning them as to what they should expect and respect from their countryside visit. As Aldridge (1975a) explains, "Without the application of resource management countryside areas will suffer from erosion in the physical sense; without interpretation it would suffer from erosion in that other sense which destroys the atmosphere or special character of the place."

Although semantic variations exist as to its definition, most interpreters agree with Aldridge as to the general purpose of interpretation and its objectives: the stimulation of visitors' interest; the promotion of his awareness and understanding of our natural, historical and cultural environment thus making a visit more meaningful and enjoyable, whilst at the same time engaging support for the conservation movement. This provides us with an adequate conceptual base, but the translation of this theory into an inspired, and appropriate interpretive service at site and regional levels illustrates remarkable variations in the selection, co-ordination and development of facilities resulting in varied effectiveness and quality (Sandford, 1974). The diversity of opportunities provided is encouraging since it reflects matters of judgement and personality emanating from the interpreter, the promoting agency, or the resource. Low standards and poor quality cannot be tolerated. Contemporary efforts to improve the interpretive delivery system initiated by the two Countryside Commissions and the Society for the Interpretation of Britain's Heritage must be extended and encouraged.

DEVELOPMENT

The past decade has witnessed a dramatic transformation in the approach to interpretation in Britain following an exaggerated gestation period characterised by unsystematic, *ad hoc* provision of information and education for visitors to the countryside. The recent fruition and realisation of the benefits accruing from interpretive programmes, developed and monitored in the wake of the 1968 Countryside Act, has prompted and ensured their further application. This piece of legislation — part of the 'new machinery' mentioned earlier — provided the necessary impetus for the creation of interpretive agencies together with the upgrading of existing ones. It also fostered the quest for fresh opportunities to which the recently acquired but adapted interpretive skills, pioneered in America, could be applied. A more critical and cost-effective attitude, questioning our early faith in visitor centres, the ubiquitous self-guided trail and those early developments born more out of "enthusiasm than understanding" (MacEwen, 1976) also grew out of this period.

The progress made at practical levels of management has, unfortunately, not been reinforced by consistent legislative, professional or financial commitment, especially from central and local government. The enlightened attitude of Gwent, Cheshire and Hampshire County Councils, amongst others, indicates the potential of a determined policy. Equally the contribution from the private sector has been varied but encouraging, although their motivations may not always prove totally altruistic (Stevens, 1975). These vagaries in supply indicate different degrees of acceptance of interpretation as a valid countryside management technique, particularly by our elected representatives and countryside visitors, despite the plea from a former director of the US National Parks service that "interpretation is as important as the initial purchase of the land". This is due in part to the nature of the subject, the ambiguity, and the difficulty of defining it satisfactorily (Hammond, 1976). "If you add (to these) the problems of drawing acceptable distinctions between it and education (and) of proving that it actually achieves anything" (Moore, 1975) then these constraints obviously prevent the full development or acceptance of interpretation. It is not surprising therefore that some interpreters question the success we have had in 'selling' the technique to the public, and to the decision makers.

THE PLAN

Interpretation in upland Britain closely reflects these trends. Appropriate provision in an upland context offers managers an exciting potential to establish effective communication with their visitors and to achieve a variety of management objectives, a fact recognised by Joad (1937): "Citizens (of Britain) educated in rural lore will not want to walk through fields of corn, or leave behind a trail of open gates." The systematic, articulated explanation of the objectives, and their operation constitutes the site or region's interpretive plan. The regional plan must establish the strategic approach to the interpretation of an upland area; comprehensively identifying the 'why', 'what', 'where', 'how' and 'when' of interpretive provision in the light of detailed research involving visitor surveys and site inventories. The plan, formulated in conjunction with other management interests, must identify sites where visitor access is considered inappropriate as well as those locations where interpretive input is to be concentrated.

The ultimate success of this areal approach depends upon the rational co-ordination of effort ensuring that site operation, and the use of media to develop chosen themes complies with the agreed plan. This unified approach to interpretation in upland areas helps to secure an orderly development, reduces duplication, produces priorities as well as facilitating monitoring, evaluation, and the essential re-appraisal of the service. Structured in this way it proves a useful lever for securing financial or other forms of support (Thompson, 1967) . Interpreters have all too often failed to adopt this regional approach in their attempts to interpret upland areas or sites within them, even though the necessity to do so has often been stated (Hookway, 1974; Stevens, 1975). On-going experimental projects sponsored by the Countryside Commission in Exmoor and Nottinghamshire, and completed Carnegie UK Trust sponsored studies of Wales and Norfolk aim to stimulate this procedure, whilst the work of the Peak District National Park Authority closely resembles our model.

The objectives of interpretation are easy to write, as policy statements appearing in the recent National Park consultative documents illustrate, eg "specific activities will be discouraged if they are likely to destroy the remote qualities of open country . . . interpretation and the use of the warden service will secure the good management of sites" (Brecon Beacons National Park, 1976), and "the capacity of certain sites can be adjusted by the use of selective interpretation . . . future policies for recreation will be related to the particular qualities and capacities of different types of areas" (Pembrokeshire Coast National Park, 1976). The crucial step is the translation of these proposals into action through the identification of sites and/or themes, together with the allocation of resources, including the media to be used. A comprehensive review outlining the suitability of particular media with empirical examples of their application in Britain has been produced by the two Countryside Commissions (Pennyfather, 1975; Aldridge, 1975b).

In upland situations the practical difficulties of implementing strategic policies and site proposals are compounded by the character and personality of these areas, reinforcing the need for a flexible yet comprehensive interpretive plan.

INTERESTS AND ATTITUDES
The present division of ownership and responsibility resulting in an overlap of

interests in upland management, plus varying spatial and functional designations or definitions (eg as National Park, Nature Reserve, or Country Park), does little to engender the prescribed approach to interpretation. Provision in Wales is indicative of this confusion with 225 separate managing bodies being identified, 32 of which were statutory agencies — including county councils (8), national park authorities (3), district councils (11), among others. The contribution of the private sector is considerable, even to the extent of monopolising provision in certain situations, ranging from the small-scale craft workshop to the larger commercially marketed attractions such as Llechwedd Slate Caverns, Gwynedd — with 199 410 visitors in 1974 (Wales Tourist Board, 1975b) and Dan-yr-Ogof Caves with 140 800 visitors.

The dominant productive land uses of upland Britain, including agriculture, forestry and water catchment/supply but excluding military uses, have recognised their responsibility to embrace objectives other than those of primary production, especially in terms of recreation, amenity and education (Douglas, 1975; Goodall & Whittow, 1973). This trend initiated by the statutory undertakers, and reaffirmed by central government (eg Forestry Commission, 1972) was soon followed by non-statutory and private enterprise. In these cases the use of interpretation as a public relations technique, whilst not being an overt principle explicitly used by all of the organisations involved, may certainly feature alongside the more usual purposes of interpretation, which include:

(i)   The protection of the resource from the visitor;

(ii)   The protection of the visitor from the resource;

(iii)   The stimulation and catalyst for positive environmental action and participation by the general public.

Sanctioned public enjoyment of these resources represents a healthy, if a somewhat reluctant change in attitude on behalf of the manager. As recently as the late 1950's the Government was refusing access orders in upland water catchment areas on the grounds of possible pollution risk (Gibbs & Whitby, 1976), and recent research indicates that a complete change of attitude is still a long way off (Bayfield & Barrow, 1976). The potential of open days acting as a synthesiser, allowing users and managers to assess the value of establishing a dialogue, can hasten this change and provide an effective form of interpretive provision in their own right (Countryside Commission, 1974). Occasional open days present an important opportunity to interpret in situations where permanent opening is impossible, or undesirable (eg working farms, industrial units, arboretum, Ministry of Defence lands or experimental centres), utilising techniques regarded as the essence of good interpretation, with minimal environmental impact.

THEMES

The theme chosen for interpretation at a particular site, or the selection of a series of themes to tell the region's story, must:

(i)   form a vital element of the heritage;
(ii)   be capable of interpretation;
(iii)   contribute to telling the whole story;
(iv)   relate to what is visible from the point of interpretation;
(v)   relate to the personality or experience of the visitor.

Even working within this framework certain aspects of the environment suffer from being considered relatively 'easy' to interpret and often this imagined simplicity dictates programme planning and content. Effort is concentrated upon those visually pleasant and physically permanent aspects of the upland areas whereas the more intangible, less dominant facets of life, which are arguably the most important, are neglected. Particular caveats exist in the eg interpretation of oral tradition (including folk songs and dialect); folk customs; settlement patterns and rural vernacular architecture. Upland Britain generally coincides with distinct, cultural and ethno-geographical areas, consequently the survival of this essentially human heritage depends upon our involvement in its interpretation.

An opportunity exists in this situation for encouraging participation by the resident community through fostering a 'self-help' philosophy, with a view to developing local museums, special events, village exhibitions which have the purpose of explaining the local heritage to visitors. At the same time such involvement of local people would contribute to the positive conservation of this heritage. The potential of this essentially heritage-based interpretation has been realised by the Wales Tourist Board (1976) in their written strategy for tourism in Wales, and also by Lewis (1975) who recognises that "visitors are anxious to experience a country or region's culture and not a plastic substitute created to please them." Equally it is important to realise that "we (planners and managers) are too obsessed with the visitors and we are not paying enough attention to making sure that the resident population . . . understand the environment in which they are living and understand the tremendous responsibilities upon their elected representatives and themselves for protecting that (environment) for their own purposes" (Pritchard, 1976a).

The direct and indirect benefits accruing from such involvement are likely to be considerable. Directly, through job opportunities, both seasonal and full-time, requiring varied skills many of which could be filled under the Manpower Commission's Job Creation Programme. This contribution to alleviating unemployment in upland areas will induce a multiplier effect underpinning the local economy as a whole. Indirect benefits from interpretation can develop by improving the visitors' understanding of indigenous life styles and attitudes (and

149

vice versa), thus reducing points of conflict between the two groups, which, in conjunction with the development of a better environment, can form a base for a community's healthy survival.

If we agree that imparting a conservation message is a major objective underlying interpretation, then our programmes must illustrate all aspects of the contemporary environment in these upland regions, including the less attractive or less aesthetic elements. Several agencies whose activities are particularly incongruous provide guided tours, trails, exhibitions and literature on-site, whilst others have offered 'generous' donations for facility development, each attempting to ameliorate their environmental impact in some way. The proposed Environmental Centre at Llanberis, North Wales, is an example of this type of involvement: the Central Electricity Generating Board realising the impact of their £150 million pound nuclear powered pump storage scheme at Dinorwic upon the Snowdonia environment, are making finances available to a group of experts to advise on the construction of the centre to be run by the National Museum of Wales (Pritchard, 1976b; Bassett, 1976).

CLIMATE

Climate is an essential factor to be considered in the planning of any interpretive facility. This is even more crucial in upland areas where local weather conditions are unpredictable and unco-operative thereby affecting day-to-day planning and producing problems affecting the demand and supply of services (Van Lear, 1973). Technical aspects of design, materials used, and the siting of a facility, whether a prestigious centre or a simple orientation table, must show a regard for these climatic factors. On the other hand visitation will be controlled by the prevalent conditions. Outdoor events, particularly guided walks, may suffer from poor attendance, and effective communication may be forfeited in conditions which adversely affect the psychological or physical comfort of our visitor.

However, certain weather conditions, contribute positively to the character of an area, creating an ambiance enhancing the visitor's enjoyment, or which may require interpretation in its own right (Van Duin, 1971).

DEPLOYMENT OF RESOURCES

The Interpretive Plan should identify areas of provision for the allocation of interpretive resources. Three types of areas exist in upland Britain, although the distinction between them is often blurred:

(i)   Focal points — sites warranting a concentration of effort in response to an existing or planned congregation of visitors.

(ii)   Supervised access — the direction or channelling of visitors in an acceptable manner to allow them to explore other areas capable of absorbing this controlled use.

(iii)   Remote areas — where visitation is discouraged and any form of interpretation is inappropriate.

(i)   Focal points: within mountain and moorland areas there exists a hierarchy of sites which, because of their inherent natural quality and charisma, or the introduction of man-made facilities, make them attractive and accessible to varying numbers of visitors. The accessible sites are used by the informal, casual visitor whilst others remain the prerogative of the active recreationalist. Interpreters have a duty in these situations, whether a visitor centre, viewpoint, or a climbing hut, to establish contact and communicate with as many of this 'captive' audience as possible. The aim must be to orientate the users by positively indicating legitimate access and activities in the upland region together with the opportunities to pursue them, including access supervised by interpreters (see (ii) below).

Interpreters should not be content simple to use their skills in situations where a problem exists, or is likely to develop, as a result of visitation. A much more extrovert approach is necessary, taking interpretation to the visitor, thus establishing new points of contact involving subtle, persuasive techniques.

Potential situations include: picnic sites and refreshment places (talks and exhibitions at the Brecon Beacons Mountain Centre); visitor accommodation (talks provided by Pembrokeshire Coast National Park Authority); public or alternative transport (Tape cassette sound guide, and literature on the Pembrokeshire Coast National Park Authority's Hiker Bus Experiment); information centres (an exhibition explaining the local industry in the vicinity of the Kilgetty Centre, run jointly by the Wales Tourist Board and Pembrokeshire Coast National Park Authority); additional flexibility may be obtained by using travelling exhibits housed in purpose built units (the Mobile Centre of the Peak District National Park Authority).

The effectiveness of interpretation is often constrained because its application is confined to a particular area. Interpretation in upland Britain should not always be restricted by geographical limitations. Viable multiple use of upland areas in the future depends upon a rapport being established with potential visitors in recreational settings in closer proximity to the visitors' home, and in ambushing the visitor with interpretive opportunities before he arrives in the upland countryside. This policy is explicit in the Country Park concept, and the concentration of effort in rural-urban fringe areas advocated by the Countryside Commission — a policy which is physically practised by many County Councils eg Cheshire with Teg's Nose Country Park (Cheshire County Council 1975) and Clwyd with Y Mynydd Hiraethog (Clwyd County Council, 1977).

(ii)   Supervised Access: If visitors are to be encouraged to explore and venture out into the upland countryside away from the 'focal points', then it is imperative that interpreters retain their ability to influence and control their movements to prescribed routes and predetermined sites, previously confirmed with other resource managers. This control can be used to channel people away from 'fragile' areas whilst at the same time allowing access in situations not otherwise available. A full exposition of the many forms of media and facilities available to attain this is detailed in the Countryside Commission's handbook. Those techniques involving personal services — guided walks, pony treks and tours, demonstrations, site talks, and contact with members of the warden/ranger service — are proving the most successful. The Pembrokeshire Coast National Park Authority has established the value, in terms of cost-effectiveness, of these services in their guided walks and talks programme, which in 1976 involved over 150 guided walks (full and half day) attracting 4300 visitors at an average cost per head of only 19.6p (Dyfed County Council, 1977). (see Figure 3)

The most common form of interpretation used to establish contact with the visitor in the upland countryside in an attempt to influence his access for whatever purpose, is the ubiquitous self-guided trail, based upon a booklet, a series of way-markings, or orientation tables. The number of trails existing in Britain has risen steadily over the past 15 years with a dramatic increase following the impetus of European Conservation Year (1970). Unfortunately not all these trails received proper consideration as to their purpose, location or interpretation. Indeed many are poorly conceived and despite the number now in existence little research is available as to their use and effectiveness (Bayfield & Barrow, 1976). (see Figures 1 & 2)

Initial conclusions from completed research suggest that in upland areas self-guided trails must be developed, not in isolation, but in conjunction with or radiating out from other facilities, if the general public are to be encouraged to use them. The development of trails beginning at the focal points discussed earlier would therefore seem to be a sensible proposition, especially if existing footpaths can be utilised.

Trails can also function to explain management techniques to other managers, as well as the public by: routing paths around examples of the practical achievements of a particular project, indicating the application of methods; and canvassing support for future allocation of resources. The Great Langland Trail designed to illustrate the Upland Management Experiment in the Lake District is a good example of the point in question.

On extensive open mountain and moorland it becomes difficult to control access, and any permanent interpretive furniture is likely to be visually intrusive. Where interpretation is deemed necessary, emphasis should be placed

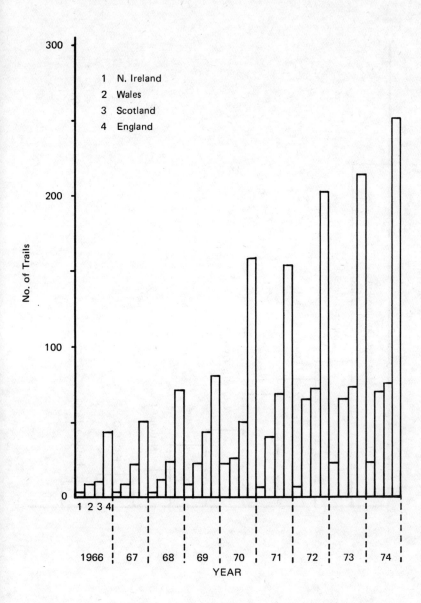

Figure 1
THE DEVELOPMENT OF SELF-GUIDED TRAILS IN BRITAIN

1 N. Ireland
2 Wales
3 Scotland
4 England

No. of Trails

YEAR

Figure 2
THE MANAGEMENT OF SELF-GUIDED TRAILS IN WALES, 1975

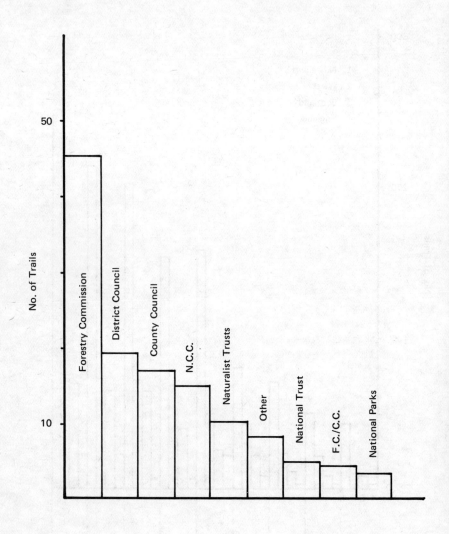

Figure 3
PEMBROKESHIRE COAST NATIONAL PARK WALKS AND TALKS – NORTHERN SECTOR PROGRAMME 1976

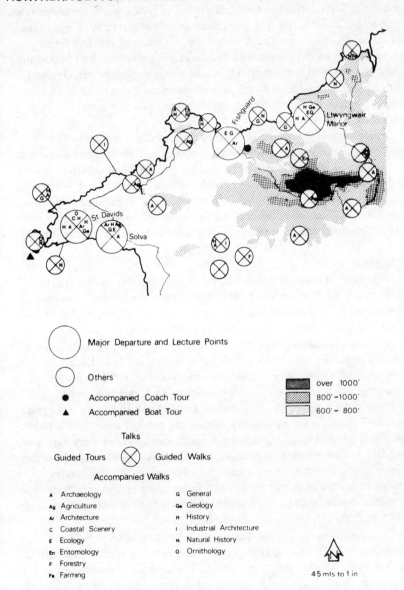

Major Departure and Lecture Points

Others

● Accompanied Coach Tour

▲ Accompanied Boat Tour

over 1000'

800'–1000'

600'– 800'

Talks

Guided Tours ⊗ Guided Walks

Accompanied Walks

A Archaeology
Ag Agriculture
Ar Architecture
C Coastal Scenery
E Ecology
En Entomology
F Forestry
Fa Farming

G General
Ge Geology
H History
I Industrial Architecture
N Natural History
O Ornithology

4·5 mls to 1 in

upon the warden service (including voluntary, if carefully trained); indeed, provision of these services exists in 92% of upland access areas, in spite of the fact that costs and man-hours required for upland wardening exceeds that for lowland sites (Gibbs & Whitby, 1976). Walking and climbing activities dominate recreational use in such areas and interpretation should aim to work within the constraints of these visitors in relation to their interests and available time. Consequently the period before and after the activity offers the best opportunity for successful interpretation which might take place in youth hostel, climbing huts or camp sites. The theme of the interpretation must also be adjusted to emphasise conduct and safety considerations appropriate to mountain environments.

(iii)   Remote Areas: In any region or at a particular site it is necessary to identify areas where people, in whatever number, would prove either detrimental to the resource eg within nature reserves on the grounds of conservation or incompatible with existing land uses eg on Ministry of Defence land. Whatever the case, interpretation must gear itself to maintaining this zonation. Situations may also be identified where any interpretive input will be inappropriate on the grounds of intrusion either upon the visual quality of the scene, or site atmosphere.

FINANCING

The achievement of management objectives through interpretation requires a financial commitment, the scale of which partly determines actual provision. Grant aid from various sources is able to supplement initial budgets. Up to 75% grant aid is available from the Countryside Commission (under the 1968 Countryside Act) to develop and maintain interpretive services in both the public and private sector. Embry (1976) points out that until the 1974 Local Government Act, Countryside Commission effort concentrated on the public sector with grants to the private sector restricted to schemes of a similar character to those supplied by the statutory agencies, which "rarely make good investments." The present inflationary climate has brought reductions in public spending and schemes involving local government capital expenditure have been frozen. This austere period does provide an opportunity for the reappraisal and evaluation of our interpretive achievements and priorities to date. Further extensions of private investment in projects interpreting upland areas backed by direct public money, with possible tax or loan repayment reductions to provide added encouragement, should be considered.

Projects qualifying for Tourist Board Assistance, (under Section 40 Development of Tourism Act, 1969) often create facilities which contribute to an area's interpretation to the casual visitors. The criteria for establishing 'development areas' apply to much of upland Britain, allowing up to 49% of the capital costs or £50 000 to be granted to private developers at the discretion of the Tourist Boards. Since the scheme's introduction in 1971 £1.4 million has been paid in grants and loans to 182 projects (year ending April 1975) with equivalent of 1 150 permanent jobs being created in Wales alone (Wales Tourist Board, 1975a).

Private interest in providing interpretive facilities is geared to obtaining a financial return upon their investment, directly or indirectly, with no apparent adverse affect upon the market demand. Indeed the opposite is true, as re-investment improving the quality of the interpretation is likely to take place. Statutory bodies must adopt this attitude and introduce pricing schemes to projects, producing an income available for enhancing future interpretive provision. Income derived in this way has the potential for replacing or supplementing uneconomical aspects of land use in upland areas creating a source of income to ensure viability of, for example, a hill farm unit.

EVALUATION AND MONITORING

The effectiveness of interpretation has rarely been evaluated, perhaps because of the absence to date of clearly defined objectives in the first instance. If interpretation is to develop as a credible management technique in the upland countryside then evaluation and monitoring of projects has to develop, together with greater emphasis upon initial research, giving an understanding of the resource and of the clientele. Successful upland management requires a knowledge of human behaviour and social organisation at least equivalent to knowledge of physical aspects. The interpretive plan can provide the structure for developing this appraisal. The vital question to be answered is, are we communicating effectively, and if not why not?

THE FUTURE

Interpreters through their programmes have got to develop a more conscientious attitude towards the total environment. Man's survival is in doubt because he has become divorced from the environment, the "nexus with nature has been broken" (MacEwen, 1976). The new challenge facing interpretation is to restore this. Past emphasis upon entertaining the visitor has often failed to communicate this more profound conservation message. Sites chosen for interpretation should become bench-marks: setting standards and encouraging action elsewhere. However, interpretation is only as good as the service providing it allows: upgrading the quality of programmes and professionalism of staff is extremely important, as the Countryside Commission recognise (Hookway, 1974), if these new objectives are to be achieved.

ACKNOWLEDGEMENTS

The author would like to thank the following friends and colleagues for their help and assistance in producing this paper: Dr Dyfed Ellis-Gruffudd; Bill Seabrooke (for their comments on the manuscript); Arwel Williams (for art work); and Mrs B Wood (for the typing).

REFERENCES

Aldridge, D (1972) *Upgrading park interpretation and communication with the public.* Second World Conference on National Parks, Session X(1), 1972.

Aldridge, D (1975a) *Interpreting the environment.* A Report on a Conference at How Hill, Norfolk Carnegie Project, CP25, July 1975.

Aldridge, D (1975b) Principles of countryside interpretation and interpretive planning. Part One of *A guide to countryside interpretation.* Countryside Commission for Scotland & Countryside Commission. London: HMSO.

Bassett, D (1976) *Llanberis project.* Society for the Interpretation of Britain's Heritage, Newsletter No 4, Summer 1976.

Bayfield, N G & Barrow, G C (1976) The use and attraction of nature trails in upland Britain. *Biological Conservation,* 9, 267-292.

Brecon Beacons National Park (1976) *Draft National Park Plan.* Brecon Beacons National Park Authority.

Cheshire County Council (1975) *Teg's Nose Country Park: interpretive prospectus.* Cheshire County Council.

Clwyd County Council (1977) *Mynydd Hiraethog: the recreational potential of an upland area.* Clwyd County Council.

Countryside Commission (1974) *Farm open days.* Countryside Commission & DART. CCP 77 & DART No 14.

Douglas, R W (1975) *Forest recreation.* Oxford: Pergamon Press.

Duin Van, R H (1971) *De inrichting van recreatieterreninen.* Band A & Band B Kandidaatscollege Cultuurtechneik, Landbouwhogeschool, Wageningen, Netherlands.

Dyfed County Council (1977) *County Council minutes.* Dyfed County Council, January 1977.

Embry, N (1976) *Financial consideration for countryside projects.* Countryside Recreation Management Association Newsletter, Winter 1976.

Gibbs, R S & Whitby, M C (1976) *Local Authority expenditure on access land.* The Agricultural Adjustment Unit, Research Monograph No 6, University of Newcastle Upon Tyne.

Goodall, B & Whittow, J (1973) *The recreational potential of Forestry Commission holdings: a report to the Forestry Commission.* Dept. of Geography, University of Reading.

Hammond, P (1976)   *Learning to Love: The science of interpretation.*
Parks and Recreation, **41,** No 11.

Forestry Commission (1972)   *Forestry Policy.*   London: HMSO.

Hookway, R J (1974)   *Countryside interpretation.*   National Park Conference,
Great Malvern, 1974.

Jenkins, J G (1975)   *Interpretation.*   Inaugural address to the Society for the
Interpretation of Britain's Heritage.   In: Newsletter No 1, Summer 1975.

Joad, C E M (1937)   The people's claim.   In: *Britain and the beast.*
(Ed) B C W Ellis.   London: Dent.

Lear Van, H N (1973)   *Determination of planning capacity and layout criteria
for outdoor recreation projects.*   Centre for Agricultural Publications and
Documentation, Wageningen, Netherlands.

Lewis, E T (1975)   Western Mail, 27 August, 1975.

MacEwen, M (1976)   The countryside explained.   *Country Life*   Feb. 1976.

Moore, P (1975)   *A hard row to furrow.*   Society for the Interpretation of
Britain's Heritage, Newsletter No 1, Summer 1975.

National Park Policies Review Committee (1974)   *Report.*   Department of the
Environment and Welsh Office.   London: HMSO.

Pembrokeshire Coast National Park (1976)   *National Park Plan Consultative
Document.*   Pembrokeshire Coast National Park Authority.

Pennyfather, K (1975)   Interpretive media and facilities.   Part two of *Guide to
countryside interpretation.*   Countryside Commission for Scotland and
Countryside Commission.   London: HMSO.

Pritchard, T (1976a)   *Session Four Report.*   National Parks Conference,
Tenby, 1976.

Pritchard, T (1976b)   *Llanberis Project.*   Society for Interpretation of
Britain's Heritage, Newsletter No 4, Summer 1976.

Society for the Interpretation of Britain's Heritage (1975)   *Prospectus.*
SIBH, 1975.

Snowdonia National Park Authority (1976)   *Draft National Park Plan.*
Snowdonia National Park Authority.

Stevens, T R (1975)   *Interpretation in Wales.*   Interim Report of the Wales
Rural Life Centre Project.

Thompson, D C (1967)   *Interpretive planning in the National Park Service.*
Report to the US National Park Service.

Tilden, F (1957)   *Interpreting our heritage.*   University of North Carolina.

United Nations (1976)   *Interpretive planning in National Parks — a manual.*
United Nations Organisation.

Wales Tourist Board (1975a)   *Annual Report.*   Cardiff: Wales Tourist Board.

Wales Tourist Board (1975b) *Summary of Tourist Statistics.* Cardiff: Wales Tourist Board.

Wales Tourist Board (1976) *A strategy for tourism.* Cardiff: Wales Tourist Board.

White, J (1973) *Managing and financing country parks: an examination.* Seminar proceedings, Seminar D, Recreational land use, planning & transport, Research & Computation Co., June 1973.

5 The recreational potential of upland areas

M A B BODDINGTON

INTRODUCTION

For the purposes of this paper recreation is distinguished from tourism as an activity involving day visitors only, whereas the latter involves overnight accommodation away from home. A tourist, however, can indulge in recreational activities by making day visits to local attractions in the area where he or she is staying. In this respect, for example, a tourist on holiday in the Lake District may be assumed to be indulging in a recreational activity if he takes a boat out on Windermere or goes on a day's pony trekking in Langdale. The latter, of course, may be borderline in definition since many pony trekking enterprises include accommodation as part of the enterprise. I shall not encompass visits to farm open days or other interpretational facilities under my heading of recreation, since interpretation is considered separately in Terry Stevens' paper.

Given these exclusions, I shall limit my review to recreational enterprises, as defined in the Dartington Amenity Research Trust/Rural Planning Services Ltd. (1974) report, *Farm Recreation and Tourism* (See Appendix 1, items B and C). The list is not exhaustive of recreational possibilities. The reader will be able to add other enterprises not mentioned as well as delete those not necessarily suited to upland areas.

POTENTIAL RECREATIONAL SUPPLY AND DEMAND IN UPLAND AREAS

Upland areas are in plentiful supply in the UK. The official figure adopted in the proposals for a EC Less Favoured Areas Directive (1974) is 7.654 million ha. Our National Parks are contained almost entirely within this and extend to 1.362 million ha. Respectively these areas constitute about 32% and 6% of the entire UK land resource. Almost all of these areas are remote from the main centres of population. Figure 1 shows the designated less-favoured areas in the UK together with the main conurban areas surrounded by 50 mile (80 km) radius.

Over a decade ago Burton and Wibberley (1965) suggested that the total amount of land available for recreational use amounted to 1.2 million ha in England and Wales and 400 000 ha in Scotland. These figures included only forest land, commons and institutional land where the public had right of access. In addition to these areas they estimated that there were some 5 million ha of private rough grazings and deer forest and a substantial area of private rough grazings in England and Wales where the public has *de facto* right of access.

Gibbs and Whitby (1975) exploring the extent of access areas (either by agreement, acquisition or order) discovered that their total extent in England and Wales, as at April 1st 1977, amounted to 35 295.5 ha, of which 30 203.0 ha were in upland areas. Of this total, 19 752.2 ha occurred in the Peak District National Park. The Gibbs and Whitby figures exclude much of the areas defined by Burton and Wibberley.

One way and another there would appear to be a fairly massive potential supply of recreational land in the United Kingdom uplands. This supply, however, is of little meaning unless it may be realistically used, and there are a number of constraints affecting the use of it. These constraints are mostly to do with demand.

Patmore (1970) noted that, ". . . of all the problems which bedevil the relationships between leisure and land use, none is more severe than the locational imbalance between the areas of greatest demand and those of readiest supply." Also that, ". . . south east England, with nearly one third of the population of England and Wales, has no National Park nearer than Derbyshire or South Wales. It is 120 miles (192 km), as the crow flies, from the centre of London to the nearest point on the boundaries of the Peak District or the Brecon Beacons, which may be compared with the average distance travelled in one direction on day trips of 50 miles (80 km) and on half day trips of 29 miles (47 km)."

Patmore's figures for distance travelled come from the survey conducted by the British Travel Association (BTA) and the University of Keele (1967). The BTA/Keele survey demonstrated the importance of car ownership in recreational activity (although car ownership itself is a function of many other variables), with car owners being up to 300% more active in certain recreational pursuits than non-car owners. Of car owners, 73% covered less than 100 miles (160 km) in their last day trip, and 24% travelled over 100 miles (160 km). These figures are reinforced by the findings of a survey undertaken by the North West Sports Council (1972) which showed that the median one-way distance travelled on half day trips was between 10 and 20 miles (16 and 32 km) and on full day trips was between 40 and 50 miles (64 and 80 km). In this case the coast was the destination for 35% of the full day trippers and for 52% of the half day trippers, whilst only 29% on half day trips and 31% on full day trips went into the countryside. These results were obtained in a region, it must be remembered, with an ample share of uplands within reasonably easy driving distance (generally, the Pennines, North Wales and Cumbria; specifically, the Peak District National Park, the Lake District National Park, the Yorkshire Dales National Park and Snowdonia National Park).

The BTA/Keele Survey also found that a greater proportion on day trips preferred the seaside to the country, although in this case 47% of half day trippers visited the countryside and only 19% the coast.

It is possible that Patmore, and others of his persuasion, are over-stating the case in considering the limited availability of the supply (notably in the uplands) of recreational land close to centres of demand. It must be recognised, of course, that these statements are quite accurate in terms of the South East. However, Figure 1 shows that a substantial proportion of the uplands of England and Wales are within the 50 mile (80 km) radii of our major conurbations. It is of interest to note that the only areas excluded are Bodmin, Dartmoor (and Exmoor in reality) central and North West Wales, and the Lake District. Nobody can claim that any of these areas suffer from a lack of demand. Ian Mercer, Chief Planning Officer of the Dartmoor National Park, is fond of stating that the area of his responsibility is now linked by continuous motorway or dual carriageway to Glasgow. He could well include Birmingham, South Wales, the Yorkshire conurbations, Tyneside, Teesside, Perth and London.

These comments should also be seen in the somewhat sobering context of recent statements by the Department of the Environment's Countryside Review Committee (1976). For example: "The number of private cars in England and Wales is expected to rise from its 1974 level of 12.6 million to about 22-23 million by the end of the century." "On present plans a trunk road network linking all the main centres of population and industry should be completed by the 1990's. This will have sufficient capacity to meet the 70% increase in traffic forecast by the end of the century . . . ". "There are too many uncertain factors to allow a worthwhile quantitative forecast to be made (of countryside recreation). However, with the prospect of a doubling of private car ownership by the end of the century, continued growth in recreational trips to the countryside seems inevitable."

This growth of recreational demand was well summarised in the Second Report of the House of Lords Select Committee on Sport and Leisure (1973): "The Scottish Office say in evidence that they expect the amount of outdoor recreation to treble by the end of the century and they mention that tourism in Scotland is increasing at the rate of 12% per annum. The Director of the Countryside Commission says that there is 'something like a 10 to 15% compound increase in

Figure 1
LESS FAVOURED AREAS IN RELATION TO CONURBATION AREAS

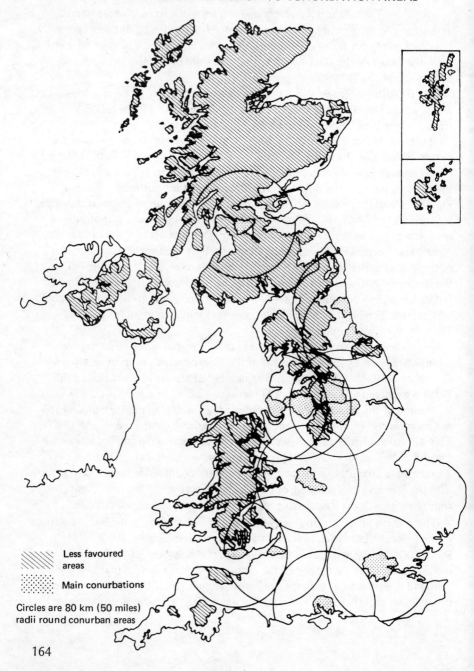

Less favoured areas

Main conurbations

Circles are 80 km (50 miles) radii round conurban areas

the rate of recreational activity in the countryside'. The British Waterways Board say that the growth of boating has to be controlled at 10% per annum to keep in line with the availability of new facilities. The Northern Region Planning Committee's Survey estimated increases between 1967 and 1980 of 74% in golf, 64% in camping, 52% in motor sports and 42% in trips to the country. The National Anglers' Council quote a growth rate for angling of 8% per annum."

These figures are, of course, national and do not necessarily reflect upon the likely increase in demand for outdoor recreation in the uplands. In any event the pressures tend very often to be localised. Because the majority of visitors to upland areas tend to be car borne the greatest pressures tend to occur on and around the road network — particularly at parking places close to good views and interesting sites. The work of Burton (1966) and Wager (1964) showed that between 70 and 80% of visitors to the countryside prefer to stay in or near their cars. Whilst the upland areas of the UK may cover nearly 8 million ha, the road network is relatively sparse, so that the quantum of land available for recreation, *de facto*, to the vast majority of the recreating public is extremely small.

This localised pressure gave concern both to the Sandford Committee (Department of the Environment, 1974) and the Countryside Review Committee (1976). The former states: "The first purpose of national parks, as stated by Dower and by Parliament — the preservation and enhancement of national beauty — seems to us to remain entirely valid and appropriate. The second purpose — the promotion of public enjoyment — however, needs to be reinterpreted and qualified because it is now evident that excessive or unsuitable use may destroy the very qualities which attract people to the parks. We have no doubt that where the conflict between the two purposes, which has always been inherent, becomes acute, the first one must prevail in order that the beauty and ecological qualities of the national parks may be maintained."

The Sandford Committee suggested a number of ways in which the pressures could be alleviated by channelling visitors away from more sensitive areas and this theme was taken up by the Countryside Review Committee: "The problems of 'people pressure' are far from academic: they are dramatically illustrated by the physical damage to the land at places of heavy visitor concentration, for instance, the top of Snowdon and the Malvern Hills, parts of the Pennine Way, and the many areas in or near the urban fringe. In the Committee's view the key factor in tackling this subject is the continued development of techniques for managing land and people. These can take many forms — nearby alternative attractions, interpretation centres, 'park and ride schemes', self-guided trails — some at least of which can make a virtue of necessity by enriching the experience offered to visitors."

Inevitably the provision of further recreational opportunities for visitors must be made and this in itself may help to relieve pressure on more sensitive sites. But what sort of facility should be provided?

RECREATIONAL OPPORTUNITIES FOR VISITORS

We know something of visitors' activities in upland areas as a result of various surveys undertaken over the past 10 years or so. Yapp (1969) interviewed 3 879 visitors to the Lake District to discover their present activities and their desire for more facilities. His findings are reproduced in Tables 1 and 2.

Table 1
LEISURE ACTIVITIES OF VISITORS TO THE LAKE DISTRICT

Activity	Half-day visitors %	Day visitors %	Holiday makers %	All not on holiday[1] %
Picnic in or around car	18	46	47	29
Picnic away from car	1	7	19	4
Meal in restaurant etc	26	38	51	29
Drink in pub	6	16	49	16
Rock climb, fell walk for over 1 mile	4	15	47	10
Walk less than 1 mile	32	44	60	34
Trip on pleasure boat	5	10	21	6
Boating/sailing	2	7	20	5
Fishing/angling	x	5	3	4
Field studies	1	2	5	1
Swimming	—	2	4	2
Sitting by lake	13	28	51	20
Others	10	11	22	13
No answer	36	11	5	29
Size of sample	666	1 211	1 955	3 879

1 Includes those staying with friends and those passing through the Lake District while on holiday elsewhere.

Source: Yapp (1969)

Table 2
FACILITIES DESIRED BY VISITORS TO THE LAKE DISTRICT

Facilities	% of respondents
None: Leave it as it is	11
Parking and laybys	9
Swimming	6
Boating and sailing	6
Camping	6
Miscellaneous outdoor sports	5
Better roads	4
Walking, hiking	4
Fishing	4
Picnic areas	4
Lavatories	3
Eating places, public houses	3
Evening entertainment	3
Access to lakes and fells	3
Caravanning	2
Indoor entertainment	2
Horse riding, pony trekking	1
Other	4
No answer	14

Source: Yapp (1969)

It is clear from Table 1 that the majority of people prefer to indulge in fairly inactive pursuits — eating, drinking, and sitting around account for between 50 and 60% of all the pursuits listed. Really energetic pastimes such as rock climbing, fell walking, boating, sailing and swimming account for a maximum of 20% of activities; and this maximum is achieved by visitors on holiday.

The category labelled 'no answer' includes, according to Yapp, those who drove about without getting out of the car. This category declines rapidly with the length of time spent in the area.

Table 2 shows that about 30% of the respondents required further provision of facilities for outdoor recreation of one sort or another — although this figure may be inflated by double counting since respondents were not limited to one answer.

A study of tourists in the Lake District by P A Management Consultants (1973) found even less desire for outdoor recreational facilities amongst a sample of

7 116 respondents (including day trippers and tourists on holiday). Of the whole sample only 2% stated that they would like to see (more) swimming pools, and no other outdoor recreational facilities were mentioned – and this was an unprompted question. The other requirements expressed by visitors ranged through lavatories, car parks, restaurants, indoor entertainment, better roads, signposting and shops. Some 55% of visitors were satisfied with the facilities offered. The P A Survey also examined the type of activity presently undertaken by holidaymakers in the area and the results are shown in Table 3.

Table 3
LEISURE PURSUITS OF HOLIDAYMAKERS IN THE LAKE DISTRICT

Activity	% of respondents
Driving around the area	70
Sightseeing in towns and villages	58
Shopping for presents and souvenirs	52
Visiting a pub	47
Climbing, hiking, rambling, caving	43
Visiting historic buildings etc	36
Visiting museum, exhibition etc	30
Going to the beach	30
Trip on steamer, other passenger boat	29

Source: P A Management Consultants (1973)

According to this break-down only 43% of the sample engaged in some active form of pursuit, whereas a more detailed table shows sailing and boating enjoying 16%, water skiing and sub aqua 3%, horse riding and pony trekking 8%, fishing 11%, golfing 3% and other sports 4%. Again, there is probably a considerable degree of double counting between all of these groups. The P A report highlights the importance of active pursuits amongst the young, of cultural activities amongst the higher socio-economic groups and of sightseeing amongst the foreign visitors.

I want to turn now to two reports on the Yorkshire Pennines. The first is the work of the North Riding Pennine Working Party (1975) and covers an area substantially the same as the administrative area of the North Pennines Rural Development Board – 1 361 km^2. It includes Aysgarth and Reeth Rural Districts, most of Leyburn and Startforth Rural Districts, and parts of Masham and Richmond Rural Districts. The report estimates that 2 800 000 people visited the area in ·1972 and of these only 116 000 were staying visitors, demonstrating the importance of the area as a day-visitor attraction rather than a holiday base.

The report lists the following activities as being important in the study area:

(i)   Informal and sightseeing activities;
(ii) Caravanning and camping;
(iii) Active pursuits on foot and horse;
(iv) Motor sports;
(v)   Winter sports;
(vi) Water sports.

In so far as the first category is concerned the report states: "Both in terms of numbers of participants and in terms of demands made upon the countryside this is by far the most important category of activity. Participation in all the activities falling within this group is overwhelmingly car-orientated." Also that, "Picnicking ranked highest but other informal activities such as 'sitting in or around the car', 'walking less than two miles', 'having a meal or a drink', and 'visiting sites of interest' all figured prominently."

Riverside sites are most important as stopping places and the report emphasizes the attraction of water as a focal point for visitors.

The third category is also important and the report suggests that there is considerable potential for the development of continuous riverside footpaths and long distance routes along ridge lines and watersheds. There are also opportunities for increased activity in caving, orienteering, canoeing and sailing. It is noted that there is a high potential for pony trekking, a pursuit growing at 7% per annum nationally. However, the experience of the Brecon Beacons may serve all authorities in good stead here: in that area pony trekking has come into oversupply and there are consequent problems for conservation.

The second study was undertaken by the Yorkshire and Humberside Economic Planning Board (1976) and covers all parishes in the former West Riding of Yorkshire in which hill cow or sheep subsidies are paid to farmers. This area is entirely outside that studied by the North Riding Pennines Study Working Party and stretches from Sedburgh in the north west to Sheffield in the south east. It has the whole of the Yorkshire and Lancashire industrial Pennines on its doorstep or within it (including Greater Manchester): "Over 1 million people can reach Grassington within one hour's travelling time by car and about 3 million are within one hour of Skipton and 7.5 million within one hour of the central part of the South Pennines."

The importance of day visitors, as opposed to tourists, in the area is demonstrated by the Planning Board's estimates that about 7 million people visited the study area in 1972 and, of these, only 200 000 were tourists staying one night or more. The planning Board anticipate that the number of visitors will increase without any attempts to attract them. The report quotes the work of Dartington Amenity Research Trust (1974) in assessing the range of recreational activities pursued by visitors in Wharfedale and this, again, stresses the importance of passive pursuits — motoring, sightseeing and picnicking — amongst visitors: an importance which tends to decrease with length of stay.

The Planning Board accept a similar classification of recreational activities to that used by the North Riding Pennine Working Party (see above) but develop this into a tabulated assessment of the degree to which potential exists and is exploited. The tabulation is reproduced as Appendix 2 to this paper.

These studies all show that the vast majority of visitors wish to engage in very passive pursuits, although tourists are often more likely to get involved in active recreation. Many of the more active recreational pursuits are resource-based — canoeing, sailing, swimming, fishing, caving or pot-holing, rock climbing, and so forth — so that it is difficult to plan for further provision. Most of these facilities which can be expanded relate to the passive enjoyment of the countryside — road improvements, picnic sites, laybys and view spots — and fall within the purview of the local authority rather than private individuals such as farmers or landowners. The next section reviews two reports prepared by my firm — Rural Planning Services Ltd (RPS) and are concerned, at least in some part, with the opportunities for private investment in recreation in upland areas.

OPPORTUNITIES FOR PRIVATE INVESTMENT IN RECREATION

In 1975 the Countryside Commission asked RPS to study the Hartsop Valley in the Lake District and one of our terms of reference was to examine the current and likely future recreation use of the area and assess this in terms of National Park objectives. We were also asked to examine the relationship between farming, landscape, recreation and the local community and to suggest the extent to which these are interdependent or in conflict.

In some respects the valley is typical of others in the Lakes but only in so far as it is one of these which is not actually a focus for large numbers of visitors. In general it tends to act as a corridor for visitors passing between Windermere and Ullswater and the main attraction is the summit of Kirkstone Pass which lies at the southern end of the valley. The main recreational activity can thus be described as pleasure motoring, generally *en route* from one location, outside the valley, to another: a very secondary activity is fell walking or mountaineering or rock climbing.

Our analysis of the potential development of tourist and recreational activities showed that the emphasis lay overwhelmingly with the former. We identified no recreational activity in which local farmers could participate as entrepreneurs, with the possible exception of establishing craft workshops in old buildings. We might also have mentioned farmbased catering as an area worthy of investigation.

The other study was concerned with the massive privately owned forest of

Eskdalemuir in Dumfriesshire. The forest extends to about 12 000 ha and is in a number of ownerships but under the common management of the Economic Forestry Group. It is some 45 miles (70 km) south of Edinburgh and 35 miles (65 km) north west of Carlisle: although the A7 and A74 trunk roads are each within 5 miles (8 km) of the forest boundary, accessibility cannot be regarded as one of its assets.

A 12 000 ha estate in the remoter parts of the Southern Uplands might appear to offer considerable opportunities in recreational development — especially when a considerable proportion is devoted to forestry. The Forestry Commission has shown the way in many respects here and their recreational sites in the Lake District, Kielder and many parts of Scotland contain many good ideas (although most are based on tourism or interpretation). The possibilities at Eskdalemuir are similarly legion but these too are heavily dependent upon accommodation since no major investment could be expected to show a satisfactory rate of return on capital if it were dependent upon a highly seasonal passing trade.

The enterprises identified for implementation were as follows:

Educational:
(i)   interpretation centre/museum;
(ii)   field study centre;
(iii) educational trails;
(iv)   observation towers and hides.

Gaming and sporting:
(i)   shooting school;
(ii)   duck flighting;
(iii) deer stalking;
(iv)   pheasant and grouse shooting.

Recreation:
(i)   pony trekking;
(ii)   picnic sites;
(iii) motor safari routes.

Accommodation:
(i)   self catering cottages;
(ii)   caravans;
(iii) field study centre hostel;
(iv)   pony trekking centre hostel;
(v)   safari lodge.

Almost every enterprise mentioned included the provision of accommodation if it were to be successful. It is thought that in most upland areas accommodation is the key to private investment in leisure facilities. A brief appraisal of Appendix 1 shows that there are few recreational enterprises which lend themselves to private investment *unless* an individual landowner happens to hold the key to a particular resource which is in demand. Such a resource might be an area of water, a pot hole, access to some site such as a rock climb or a waterfall, or simply a convenient field or wood for car parking or picnicking.

CONCLUDING REMARKS

There may well be a national demand/supply imbalance in so far as countryside recreation in upland areas is concerned but most upland areas appear to be fairly well subscribed in terms of numbers of visitors. Naturally the pressure of visitors is felt mainly in the April-October period and tends to be fairly localised within the upland areas. This concentration in time and space is giving rise to countryside management problems which may only be solved by spreading the load. There are considerable problems here since the road network in upland areas tends to be of a low density and, on the whole, visitors are not prepared to move far from the road. Considerable road building programmes in upland areas may be necessary if the recreational potential is to be realised — or even if the expected increase in visitor numbers comes about.

This emphasis upon roads as a focus for recreation in upland areas derives from observations that the majority of visitors prefer to enjoy the countryside passively from within or near their cars. Most of the facilities required or desired tend to be linked to the car. This is more the case where recreational pressure derives from day visitors (much of the Pennines, Northumberland, North Yorks Moors, North East Wales and South Wales) as opposed to tourists (Bodmin, Dartmoor, Exmoor, mid Wales, the Lake District and most of Scotland).

The whole nature of recreational supply and demand in the uplands is different from that in lowland Britain. The uplands do not generally possess the house historic, the garden beautiful or the ruin spectacular. The attractions in upland areas are more of a national character and may be enjoyed without approaching closely or are readily accessible without charge.

Under these circumstances it seems that the main onus is upon Local Authorities to provide the sort of facilities necessary for the passive enjoyment of the countryside (good roads, car parks, picnic sites, laybys etc) and to ensure that there is access to the open countryside for those who require it. The main potential for private investors would seem to be in the provision of accommodation. In many respects this is sad, especially for local farmers who need all the diversity of enterprises they can get to supplement, and give stability to, their marginal and fluctuating incomes.

Appendix 1

LIST OF RECREATION AND TOURIST ENTERPRISES WHICH CAN OR COULD BE LOCATED ON A FARM

A   Tourist Accommodation

1   In the farmhouse: bed and breakfast; farm guesthouse; farmhouse holiday; farm auto-holiday

2   Self-catering accommodation in converted farm buildings, cottages, chalets

3   Second homes, including redundant farm buildings (leased or sold) and long-let caravans

4   Camping sites

5   Caravan sites — transit/touring/static

6   Specialised holidays ie accommodation plus an activity (field studies, sketching etc)

B   Resource-based activity

7   Riding, pony-trekking, equestrian centres

8   Fishing, swimming, boating, boat moorings

9   Game — rough shooting, pigeon-shooting, pheasant and duck shooting, clay-pigeons

C   Day-visitor enterprises

10   Informal recreation — car parks, picnic sites, country parks

11   Access for caving, climbing etc.

12   Special attractions:

(i)   Rare breeds, wildlife parks, museums of farm machinery etc

(ii)   Sporting facilities: squash, tennis, swimming pool, sauna, golf driving range, golf course, grass-skiing, plastic ski slopes etc

(iii)   Wildlife hikes

13   Farm catering — teas, meals etc

14   Farm produce:

(i)   farm-gate sales to public

(ii)   home-ground wheat

(iii)   self-picking of fruit and vegetables

15   Indoor activities and events — barn dances, concerts, plays etc

16   One-day/occasional events:

(i)   Related to farming — hedge-laying, ploughing matches

(ii)   Unrelated to farming — traction engine rallies, motor cycle scrambling, archery, clay-pigeon shooting, autocross, pop concerts

17   Educational visits — farm open days, farm trails, school visits, demonstration farms etc

Source: Dartington Amenity Research Trust and Rural Planning Services Ltd (1974)

Appendix 2
RECREATION IN THE PENNINE UPLANDS

Category of Recreation	Location	Number of Visitors (where known)
Informal and sightseeing activities	The whole area has much to offer, including parts of two National Parks, and area of outstanding natural beauty and many attractive villages. Noteworthy individual sites include:	
	(i) the Malham area, famous for its limestone scenery;	
	(ii) Bolton Abbey;	About 275 000 in 1972
	(iii) Hardcastle Crags, Brimham Rocks, Rombalds Moor and the St Ives Estate;	
	(iv) historic buildings such as Browsholme Hall, East Riddlesden Hall Skipton Castle, Sawley Abbey and the Bronte Parsonage Museum;	154 000 visitors to Bronte Parsonage museum in 1972
	(v) historic towns including Haworth, Hebden Bridge and Heptonstall;	
	(vi) the Keighley and Worth Valley Railway and the Yorkshire Dales Railway	Keighley-Worth Valley railway carried over 100 000 visitors in 1972
	(vii) two National Nature Reserves in Ribblesdale, one of which is open to the public without need of permit.	
Active pursuits on foot and horseback	The study area is excellent walking country. There are rights of way throughout the area together with access agreements and *de facto* access to the Fells.	
	(i) Walking: The Pennine Way passes through the study area from Black Hill in the south to Cam Fell. There are also nature trails at Bolton Abbey, Keighley, Clapham, St Ives, Hardcastle Crags, Saddleworth, Ripponden and North Dean Wood, Elland.	A survey on four days during the summer of 1971 at six points in the study area on the Pennine Way counted 348 long distance and 295 day walkers. Use of the Pennine Way has increased approximately threefold since 1965
	(ii) Pot-holing: With at least 327 major pot-holes in the Craven district, there are considerable opportunities for caving and pot-holing. There are also pot-holes in Upper Nidderdale.	

(iii) Rock climbing: There is little serious rock climbing because of the lack of crag faces and the special climbing techniques demanded on limestone. However Goredale Scar and some crags on Ilkley Moor are popular. The character of the area means that it is more suitable for fell walking than for mountaineering.

(iv) Orienteering: Apart from Bolton Abbey area and the Washburn Valley the North Yorkshire Moors have been used more than the study area in the past, but the need for new sites means the study area may be more popular in the future. The Yorkshire and Humberside Orienteering Association has about 250 regular members, with the number increasing by about 10% per annum.

(v) There are a few centres for horse riding and pony trekking, but this activity is not well developed in the area at the present time.

Motor sports

The country is well suited to motor rallying, but various controls limit the extent to which it can be used.

Winter sports

There is little potential for winter sports because of the shortness and unreliability of the season, though some slopes are satisfactory for skiing.

Water sports

There are 114 water supply reservoirs of an acre or more in the area (many in the South Pennines) and 11 canal feeders. The main recreational activities are angling and sailing, though water sports and even access are prohibited at some reservoirs. The Leeds and Liverpool Canal is important for pleasure cruising. Little use other than angling is made of the rivers, except for the Wharfe at Appletreewick which is used for canoeing and under water swimming.

Source: Yorkshire and Humberside Economic Planning Board (1976)

REFERENCES

British Travel Association & University of Keele (1967) *Pilot National Recreation Survey.* London: British Travel Association.

Burton, T L (1966) A day in the country: A survey of leisure activity at Box Hill. *Chartered Surveyor,* **98,** 378-380.

Burton, T L & Wibberley, G P (1969) Forecasting land requirements for leisure. Regional Studies Association Conference on Regional Planning and Forecasting, University of Sussex, March-April, 1969.

Commission of the European Communities (1974) *Proposals for a less-favoured areas Directive.* Brussels: European Commission.

Countryside Commission (1974) *Digest of countryside recreation statistics.* Cheltenham: Countryside Commission.

Countryside Review Committee (1976) *The Countryside — problems and policies.* London: HMSO.

Dartington Amenity Research Trust & Rural Planning Services Ltd. (1974) *Farm recreation and tourism.* Cheltenham: Countryside Commission.

Department of the Environment (1974) *Report of the National Park Policies Review Committee.* London: HMSO.

Gibbs, R S & Whitby, M C (1975) *Local authority expenditure on access land.* Newcastle-upon-Tyne: Agricultural Adjustment Unit.

North Riding County Council (1975) *North Riding Pennines Study.* Northallerton: North Riding County Council.

North West Sports Council (1972) *Leisure in the North West.* Manchester: North West Sports Council.

Patmore, J A (1970) *Land and Leisure.* Harmondsworth: Penguin.

P A Management Consultants Ltd. (1973) *The marketing and development of tourism in the English Lakes Counties.* London: P A Management Consultants Ltd.

Rural Planning Services Ltd (1974) *Eskdalemuir: A study in multiple land use: The master plan.* Great Milton: RPS (Unpublished).

Rural Planning Services Ltd (1976) *A Study of the Hartsop Valley:* Cheltenham: Countryside Commission.

Select Committee of the House of Lords on Sport and Leisure (1973) *Second Report.* London: HMSO.

Wager, J (1964) How Common is the Land?, *New Society,* 4, No 96.

Yapp, W B (1969) *The weekend motorist in the Lake District.* London: HMSO (for the Countryside Commission.)

Yorkshire & Humberside Economic Planning Board (1976) *The Pennine Uplands.* London: HMSO.

6 The local significance of the Peak National Park

P A BENNELL

INTRODUCTION

In 1872, the government of the US acquired 809 390 ha in the states of Wyoming, Montana and Idaho and established Yellowstone as the world's first national park. The area was wilderness — vast expanses of lodgepole pine, alpine pastures and high mountains, punctuated by lakes, geyser basins and spectacular waterfalls. Buffalo and grizzly bear were the most noted inhabitants; poachers were the greatest problem, and for many years administration of the Park was left in the solidly competent hands of the US Army.

Compare and contrast the situation in England and Wales in the 1950's. After many years campaigning for the preservation of the countryside and for access to mountains, the National Parks and Access to the Countryside Act was finally passed in 1949 during the 'golden age' of socialist legislation. In 1950, the Government, acting on the advice of the then National Parks Commission, drew a line on a map around 141 643 ha, including parts of Derbyshire, Staffordshire, Cheshire, West Riding and the city of Sheffield and declared the Peak District as Britain's first national park.

None of the land was owned by the nation. All of it was used in some way, sometimes for more than one purpose, and the 40 000 inhabitants counted water gathering and impounding, grouse shooting, mining and quarrying, and cement manufacturing amongst their more traditional farming activities over the Park area. Visitors, especially day visitors, were nothing new — they had been trickling into the Peak since the Duke of Devonshire first opened the turnstiles at Chatsworth House in the 1830's. The spa town of Buxton became a fashionable holiday centre in Victorian times and the railways increased the trickle to a flood in the 1920's and 30's, when the cheap day excursion brought out hordes of ramblers to Kinder Scout, Monsal Dale and Dovedale. With 18 million people living within 81 km of the Park boundary, the scene was set for the leisure boom of the 1960's, when both active and informal recreation grew to the extent that the 4 million visitors to the Park in 1963 increased to 12 million in 1973.

Against this background, the government required the National Park Authority (NPA) to implement the following objectives:
(i)   To protect and improve the landscape of the Park;
(ii) To make provision for visitors to enjoy that landscape;
(iii) To maintain established farming uses and the general social and economic well-being of the Park.

ADMINISTRATION
In order to administer the national park, the Government set up an 'ad hoc' local authority, the Peak Park Planning Board. The Board's constitution was not, however, purely local but was rather a partnership between central government (one third of its membership) and local government (two thirds of its membership). This partnership formula was retained in the re-organisation of 1974, when the Board's membership was increased to 33; 11 appointed by the Secretary of State for the Environment and 22 by the constituent County Councils of Greater Manchester, West Yorkshire, South Yorkshire, Cheshire, Staffordshire and Derbyshire. Of the 22 members, 4 are appointed by Derbyshire to represent District Councils within the Park.

Administration is, therefore, a compromise between local and national interests. National park designation has, however, removed the administration of town and country planning from the normal local planning machinery, and this continues to cause, after 25 years, a feeling of local political antipathy towards the Board. There is a constant demand for greater local involvement in the policy formulation and decision making processes of the Board.

FINANCE
Since 1974, central government has recognised the importance of a substantial contribution towards the total costs of national park administration and management. Following the promises made during the debate on the 'Sandford Report' (Department of the Environment, 1974) that the government would provide the 'lions' share' of the cost of national parks, 75% of the total eligible national park expenditure is now provided by the Exchequer in the form of a special supplementary grant to the general rate support grant paid out to local authorities. Indeed, since the level of grant is calculated against estimated

expenditure, as opposed to actual expenditure, the underspending by some NPA's has resulted in grant levels running as high as 90%. This is not, however, a situation which is expected to last beyond 1977/78, when patterns of expenditure are expected to stabilise.

Nevertheless, the Government's commitment to increased expenditure in national parks since 1974 has provided NPA's with the opportunity to carry out an increasingly varied and widespread programme of conservation works, partly to the benefit of the local community. On the other hand, total expenditure is made up of 75% grant and 25% precept on the 6 constituent authorities referred to above. In order to maintain this proportion, the percentage increase in grant must be matched by a corresponding increase in the precept, and in 1975/76, a real growth of 34% in grant proved hard to match with the constituent authorities pegged to a 4% real growth ceiling. Such events put a great strain on the administrative partnership arrangements.

In the main, however, the net result of the administrative and financial arrangements of 1974 has been a substantial improvement in the national investment in national parks and a proportional reduction in the burden falling on the local ratepayers.

THE FORMULATION OF POLICIES

Since its inception in 1951, the NPA has been the Local Planning Authority for the whole of the Peak Park and has carried out a full range of planning and national park management duties in a comprehensive way. Policies were first set out in the Development Plan in 1959, followed by the First Review in 1969, the Structure Plan in 1976 and the National Park Plan in 1977.

The Structure Plan examines the "physical, social and economic systems of the area so far as they are subject to planning control or influence", and will provide a broad strategic framework for Local Plans and the National Park Plan. The Peak is unique in this respect in that no other national park has sole responsibility for the preparation of a Structure Plan for their area, and no other Structure Plan will be concerned solely with a national park. The National Park Plan shows how the purposes of national park designation can be achieved in the future, and contains more detailed policies and proposals.

The importance of these plans lies in:
(i) Providing clearly defined policies for the future conservation, management and development in the Park;
(ii) Providing a common framework within which all the agencies and individuals concerned can work to achieve the purposes of national park designation;
(iii) Bringing together, in the course of the plan's preparation and policy

formulation, of a wide variety of different interests, through an extensive process of consultation and public participation.

In the Peak Park, therefore, the particular combination of plans provides a framework from the strategic to the detailed and by encompassing planning issues (building construction, land use, mining and quarrying and the social and economic needs of local communities); landscape conservation; and visitor management, they illustrate a significant step towards the 'total approach' to countryside matters recently advocated by the Department of the Environment's (1976a) Countryside Review Committee. In particular these plans emphasise that implementation of policies in the Park is a matter of agreement and common understanding, rather than a matter of legal powers and bureaucratic bull-dozing.

THE IMPLEMENTATION OF POLICIES

The regional situation of the Peak Park, its resources and traditional activities combine to emphasise that conservation in England and Wales can never be a static concept and implementation of the Park's basic objectives must always be considered against this background. The need for 'give and take' was recognised by John Dower in his widely respected pioneering report for the Ministry of Town and Country Planning (1945), but as pressures continued to increase, the government endorsed, in Department of the Environment Circular 4/76 (1976b), the fundamental principle propounded in the 'Sandford Report' (Department of the Environment, 1974), that the public enjoyment of the Parks must be such as "will leave their natural beauty unimpaired for the enjoyment of this and future generations". Where the twin objectives of conservation and public enjoyment are irreconcilable, priority must be given to the conservation of natural beauty.

Generally, policies are implemented in the following ways:

(i) By the control of development under the Town and Country Planning Acts.
The NPA handles approximately 1 000 planning applications each year, dealing with both the strategic and the local. There is no system of delegation to the District Councils within the Park and all decisions are made by the NPA following consultations.

Planning control is, generally, the most effective means of protecting the landscape of the Park, through sifting out and refusing potentially harmful development and also by ensuring sympathetic design, siting and materials for development which is carried out. In this respect, the NPA adopts a positive attitude towards development, and apart from the general policy guidelines contained in the various plans already referred to, has published a comprehensive 'Design Guide' in consultation with local architects, builders and local authorities.

Protection in the face of pressure implies restriction; for new buildings the requirement to use stone or artificial stone adds to development costs. In the local context, the NPA is often accused of being too restrictive in not allowing adequate village expansion and in not allowing cheaper materials to be used to build cheaper houses for 'local people'. Pressures from Sheffield/Chesterfield commuters keep the prices of the housing stock at a relatively high level in the eastern part of the Park. Whilst policies aim to maintain the local communities, planning decisions cannot differentiate between 'local' and 'non-local' and, as in other issues, agreements with the managing party — housing authorities and/or co-operatives — are required to effectively implement the policies.

It is however, in the reconciliation of mineral working with landscape conservation that the Park experiences its greatest problems and raises one of the most strongly contested local issues. The Peak is one of the largest and most accessible mineral fields in the country, producing 5.4 million tonnes of limestone and over 200 000 tonnes of processed fluorspar in 1971. Laporte's, who process fluorspar at the Cavendish Mill near Stoney Middleton, have recently been granted permission, on appeal, to use a 70 acre (28 ha) site at Combs Dale in the Park for tailings disposal; a site that is predicted to satisfy the present needs of the processing plant for 14 years. The national demand for fluorspar and the fears of local unemployment undoubtedly played a large part in the decision. On the western boundary of the Park, a public inquiry into the NPA's refusal to grant ICI Ltd permission to extend the Tunstead Quarry over 240 acres (97 ha) of the Park lasted for 10 weeks. The decision is awaited.

By way of contrast, a great deal of the Park landscape, under farming and forestry, lies outside planning control. The Landscape Areas Special Development Order (LASDO) at present applies to only part of the Park, enabling some control over the design and materials of farm buildings. In the Department of the Environment Circular 4/76 (1976b), there is agreement that LASDO should also cover control of siting and should apply to the whole of every national park. At the same time, the concept of compensation for farmers who are required to incur additional costs in the interests of amenity is introduced, although the opposite principle is, of course, enshrined in the planning legislation which controls most non-farming development. This move, taken together with the farmers claim to be compensated for not ploughing moorland, indicates a potentially effective, albeit costly, approach which is likely to be more widely adopted in the future.

(ii) By agreement between the NPA and a third party, normally involving grant aid or compensation.

When the Peak Park Planning Board began work in 1951, one of its most immediate problems of visitor management was the 'Battle for Kinder Scout'.

Thousands of hectares of moorland were owned by water authorities and grouse shooters and access for hill-walking was fiercely opposed. The mechanism to resolve the bitter conflict between walker and grouse-shooter was the access agreement provisions of the 1949 National Parks Act. In 1955, the first agreement was concluded, and since that time, 19 such agreements have been voluntarily entered into with the NPA covering 19 425 ha. The principle is relatively simple — the landowner and tenants allow the public the right to roam, and in return receive compensation, bye-laws and a ranger service. Agreements are now based on the Countryside Commission's model form and compensation (based on 9.9p per ha consideration, £10 per 100 breeding ewes, £16.2 per km of boundary wall, and £8.4 per km of internal wall) is finalised by the District Valuer and paid annually. Those moorlands which are used for grouse shooting are closed on 12 days each year and extensive publicity and ranger patrols ensure minimum interference with either shoots or walkers. An annual meeting is held between the NPA and all access agreement parties, to resolve problems.

This principle works well, and its extension into the wider field of the management agreement is now being considered. Wager (1976) in a report for the NPA, concluded that this technique could be effective in bringing together the varying, and sometimes conflicting, objectives of the landowner, the tenant(s), the naturalist, rock climbers etc. and the NPA, to produce an agreed management plan as the basis for future action. Compensation, direct works, a ranger service and organised voluntary efforts might form the NPA input. Access to the land, revised grazing regimes and woodland management might form the landowners input. In this way both short term visitor management problems as well as long term landscape management problems might be overcome, with the NPA acting as a catalyst, injecting grants, expertise and manpower into the private sector so that national park objectives, as defined in the National Park Plan, can be achieved on a broad front.

In both these examples, reference has been made to the Ranger Service, which forms a vital link between the Park resident and the Park visitor. In the Peak Park, the Service was developed to patrol the access areas, advising visitors and enforcing bye-laws. Now, under the direction of the Chief Ranger, 11 Field Rangers cover the whole 140 378 ha of the Park, building up the day-to-day liaison with the farmers in particular, advising and guiding visitors, and carrying out a programme of litter clearance, footpath maintenance, including repairs to stiles and gates, waymarking, drystone walling, drainage and fencing. In association with a growing number of volunteers, some of whom are acquiring a good standard of skills, the Rangers are providing a modest level of rural estate work which is welcomed by the farmer in the Park. In this very practical way, the farmer is beginning to receive some recompense for the problems created by visitor pressures in some areas, and the process forges stronger links and a better understanding of mutual problems between the farmer, the visitor and the NPA.

(iii) By acquisition, development and management by the NPA.

In order to take effective action to promote new approaches to problems, the NPA has consistently taken a positive attitude towards opportunities arising in the Park, and continued opportunism allied to sound policies and programmes, will always be an essential element of Park management. Derelict railways became a 53 km Trails system for cyclists, horseriders or the casual stroller, with several car park access points, but free of vehicular traffic throughout. Derelict quarries, with machinery and buildings cleared away have become picnic areas as at Tideswell Dale or nature conservation sites as at Millers Dale. A disused farm in the Snake Valley is now the Hagg Mountain Hostel and an empty row of cottages in Longdendale were restored to provide the 45 bed Crowden Youth Hostel on the Pennine Way. The caravan and camping sites at Castleton and Hayfield set high standards of design and provision and 304 ha of woodland scattered throughout the Park are managed on a selective felling and group regeneration system.

The importance of these provisions goes beyond the value of the facility itself. They draw problems away from the surrounding area, they provide test beds for new ideas and improve management expertise, they set new standard and they bring back some life and employment to former derelict scenes.

CONCLUSIONS

In the Peak District, the national park designation has had a significant impact on the local scene, through administration, finance and the implementation of Park policies. Taken against the time-scale of landscape change, the super-imposition of the Park administration is still relatively new, and changes are constantly being made to seek more effective co-operation between the 'planners' and the 'planned'.

The early specific problem solving days were replaced by the broader co-ordinated schemes of the late-1960's and early-1970's, when traffic management was increasingly becoming the basis of visitor management schemes such as the Goyt Valley Traffic Management Scheme and 'Routes for People'. Now the trend is towards the joint approach, co-ordinating the many agencies responsible for making things happen within the Park area, and by agreement, persuasion, subsidies, incentives, grants, and controls endeavouring to ensure that Park policies are effectively implemented on a Park-wide basis.

REFERENCES

Department of the Environment (1974)   *Report of the National Park Policies Review Committee.*   London: HMSO.

Department of the Environment (1976a) *The Countryside — problems and policies.* Countryside Review Committee. London: HMSO.

Department of the Environment (1976b)   *Report on the National Park Policies Review Committee.*   Circular 4/76. London: HMSO.

Ministry of Town and Country Planning (1945)   *National Parks in England and Wales.*   London: HMSO.

Wager, J (1976)   *Management agreements in principle and practice — a case study in Monsal Dale.*   Bakewell: Peak District National Park Authority.

17 The economic potential of farm tourism in the uplands

E T DAVIES

INTRODUCTION

The upland areas of Britain, estimated to account for about one-third of the total agricultural area and for one-seventh the number of full-time farming units of the country, have always possessed problems of climate, soil quality and topography which have posed difficulties to those who work and live there. The economy of the uplands is basically dependent upon farming but, because of these inherent physical constraints, the areas are largely confined to the production of store and breeding stock for more favourably situated farms, a system which has long been associated with low levels of profitability in comparison with other areas and forms of production. Sharp fluctuations in returns from year to year, due to severe climatic conditions and/or instability of store livestock prices, contribute in large measure to this differential but, basically, the general weakness of upland farming from an economic standpoint is one of low output relative to costs. Certain farmers have reacted to the situation by expanding output through the acquisition of more land, others, through the improvement and intensification of existing land.

But to the majority of upland farmers, even allowing for the availability of suitable land for purchase or improvement, the capital requirements of either undertaking is frequently prohibitive. In these instances the choice often lies between hanging-on and relying heavily on subsidies as income, or quitting farming and the uplands altogether. Undoubtedly the latter would aid the restructuring of upland farming into larger and, hopefully, more viable units, but it would also exacerbate further the problem of rural depopulation and the social and amenity consequences arising therefrom. Neither alternative, therefore, provides an acceptable long term solution to the future of our uplands. The question thus remains, what can be done to achieve economic and social stability in these areas

There is no doubt whatsoever that the economy of the uplands is, and always will be, largely dependent upon agriculture. Indeed, the maintenance of farming is an essential prerequisite to the preservation of those scenic attractions of our uplands which are becoming of increasing appeal to large numbers of the population in their pursuit for leisure and recreation activities. The answer to the question posed above may lie in part, therefore, in the opportunities afforded to farmers to 'cash-in' on the tourist influx to the uplands. Studies undertaken in the West Country have shown that the countryside is rapidly extending its appeal to an ever widening spectrum of the populace, and that farmers can derive a significant income supplement from their participation in tourism. In fact, tourism has been the salvation of many a West Country farmer in that it has provided capital for the expansion or intensification of the farming enterprise into a viable whole; indeed, the potential of tourism and other ancillary activities in this respect was expressly recognised in the European Community (1972) Directive 161, which charged member states with the task of "informing the agricultural population as to the possibilities open to them for improving their socio-economic situation."

What opportunities exist, therefore, for upland farmers to cater for the leisure needs of the country visitor? The word 'tourism' as applied in the farming context is not an easily defined homogeneous entity. It can mean the provision of certain sporting and recreational facilities, such as shooting, fishing, pony trekking, and so on, or it can have an educational connotation in the form of nature trails and farm open days. But the aspect of tourism which perhaps offers the greatest scope to the majority of farmers is the provision of holiday accommodation, and it is with the need and potential for such a service that this paper is specifically concerned.

DEMAND CONSIDERATIONS

Naturally, the opportunities to participate in the holiday trade are greater for some farmers than others. Those located along main holiday routes or in the hinterlands of our more popular holiday areas will always be, perhaps, the main beneficiaries, but one believes that there will be increasing opportunity in the years ahead for farmers in our remoter, upland areas to participate in the business, and that this will arise as a result of the combined effects of two main factors.

Firstly, the evidence presented in Table 1 indicates that the rates charged on farms for various forms of holiday accommodation are more attractive than those currently charged for similar accommodation in more traditional holiday establishments. Furthermore, it would appear from studies undertaken in south-west England that as inflation has increased so has this tariff gap widened. Hence, on economic grounds alone, the appeal of farm based holidays could well be

Table 1

COMPARATIVE HOLIDAY ACCOMMODATION TARIFFS,
HIGH SEASON RATES 1977

Accommodation type	Farm enterprises	Guest houses and small hotels	Hotels
	£	£	£
Bed and breakfast (per person/night)	3.00	4.40	7.20
Bed and breakfast plus evening meal (per person/week)	29.75	38.50	58.50
Self catering units (per week)		Non farm units	
Sleeping up to 6	50.00	70.00	
Sleeping over 6	80.00	97.00	
Caravan and tent sites (per night)	1.25	1.20	

Sources: University of Exeter study farms, and English Tourist Board Guide (1977)

stimulated in the years ahead and, indeed, there is some evidence to indicate that this is already taking place in the West Country.

But, financial considerations apart, the countryside itself, with its aesthetically appealing combination of landscape and wild life, is fast assuming a therapeutic role in providing scope for relaxation and the enjoyment of one's leisure time. This function stems from the fact that the pressures of life today are such that more and more people in all walks of life are finding the need to break away completely from the rush and bustle of modern society. And since such pressures are more likely to increase than diminish in the future, the farm could well assume a new and increasing role in satisfying a hitherto unprecedented demand for the peaceful and restorative qualities of the countryside.

The uplands possess these attributes in abundance, thereby affording the opportunity for those who work and live there not only to share what is essentially everyone's heritage but, also, to benefit financially from so doing. Non-participation in farm tourism is frequently attributed to lack of effective demand, but it should be remembered that demand can often be a latent one, emerging only when a supply of the product or service becomes available. Such a situation undoubtedly has much relevance in our upland areas at the present time and, conceivably, could be more so in the future.

It is a consideration which must not be overlooked, therefore, in any appraisal of the potential for farm tourism in these areas although, equally, it must be appreciated that additional efforts may be required on the part of farmers both to increase the range and attractiveness of the facilities they have to offer and to increase the general public's awareness of their availability if the full potential of tourism is to be realised.

FINANCIAL CONSIDERATIONS

To what extent can tourism contribute to the income situation of upland farmers? Naturally, the answer to this question depends on many factors. The type of tourist accommodation offered is an important consideration in this respect whilst, for any given type of holiday accommodation, the scale of the enterprise, the occupancy rate of the available accommodation over the holiday season, the nature and extent of the costs incurred and, of course, the rates charged can all influence the profitability of a farm tourist enterprise. Despite these varying factors, however, some common basis of comparison has to be established if a broad indication of the relative profitability of each main type of holiday enterprise is to be obtained and, in this respect, one such measure which is comparatively easy to calculate is that presented in Table 2, namely, the gross margin attained per £100 of receipts or turnover. In this respect, four main forms of facility are considered:

(i)   Farmhouse bed and breakfast;
(ii) Farmhouse bed and breakfast plus evening meal;
(iii) Self catering units;
(iv) Touring caravan and tent sites.

On the evidence of the data in the following table, which have been compiled on the basis of the average rates to be actually charged during 1977 on south-west farms and the likely level of direct costs to be incurred (excluding family labour costs), it is abundantly clear that it is the touring caravan and tent site which currently yields the highest margin of profit. But how feasible a proposition is this type of enterprise for the majority of upland farmers bearing in mind the question of suitable approach and access roads, its dependence, in most instances on planning approval and the high capital requirement normally associated with such a venture? The two latter constraints apply also in the case of the self catering units, be these in the form of flats in the farmhouse itself, in converted farm buildings and cottages or in purpose built chalets. Obtaining the necessary planning approval for these two types of development has always been a difficult

188

Table 2

AVERAGE DIRECT COSTS AND MARGINS PER £100 OF RECEIPTS

Returns and costs	Bed and breakfast £	Bed and breakfast plus evening meal £	Self catering units £	Touring caravan and tent sites £
Receipts	100	100	100	100
Direct costs:				
Food	21	39	–	–
Hired Labour	2	2	4	3
Repairs, renewals and maintenance	5	6	16	4
Fuel and electricity	1	2	8	1
Advertising, postage and insurance	2	2	8	2
Other	2	1	7	8
Total direct costs	33	52	43	18
Gross margins	67	48	57	82
Family labour input (hours)	29	36	11	12

undertaking for most farmer applicants, but for upland farmers, especially those in designated areas, the likelihood of such consent is even more questionable. However, bearing in mind the income problem of upland farming generally, as well as the immeasurable role farming plays in maintaining the scenic beauty of these areas, a case could well be advanced for a more tolerant and flexible attitude on the part of planners in respect of developments of this nature in the uplands. Justification for such action could also be stressed on the grounds that the demand for self catering accommodation on farms is increasing rapidly, a situation which is inducing many West Country farmers to switch over this type of development in preference to farmhouse catering.

The current constraints imposed by planning regulations means, however, that for the majority of upland farmers the only feasible holiday enterprise may well be farmhouse catering. The data in Table 2 show that such an enterprise can yield worthwhile returns. It has the further merit, as will be shown later, of being least demanding in terms of capital requirements while, also, it is the type of enterprise which is least likely to interfere with normal farming routines and practices. On the other hand, it demands from the farm family a high labour input and, also, it inevitably intrudes on the privacy of family members. For these reasons, it should be of appeal only to those farm families who possess a sincere interest in meeting people and who have the capacity to socialise with their guests.

The figures presented in Table 2 provide some indication of the relative profitability of the most popular forms of farm holiday enterprises in terms of margins over costs. A prospective entrant into the business of tourism will require some knowledge, however, as to whether or not the margins he can expect to earn from the business will be adequate to both service the capital he is likely to invest and provide him with a profit. Some indication of such a measure is presented in Table 3. This table has been compiled on the basis of the average occupancy rates encountered on West Country farms and the current charges and costs associated with these farms as depicted in previous tables. The capital sums reflect typical rates of investment when conversions and other structural works are undertaken by contracting firms.

Table 3
COMPARATIVE FINANCIAL MEASURES FOR VARIOUS HOLIDAY UNITS

| Returns and costs | Per double bedroom in farmhouse | | Per self catering unit | Per caravan or tent pitch |
	Bed and breakfast	Bed and breakfast plus evening meal		
Occupancy rate per season	83 nights	83	16½ weeks	84 nights
Average charge per night/ week	£6	£8.5	£60	£1.25
Total returns per season	£498	£705	£990	£105
Total direct costs per season	£164	£367	£426	£19
Gross margins per season	£334	£338	£564	£86
Average capital requirements	£300	£300	£4500	£500
Gross margin as a percentage of capital	111	111	12	17

On the evidence of the data in this table, it would appear that the economic viability of both the self catering and the caravan/tent site type of holiday accommodation is rather questionable in terms of their ability to yield sufficiently high margins to both service the likely levels of capital investment required and provide an adequate measure of profit for the operator. In practice, however, it is known that capital investments on these enterprises can be considerably lower than those quoted in the table when much of the conversion and structural work is undertaken by the farm staff. In fact, on the evidence of the West Country studies, such an arrangement can virtually halve the capital commitment. But, in any event, it behoves every prospective entrant to the business of farm tourism to consider most carefully whether his capital outlay is likely to yield a higher return than if the same amount of money were invested in the farming enterprise itself, or, indeed, outside the farming industry. In his deliberations, however, he should also bear in mind that returns to capital may well reflect only in part the true investment potential of a farm tourist enterprise, since the presence of a range of self catering units or a licensed caravan/tent site can substantially enhance the market value of a farm.

CONCLUSIONS

The financial information presented in this paper gives some indication of the potential of tourism to augment farming incomes. The nature of the data, however, suggests that the role of tourism on farms can never be more than that of a supplementary enterprise. That is to say, it must represent an extension to, rather than a replacement for, the farming business. There is ample evidence to show that both interests can exist harmoniously side by side, and it is in this capacity that tourism has a future on our upland farms. But, in addition to its potential in financial terms, farm tourism could well play a further important role in the uplands. It is well known that public access to our rural areas has frequently led to conflict between residents and visitors. In very many instances there have been justifiable grounds for this reaction but, more frequently, arguments and disagreements have arisen largely because there has been a lack of understanding on the part of both parties as to the social and economic attitudes of the other. With the prospect of demand for countryside resources likely to increase in the future, these conflicts could well grow much sharper in the years to come. It would appear, therefore, that there is an unquestionable need to establish a better social cohesion between those who live and work in the countryside and those who spend their leisure time there.

Greater participation in the business of farm tourism could go a long way towards achieving this objective. As custodians of much of our natural heritage, participation in tourism provides farmers with the opportunity to educate their guests in the ways of the countryside and to prevail upon them not to abuse and despoil the very things they have come to enjoy.

In this sense, therefore, as well as in the direct economic context, farm tourism could play an important role in the future of our uplands. But a word of caution may not be misplaced at this juncture. Catering for the tourist is not an undertaking which any farm family can pursue. As a service it does call for a real interest in people and, frequently, for a great deal of understanding and tolerance. The farm visitor of today is no longer content to accept sub-standard conditions and service; he has become a far more discriminating being, expecting to receive full value for his money and not being afraid to express himself when he does not get it. Farm families must be confident, therefore, that they can provide acceptable standards of accommodation and service and, also, be able to deal courteously, but effectively, with any problems of discontent, conflict and misunderstanding which may arise.

REFERENCES

English Tourist Board (1977)   *Where to stay '77.*   London: English Tourist Board.

European Community (1972)   Council directive 72/161.   Brussels: European Community.

8 Tourism potential and influences on development objectives

E TAYLOR

INTRODUCTION

This paper considers some of the influences of tourism and recreation demand, and of the nature of receiving-communities in upland areas, with particular reference to Scotland. The purpose is to sketch in a broader background of influences than may be more commonly considered when investigating potential in rural areas, to point out those salient factors which have to be considered when evolving development objectives.

DEMAND

Long term market trends for tourism indicate that there is tremendous growth potential in Scotland. Various recent marketing·studies indicate that about 30 million British adults would like to visit Scotland on holiday. A large proportion of these — 20 million — are in ABC1 social class groups. However, the actual numbers, including children, holidaying in Scotland take only about 5 million long holidays each year, around half being repeat visits.

Scotland's potential is seemingly constrained by four main factors: distance, cost (itself a function of distance), perceived lack of activities for children, and the weather.

The attraction of Scotland's highland scenery is cited as one of the main reasons for visiting the country and the uplands generally offer a wide variety of moor, mountain, loch and river in a relatively small area. One of the added attractions for tourists is the proximity of the sea to mountain scenery.

The upland (Highland and Island) geography offers a high quality of resource for activity holidays: fishing, sailing, hill walking, mountaineering and skiing all have various degrees of development potential. Sporting and special activities are highly rated by car borne tourists to Scotland (Professional Studies Ltd., 1977), with the 40% indicating an interest in hill walking being the largest activity group. There are also indications that horse riding and pony trekking potential is not fully exploited. Between one in four and one in six tourists expecting to take part in these sports when interviewed on their entry to Scotland, failed to do so.

A general conclusion on the marketing of activity holidays in upland areas is that tourists require prior knowledge of facilities and need to know in full details of booking and costs as an input to their pre-holiday planning.

Of immediate interest is the effect inflation has had and is likely to have on holidaytaking trends and the subsequent effect on supply. As far as Scotland is concerned, certain demand patterns are emerging which may be wholly ascribed to price inflation.

Firstly, the results from the 1976 tourist season in Scotland indicate that although the number of holiday and business tourist trips taken in Scotland increased by 5% and 7% respectively, the number of nights spent dropped by 15% and 20%, and expenditure by 5% and 14% (Professional Studies Ltd., 1977). Overseas visitors increased by 15% on 1975 figures, and the European market provided the highest increase.

A further indicator of interest in Scotland as a holiday destination has been the decrease in the number of personal callers at the Scottish Tourist Board's Information Centre in London; this has fallen by 26% when compared with 1975, which also revealed a decrease from 1974. The cost of travel to Scotland and the higher petrol costs in remoter areas are doubtless having an effect on holiday budgeting by British residents, while the drop in total holidaytaking by all British residents, first apparent in the 1974 season, is likely to continue. A study (Business and Economic Planning, 1977) recently commissioned by the national tourist boards forecasts an increase of only 1% in all tourism nights by British tourists in Britain, and a decrease of 1%-2% in holiday tourism nights for 1977. This forecast is founded on the expectation that real disposable income will fall by 2%, as prices rise at a considerably faster rate than wages. Recently published statistics have shown that average wages at the end of the Government's Phase II policy were indeed more severely constrained than prices.

Demand for accommodation by all tourists in Scotland in the twelve months of 1976 produced a drop of 1% in hotel occupancy (to 43%), although occupancy by overseas visitors continued to rise, but one bright feature has been the continuing growth of self-catering demand in Scotland. Market studies show an improvement for built properties for most months of 1976, most significantly in the early season (Professional Studies Ltd, 1977).

These demand trends can be summarised and ascribed to price inflation and the value of the pound:

(i) Holidaytaking: British residents are taking more but shorter holidays in Scotland. They are also spending proportionately less than the average rate of retail price inflation, reflecting lower disposable incomes. Overseas, and particularly European, visitors are on the increase and are as attracted to self-catering accommodation as British residents. Europeans are used to self-catering holidays in their own countries and are keen on outdoor, sporting activities.

(ii) Business tourism: the effects of North Sea Oil and a projected increase in general industrial activity (Business and Economic Planning, 1975) will see a continuing marginal increase in business tourism, most likely to be supplied by the hotel sector.

The longer term implications for Scotland and for farm holiday enterprises in particular can be considered as:

(i) A trend towards centre-based holidays with perhaps more frequent holidays taken in the 'shoulder' months, and demand for self-catering accommodation.

(ii) A need for budgetable holidays, with costed activity choices related to accommodation.

(iii) A trend towards an increased average party size, with perhaps families travelling together to share expenses.

(iv) An increase in demand by tourists for cheaper local produce to supplement 'imported' foodstuffs; this could be of marginal but significant importance to farms making self-catering provision.

(v) The need to market skillfully a holiday experience as value for money; in particular the European market would respond to this kind of selling approach.

POTENTIAL SUPPLY

A major study of the potential for tourism and recreation on farms, crofts and estates in Scotland has been commissioned by the Scottish Tourist Board, the Highlands and Islands Development Board (HIDB) and the Countryside Commission for Scotland. Although not yet complete, this study (Denman, in preparation) gives strong indications that both tenants and owners have open minds about developing recreation provision on their land. Any conflict of land use hinges on the matter of scale, and on the location of land holdings affecting impact from day trip demand. It appears that farmers are less opposed to the 'tourist' than might be supposed.

The crofting system of land tenure which predominates in the Highlands and Islands has its own characteristics and has a strong influence on patterns of community life. Recently the HIDB has been looking to the Irish experience in the Gaeltacht and in particular at the kinds of encouragement offered to cooperatives by the Irish Government. Crofting in Scotland depends on grants and loans for its viability and recent legislation, ensuring crofters have rights to purchase their croft lands, is intended to reform the crofting system by injecting new capital. The theory is that crofters purchasing their crofts will be able to raise capital by using their value as collateral. But the basic problem is still that crofters have little capital initially at their disposal, and many are reluctatnt to enter into a new way of life while the existing system continues to ensure their security of tenure. The word 'community' often follows 'crofting' in the Highlands and Islands, and shared work is an expression of this community life. But there are more issues than those of traditional sharing of labour. MacDonald (1977) points out: "Six tractors sitting side by side on six acre crofts and working six days a year may be an exaggeration of what happens, but not a very big one. The fact that 44.5% of inputs in crofting counties is tied up in machinery compared with only 28.4% in the whole of Scotland bears this out. The logic of this is that various forms of co-operative effort ought to be explored as the way to more intensive use of machinery."

As with capital expenditure on machinery on upland farms and crofts, so with newly built provision in any recreation enterprise. We have not yet begun to realise the potential of accommodation and recreation facilities, and its marketing on a cooperative, community basis. The past success of bed and breakfast has established it as the most popular form of accommodation in rural Scotland. Crofts and farms are also allowed two or three caravans on their land for seasonal letting. Both of these types of accommodation are becoming less satisfactory: bed and breakfast because it became popular in the car-borne tourist boom of the 1960's and the early 1970's, and fuel costs are only one item likely to curtail demand in the future. Static caravans present the kind of visual intrusion which is extremely difficult to offset in the open treeless landscape of crofting and upland farm areas. Public awareness of environmental factors and the planning policies of local authorities will continue to restrict static caravan proliferation: camp-sites for touring caravans, some statics and for tent pitches, located in valley floors and screened by coniferous planting, will be more acceptable than a scatter of caravans across open hillsides.

Local development control policies are now turning in favour of vernacular building forms and local authorities and other statutory bodies are in the field with guidance on development (Peak Park Planning Board, 1976). Redundant farm buildings are of course a valuable resource for new types of accommodation and facilities. Much more could be made of converting existing buildings so that their character is retained and the value of the farm landscape enhanced, incidentally adding to the value of the holiday experience itself.

NATIONAL AGENCY POLICIES
Besides the market and the effects of inflation, one other external factor — government development policy — will have an influence on unrealised potential

and tourist accommodation supply in particular. Since 1975, the Scottish Tourist Board with other national agencies have been working corporately to evolve compatible policies for tourism, countryside recreation and sport (Countryside Commission for Scotland, 1976a & b). This work is of a long-term, strategic nature but is being carried out in collaboration with the Scottish Regional Councils, the aim being to effect implementation in accordance with the objectives of regional, social and economic development. In the context of the scale of such work, farm tourism is very much a tactical matter: but there are characteristics of rural communities which have strategic significance for recreation development in Scotland. First among these is the process of farm amalgamation and increasing productive efficiency on arable farms, producing fewer jobs and promoting a movement of scattered rural populations into existing settlements. This pattern is by no means uniform, especially throughout Scotland's uplands. Population movement from upland areas in particular may be caused by other more onerous factors, such as remoteness from services and the land use policies of estate owners and local authorities. There are indications that population loss in rural areas has been generally reversed since 1971. Between 1961 and 1971 there was a population decline in rural Scotland, with continuous negative net migration rates and low rate of natural increase. However, the increases in population in rural areas since 1971 have not been wholly due to natural increase but to positive net migration. This may be ascribed to the job opportunities created by the exploration and early exploitation stage of North Sea Oil, and not to any increase in agricultural manpower. Once these labour intensive stages of oil-related development are past, the employment scene will probably revert to pre-1971 conditions.

Employment in agriculture and other primary sectors in rural Scotland shows considerable variation in volume between regions. If we accept that primary sector employment will continue to show a decline, then those regions of Scotland which have proportionally high volumes of employment in this sector are likely to face the severest future employment losses. In regional economic terms, those regions would benefit from new diversified job opportunities, which may partially be supplied by the encouragement of tourism. Again, areas with an already high incidence of employment in the service sector might be less appropriate for tourism development. Essential for these areas will be a developing manufacturing sector, to raise activity rates and to offer a spread of jobs beyond service employment.

Such wider implications of population and employment are introduced here to affirm that issues of tourism development are not only important at the individual tactical level of farm tourism: there are wider implications, and in particular it is important to see tourism as a device to complement the employment structure of any one area. Often it may be more important to promote tourism as a means of raising family incomes through providing seasonal and part-time jobs, than by creating full-time work. It is this ability to be utilised in a small-scale and diversified fashion which characterises tourism's potential for local economies and emphasises its importance in rural areas.

Implications of these broader background factors for national policy must be that tourism development should relate to local needs. The aim should be to direct tourist expenditure where it would benefit local economies in a form most fitting their needs. These are the kinds of considerations which will help (along with the policies adopted by Regional Authorities) to direct central government expenditure through such media as Section 4 grant-aid under the Development of Tourism Act.

Work on assessing the economic benefit of tourism (Henderson & Cousins, 1975) has shown the degree to which expenditure on differing kinds of accommodation and facilities has a direct effect on local economies. One of the more revealing findings of this work was the relatively low economic benefit accruing to rural areas, even those areas providing tourist accommodation, since purchase of goods and services were predominantly outside rural areas. There is therefore an obvious need to encourage tourists to spend money in local facilities and, where possible, on local produce and locally produced products.

CONCLUSIONS

This paper has briefly summarised the main factors influencing tourism development in rural and upland areas, with particular reference to Scotland. Some general guidance on development objectives can be set out:

(i) Tourism provision and the tourist industry is diverse and dispersed. Its development in rural areas depends upon external factors influencing demand, upon private sector entrepreneurs willing to take risks (not necessarily only on farms), and upon the levels and trends of employment in agriculture and forestry.

(ii) The impact of tourism needs direction and control. But because the tourist industry exists predominantly as a free market activity, its development is ultimately controlled by the market. National agencies with the remit to encourage tourism must seek to encourage the right kind of scale of provision, and in partnership with the private sector.

(iii) The issues facing farm tourism are essentially those of demand trends and there is every indication of a current and foreseeable demand for centre-based, budgetable holidays offering access to countryside recreation activities. Farm tourism has a marketable image, but price inflation must point to a cooperative approach by providers to cut costs to consumers at a time when the market is potentially widened by consumers 'trading down'.

(iv) Farm holidays are naturally attractive to families. Operators will have to consider the kinds of package most attractive to families both in the form of accommodation and activities. The special needs of children should be anticipated. Travel will begin to be the most onerous cost factor, even for British residents seeking home-based holidays. Even on holiday, the centre-based tourist will be looking for ways to economise on travel to centres of attraction.

(v) Upland recreation has been traditionally seen to pose physical impact problems: visual intrusion, noise, erosion and conflict with other land uses. Public awareness of such problems has been heightened and more sensitive development control policies have been the result. Such impact problems are a matter of scale to fit capacity and underline the need to relate tourism development closely to complement local needs rather than supplant them. The most significant development for remoter areas is the effect of increasing fuel costs and the likely reduction in car-based touring holidays.

(vi) The economic benefit of tourism to receiving areas is not the only determinant of scale: there is a continuing need to conserve the built and landscape heritage which are the generators of public interest.

(vii) Not all upland areas are identical. In Scotland there are traditional differences between crofting communities and other farming communities. There is a danger in assuming that the geographic homogeneity of the uplands might produce a common programme of recreation and tourism development. The issues are essentially local, but strategy must be related to the wider background.

REFERENCES

Business and Economic Planning (1975) *Demand for tourism in Scotland and the regions of Scotland.*   Edinburgh: Scottish Tourist Board.

Business and Economic Planning (1977)   Forecasting study commissioned by national Tourist Boards.   Unpublished report.

Countryside Commission for Scotland (1976a) *Guide to the preparation of initial regional strategies.*   Edinburgh: Countryside Commission for Scotland.

Countryside Commission for Scotland (1976b)   *Strategic issues.* Edinburgh: Countryside Commission for Scotland.

Denman, R (in preparation) *Tourism and recreation on farms, crofts and estates.* Unpublished report for Scottish Tourist Board.

Henderson, D M & Cousins, R L (1975) *The economic impact of tourism: a case study in Greater Tayside.*   Tourism and Recreation Research Unit Report No 13, University of Edinburgh.

MacDonald, M (1977)   Crofting's role.   *North 7,* **25,** 8-11.

Peak Park Planning Board (1976) *Building design guide.*   Bakewell: Peak Park Planning Board.

Professional Studies Ltd. (1977) *Holiday marketing and information survey, 1976.* Unpublished report for Scottish Tourist Board.

19 Likely future trends in countryside recreation in upland areas of Britain

M DOWER & P DOWNING

INTRODUCTION

This is a paper of ideas rather than numerical forecasts. A timescale of nearly 25 years (to the year 2000) is too great for sensible forecasting; and, as we shall show, demand for countryside recreation will be heavily influenced by the nation's economic state (which is unpredictable) and by attitudes and policies affecting the uplands (to assume which would beg the questions posed to the symposium).

Recreation — and, even more markedly, recreational demand — is no independent variable: rather does it mesh most closely with other aspects of land use, life, economic activity and politics in the uplands. While sticking to our subject, we shall try to show some of these links.

A word of definition — we take 'countryside recreation' to be recreational activity, mainly outdoors, in the countryside, villages or country towns of the upland areas, pursued both by those who live in those areas and by those who visit them. These visitors from outside the uplands will include many who are merely there on a day trip, but also many 'tourists' who are away from home for a night or more. Thus the subject is closely meshed to that of tourism.

In this paper, we look in turn at two aspects of 'likely future trends' namely:

(i) trends of demand and factors affecting demand;

(ii) attitudes, policies and other factors affecting supply.

TRENDS OF DEMAND

Much has been written (eg Patmore, 1970; Tanner, 1973 & 1974; Davidson &

Wibberley, 1977) about the enormous growth in many aspects of countryside recreation from about 1950 to the energy/economic crisis of 1973 — a growth in numbers of people walking, rambling, riding, sailing, canoeing, pursuing manifold other activities and (above all) going on car-borne pleasure trips into the country-side which prompted the passing of the Countryside Acts, the creation of many country parks and much other action by public and private bodies.

This growth in countryside recreation was made possible primarily by the rise in average disposable incomes and in car ownership. The significance of these factors has been confirmed by the slowing down or even halting of growth in many aspects of countryside recreation during the last four years of faltering economy and higher energy prices as recorded, for example, by Duffell (1975) in relation to recreational motoring, and by Dartington Amenity Research Trust (1977a) in relation to second home numbers in Scotland.

The future scale of demand for countryside recreation by visitors to the uplands may thus depend substantially on the state of the economy, the rate of change in disposable incomes, and the price of petrol. The Countryside Commission for Scotland and others (1976) attempted to assess the forward prospects in these and related factors, and their possible effect upon trends in countryside recreation; and concluded that further growth could be expected but might well be accompanied by a shift in emphasis towards shorter average recreational journeys, greater use of public transport (which remains available) and lower cost activities.

Even before the rise in petrol prices, it was very noticeable how most city-dwellers wishing to visit the uplands (whether on day trips or longer visits) would choose those uplands which were nearest to them. Thus the Highlands are visited mainly by Scottish residents, the Yorkshire Dales by Yorkshire people and Mid-Wales by people from the West Midlands. This pattern gives a strongly regional flavour to the participants in recreation in many areas, and may lead to marked patterns of repeat visiting. This, in turn, is related to an evolution in the relations between townsman and countryside which we believe may have growing significance over the next quarter-century.

Since before the campaigns of a century ago to secure 'access to the mountains', there has been a strong minority of town-dwellers who sought recreation, often of strenuous kind, in the hills, and who made their way to the hills by train, bus or on foot. It was largely for them that access provisions finally became law in the 1949 National Parks Act.

Within a year or two of the passing of that Act began the flow of that very different tide of visitors, arriving in their tens and (within a few years) their thousands of cars into the uplands. Many of them were wholly unfamiliar with the country-side separated from its traditions by five or more generations of urban life, eager to see it, but timid. Therefore, they tended to keep to the main roads shown on their small-scale motoring maps, to venture off the road only where land was clearly open to them, and to gain little serious contact with the countryside or the country-dweller. . .

. . . until, that is, they gained a measure of confidence. Looking over the hedge, reading the AA Book of the Countryside, listening to the Archers, visiting a nature trail or a farm open day, many such townsmen become familiar with the countryside. They buy larger-scale maps, they explore the side roads, they seek out the footpaths and the country pubs, they talk to farmers, they launch into active pursuits such as fishing, canoeing, sailing and pony-trekking. As tourists, they may forsake the familiar coastal resorts and bring their caravan into the hills; they may partake of farmhouse holidays; they may even buy a country cottage as a second home.

The National Household Survey of Countryside Recreation, currently in hand for the Countryside Commission, should throw some light on how far this evolution of the townsman's awareness of the countryside has yet reached. Clearly, there are many still unfamiliar with the countryside and limited in their activity after years of visting it: more people are joining their ranks as car ownership gradually expands. But a single post-war generation of mass motoring has produced a growing army of people who are not only visiting the uplands but penetrating it in their recreation and increasingly identifying themselves with it.

This has formidable implications for many upland areas. On the debit side lie the physical impact of traffic, trespass and witting, or unwitting, damage to crops and stock; the inflated prices in popular tourist areas; the competition by second-home purchasers on the local housing market; the cultural impact of outside language and customs. On the credit side lie the injections of visitors' money into the local economy; the support given to local bus and other services; the income and employment for local people; and, less easily measured but of possibly high significance for the future of the uplands, a new constituency sympathetic to political support of their well-being.

FACTORS AFFECTING SUPPLY

Upon the balance between such debits and such credits, as perceived by the residents of the uplands and their political spokesmen, may depend much of the attitude and policy which affects the supply of countryside recreation in the uplands.

The last few years have seen a welcome emphasis upon the need to reconcile the demands of recreation (and of that other purpose of the National Parks Act, the protection of upland landscapes) with the social and economic needs of those who live and work in the uplands. This emphasis was expressed in the Sandford report (DoE, 1974); the Government's response to it (DoE, 1976; Countryside

Review Committee, 1977 a & b); several of the new generation of National Park Plans; and is indeed already reflected in a range of policies and actions in the uplands.

In places, these policies will have the effect of dampening or diverting demand. Examples are the measures of traffic control proposed in the Dartmoor National Park Plan; the Lake District National Park's new policies designed to restrict new housing to local people; and three of the four optional strategies for outdoor recreation in the Hadrian's Wall area proposed by Dartington Amenity Research Trust (1977 b). Such measures, of course — where they are successful in dampening demand in one upland area — are likely simply to divert it to another (possibly upland) area.

Many other policies, however, are aimed directly to meet recreational demand in ways compatible with the interests of local people. These include provision of facilities on land not in other productive use, or as secondary use of suitable resources; means of easing the movement of visitors through the countryside; development of recreation and tourism enterprises on farms; and measures of information and interpretation of the countryside to the visitor. We comment briefly below on each of these four kinds of action.

Many upland areas already have quite a range of recreation facilities — caravan and camp sites, chalets, walks, scenic drives, nature trails, picnic sites, car parks, visitor centres and so on — established in places where they are unobtrusive and do not much impinge upon productive land. The Forestry Commission has done much in this field, as have some water authorities, thus securing not only some extra use, but also some extra financial return and political justification, for the resources they have invested; and recreational use could well help to justify future investment by these bodies in the uplands. Some disused and derelict land in the uplands has been put to new use for recreation, thus sometimes generating new employment to replace that lost: examples are the disused railways of the Peak District (now laid out as trails), the Llechwedd slate quarry at Blaenau Ffestiniog (now a visitor centre), and the army camp near Trawsfynydd (now a holiday chalet centre). Such facilities permit recreation to take place in the uplands without impact on productive land.

Some much-visited upland areas, however, have few resources suited to such segregated use for tourism. In these areas, visitors are bound to penetrate hill farming land and may well have adverse impact upon the farming community. The Lake District is one such area: and in that National Park has been pioneered, through the Upland Management Experiment, a set of techniques for reconciling the visitor and the farmer. By the creation of small lay-bys, the provision of stiles, the repair of walls, the building of footbridges and the like, it has been shown possible to take the visitor through the uplands without damage to farms. In the process, the physical works have provided employment for local people, and the landscape has been improved (Countryside Commission, 1977).

But the farmer and the visitor do not everywhere need or want to stay at arm's length. Farming families in many upland areas have chosen to cater for visitors by providing farmhouse accommodation, caravan or camping sites, farm teas, sales of farm produce, pony-trekking or other facilities — and thereby to gain extra income or to permit a son or daughter to find work in the area (Davies, 1971 & 1973; Dartington Amenity Research Trust, 1974). Since the uplands are generally areas of marginal farming, in which farm incomes are precarious and the EC's socio-economic directives may be of high relevance, the economic benefit offered by recreation may be of real significance over the next 20 years. The extent to which farm-based recreation develops may depend, however, on the attitudes of farmers (which vary greatly, on this subject, from area to area), on the evolving nature of agricultural support and advisory systems, and on the reaction of planning authorities to recreational development on farms.

The last decade has seen the provision, on quite a wide scale, of facilities to inform the visitor about the countryside and to interpret it to him. These include National Park (and other) information centres, wayside signs, a variety of interpreted trails, farm (and other) open days, guided walks, visitor centres, leaflets, booklets, books, films, radio and television programmes. The townsman has the opportunity to learn a great deal about the countryside. Our impression (from research by the Dartington Amenity Research Trust for the Countryside Commission and others) is that people are progressively taking advantage of that opportunity, though there is clearly a lumpen mass who are content to regard the countryside simply as a place to find 'peace and quiet and a bit of scenery'. Despite the distortions and romanticism in some of the interpretation, this increasing knowledge of the countryside is bound to give a strong extra twist to the process of identifying the townsman with the uplands, and even of integrating the visitor to a degree into the upland community. It is now common, for example, to see urban visitors taking a competitive part in annual shows and fairs in the uplands, or helping the hill farmer as part of regular holidays there.

Thus the strong impression is of upland communities who have reconciled themselves to acting as hosts to visiting townspeople, and who are rapidly developing a set of facilities and techniques to cope with those visitors and to turn this invasion into a benefit to the hill community. This process seems certain to continue over the next two decades, with countryside recreation becoming a part of what might be called the multi-purpose management not merely of hill land, but of the upland society and economy. It is not by chance coincidence that we see National Park authorities (with a brief to provide for countryside recreation in their upland areas) searching for ways to assist the social and economic well-being of hill communities, while the Development Commission (with a brief related to that well-being) moves towards the production of 'action plans' which incorporate elements of tourism and recreation.

This coming together of different arms of public concern and action is of high significance for the future of the uplands, and echoes the wide scope of the present symposium. Our hope and expectation is that, within the present century, we shall see multi-purpose management and support for hill lands, societies and economies, with countryside recreation — for hill resident and visitor alike — as an integral element.

REFERENCES

Countryside Commission (1977) *The Lake District Upland Management Experiment.* CCP93. Cheltenham: Countryside Commission.

Countryside Commission for Scotland, Scottish Sports Council, Scottish Tourist Board & the Forestry Commission (1976) *Strategic Issues.* Scottish Tourism and Recreation Planning Studies, Volume I: a report prepared by the Dartington Amenity Research Trust. Edinburgh: Countryside Commission for Scotland.

Countryside Review Committee (1977) *The Countryside — Problems and Policies: a discussion paper;* and *Leisure and the Countryside,* Topic Paper No. 2. London: HMSO.

Dartington Amenity Research Trust (1974) *Farm Recreation and Tourism in England and Wales.* A report to the Countryside Commission, English Tourist Board and Wales Tourist Board. Dartington Amenity Research Trust Publication No. 14/Countryside Commission CCP 83. Cheltenham: Countryside Commission.

Dartington Amenity Research Trust (1977 a) *Second Homes in Scotland.* A report to the Countryside Commission for Scotland, Scottish Tourist Board, Highlands and Islands Development Board and Scottish Development Department. Dartington Amenity Research Trust Publication No. 22. Edinburgh: Countryside Commission for Scotland.

Dartington Amenity Research Trust (1977 b) *Hadrian's Wall.* A strategy for conservation and visitor services, prepared for the Countryside Commission. Cheltenham: Countryside Commission.

Davidson, J & Wibberley, G P (1977) *Planning and the Rural Environment.* London: Pergamon.

Davies, E T (1971) *Farm Tourism in Cornwall and Devon: some economic and physical considerations.* Report No. 184, Agricultural Economics Unit, University of Exeter.

Davies, E T (1973) *Tourism on Devon Farms: a physical and economic appraisal.* Report No. 188, Agricultural Economics Unit, University of Exeter.

Department of the Environment (1974) *Report of the National Park Policies Review Committee.* London: HMSO.

Department of the Environment (1976) *Ministerial Conclusions on the Report of the National Parks Policies Review Committee.* DoE Circular 4/76. London: HMSO.

Duffell, J R (1975) Car travel, 1965-75, with particular reference to pleasure travel and highway planning. *Traffic Engineering and Control,* **16,** 557-559.

Patmore, J A (1970) *Land and Leisure in England and Wales.* Newton Abbott: David and Charles.

Tanner, M F (1973) *Water Resources and Recreation.* Water Recreation Series, Study 3. London: Sports Council.

Tanner, M F (1974) *The Management of Water Recreation Areas.* Unpublished report to the Sports Council and Countryside Commission.

20 Landscape conservation in upland Britain

M J FEIST

INTRODUCTION

The importance which society attaches to the landscapes of upland Britain is evident from Figure 1. This shows that a high proportion of the uplands, as defined for this symposium, has been officially recognised as being of high scenic quality: the National Parks were designated specifically on account of their 'beautiful and relatively wild country'; Areas of Outstanding Natural Beauty have been similarly selected as having a national signficance by virtue of their landscape quality and unique character. These two forms of designation are accompanied by certain legislative and administrative measures intended to ensure that the characteristic beauty of the designated areas might be maintained and even enhanced.

Despite these measures, however, there must be reservations regarding the effectiveness of current arrangements for conserving upland landscapes. The subjective nature of landscape appreciation means that even in our most valued scenic areas we are by no means unanimous as to what exactly it is that we wish to conserve (the objective) or at what cost. Since other objectives, such as food production, can be more easily and precisely defined and quantified, particularly in economic terms, the objective of conserving landscape quality has tended to suffer by default.

The purpose of this paper, therefore, is twofold: first to reiterate the importance of the landscapes of upland Britain and second to point out inadequacies in the present arrangements for landscape conservation so that such inadequacies may be remedied in formulating future strategies for the uplands.

The paper is divided into three sections: the first section assesses the value of upland landscapes from various standpoints and seeks to answer the question,

Figure 1
DESIGNATED AREAS FOR COUNTRYSIDE CONSERVATION IN UPLAND BRITAIN, 1976

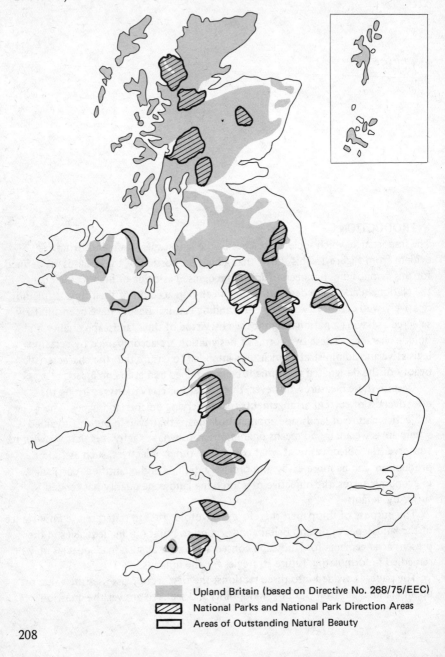

Upland Britain (based on Directive No. 268/75/EEC)

National Parks and National Park Direction Areas

Areas of Outstanding Natural Beauty

"Why bother to conserve them?"; the second section briefly analyses the main
threats to landscape qualities; the final section suggests how the goal of conserving
these qualities might be integrated into an overall upland strategy.

THE VALUE OF UPLAND LANDSCAPES

Any assessment of the value of upland landscapes must of necessity be very
generalised since the uplands contain a wide variety of landscapes. This variety is
evident in a number of respects. Each upland region has a distinct character due to
differences in topography, geology, climate, vegetation and other factors. For
instance, the Lake District (with its mountains, crags and deep glaciated valley
profiles) differs fundamentally from the moor-clad granite dome of Dartmoor.
In addition, there are considerable landscape variations within each upland region
which reflect the influences of altitude, agricultural practice and cultural considerations. The difference between fell and in-bye, between high exposed moors and
sheltered dales and between the landscape patterns of the central uplands and their
lower fringes, all illustrate these variations. Finally, landscapes vary in terms of
quality. Even taking into account differing tastes in landscape appreciation, it is
evident that some landscapes are considered less interesting and less attractive than
others either because of the absence or the poorer quality of the features that
characterise that landscape type, or because the landscape has been 'spoilt' by
industrial activities and incongruous development.

Despite this high degree of landscape diversity certain characteristics can be
recognised as being common to most or all of the uplands of Britain. Their height,
topography and climatic conditions combine to create a dramatic landscape and
a harsh environment, the severity of which increases with altitude and exposure.
Such an environment has constrained the activities of man to the extent that the
uplands today are sparsely populated and relatively free of the signs of 20th
century civilisation. This, together with economic and physical limitations on
the productive use of upland areas, has led to them being regarded as the nearest
thing to 'wilderness' that exists in the British Isles.

Collectively these characteristics create a completely different environment
than that of lowland Britain and much of the particular value of the uplands as
a national resource is based on this contrast. The theme of this paper is that the
landscape is a vital part of that resource.

To many people the case for landscape conservation rests on the intrinsic
value of high quality scenery. Upland landscapes have a sense of drama and
grandeur. The rugged mountainous scenery, the snow-clad peaks obscured by
mist and cloud, the bleak moorland plateaux, the turbulent mountain streams
and waterfalls — all have power to awe and stir the imagination, and have inspired
and enriched our artistic, musical and literary heritage. A parallel is often drawn

209

between attractive landscapes and the valuable paintings and sculptures in our art galleries. Both appeal to the visual senses; both should be regarded as national treasures and protected accordingly.

The uplands also possess other qualities that enhance the purely visual experience of landscape. Much of the higher, more remote land has a wild untamed appearance and although it would be stretching a point to describe this as 'wilderness', such land possesses a certain primeval atmosphere in the eyes of those accustomed to the comparatively domesticated lowland landscapes. This wilderness has value in its power to evoke the sense of man's primitive past and as a salutary reminder of man's place in the natural order of things. The upland environment is also noted for the element of danger inherent in its topography and climatic conditions and thus provides a locus for those who wish to test themselves and their ability to do without the creature comforts of modern society. Some would argue that the well-being of the human race itself is largely dependent upon the character-moulding experience of facing such dangers and discomforts and the uplands take on a new significance in this respect.

In addition to the atmosphere of wildness, the uplands contain most of the few remaining places where it is still possible to get away from concrete and glass, the infernal combustion engine, and other humans. The quality of remoteness, the opportunity to enjoy peace and solitude and the freedom to roam across wide open spaces are becoming increasingly precious as a respite from the myriad pressures of a highly urbanised society. Professor Grieve of the HIDB has expressed the psychological value of this resource to the nation as follows (Brasher, 1977):

"It is necessary for the sanity of the nation that people know that there are still remote areas of Britain which offer an alternative: they may never go there, but the knowledge that they exist preserves our balance."

Apart from the aesthetic and psychological value of upland landscapes, an increasing environmental consciousness among the public means that more people now associate an attractive landscape with one that has a high wildlife value and vice versa. As Darling (1970) has put it, "All in all the most general consensus of beautiful landscape would be found to be that which is in ecological repose or near to it". For instance a mature woodland with little age gradation and no natural regeneration implies loss of that feature in the landscape with a consequent deterioration in overall visual quality and a reduction in species diversity. Similarly, the effects of various forms of pollution on semi-natural ecosystems are generally held to detract from landscape value and to disrupt the food chain; an example is the impoverishment of meadow flora following fertiliser and herbicide applications. It is argued that by conserving landscape quality the equally important objective of maintaining habitat diversity and a healthy ecosystem will also be achieved. By way of illustration, the retention and management of several hundred hectares of scenically attractive heather moorland will safeguard the continued existence of species of flora and fauna that depend on a fairly extensive habitat of this type for their ecological viability.

Finally a case can be made for conserving particular types or areas of landscape in the uplands on the basis of their importance to our heritage. Much of the uplands still remain substantially the same in appearance as they were some 200 years ago at the time of the enclosures while some areas have remained largely undisturbed since the neolithic period. The relatively unchanged nature of upland environments is of great value in furthering our understanding of their history and cultural development ranging from medieval farming systems to rural manifestations of the Industrial Revolution. It should also be noted that there is a measure of support for those who regard the landscape of the Brontes and the Doones as part of our cultural heritage and hence worthy of protection, although the interest in this aspect of landscape may be more commercial than literary.

The aesthetic, ecological and cultural value of upland landscapes, therefore, constitute good grounds in themselves for conserving them. Collectively, however, they add up to a far more important reason why our best landscapes should be safeguarded: the landscape is the basic resource of the tourist industry. For many thousands of visitors the scenery is the primary attraction of the uplands, whether it is admired for its own sake or as an essential ingredient in the enjoyment of those more actively involved in the upland environment through such activities as mountain-eering, fell-walking, skiing, pony-trekking or hang-gliding. In simple terms, a lot of people get a lot of pleasure from the particular attributes of upland landscapes, and the importance they attach to this can be gauged by the willingness of the pre-dominantly lowland population to spend time and money on travelling to upland areas.

Apart from the quality of the landscape, the uplands have few other attractions to tourists and visitors; they are mostly considerable distances from the main population centres, they are not readily accessible by public transport, they contain fewer facilities and nothing like the range of entertainments to be found in seaside resorts. If the quality of upland landscapes is allowed to deteriorate through default or by adverse development, the tourist industry will suffer as a result. Since tourism plays a major role in the economy of the uplands, generating income, jobs and subsidies for otherwise unprofitable services (shops, garages, etc) the effect of a decline in tourism would be severe. Upland landscapes thus have a very real economic significance on a local, national and international scale, and this fact should carry some weight with those elements of our society that have the unfortunate tendency to regard something as being of value only insofar as it can be expressed in monetary terms.

THE THREATS TO LANDSCAPE QUALITY

The particular valued attributes of upland landscapes have been discussed at some length in the preceding section because an understanding of these qualities is essential to an appreciation of the ways in which they are threatened. For the most part, public concern over adverse changes to landscape quality has been concentrated on the lowlands. This is understandable since changes in the uplands have appeared relatively minor by comparison. However, with the exception of a few well-publicised cases involving mining, reservoirs and major road proposals in National Parks, an unfortunate tendency has arisen to regard upland landscapes generally as being safe from pressures for adverse change. This view has been based on three main lines of argument. First, topographical and physical constraints limit man's ability to re-shape the appearance of the landscape as in the new agricultural landscapes of the lowlands. Second, it is held that there are a number of reasons why the uplands are highly unlikely to experience the development pressures and degree of urbanisation that exists in the lowlands. Finally, there is the belief that the top quality landscapes in the uplands are safeguarded by virtue of their designation as National Parks and Areas of Outstanding Natural Beauty, and the higher standards of planning control exercised in these areas, (See Figure 1). There is much to be said for these arguments but unfortunately they have tended to foster a false sense of security.

Although there seems no reason to suppose that the uplands of Britain as a whole are likely to undergo drastic changes in the foreseeable future, there are certainly a number of ways in which the landform and appearance of the landscape can be considerably transformed on a local scale:

(i)   Extractive industries — The increasing demand for aggregates and minerals, both of which are found primarily in the uplands, will find expression in more and larger mines and quarries with all their attendant plant and spoil heaps. These extractive industries generate a sizeable amount of heavy traffic which in turn requires better roads so that the effects of mining activities extend some distance beyond the actual site. Quarrying literally carves up the landscape. Past experience shows that the landscape rarely benefits, as can be readily seen in the area around Buxton in the Peak District.

(ii)   Road construction — The nature of upland terrain invariably means that modern road design standards can only be achieved at the expense of the landscape. The construction of the M6 over Shap Fells, the M62 Trans-Pennine motorway and the extensive enlargement of the A66 in the Lake District have all had a major impact on the scenic qualities of the areas affected, despite attempts to minimise damage. On a smaller scale there has been widespread criticism of the practice of piecemeal 'improvements' to rural roads that have been carried out with little regard for landscape character, while in Scotland there has been increasing concern over the scarring of the landscape through the construction of estate roads for forestry and sporting purposes.

(iii) Afforestation — This can have a major impact on the appearance of an area since large-scale afforestation alters the scale, colour, ecology and indeed the whole nature of the landscape. The changes that have taken place in the Snowdonia and Northumberland National Parks illustrate this. Similarly, the felling of mature broadleaf or mixed woodlands and replacement with commercial coniferous species has a substantial effect, especially in the short-term.

(iv) Reservoirs — That the building of a dam and the drowning of a valley has a profound effect on the character of an area hardly requires elaboration.

(v) Agriculture — Changes in farm management together with various agricultural operations (hedge and bank removal, drainage schemes, reclamation of rough grazing, scrub clearance and bracken spraying, etc) can all have a very significant impact on the colour and texture of landscapes by changing the vegetation and other natural features.

Two points should be noted regarding the development of the uplands and the degree to which they might become urbanised. Because upland areas currently exhibit such a contrast with lowland Britain (in terms of settlement size, urban sprawl, industrialisation and much of the other paraphernalia of the 20th century) any substantial increase in these factors would appreciably diminish the un-developed and strongly rural character of the uplands. By and large, there seems no reason to believe that any such substantial increase is likely. Nevertheless, the uplands are being subjected to three main forces for development. The first of these is the power industries in their search for sites for power stations; routes for further power and energy supply lines; and more recently sites for the disposal of nuclear waste. The second main pressure for development comes from tourism and recreation and takes the form of demand for more caravan and camping sites; more chalets and homes for holiday or retirement; better access roads to beauty spots and more car parks, toilet blocks, refreshment facilities and so on. These pressures, together with the unsightly commercial garishness that tends to accompany tourism, pose a considerable threat to the beauty of the upland environment. The third threat comes from the increasingly industrialised appearance of modern farm buildings which, through their size, design and materials are not easily harmonised into the popular conception of a 'traditional' landscape.

The belief that protective designations alone are sufficient to safeguard officially recognised landscapes is very much open to question. The controversies over quarrying in the Peak District, the reclamation of heather moorland on Exmoor, the A66 'improvement' in the Lake District, potash mining in the North Yorks

Moors, Swincombe reservoir on Dartmoor, and many lesser known examples all serve to illustrate that landscape and amenity considerations can be effectively overridden by other interests. Furthermore, the designation of scenic areas has drawn wider attention to their attractiveness and, to some extent, increased the tourist and recreational pressures. Where these visitor pressures have been concentrated, the landscape quality has often been marred by the erosion of ground vegetation; the flanks of Snowdon and Kinder Scout (Peak District) are two examples of the problems affecting almost any popular beauty spot.

So far the emphasis in this paper has been on the threats to landscape values that stem from pressures for various kinds of development. These pressures, whether they involve the introduction of new elements or the alteration of existing features in the landscape, require positive actions. There are, however, less dramatic but nevertheless significant threats to scenic quality arising from inaction. The characteristic appearance of different landscapes has been and continues to be dependent on particular methods of management. If, for economic or other reasons, former management practices are abandoned or neglected, then certain landscape features will change. Poorly-maintained hedges, broken down walls, dilapidated farm buildings, and moribund woodlands are all signs of a landscape at risk through the withdrawal of farm labour or a depressed farm economy.

From the foregoing discussion it will be evident that, whether officially designated or not, upland landscapes are subject to a variety of pressures that will affect their essential character and qualities to varying degrees. It is not claimed that all these pressures are necessarily harmful to landscape values. Indeed, in some circumstances the landscape may be enhanced by a reservoir, by sympathetic tree-planting, by agricultural improvement schemes and even by the likes of the radar installations at Fylingdales on the North Yorks Moors. However, it is important to recognise that the continued maintenance of our valued upland landscapes and particularly of certain scarce qualities, cannot be taken for granted. If we are seriously concerned to preserve scenic values for this and succeeding generations then the appropriate conservation measures must be taken to counter the threats and pressures described above.

A STRATEGY FOR CONSERVATION

"The art of conservation stems from the science of ecology, a delight in knowing how nature works and a love of beauty which may or may not be conscious. Every acre . . . demands thought before its biological and visual relations are altered." (Darling, 1970).

To many people such a principle might be regarded as self-evident. However, actions affecting the landscape are frequently dominated by short-term considerations and the private rather than the public interest. By almost any socio-economic criterion, the uplands constitute the most disadvantaged regions of Britain and those who live and work there cannot be blamed for regarding landscape protection as a luxury when it threatens their livelihood or standard of living. The position of the upland farmer illustrates this viewpoint. The attractiveness of many landscapes is dependent upon the way in which the land is farmed but the farmer is concerned with earning a living by producing food not with managing his holding for scenic reasons. He is not paid for the latter function and to paraphrase the point tellingly made by Jeffries (1865) 'loveliness gives him no cheese for breakfast'.

A similar situation applies when companies propose to open or extend quarry workings or to undertake other developments that are generally held to have adverse effects on the upland environment. Here the conflict is expressed as being between much-needed jobs for local people and the fleeting pleasures of visitors from further afield. Another variation on this socio-economic argument is advanced in favour of road improvements. In almost every case the application of cost-benefit techniques means that the objective of conserving landscape beauty is subordinated to technological and economic objectives because landscape is too intangible a concept to be a meaningful part of the equation. For the political decision-takers in upland areas there are few if any votes in landscape conservation.

Theoretically, these problems should be resolved on a national level by government acting in the wider interest to ensure that the needs of environmental conservation are both considered and implemented. Unfortunately at this level the picture is further confused by the conflicting mandates of government departments. On the one hand Ministers are required in Section 11 of the Countryside Act to "have regard to the desirability of conserving the natural beauty and amenity of the countryside" (HMSO, 1968). On the other a duty is laid on them in Section 37 of the Countryside Act "to have due regard to the needs of agriculture and forestry and to the economic and social interests of rural areas" (HMSO, 1968). Faced with such ambiguous, ill-defined and conflicting instructions the various ministries have invariably plumped for their main mandates because these are more precisely expressed in terms of achieving target figures or balancing the books and thus carry more weight.

Since agriculture is the most potent influence on the landscape of the uplands the nature of conflicts between government departments can best be illustrated by reference to the current controversies surrounding farming in National Parks. Farmers are encouraged, through the grants and subsidies paid by MAFF, to undertake schemes that often have adverse landscape effects. The reclamation of areas of heather moorland and the erection of fences in formerly open areas in Exmoor National Park is a case in point. Without the aid of MAFF such schemes

215

would generally be uneconomic so that the tax-payer is in effect subsidising the loss of scenic quality in return for little or no increase in agricultural output. Under the existing system there is little that local authorities or the Department of the Environment can do other than try to secure an unsatisfactory compromise.

The clash between amenity and agricultural interests in the uplands is all the more unfortunate because it is unnecessary, particularly in strategic terms. The hills and the uplands of Britain produce only 7% of our gross farm output and MAFF statistics indicate that the national aim of producing more food from our own resources would be far better served by diverting the bulk of current investment in upland agriculture to lowland farms. A further factor to consider is the need to safeguard the better agricultural areas of the lowlands from pressures such as the recreational demands of the urban population; these pressures should be diverted to land of relatively poor productive quality, ie to the uplands. But will the public still be attracted to upland areas if landscape values are diminished through the actions of farmers and other interests?

From an agricultural standpoint, therefore, there seems little justification for damaging environmental qualities in the uplands in the interests of national food production. However, quite apart from social considerations, the continued survival of the farming community is vital to landscape conservation so that in any future strategy the national interest would best be served by emphasising that upland farmers are being subsidised primarily for their contribution to community life and their role in maintaining an attractive environment rather than for their ability to produce food. This is already implicit in MAFF's system of support, and the principle that farmers should receive financial assistance on social grounds to maintain a minimum population and "to ensure the continued conservation of the countryside" has been accepted on an EC level in the Less Favoured Areas Directive.

This examination of the role of agriculture in relation to landscape conservation shows that it is possible to harmonize amenity considerations with other objectives in the uplands. It is appreciated that there are situations where society, on a national or local scale, has greater need of amenities (such as water or good television reception) than of a particular view. In such circumstances there is little room for compromise; the most that can be done is to minimise the damage to landscape values. The key question is whether the development is absolutely essential in the first place and whether there are alternative and less environmentally damaging means of achieving the same ends. There must be some reservations about the assumptions that have been used in the past to construct cases proving the 'demand' for more roads, more quarries and more power stations, for example. A landscape conservation strategy should ensure that attractive environments are only despoiled if there is no alternative, and that the

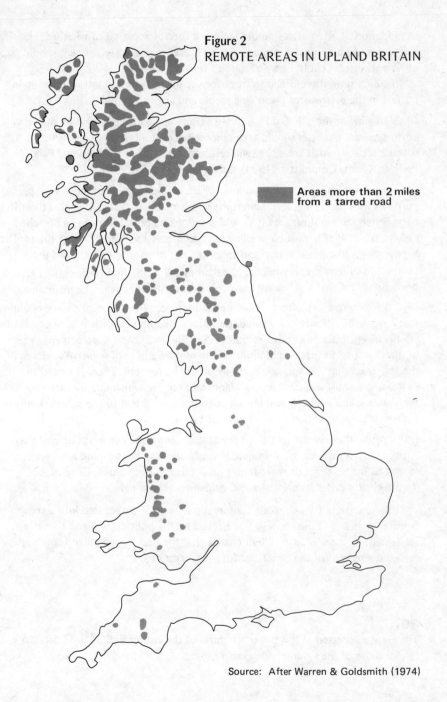

Figure 2
REMOTE AREAS IN UPLAND BRITAIN

Areas more than 2 miles
from a tarred road

Source: After Warren & Goldsmith (1974)

217

examination of alternatives should include a careful appraisal of whether the threatened development is necessary at all rather than merely where it should go, or how its effects could be ameliorated.

In conclusion, therefore, a strategy for the uplands should satisfy three main criteria in the interests of preserving scenic and environmental quality:

(i) In view of the value of high-quality landscapes, the conservation of environmental qualities should take precedence over all other objectives in specific areas. In such areas the twin recommendations of the National Park Policies Review Committee (1974) should apply:

"the presumption against development which would be out of accord with park purposes must be strong throughout the whole of the parks: in the most beautiful parts which remain unspoiled it should amount to a prohibitioñ to be breached only in the case of a most compelling national necessity."; and "where the conflict between . . . (the preservation and enhancement of natural beauty, and the promotion of public enjoyment) . . . becomes acute, the first (purpose) must prevail in order that the beauty and ecological qualities . . . may be maintained."

(ii) Elsewhere every effort should be made to conserve those landscape qualities that have an additional rarity value. Remoteness combined with wild open country is a prime example of a scarce resource. (See Figure 2). Any development or sign of man's intrusion that would diminish the remote and semi-wilderness nature of the few areas that remain should consequently be resisted. There is a need to examine our most attractive upland landscapes to see which qualities are rare or even unique and which would represent an irreparable loss to the nation should the appropriate conservation measures not be taken.

(iii) Where there is outright conflict between landscape conservation and alternative land uses it is clear that valuable landscape resources should not be sacrificed for marginal or short-term gain if this can be avoided. Government should clearly order its priorities and guidelines accordingly.

If these criteria for landscape conservation can be incorporated into a comprehensive upland land use strategy and backed by the political will and resources to implement it, there is an excellent chance that the best of our upland landscapes can be conserved for the benefit of future generations.

NOTE
The views expressed in this paper are those of the author and do not necessarily reflect those of the Countryside Commission.

REFERENCES AND BIBLIOGRAPHY

Appleton, J (1975) *The experience of landscape.* London: Wiley.

Brasher, C (1977) His enemy — bureaucracy galore. *The Observer Review,*
19th June, 1977.

Countryside Commission (1976) *National Park Policies: A Statement.*
(CCP 95). Cheltenham: Countryside Commission.

Countryside Commission (1977) *New agricultural landscapes — issues, objectives
and action.* (CCP 102). Cheltenham: Countryside Commission.

Darling, F F (1970) *Wilderness and plenty.* The Reith Lectures, 1969. London:
BBC.

National Economic Development Office (1973) *UK farming and the Common
Market: hills and uplands.* A report by the Economic Development Committee
for Agriculture. London: NEDO.

Fairbrother, N (1970) *New lives, new landscapes.* London: Architectural Press.

Feist, M J, Leat, P M K & Wibberley, G P (1976) *A study of the Hartsop
Valley.* Cheltenham: Countryside Commission.

HMSO (1968) *Countryside Act.* London: HMSO.

HMSO (1976) *Sixth Report of the Environmental Sub-Committee of the
Parliamentary Expenditure Committee on National Parks and the Countryside.*
London: HMSO.

Jeffries, R (1885) *The open air.* London.

Lake District Special Planning Board (1976) *National Park Plan: Ideas for
discussion: Landscape.* Kendal: Lake District Special Planning Board.

Laurie, I C, Robinson, D G, Traill, A L & Wager, J F (Eds.) (1976) *Landscape
evaluation.* University of Manchester.

MacEwen, M (Ed.) (1976) *Future landscapes.* London: Chatto and Windus.

National Park Policies Review Committee (1974) *Report.* (under the chairmanship
of Lord Sandford.) London: HMSO.

Sayer, Lady (1970) *Wild country: National asset or barren waste?* London:
Council for the Protection of Rural England.

Warren, A & Goldsmith, F B (1974) (Eds.) *Conservation in practice.* London:
Wiley.

21 The future of the extractive industries in upland Britain

J R BLUNDEN

THE CHANGING NATURE OF MINERALS PRODUCTION

The upland areas of Britain, as defined by the appropriate EC directive, have long had considerable significance in terms of the contribution they have made to our mineral wealth. Non-ferrous ores, for example, have an extensive history of extraction in three main types of upland geological environment: the granite masses of Devon and Cornwall; the Lower Paleozoic rocks of the highland zones such as Central and North Wales, the Welsh border, the Lake District and the Southern Uplands of Scotland; and parts of the Carboniferous limestone outcrop of Derbyshire and the Northern Pennines.

The production of these ores, frequently dating from the pre-Roman period, may be divided primarily on the basis of value into the precious metals (gold and silver) and the base metals, of which tin, lead, zinc, copper, tungsten ore (wolfram), arsenic and nickel have at various times been extracted in upland Britain. Precious metals have never been located in any great quantity. Silver, usually found in association with lead, has been obtained from argentiferous ores of lead in Derbyshire. A little gold has been obtained, notably from the Dolgellau area of North Wales where at least 13 gold mines have been operative. A well-known working, the Ogofau gold mine, was also in production in south-western Dyfed. Alluvial deposits of gold have been worked in streams in Selkirkshire and Sutherland. The base metals, lead, copper, zinc and tin have, on the other hand, been located and worked in very substantial quantities, notably lead from the Pennines, Clywd, Shropshire and the Scottish borders, copper from Shropshire, tin from Dartmoor and zinc from the Pennines. Although lead and tin were worked substantially in Roman times (zinc was of little commercial value until the end of the 18th century), the height of extractive output occurred in the 19th century, interacting with the rapid industrial expansion of the period.

Lead mining was also approaching its most active phase; there are now some 4 000 disused lead mines in Derbyshire alone. The peak period for lead mining was 1850-1870 when an average of more than 91 000 tonnes of ore were produced annually (chiefly from Derbyshire, the Northern Pennines and North Wales). However, all these base metals were severely affected by a recession in demand and sharply falling prices during the late 19th century, influencing different metals at slightly different times. The marked decline in British base metal mining resulted from the discovery of new large deposits overseas, notably copper from the United States and Chile, lead from Spain and tin from Malaya and Bolivia. In important instances, the deposits occurred in countries over which Britain then enjoyed economic or political influence. The rapid growth of steam shipping facilitated imports at prices which greatly undercut home supplies, obtained in many cases from areas where mining conditions were becoming more difficult as the best and/or most accessible ores were being worked-out.

Output of almost all these base metals has remained at a continuously low level this century and that of copper has virtually died out. In 1974 the domestic mining of metallic ores provided about 2% by value of metals consumed, including the output of the Cornish tin mining industry which has undergone a considerable renaissance since the mid-1960's. That necessary prerequisite of continued mining activity, an active search for new ore bodies to replace those that had become exhausted, was, until recently, hardly undertaken. Apart from tin, only in one case was there a partial revival. Between 1950 and 1970 the output of lead and zinc ores (principally lead) increased by 39.7% (from 4 332 tonnes to 6 055 tonnes). This was due almost entirely to its coincidence in the Pennines with fluorspar, in earlier centuries considered a waste material, but for which demand in the 1950's and 1960's was accelerating rapidly. Of the total British output of lead in 1974, most of it, approximately 5 500 tonnes, was produced in Derbyshire as a by-product of a fluorspar processing plant near Eyam and another south west of Matlock which also produced a limited amount of zinc concentrate. In the Northern Pennines lead was also concentrated at two plants, primarily processing fluorspar, at Blanchland and Rookhope. Thus the factors influencing the increase of lead output in the last two decades were not related essentially to the economics of lead mining itself.

Fluorspar is but one example of a non-metallic mineral once not valued as a commodity to be won from upland Britain but which has become of significance in the 20th century. Another is barytes, also primarily associated with lead and zinc veins of the North Pennines. Whilst china clay, now produced from workings on the edge of Dartmoor, has an extractive history going back to the

18th century, only in recent years has its diversity of usage been fully realised and the winning of these deposits opened up on a considerable scale.

Other more recent developments in upland Britain have involved extractive activities of a quantitatively more limited nature with the working of talc in the Shetlands, diatomite in Cumbria and silica sand at Loch Aline in Scotland as well as the opening up of Britain's only and not inconsiderable reserves of potash under the North Yorkshire Moors. All of these commodities are traded internationally and are subject to a world supply and demand situation and therefore variations in price and profitability, and their future output to some extent must be considered within such a global context.

However, perhaps the key significance of upland Britain in terms of its history of mineral production and its on-going importance is as a supplier of hard rock materials. With the notable exception of silica rock and ganister used for blast furnace lining (a fast diminishing market) these are utilised for construction purposes. For centuries, block stone in the form of indigenous limestone, sandstone or igneous rock has been used throughout upland areas and beyond as far as the prevailing transport mode of the time economically permitted.

The material which spread furthest in the wake of the great increase in population and house building at the time of the Industrial Revolution was slate. Production continued to expand through the 19th century until in 1898 it reached its peak, with the chief source, North Wales, providing nearly half a million tonnes of roofing materials. With the development of clay and concrete tiles in the twentieth century and the increased use of brick and concrete in construction, the use of slate and stone blocks for building fell away rapidly.

With the change in building technology, first sand and gravel came into its own. But since World War II, the need to make good the shortfall of this material in many areas of Britain where its occurence is naturally limited, the increasing scarcity of sand and gravel in districts where it was once plentiful and the growth of the construction industry (at a rate double that of the gross national product for the 12 years up to 1969) have led to the increased utilisation of limestone, sandstone and igneous rocks in crushed form, mostly from upland Britain. This rising trend for all three minerals was also encouraged by the upsurge in road construction with the commencement of the motorway programme and the need for better and more frequent maintenance of other highways resulting from greatly increased levels of traffic. In the case of limestone, additional demands also came from the agricultural, chemical and iron and steel industries. However, upward trends here have only been tempered by the greater efficiency with which the limestone has been used in the last mentioned, and a modest fall in the amount of lime required by farmers.

Since, because of their relatively low value, aggregate materials as well as chemical limestone are supplied only from home sources, the uplands will continue to be prime sources from which future needs are met. Reserves of all these materials, taken as a whole, are prodigious and, except in the case of specific point sources, are likely to be able to meet any foreseeable demand. But whilst needs up to the turn of the century are likely to be determined by the growth of the home economy, the availability of supplies cannot be seen simply as a matter of increasing the output of any or all of the materials in question at any or all point sources. This is because the extractive industries of Britain, producing aggregates or chemical rock, or any other type of industrial mineral, must work within the context of a clearly defined legislative framework.

LEGISLATIVE CONTROLS ON THE EXTRACTIVE INDUSTRIES

All mineral operations must, of course, be licensed by the Department of Trade and Industry in order that they comply with safety and other regulations administered by the Mines and Quarries Inspectorate. Moreover, there may well be some constraints exercised upon the activities of extractors through the 1974 Control of Pollution Act to prevent water, air and noise pollution, though the Alkali Inspectorate has more specific responsibility to supervise and enforce pollution controls with respect to the processing of minerals once they are removed from the mine or quarry face.

Much more significant to the extraction of minerals is that legislation which governs the planning and development of mining and quarrying operations, since it determines not only the physical limits of individual production units but whether minerals shall be extracted from a particular site at all. This body of legislation stems initially from the Town and Country Planning Act 1932 which enabled planning authorities for the first time to bring mineral extraction within some degree of control, though few exercised their option. It was for this reason that in 1946 an Interim Development Order was added to the Act of fourteen years earlier which made it obligatory for planning permission to be sought by any firm wishing to begin working minerals at a specific site. In 1947 the Town and Country Planning Act made controls on mineral extraction even more explicit and though existing workings begun before or during the Second World War remained outside planning constraints, this new legislation recognised the need for some element of forward planning for all land uses. The 1947 Act, which was further consolidated in 1962 and modified in 1968, essentially charges the local authorities with the task of preparing Development Plans, or since 1968 Structure Plans for their areas which are supposed to zone districts for various classes of development including mineral extraction.

Equally important, the framework of law necessitates the mineral extractor, when wishing to exploit new ground, submitting a detailed application to the planning authority for the area in which the site is located. This has to show the direction of working, the situation of the proposed plant and buildings, as well as details of the mineral to be extracted, the rate of extraction, the life of the deposit and, not least, that a genuine demand for the mineral exists which cannot be economically met elsewhere.

If the extractor wishes to break new ground not already designated for mineral working his application will have to be referred to the Secretary of State for the Environment or the Secretaries of State for Wales or Scotland if those countries are concerned, since a major change in land use contrary to that set out in the Development Plan is involved. In such situations the planning authority will certainly make its own views known to the Secretary of State concerning the application. However, in all planning permissions for mineral extraction, the Secretary of State, knowing the local authority view, will decide whether to 'call-in' the application, which means he will deal with it himself or whether to leave it to that planning authority to make a decision on its own.

In spite of these controls and contrary to the view often held, the planning legislation described is not designed unreasonably to restrict the activities of extractors or to fight a running battle for the preservation of amenity. Nevertheless, in recent years, increasingly stringent conditions have been imposed on mineral operations. In the 1960's the emphasis had been more heavily placed on the role of planning authorities (using the legislation they have at their disposal) in the resolution of conflicting demands on land, aiming at some degree of reconciliation between mineral extraction and amenity interests, although this had always been accepted to some degree as an aim. Thus, when permission for mineral extraction has been granted, increasing weight has been placed on the need for the restoration of land to a stipulated standard, adequate disposal of waste materials and the minimisation of disturbance to other amenities and land use functions. Indeed, the Countryside Act of 1968 imposes a definite duty on decision makers exercising powers under the Town and Country Planning Acts to have regard for natural beauty and amenity in using their statutory powers in relation to land. Certainly conservationists would accept the view that landscaping conditions associated with a planning consent often result in the ultimate restoration of the land in a satisfactory way. But since permission for mining as recommended in the Ministry of Housing and Local Government's (1960) publicatio *Control of Mineral Working* should "afford (not) less than fifteen years' working" ar in some cases "a working life of up to sixty years or sometimes longer", it is not surprising that those concerned with the quality of the environment should feel that it i the loss of amenity during the quarrying operation that is of most significance. On th grounds they would argue that in many more cases applications to extract minerals should be refused, particularly in upland areas where landscapes are invariably of high quality. The contention of damage to amenity is one which the extractive industry finds difficult to refute, in spite of the fact that it is heavily constrained by planning legislation. Almost all applications for mineral workings are now opposed by amenity interests of some kind, whether local or national, and the industry is alarmed at the rate of refusal of consent by local authorities, leading to the expensive and time-consuming process of appeals to the Secretary of State and the holding of public inquiries.

Whilst the extractive companies argue the need to meet the demands of industry for minerals at least cost and the virtues of minerals operations in that they provide much needed employment in upland areas where other opportunities are scarce, the planners are left to resolve the conflict between allowing development in a way which offers some concession to amenity or even prohibiting it in the interests of total environmental conservation. This can be particularly difficult in areas designated as National Parks for whilst it was envisaged by the Act setting them up that mineral extraction was an acceptable activity within the defined zone, no-one in 1947 could foresee the scale or the level of output of the modern quarry, let alone the extent of its working life.

These issues are central to the discussion of the current and future production levels of each of the minerals produced in upland Britain which follows.

THE MINERALS CURRENTLY EXTRACTED
Limestone
Of all the hard rock materials quarried in upland Britain, limestone is by far the most important economically; indeed it represents the largest single source of crushed aggregate (Figure 1). In the light of what has been said about the changing nature of aggregates supply to construction industry, it is not surprising that extraction has increased by 115% in the period 1950-1974, compared with only 41% for sand and gravel, and that this market consumes about 72% of all output. The only other expanding market for limestone has been the chemical industry where increased utilisation has kept pace with growth in the gross national product.

Limestone, although more expensive to work than the softer sand and gravels, incurs lower extractive and processing charges than sandstones and igneous rocks and has a much wider usage even in the construction industry. Both sand and gravel and limestone can be used in the base courses of roads but only the latter is suitable for surfacing. In the concrete market its fire resistance helps to make it preferred to alternatives but in the production of cement, chalk still predominates. Nevertheless, since 1960 there has been an almost 30% increase in its utilisation for this purpose and only one new cement works based on chalk has been constructed.

Figure 1

LIMESTONE PRODUCTION IN UPLAND BRITAIN 1967 AND 1974

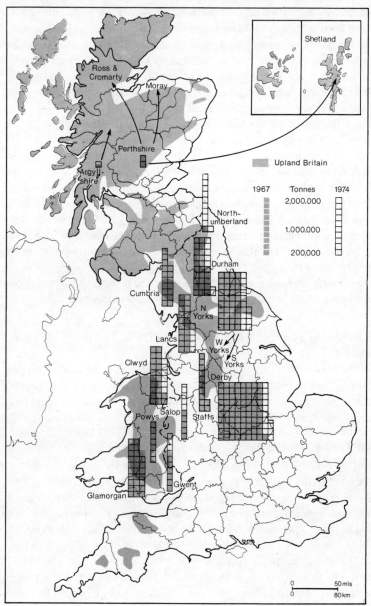

Limestone, whatever its ultimate usage, must remain a relatively low value product which cannot be moved over great distances because of the transport ` costs involved, though plainly this dictum applies more to aggregate materials than processed chemical lime. Although the shortfall in sand and gravel supplies in south east England has led to the transport of limestone from the Mendips (not part of upland Britain) as far as Greater London, this material is mainly used in the large conurbations adjacent to production areas, particularly in the North of England and in Wales. Certainly in both areas it has always been the mainstay of the growing cement industry because of the lack of chalk supplies and has been of fundamental importance for the chemical industries. However, as their very limited areas of sand and gravel have become exhausted, limestone from local sources has increasingly taken its place as the main aggregate material. These demands have led to the development of three major quarrying areas together with two lesser zones of production, in the Lake District and North Wales.

Of foremost importance is the South Pennine area of Derbyshire and Staffordshire, known as the Peak District (Figure 2). There are 35 quarries active here either in or adjacent to the National Park. Although the majority of the workings in the Park produce limestone for aggregates, the purity of much of the material (98-99% calcium carbonate) has meant the area is important for the supply of the chemical industries of Lancashire and Cheshire and the steel industry of Sheffield. The largest quarry in the area, Tunstead near Buxton and adjacent to the Park, is owned by the chief British manufacturer of chemicals, ICI. This quarry produces over 5 million tonnes of material a year primarily for ammonia-soda works in mid-Cheshire. However, of this total output some 200 000 tonnes is sold as coated roadstone, whilst its associated on-site cement works is also a major consumer of the quarried output. Reserves are estimated at 125 million tonnes. Two other workings are also associated with cement manufacture, at Hope and Cauldon and although not on the scale of Tunstead, output at each is over 1 million tonnes a year and both have very substantial reserves. Those at Cauldon will last 65 years at current production rates. Quarrying in the area of Middleton by Wirksworth specialises in the production of pure limestone for the extraction of magnesium used in making light alloy metals.

The North Pennines area is centred on the Craven District of the Dales National Park (Figure 3). Again chemical limestone is a key feature with lime works at the two largest quarries, Beecroft in Ribblesdale (owned by ICI) and Swinden near Threshfield. There are two other chemical grade quarries but all of them, along with other workings in the area, produce some aggregate materials mainly for the Leeds-Bradford conurbation. Chemical limestone which has been converted to lime travels as far as Teesside, Consett and Liverpool. Although the average quarry output is smaller here (even the largest produces under 1 million tonnes a year),

227

Figure 2
LIMESTONE QUARRIES IN AND ADJACENT TO THE PEAK DISTRICT NATIONAL PARK

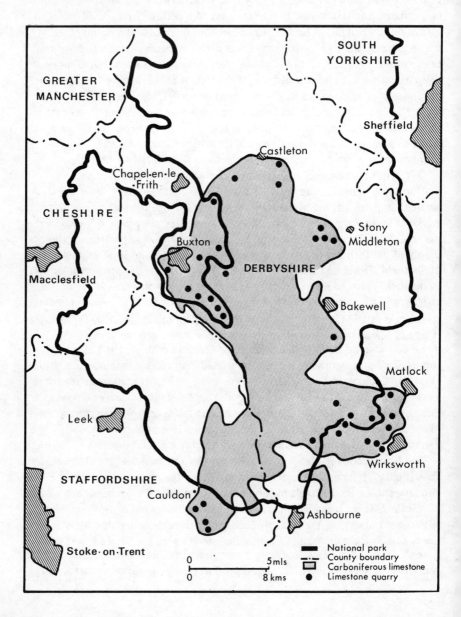

SOUTH YORKSHIRE

GREATER MANCHESTER

Sheffield

Castleton

Chapel-en-le-Frith

CHESHIRE

Buxton

Stony Middleton

DERBYSHIRE

Macclesfield

Bakewell

Matlock

Leek

Wirksworth

STAFFORDSHIRE

Cauldon

Ashbourne

Stoke-on-Trent

| 0 | | 5mls |
| 0 | | 8 kms |

━━━ National park
─·─·─ County boundary
▨ Carboniferous limestone
● Limestone quarry

Figure 3
QUARRIES IN AND ADJACENT TO THE YORKSHIRE DALES
NATIONAL PARK

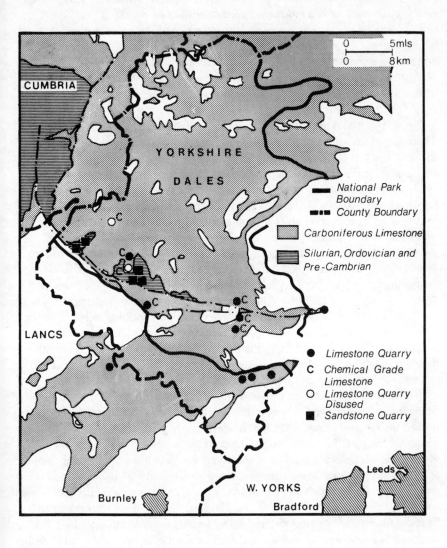

229

reserves are substantial enough for the remainder of the century with the exception of the more limited operations east of Skipton.

The third major production area is that of South Wales and is located primarily inside the Brecon Beacons National Park or just across its boundary. This particular zone is characterised by a much less spectacular increase in output over recent years compared with the Pennines mainly as a result of the lower levels of demand for aggregate and the fact that whilst the purest forms of limestone supply the iron and steel industry of South Wales, this has not been a growing market. Thus of the four major quarries (out of a total of seven), one of which is owned by the British Steel Corporation, production in no instance exceeds half a million tonnes a year and all have ample future reserves.

Figure 1 indicates the other production areas in Britain. Certainly of these, the limestones of Clywd are of greatest importance, supplying both the aggregates and chemical markets of Lancashire and Cheshire. Least significant of all the deposits are those of Scotland, producing only about 3% of total British upland output in 1974, which amounted to 66% of all our limestone supplies. There, more than anywhere else, deposits are worked to supply the need for agricultural lime.

All of these production areas are coincident with locations valued for their scenery and in the majority of instances lie within National Parks. They may, therefore, be said to pose some amenity problems which either constrain current extractive activities or are likely to do so in the future, irrespective of the availability of susbtantial reserves. Even the Peak Park boundary which was deliberately drawn in 1950 to exclude the then major complexes, particularly of the Buxton area, has within it a considerable number of workings, most of which have increased their output markedly in recent years. In the South Wales area, six out of the seven quarries are in the Brecon Beacons National Park, whilst the four worked sources of limestone in the Lake District fall in just those areas of greatest conflict with amenity.

The most obvious problem caused by limestone extraction is its impact on the landscape and the changes in topography which result. Some extraction may even involve the removal of entire small hills, leaving only grassed-over stumps, although modern planning stipulations usually insist on the preservation of hill profiles. Many more workings are bluff (perpendicular) sites which it would be impossible to restore. In the Peak District many quarries are sited on high slopes such as the outer bluffs of limestone outcrops and the sides of the dales, particularly prominent and attractive features of the landscape. The great bulk of these workings cannot be restored; even where pits exist and filling would be technically possible, their location is in rural areas remote from the vast quantities of fill required. The main hope of ameliorating the impact of worked-out areas in the majority of quarries lies in the natural mellowing of the face. This, in the Carboniferous limestones to which we have been referring, occurs in 3 to 4 years. However, the limestone does not begin to weather substantially until after 20 to 30 years.

But of more significance is the question of mitigating the impact of active quarries, most of which now have working lives of some 30 years and some working lives of more than 60 years. Certainly the association of active quarrying with large processing complexes does constitute an undeniable intrusion in otherwise rural surroundings.

The problem of the visual impact of machinery at limestone quarries is a serious and in some respects a growing one. The increase in numbers of very large quarries does have the merit of permitting the closure of more smaller works elsewhere — the expansion at Tunstead has permitted the closure of 17 of ICI's smaller quarries — but these larger workings are correspondingly much more difficult to screen. A large quarry supplying aggregates is likely to have an on-site complex of crushing, asphalt, concrete batching and mixing plants. A modern, high output lime burning kiln will probably be nearly 31 m high. A modern cement works may contain a large kiln complex, preheater tower and chimney, limestone crushers, clinker stores, cement silos, laboratory and control rooms. The growing size and complexity of plant of all types may be partially offset by the improvements in landscaping techniques, especially if tree planting, the construction of banks on which these may grow and other screening operations are carried out in advance. The optimum choice of site from both an economic and environmental point of view is, however, only possible in the very rare case of an entirely new quarry; in most instances new plant is added to an existing site where scope for concealment or landscaping can be limited.

The problems associated with the day-to-day working of limestone quarries are common to all types of hard rock extraction, and are primarily noise, vibration, dust and traffic generation. One reason why some of these problems appear to have increased recently is that, apart from the greater consciousness of such questions, more people are living in close proximity to quarries as commuter villages in rural areas are expanded. The most frequent cause of complaint, as far as local residents are concerned, is the noise and vibration of explosive charges which, apart from disturbance, may very occasionally result in ground movements and even damage to property. From the planning authorities point of view, these levels are difficult to control or alter.

More continuous noise is generally the product of plant operations and internal transport within the quarry. Plant noise may be substantially reduced by the installation of proper cladding on equipment. In the case of recent quarries, planning stipulations may be imposed on plant noise, but the enforcement of specific standards is not easy as sound levels are difficult to monitor, especially where differences between day and night are concerned.

The hard rock quarrying industry, and in particular limestone, is one of the largest producers of dust in the country. Dust may be produced at the workface, by the crushers, drying plant, screens and elevators, by stockpiles and by dumpers operating on unmetalled internal roads. The trend towards finer and finer crushing requirements in the 1960's involved a steadily increasing production of dust, which took the industry unawares and brought considerable operational and public relations difficulties. Large crushers, dealing with about 1 000 tonnes of material an hour, can create clouds of dust visible for miles, which may settle heavily on fields and trees close to the quarry and be carried in small quantities as far as about 1 000 m by the prevailing winds. With efficient modern dust suppression equipment at all points in the processing cycle, it is possible to reduce this nuisance. Very substantial improvements can be brought about by such measures as metalling internal roads, washing wheels, covering stockpiles of all but the coarsest material and sheeting lorries. Recently standards have improved as a result of the concerted efforts of some local authorities and by the Alkali Inspectorate, but complaints about high dust levels continue. These may result from the overloading or imperfect maintenance of dust suppressors at modern quarries or from lack of adequate facilities at older units which may pre-date effective planning controls.

Certainly, although the disturbance caused by quarrying operations in terms of noise, dust and visual intrusion can be greatly reduced by careful planning stipulations or the voluntary efforts of the extractor, many current workings do, in fact, date from a period when planning constraints were few. In the Peak Park a number of limestone quarries still operate under permissions granted during the 1950's which, in the main, only contained conditions about waste disposal, not the most serious problem. In some cases backfilling was required on completion of the workings but nothing was done to mitigate impact during a very long working life. Because of the long-term permissions granted at that time, the Planning Board, which does impose controls, has only had occasion to approve comparatively minor extensions to workings.

The problems of traffic generation cannot readily be eased by the planning stipulations even where they apply. The bulk of movements in and out of quarries are by road and involve increasingly large capacity lorries. The development of fewer, larger quarries inevitably creates heightened congestion in some localities. There is, in addition, a heavy inward traffic of lorries carrying bitumen and other coatings, and cement, to the aggregate quarries. The chief problem in the Peak District and elsewhere is created by the concentration of heavy traffic on roads which are unsuitable by reason of their width, gradient, or route through settlements. Some planning consents stipulate the use of specific approach roads and attempt to steer traffic away from unsuitable routes, but the scope for this is clearly limited. Significant long-term improvements can only result from the creation of new road links or the improvement of existing ones to serve quarry traffic, or if widening market radii and technical improvements encourage a more extensive use of rail transport, or if a new transport mode becomes viable.

All of these environmental problems must be entirely inimical to the use of such areas for recreational and other outdoor pursuits, a point which the conservationist lobby vociferously continues to make. The question of how far they can be reasonably tolerated or ameliorated in the longer term has been exercising the minds of planning authorities in the main production areas described. All three have based their response upon the supposition that there may well be a six-fold increase in the demands for aggregate materials by the year 2000 (though in the light of recent performance of the British economy this seems a considerable overestimate); all three have reacted differently in terms of articulating a future policy.

In the Brecon Beacons area a report from the Welsh Office recommended a dimunition in the overall impact of quarrying and the disturbance caused by it through future concentration on the development of just three of the four major quarries already mentioned to meet total demands on the area up to the year 2000; the rest would be shut down. One of these proposed giant quarries located outside the National Park currently produces only aggregate, whilst of the other two within its boundaries, one again concentrates on aggregate whilst the other is the British Steel Corporation holding. The report also suggested that a large 1 250 million tonne reserve of oolite limestone of high purity suitable for the steel industry might be economically mined with a view to further diminishing surface environmental impact in the longer term.

In the case of the Dales National Park, the policy articulated is again a pragmatic response. In its attempt to diminish the environmental impact of quarrying, it proposes to steer future expansion to those areas with large quarriable reserves of all the appropriate grades of stone but which are in locations of least environmental merit. In this respect it has already identified such sites in areas such as Ribblesdale. The planning authority have certainly rejected the notion of attempting to force quarrying out of the Park on the grounds that it would lead to abnormal pressure on areas immediately beyond its boundaries which are also of great scenic value. What their proposals describe as the "improper philosophy of attempting to off-load a minerals problem onto another authority" is just the one the Peak Park Planning Board is embracing.

As a result of pressure on their planning area, the Peak Board would like to see as much limestone extraction as possible carried out beyond the Park and have suggested the phasing out of all present workings. Indeed, they have resisted an attempt by ICI to engage in long term planning when the company recently proposed a new quarry at Old Moor to replace Tunstead at the end of the century. 81 of the 121 ha needed would have been in the National Park and it was ICI's purpose to establish the relevant landscaping work in the immediate future so that tree screens, etc., would have matured by the time quarrying commenced. Whilst the problems of this Planning Board are extreme in that they have to contend with visitor pressure from the conurbations of Manchester and Sheffield, as well as the difficulties caused by fluorspar and limestone working, their policy, if carried through, could have major repercussions on the availability of limestone in that area of Northern England unless adequate extractive sites could be developed in the remaining limestone areas surrounding the Peak Park. But here again such a policy would merely export their problem to the planning authorities of Derbyshire and Staffordshire County Councils.

Sandstone

The term 'sandstone' at its broadest denotes rocks consisting largely of quartz sand, welded into solid form. Such rocks, which are normally of sedimentary type, differ widely in chemical composition, particle size and shape, degree of compaction and the geological period of their formation. Sandstones, from a variety of geological epochs, occur extensively throughout the stratified rocks of upland Britain. The main deposits, in chronological order of formation, are as follows. First, the numerous gritstones and quartzites of the Pre-Cambrian deposits to be found notably on the Welsh border, in a small part of Yorkshire and in North-West Scotland. Then Cambrian sandstone, mainly quartzites, which are met with on the Welsh border, and other Lower Palaeozoic sandstones which occur in Mid- and North Wales, the Lake District and the Southern Uplands of Scotland. Sandstones in the Devonian series appear as Old Red Sandstones on the Welsh border, in the Brecon Beacons, and adjacent to the Central Lowlands of Scotland. Old Red Sandstones also extend along the eastern border of the Highlands from north Aberdeenshire to Caithness and recur in the Orkneys. The most abundant source of sandstone is the Carboniferous system. Sandstones in this system (which include the widespread Millstone Grit) are found in South Wales, Lancashire, Derbyshire, Yorkshire, Durham and Northumberland.

In 1974 the upland areas supplied 70% of the sandstones worked in Britain, an increase of 6% on 1967 (Figure 4). The aggregates market is now the major consumer of sandstones and in 1974 accounted for just about 66% of their sales. Their commercial viability for this use inevitably depends on the properties of the various deposits. Hard types with high crushing strengths are used for concrete aggregates, railway ballast and roadworks, whilst poorer grades are used as hardcore or fill. But wide variations in the chemical specification and physical properties of sandstone make limestone, which in any case has a wider range of

Figure 4
SANDSTONE PRODUCTION IN UPLAND BRITAIN 1967 AND 1974

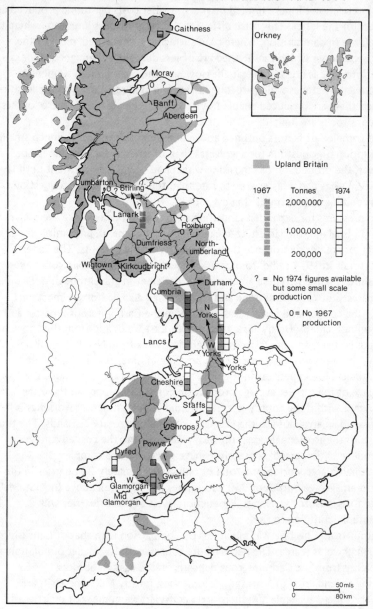

applications, preferred at those locations where both are equally available. As sandstone quarries have on average an output of 48% less than those of limestone (itself a reflection of more limited markets), higher costs per tonne produced are incurred for the latter. This price differential further favours limestone where the minerals are in competition. Where road surfacing is concerned, most of the harder sandstones which can be used are of less durability than igneous rocks, whilst limestone is not suitable at all. However, there are limited supplies of high quality gritstones which are long lasting and skid resistant, and the locations at which these are produced enable them to compete in markets where sources of igneous rocks are limited.

The complex of factors outlined above does help to explain the much smaller consumption of sandstone for aggregates than of igneous rocks or limestone. However, the production of sandstone which had been fairly constant until the early 1960's has had a faster growth rate than the other minerals in question over the last decade with output rising by 230%.

The pressures for expanded sandstone output continue to make themselves felt mainly in England, the largest aggregates market. In general, proximity to markets has been of greater significance than the quality of the deposits. The largest upland totals in 1974 came from areas adjacent to the large urban complexes of Lancashire (Figure 4). These areas are very deficient in gravel though not sand. The nearest sources of limestone and igneous rock also lie, for the most part, outside the county; the former is derived from the Carboniferous limestone of the Pennines, chiefly Derbyshire, from North-East Wales and from the fringe of the Lake District, and the latter is brought in by sea from North-West Wales. Clearly, the transport costs involved in bringing in limestone and sand and gravel, the chief competitors in the bulk aggregates market, cancel out the advantage of their lower average production costs. Sandstone, on the other hand, is abundant within the county itself. The chief concentration of workings is in the Rossendale area close to the markets with high aggregate demands. The thick deposits of the Rossendale area, the heavy demand and the cost advantages of sandstone over 'imported' competitors have given rise to a complex of exceptionally large workings: a total of only approximately 27 quarries in the area had an average output of 250 000 tonnes in 1970, well above the national average for sandstone workings. Production levels at these quarries will undoubtedly continue to rise.

Output from Cheshire was much less by comparison with that of Lancashire, although gravel is scarce. The needs of the county with its smaller population are met mainly from the Carboniferous deposits on the eastern borders.

In the upland areas of Yorkshire, sandstones, mostly Millstone Grit, are relatively widely available and there are a considerable number of quarries of small size, largely producing poor quality materials for road bases, especially in North Yorkshire. Only the quarries working Pre-Cambrian materials (Ingletonian 'granite') produced a high quality wearing course aggregate (Figure 3) with output in 1974 running at three quarters of a million tonnes.

Derbyshire, which also has extensive areas of Millstone Grit, had only modest quantities of this material won in 1974. The presence of extensive limestone deposits in the county is probably the main reason for its low sandstone output. The 13 quarries in Derbyshire, mainly small units, are chiefly in the Matlock district.

Output of sandstone from upland Wales is small by English standards in spite of an absence of sand and gravel. Production levels have tended to reflect the abundance of limestone in the south and in Clywd, the low aggregate demands of much of the country and the poor quality of many of the Welsh sandstones. Only in Mid-Wales, where alternatives are particularly lacking, are these inferior sandstones worked for ballast and fill. Production figures in South Wales are boosted by the winning of the Pennant sandstones north west of Newport. As a valuable source of wearing course roadstone, they are not in competition with the nearby limestones.

Sandstone output from upland Scotland totalled only 590 000 tonnes in 1974. In the Central Valley, high levels of aggregate demand were met by the nearby Old Red Sandstones and Carboniferous sandstone deposits, although readily available igneous materials are now becoming more important. There are high quality sandstone deposits in the north of Scotland of Pre-Cambrian origin but these are too remote from major markets to be of importance even as good wearing course material. In the Orkneys, composed almost entirely of sandstone, this material has necessarily to provide most of the stone for the islands' roads and of the 13 quarries worked there in 1974, 11 were retained by the local authorities.

The environmental problems that increasingly impose themselves on limestone working and may well constrain its future availability are considerably less in the case of sandstone. Whilst any hard rock quarry operation has its attendant impact on the landscape, the production of sandstone not only takes place in areas outside National Parks, but at workings which are still much smaller in scale and thereby have less impact on the landscape. Moreover, whilst sandstone quarries consume a similar amount of land per tonne worked to limestone, the overall land take is less. Traffic generation on steep, narrow country roads around a quarry remains a difficulty but the environmental nuisance caused by dust at limestone quarries is very much less at sandstone workings. However, if recent growth rates for sandstone are sustained, some environmental problems will increase in those areas, like Rossendale, where markets are close at hand and alternative materials in short supply.

Igneous and Metamorphic Rocks

An igneous rock is any rock which has formed from molten magma or lava. Metamorphic rocks which are, with the notable exception of slate, grouped with igneous rocks in the official statistics of production, are rocks whose appearance, mineral composition or sometimes chemical composition have been changed by intense heat or pressure or both.

In Britain, igneous and metamorphic rocks are really less dispersed than either limestone or sandstone and are heavily concentrated in the upland zones of North and West Britain. Like sandstone, they date from a variety of geological periods. The chief deposits can be considered in descending order of age. Thus, starting with the Pre-Cambrian metamophic rocks, these occur mainly in North-West Scotland, and cover the larger part of the Scottish Highlands. In upland England and Wales, Pre-Cambrian metamorphic rocks occur only in Shropshire. During the Ordovician period, lavas or sub-volcanic intrusive sheets were emitted in the Lake District and in Wales (particularly the Snowdon region). The Devonian period was an active period of igneous rock formation; volcanic lavas were emitted in Devon and Cornwall and in Scotland (Lorne, Glen Coe, Ben Nevis, Ochil and Sidlaw Hills, Cheviot Hills). Intrusive rocks of this period were formed in Scotland (Glen Coe and Ballachulish, the Eastern Highlands between Aberdeen, Peterhead and Inverness and the South-West Scottish Uplands) and the Lake District (the Ennerdale and Eskdale granites, the Skiddaw granite, the Threlkeld microgranite and the Shap granite). In the Upper Carboniferous/Permian period, igneous activity resulted mainly in the intrusive granite masses of Bodmin Moor and Dartmoor. During the early Tertiary period, the last geological epoch of igneous activity, isolated lavas were extruded in North-West Scotland (Skye, Canna, Rum, Eigg, Ardnamurchan, Mull and Arran). Igneous activity ended with the formation of basaltic dykes, present from Mull to Yorkshire.

Amongst the economic usages of igneous and metamorphic rocks, the aggregates market is of supreme importance. In 1974, well over 90% of sales (by tonnage) of the larger extractive enterprises consisted of aggregate material. Although igneous and metamorphic rocks can provide useful wearing course material for roads, their higher costs of extraction and processing than competing hard rock materials and their relative remoteness from areas where they are needed in quantity has so far largely precluded the development of upland Britain's resources of these materials to do more than meet localised markets. Some of these markets are quite small. Indeed the higher production costs also mean that it is only where there are plentiful supplies of igneous and metamorphic rocks and therefore little need to transport them far, and few if any competing materials, that they come into their own. Their primacy as a general aggregate material for ballast, fill, hardcore and concrete manufacture over much of

Scotland is, therefore, hardly surprising; nor, given these circumstances, is the small size of most of the quarries with an average output in Scotland of around 65 000 tonnes per year.

The only area to be distinguished from the above generalisation in the Highland zone is Aberdeenshire (Figure 5). This has the highest density of population of any county outside the Lowlands and has recently been rapidly developing on-shore facilities for North Sea Oil. (The rapid expansion in the output of the eleven Shetland quarries working igneous rocks is again due to the need to provide land-based facilities for this new development.) The only other counties with high levels of output are those adjacent to the Central Valley. Here, larger quarries producing about 90 000 tonnes per annum exist in the Pentland Hills and the relic plateau lavas of the Clyde area. Production falls away in the more distant parts of the Southern Uplands and the Border region. The Cheviots are only worked on the southern side where the material comes within the market radius of the populous Tyneside area. But in the southern areas of Scotland, as in the greater part of the Highlands, population levels are low and quarries serve small limited markets.

The question of distance from centres of demand is again a strong determining factor regarding the exploitation of igneous and metamorphic rocks in Wales though here the availability of alternative aggregate supplies is also pertinent. Thus whilst upland reserves are at least as large as those in the whole of England, which includes the highly productive deposits of Cornwall and Leicestershire as well as those of upland areas, they are little exploited with output totalling only 2.5 million tonnes in 1974. The South Wales markets, for example, are mainly satisfied by the more cheaply won and more versatile limestones to be found adjacent to the area and are therefore not served by the extensive but distant and relatively inaccessible Gwynedd igneous deposits. The quarries of the interior of that county are therefore small and meet local needs. Only at coastally located quarries, formerly exporting stone by sea and now using mostly the good rail and road communications, has there been an achievement of anything more than local sales. The quarries of the Lleyn Peninsula, particularly those of the north coast, together with Penmaenmawr, between Bangor and Conway, serve markets in Cheshire, Lancashire, Merseyside and Greater Manchester which suffer from a scarcity of hard rocks (except sandstone) and gravel. But the low level of growth in output of the coastal quarries of Gwynedd (Figure 5) is indicative of increasing competition in these markets from the large capital intensive quarries of the Peak District and North-East Wales and the expansion of the Rossendale sandstone workings.

Resistance from environmentalists to igneous rock quarrying in upland areas of Britain has, on the whole, been muted in spite of their occurrence primarily in areas of outstanding landscape valued for recreation purposes, some of which are

Figure 5
IGNEOUS ROCK PRODUCTION IN UPLAND BRITAIN 1967 AND 1974

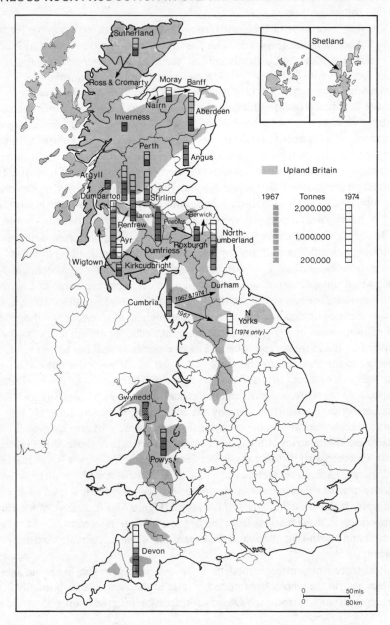

in National Parks, and in spite of the fact that quarrying technologies are similar to those deployed for the working of other hard rocks. The reasons for this are two-fold. First, quarry size is much smaller than those generally producing other aggregate materials and their occurrence relatively scattered. Secondly, quarry faces, once disused, are rapidly assimilated into the scenery and according to many Scottish planning departments soon become a not unacceptable feature of the landscape. Unless production is expanded quite considerably, it is unlikely that igneous and metamorphic rock quarries will become an environmental problem. Since their locations are generally characterised by their remoteness and by processing costs which are greater than those for alternative materials, such an expansion is not to be expected. Only the achievement of economies of scale resulting from the operation of a super quarry (over 10 million tonnes a year) and the transport of materials from that location to distant but major markets by a low cost means could change the situation.

Slate

The term 'slate' refers to fine-grained, compact rocks with the property of cleavage. The process of metamorphosis which the material has undergone has rendered it highly resistant to weathering and this characteristic, together with its fissility, gives the material its economic importance.

Three of the principal areas of upland Britain where slate has been formed are North Wales, the Lake District and the Grampian Mountains of Scotland. In Wales the chief areas are in Northern Gwynedd, which contains slates of Cambrian age, and in the Tremadoc/Blaenau Ffestiniog/Betws-y-coed area, and the Corwen/Corris area, which both contain slates of the Ordovician and Silurian ages. All these deposits form part of the old mountain chain known as the Caledonides, another fragment of which appears in the Lake District. There, slates occur in each of the three main geological bands extending south-west/north-east across the area. The oldest of these bands contains the Skiddaw 'slates', which are poorly cleaved and are only used locally for building and walling. To the south is the Borrowdale Volcanic series, forming the highest hills in the Lake District. This series contains the Lancashire green slate of Ordovician age, varying in colour from light and dark green to purple green and consisting of metamorphosed volcanic ash. Further south still lies a Silurian formation which contains the Bannisdale slates. In Scotland slate occurs among the metamorphic rocks of the Dalradian series but extraction is now limited to very small quarries in the Easdale slates which occur in a belt extending south-westwards from Oban in Argyllshire. Although slate production has everywhere declined from its high point in the late 19th century (as was mentioned in the first section), it is particularly striking in Scotland. In 1880 the Scottish industry employed 1500 men and produced over

50 000 tonnes. The decline has also been especially marked in North Wales where, by 1974, output was reduced to a twenty-fourth of its peak figure (Figure 7). Indeed, in upland Britain as a whole in that year, output of cut slate was only 38 000 tonnes, though in addition there was also a considerable production of high bulk/low value slate powders and granules.

The slate industry, even in its most modern and capital intensive form uses a good deal of labour. The degree of mechanisation and improvement in productivity achieved at other types of hard rock quarries has consequently not been possible in the slate industry. Output per wage-earner (by tonnes) at slate quarries went up by over 140% in the period 1950-74, while output per wage-earner at limestone quarries went up by over 390%. The high cost of the skilled labour needed, for instance, in splitting slabs of slate from the quarried blocks, a process which has defied mechanisation, has been a major factor in the very large price increase of the product. These rapid increases over the past two decades, added to the costs of transporting the material to markets from the generally remote deposits, has reduced sales in the housing market. Slates needed for the maintenance of existing buildings now constitute a larger percentage of the roofing market than those for new houses.

Somewhat different factors are operative in certain speciality markets, where slate as an architectural feature can be sold essentially on its special qualities of colour, pattern and texture, rather than on price. Demand for slate for wall cladding and facing, flooring and paving was growing in the 1960's, especially for use in public buildings, large commercial buildings such as banks, and for the small number of individual, high budget private houses. A notable part of this demand comes from overseas markets, mainly in Western Europe and the United States. Indeed, slate exports which in 1974 totalled around 19 000 tonnes consisted largely of such speciality products. One firm in the Lake District which has concentrated heavily on this type of slate has achieved an export figure as high as 50% of total production. In doing so it has increased its work force from 15 in 1968 to over 50 in 1976, though this should not be allowed to obscure the fact that the operation is a capital intensive one. Only very recently has the largest of the five slate quarries still active in Gwynedd begun to interest itself in architectural slate and this as a result of being taken over by a large combine and a large injection of capital. Whilst the production of this form of slate is increasing at this quarry (Penrhyn) it has to be said that the characteristics of the green slates of Cumbria make them better suited to the architectural market and opportunities for other Welsh quarries to get into this type of output are not great. However, the high value of architectural slate compared with most other building materials (up to £90 a tonne) means that the product can bear transport costs to the west coast of the USA or to markets as distant as Australia. In the period 1967 to 1974, there has been a 300% rise in output from Cumbria (Figure 7), largely as a result of rising demand for this product and further market growth is confidently predicted for the late-1970's and 1980's.

Another growing market is that of slate powders or granules, prepared by crushing and screening of selected material previously rejected as waste. Crushed slate is being used increasingly for surfacing asphaltic roofing felts, for inert fillers in a variety of products such as bitumen and bitumen compounds, coal-tar-based coating materials, insecticides, thermal insulation, polyester resins, pipeline coatings, motor car underseal, paints and plastics and as a filler for concrete blocks. Crushed slate constituted much the largest part of the tonnage from several large slate quarries in 1974; one of these had increased output of powder and granules by near 400% since 1964. However, slate for many of these applications competes with other mineral products and current usage depends to a large extent on its comparative cheapness. Consequently, the value of slate powders and granules is very much lower than that of cut slate.

The main environmental problem created by slate workings is derived from the need to dump waste material. The waste to cut slate ratio is estimated to range between 20:1 and 50:1 and in spite of the vigorous programme to sell this residue as powder and granules, quarries only dispose of a limited amount. Currently Penrhyn only gets rid of a tenth of its waste in this way. But the real difficulty in North Wales derives not so much from the present limited production levels but from the enormous back-log of waste produced in times of greater prosperity when land dereliction from dumping was created on a substantial scale. The worst area, Balenau Ffestiniog, was deliberately omitted from the Snowdonia National Park when it was set up for this reason. More recently, as a result of environmentalist pressures, some attempt has been made to vegetate these tips, but this is slow and difficult. Only the current low levels of Welsh slate production and prospects of only limited growth, together with the efforts being made to increase slate powder sales, prevent the waste problem from becoming a contentious one. Fortunately, in the Lake District the industry has always been on a limited scale and is only now undergoing rapid expansion. However waste output is at the lower end of the scale and with some sales of powder, dumping, even in the National Park, is unlikely to become an issue providing tips are first screened and then later graded and vegetated.

China Clay

It is the question of waste disposal adjacent to and in a National Park that has been the significant factor affecting the development of china clay workings. This mineral, a kaolinized granite originating about 290 million years ago, is produced from two areas of Britain: in Cornwall near St. Austell and at Lee Moor on the edge of the upland area of Dartmoor.

The deposit with which we are concerned only produced 19% of total output in 1974 (Figure 7) but is of high quality and is used in paper making and coating and in the making of pottery. With world wide deposits limited and best grades fetching £44-50 a tonne, this commodity is a major export earner. Unfortunately the working of the clay also necessitates the removal from the quarry sites of large quantities of quartz sand with which it is intermixed. As the ratio of quartz, largely a waste product, to china clay is about 8:1 at Lee Moor, the problem of disposal is not inconsiderable. Thus a planning application in 1971 to work the rest of the reserves of the area, estimated at 26 million tonnes, also made it clear that a further 328 ha, in addition to the present sites, would be needed to dump 200 million tonnes of quartz sand; 106 ha of this would be in the National Park.

Not surprisingly, these proposals were vigorously resisted by amenity bodies on the grounds of irreparable damage to part of the landscape of Dartmoor. It was certainly the balance of payment advantages to working this deposit, plus the fact that 1 000 male jobs were immediately at stake in the area, that led the Secretary of State for the Environment, after a planning enquiry, to recommend in favour of the mineral operator. The operation, though, was to be curtailed to the extent that the tipping areas were reduced where their impact on the environment would be greatest, and the rehabilitation of tips through grading and vegetation made obligatory, whilst it was implied that greater efforts should be made to use the waste material as concreting sand, building sand, and for brick making and fill.

The utilisation of the quartz locally, however, is constrained by a lack of coarse aggregate to supply with it, and by the fact that particle shape and mica content raise the amount of cement needed per unit of quartz in the manufacture of concrete. In terms of its wider use, transport costs limit market radii to 32-42 km. Currently, the difference between the price for sand produced in the South-East of England and that delivered to this area from Lee Moor sources is £3-4 a tonne, otherwise the latter could undoubtedly contribute to the growing short fall of such material in the most populous part of Britain.

Whether quartz sand does find its way to the South East will depend on two factors. First, there is the possibility that a cheaper alternative form of transport will become available. Secondly, the speed with which the problems of meeting rising demands in the region become acute will also be a determinant. Certainly it is likely that as old consents for sand and gravel run out they will not be renewed, either because locally-won resources are not available or their working will cause too many difficulties in a largely urbanised area.

Fluorspar; Barytes; Lead and Zinc Ores

Fluorspar, like china clay, is worked within a world market context. Its production growth rate is one of the fastest of any of the minerals found in upland Britain (Figure 6). World consumption, which is allied to the growing requirements of the steel, aluminium and fluorine chemical industries, has been increasing rapidly for a number of reasons. First of all, the change over to the basic oxygen method of making steel, which accounted for 30% of world output in 1970 and is expected to account for 75-80% by 1985, is already vastly enhancing demand. This requires 4.5-6.7 kg of fluorspar per tonne of steel compared with 3.6-4.5 kg for the electric furnace and 1.3-2.2 kg for the open hearth methods. At the same time the need for hydrofluoric acid in the fluorocarbon and aluminium industries is growing. Although the requirement per tonne of aluminium smelted has fallen, the output of the metal has been rising in the 1970's at a compound annual rate of 9%. In the fluorocarbon industry, which supplies the makers of refrigerators, aerosols and methane foams, growth has been around 8% through the 1970's.

Overall estimates of increased world consumption of fluorspar in the period 1969/1975 have been in the region 60-70%, figures which tie in well with the increased British production. Levels of home production should also be seen in the light of increased steel output at Port Talbot and Scunthorpe and a progressive change to the basic oxygen process, the construction of three new aluminium smelters at Tynemouth, Holyhead and Invergordon, and increased demands (20% a year) from the fluorine chemical manufacturers, especially ICI.

Fluorspar obtained from fluorite is found in veins in the Carboniferous limestone in two main fields in the Pennines and is frequently associated with galena (sulphide of lead), blende (sulphide of zinc) and barite. The Southern Pennines orefield, the main centre of fluorspar production in Britain, stretches from Castleton in the north through Bakewell, Darley and Matlock as far as Wirksworth. Fluorspar production comes from two main districts, one centred on Eyam at the northern end and the other around Matlock to the south. Output is mainly associated with the chemical and steel industries of nearby Sheffield.

The Northern Pennine orefield also falls into two main districts. The more important northern district extends from west Durham into south Northumberland and east Cumbria, from the headwaters of the Derwent at Hunstanworth southwards to Teesdale. The crude ore is usually higher grade than that of the Southern Pennines although silica impurities are greater. The deposits in north-west Yorkshire have a leaner fluorite content whilst those on the extreme southern margin are comparable with the Southern Pennine field.

British reserves of economically workable crude ore are conservatively estimated to be 25 million tonnes; 20 million tonnes in the Southern Pennine orefield and the remainder in the Northern Pennine orefield. (The difference between the two fields in terms of fluorite is of course substantially less than these figures

Figure 6
FLUORSPAR, BARYTES, LEAD AND ZINC PRODUCTION 1967 AND 1974

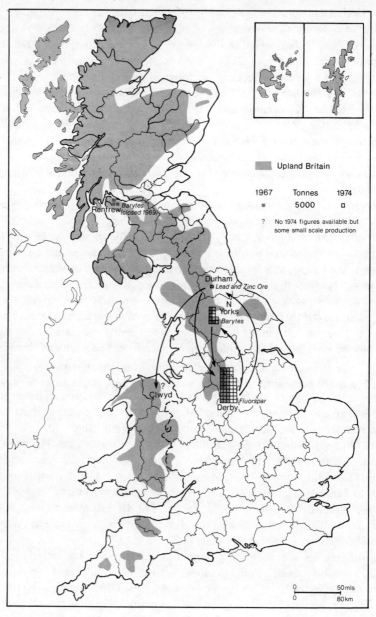

suggest, in view of the higher grade of the northern orefield.) The bulk of these reserves are unproven, and probably proved ore amounts to only 5 million tonnes. Further workable reserves may well be found, especially at deeper levels, since the amount of detailed information relating to deposits is in most cases incomplete, and exploration has been relatively superficial by world mining standards.

Although the areas concerned have a long mining history in terms of lead, fluorspar production has only reached major proportions in the 20th century, particularly since 1960. The expansion of output during that decade was largely due to increased production in Derbyshire from the operations of Laporte Industries Ltd., whose Cavendish mill and mining operations contributed more than 60% of total British output in 1970 when an expansion programme at the mill was completed. Laporte Industries Ltd., has extensive holdings in the two fluorspar producing regions in Derbyshire but its main operations are located in the northern one. The original focus of activities in this area was the Glebe mine at Eyam, formerly worked for lead.

Laporte's mining operations now centre on the Ladywash working to the north and a new project, the Sallet Hole mine, which exploits the extensive deposits of Longstone Edge to the south of Eyam, described as "one of the world's largest and most spectacular deposits". The company also holds a number of properties in the southern fluorspar-producing district around Matlock and has negotiated a number of long-term contracts for material to be supplied by tributers. 'Tributers' is the term applied to individuals or small companies extracting the material mainly from dumps which they own or lease in the area.

The Cavendish mill, completed in 1965, removes both galena and barytes as well as fluorite from the ore. Barytes (Figure 6) is now sold mainly as a filter cake, whilst the lead concentrates (Figure 6) are shipped to smelters on the continent of Europe. In 1974 Laporte produced over 90% of British fluorspar used for making hydrofluoric acid as well as exporting about 50 000 tonnes of acid grade fluorspar to the USA, Japan, Canada, Australia and a number of western European countries. Clearly the price of acid grade fluorspar (now £40-55 per tonne) means that it can be economically transported to world markets. Laporte operations are now expanding in view of home and export demand; their widespread holdings and contacts with tributers place them in a strong position for an extended period of production and expansion.

The first significant addition to British fluorspar processing plant in recent years has been the new 8 000 tonnes per year capacity mill of the C E Guilini Group, Europe's largest producer of acid grade fluorspar. The plant is housed in the Hopton works south-west of Matlock and the Group's interest in Derbyshire is a significant indication of the potential of the area. Its output will add considerably to British output of acid grade fluorspar and should put her in second place behind

Italy as Europe's leading producer. By-product barytes, lead and zinc concentrates mainly for export are produced at Hopton, the first by-product zinc to be obtained from fluorspar operations in Britain (Figure 6).

Supplies to the Guilini mill should be enhanced by expanded output from two medium sized companies. Deepwood Mining, a company who produced about 30 500 tonnes a year from four deposits near Bakewell during the early 1970's has discovered a new deposit of significant size with a high percentage of fluorite in addition to barite and lead. Spar Mining Ltd. is a new company formed to work veins near Matlock.

Major expansion of output is also taking place in the less important Northern Pennine orefield. The three main extractive operations, one controlled by ICI and two by the British Steel Corporation, are concentrated in the area between Weardale and the River Derwent in the northern district of the field. ICI, the largest operator, produced over 20 000 tonnes a year in the early 1970's (two thirds acid grade and one third metallurgical), with lead concentrates as a by-product. The company operates a processing plant at Rookhope, north of Weardale and this is now fed by a new mine on a virgin section of the vein between Stotfieldburn and the Groverake mine.

The major expansion in the Northern Pennines is that of BSC properties where metallurgical fluorspar is being produced to meet their annual demands which are estimated to be well over 100 000 tonnes by the end of 1977.

The general steels division at Scunthorpe is developing old lead mines including Blackdene which, according to the Geological Survey, "probably contains substantial reserves of fluorspar both in ground previously worked for lead ore and also in virgin ground beneath Blackdene level".

A few kilometres further north near Blanchard, BSC has a larger operation based on a group of mines including West Whiteheaps, East Whiteheaps and Groverake. In the early-1970's the Whiteheaps mines produced over 11 000 tonnes of fluorspar, mostly metallurgical, whilst the Groverake working produced around 21 000 tonnes. The last named appears capable of considerable expansion.

Slightly west of these mines is the site of the BSC's third and newest operation, the Allenheads mine, now employing 50 men. According to old records the potential of this fluorspar working has hardly been tapped. The Corporation has now completed development and it is hoped that this mine plus those at Blanchard and Blackdene could take output up to over 142 000 tonnes by 1980, a considerable level of expansion to have been achieved in a decade.

Mention has been made of lead, zinc and barytes as by-products of fluorspar production. Of these, only barytes is also worked independently to any extent, but production is now reduced to one mine at Closehouse on the north side of the Lune Valley on the outer edge of the Northern Pennine fluorspar field. This situation is probably a reflection of the contraction of British output in the 1960's of a mineral which is common by world standards and relatively low cost. Certainly many of the British upland workings had by then exhausted their known reserves of quality and the cheapness of foreign imports did not encourage investment in fresh workings. Thus in that decade mines closed in Cumbria, Ayrshire and most recently in Renfrewshire.

However, since on a world scale the barytes industry is largely dependent on the oil and gas well drilling market (notwithstanding its use in the chemical, paint and rubber industries) it is perhaps not surprising that intensive drilling in British waters has brought about some recovery in the home product in the 1970's (Figure 6) from sources adjacent to areas in which it is needed. Indeed the company owning Closehouse is considering opening a neighbouring mine, Lunehead, whilst exploration is taking place in a vein running south west in Cumbria. However, at present the more buoyant home demand seems unlikely to outrun hydrocarbon exploration around British coasts.

Resistance to fluorspar working on environmental grounds has come almost entirely from operations in that part of the Southern Pennine orefield which lies inside the Peak District National Park. This area, it will be recalled, is already under pressure from limestone workings and the needs of the large urban populations adajcent to it. The large number of small operators carrying on surface workings tend to have a cumulative rather than an individual impact but with the ratio of waste to commercial product at 3:1, back-filling of pits is a condition of planning consents and the problem is diminishing. Modern fluorspar workings are, though, mostly underground and since subsidence can be avoided, problems do not arise. However, where the material is processed as at the Cavendish mill, a considerable amount of fine waste is produced (tailings) and its deposition in lagoons in the neighbourhood has been increasingly resisted by the Planning Board.

When Laporte applied to extend their lagoon to around 30 ha in 1969, although they were given short term additional dumping capacity, this plan was rejected in favour of research into alternative schemes. The Board would favour the filtration of the material and its stabilisation using chemical additives to allow it to be dumped into old excavations but believe that its use in concrete manufacture or its pumping by pipeline to a disposal site outside the National Park might be viable alternatives. Laporte believe these wastes to be technically unsuitable and produced in too large quantities to be of value to the local aggregates market, whilst the alternatives accordingly look expensive solutions adding up to 20% to production costs. This problem has yet to be resolved.

Since the Guilini plant lies outside the Park and is discharging into old silica sand pits, environmental difficulties are not produced, but the local authority finds it hard to enforce planning consents on the large number of small surface

249

excavations; it also lacks the advantages of the National Park with its wardens and its influx of middle class newcomers acting as vigilantes.

In the Northern Pennine orefield, although the southern part of it falls inside the Dales National Park, and the rest mainly in an 'Area of Great Landscape Value', the greater incidence of underground extraction, the absence of a very large processing plant, the general remoteness and lack of population pressure, have all tended to lessen environmental problems. Moreoever, the poor employment situation in many parts of this field gives fluorspar extraction an especially high socio-economic value there. Expansion appears to be proceeding unhampered.

Silica Rock and Ganister

These materials, containing at least 97% silica and little alumina or alkaline material, are used to make silica bricks for the iron and steel industry and gas plants. The latter have, of course, been phased out, whilst changing iron and steel technology has reduced demand and this has been the chief factor in recent production decline. Output is likely to eventually stabilise simply because of the needs of coke ovens, but demand is still falling, as Figure 7 indicates.

The decline applies more specifically to silica rock. The Basal Grits of the southern upland area of Wales were a major source of supply of high grade rock (42% of total Welsh output in 1967) and are alleged to contain the greatest known reserves of high grade silica rock in Britain. But in spite of the close proximity of the South Wales steel industry, decline of output has been rapid. In 1970 only six silica quarries were active in the area whilst by 1974 output had fallen to a figure not recorded in the official statistics.

The decline in the relatively small production capacity of South Yorkshire to almost nothing and the closure of the quarries in Stirlingshire (associated in the official statistics with the always very limited output of upland Northumberland) is further symptomatic of this trend.

Although the official statistics do record some output of silica rock from areas bordering on the uplands of the Southern Pennines, amounts are very small and British production is almost entirely centred on a district in the county of Durham. There in the uplands between Teesdale and South Tyne the Millstone Grit and Lower Coal Measures offer supplies of both silica rock and ganister but it is the former which makes up most of the output and is worked using open pit methods. The limited scale of operations offers no particular environmental difficulties and the workings are not constrained in any way.

Silica Sand

Highest quality sands for optical glass and crystal are not widely available in Britain. Using the relatively more ubiquitous Cretaceous Lower Greensand would

Figure 7
SLATE, CHINA CLAY, SILICA ROCK & GANISTER, POTASH, TALC AND DIATOMITE PRODUCTION, 1967 AND 1974

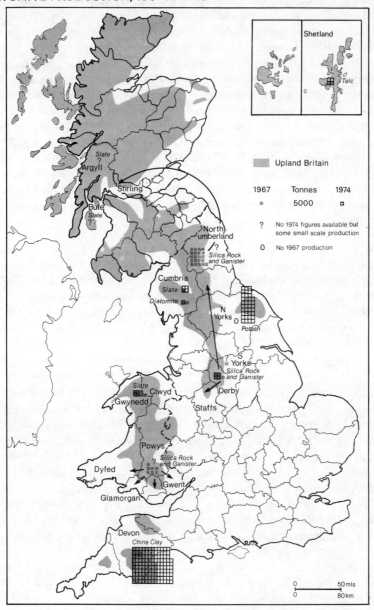

involve the use of expensive and sophisticated benefication techniques. Since the market is in any case small, these costs could not be spread over a large tonnage. Only one British deposit, and that in the upland zone, produces untreated glass sand of the quality needed, the sandstone of Loch Aline in Argyllshire, on the northern coast of the Sound of Mull.

The deposit extends over 32 km and by 1970 output had reached two million tonnes. But in spite of its quality the working suffers from two disadvantages. The occurrence of the mineral, overlaid by Tertiary basalt, necessitates the more costly mining rather than quarrying, using the comparatively wasteful room and pillar method. Although environmentally beneficial, it involves leaving about 40% of the mineral as pillars for support. More serious is the locational disadvantage of the deposit, remote from the main glass manufacturing centres. Although it is shipped to St Helens, Stoke-on-Trent, Stourbridge and Waterford, freight charges are all but comparable with imports from Belgium and Holland where deposits lie adjacent to the canals system. However, there is no doubt that the large Loch Aline reserves will continue to be exploited as Britain's only indigenous quality sand resource.

Potash

Although potash, a valuable chemical fertiliser, was discovered in what is now part of the North York Moors National Park in 1939, it was not until the late 1960's that resumed investigations in the Staithes area came up with a workable deposit that could yield between 0.86 and 1.27 million tonnes a year. Calculations made in 1968 suggested the production of this mineral at a newly developed mine (the first in Britain) could save £14 million a year on our import bill, assuming a productive capacity of a million tonnes a year (£45 million at 1977 prices). This fact, plus the work potential of the operation (500 permanent employees) in an area of high unemployment, led to the granting of planning consent in spite of the National Park location. However, this was not obtained without careful siting to minimise the impact of the minehead complex on the surrounding country and an expenditure of £100 000 (1970 prices) on landscaping the site. Production began in 1973 and by the following year output had reached 183 000 tonnes.

However, shortly after the validation of the Staithes deposit by ICI, two other companies established the presence of large potash fields in the National Park, possibly yielding a further million tonnes a year. Planning consents were again granted but depressed world potash prices and over-supply led to the deferment of the additional projects. In 1977 these have still not gone ahead and estimates of current output from the ICI mine are below predicted levels.

The case of potash is a good example of the problems of production forecasting for minerals, especially where the commodities in question have their price determined on a world market which can at times prove volatile.

Talc and Diatomite

The last two minerals considered in this section are paired not only because of the very limited scale on which they are worked and their trifling impact on the environment, but their common potential in terms of development in an area where any job opportunities need to be maximised.

Talc, a magnesium silicate used in cosmetics manufacture and in the electrical industry where it is important as an insulator, has been worked since the mid-1960's. The remoteness of the one productive location in Shetland is offset by the value of the mineral currently priced in a range depending on quality from £75-£100 a tonne. Production has been rising rapidly as Figure 7 shows.

Diatomite, which consists of the fossil remains of a minute primitive plant laid down in Tertiary times in freshwater lakes, on the other hand, has been declining in output (Figure 7). In spite of prices between £150-£200 a tonne for top grade pure material, the only source now worked, in the Lake District, is of poor quality and can be used only as a filler for paints, rubbers, etc. Better qualities are used in water filtration plant, though the product is also important as an insulation against heat, cold or sound. The Lake District deposit is therefore not of great value in a 23 million tonne world market which seems to be expanding at about 5% a year. However, better quality diatomite is known to exist on Skye and the good prices currently fetched could help negate distance from markets. Certainly the HIDB has had the deposit evaluated and is actively trying to interest a company in working it.

The approach of the HIDB in the case of diatomite is in keeping with its philosophy since it was set up in 1965. It believes that the stimulation of such a mineral development here as elsewhere in its area is likely to create the direct employment of between 10 - 40 men but will be of such a limited scale as not to have an undue impact on the environment. Thus several HIDB appraisals of minerals have so far taken place (Figure 8), and it has on its books what it considers to be viable projects for working feldspar (a flux used in the manufacture of ceramics), garnetiferous rock (used as an abrasive), marble, granite (suitable for architectural facings) and anorthosite (valued for its alumina, as a filler, and for its garnetiferous fractions).

NEW MINERAL RESOURCES AND THEIR DEVELOPMENT POTENTIAL

While Figure 8 gives some indication of the HIDB's policy towards an assessment of the mineral potential of North West Scotland and its possible exploitation, legislation at a national level has encouraged private mining companies to undertake a much more rigorous analysis of Britain's upland mineral wealth than ever before. In particular, the Mineral Exploration Act, 1971, made £50 million available from government sources in the form of loans which could cover up to

35% of the cost of exploration for non-ferrous metal ores to be repaid only out of the profits of exploitation.

The passage of this Act must be seen as a response by government to rising world demand, an unprecedented escalation of some metal prices, the need for long term security of supplies and a desire not only to improve the balance of payments position but to provide additional job opportunities in areas where unemployment is well above average. But the response of the mining companies has to be seen not only in the light of the 1971 Act and their own concern to secure additional working reserves, but also the potential availability of investment grants by way of free depreciation of plant for mineral operations in Development Areas which also happen to be largely coincident with upland Britain. The interplay of all these factors is manifest in the rash of exploratory activities set out in Figure 8.

To date some resources identified have been taken to the production stage, particularly where there was a degree of primary development work undertaken prior to 1971. Of the rest it will remain to be seen whether, in the light of world markets and production incentives, firm proposals for working operations will emerge. If they do, another factor of major importance already alluded to in the last two sections of this chapter will need to be reckoned with at the preparatory stage, for whilst the HIDB may presume a freedom from environmental and competing land use problems regarding mineral exploitation, this cannot be taken for granted elsewhere; indeed the planning consents that will be necessary could severely restrict an operation or, in certain instances, could be withheld altogether. Such a situation could be envisaged where an ore body turns out to be a low grade disseminated metal ore (say at about 0.5%) and is located in an upland area noted for its landscape value or in a National Park. Deposits of this kind by their nature could not be economically worked by underground techniques which reduce environmental hazards. Open pit methods would have to be used and taking a not unreasonable assumption of a disseminated ore body of just over 60 million tonnes, it is possible to suppose the operation might require up to 1200 ha of land, depending on site topography. This hypothetical working is about the size of that proposed by RTZ for the copper deposits found in the Coed-y-Brenin area of Snowdonia, one which has been temporarily withdrawn from further consideration primarily because of the immense weight of opposition to an undertaking of this type in a National Park, involving not only a pit of around 80 ha but a large area set aside for the disposal of tailings.

Certainly should other proposals to undertake large scale mineral exploitation projects in National Parks or in areas of great landscape value come forward for evaluation, the processes involved in attempting to balance environmental considerations against other economic and social benefits will be exceedingly complex. To begin with, the employment opportunities afforded by an exploitation project

Figure 8
MINERAL PROSPECTING IN UPLAND BRITAIN, 1971-6

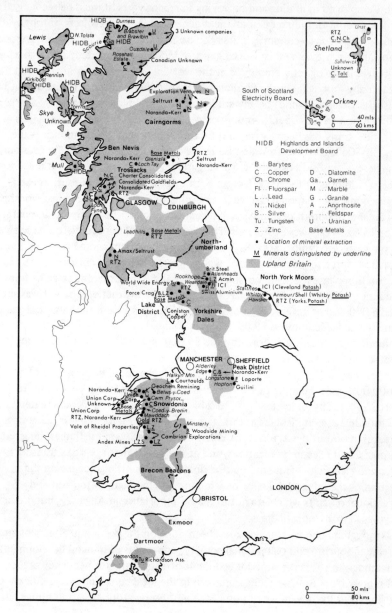

are often difficult to finally predict at the planning stage and are usually over-estimates, but whilst one may point to the general rapid fall in the number of wage-earners employed in mining and quarrying in recent years, it must be recognised that the amount of indirect employment generated by such projects, through stimulus of the local economy, is likely to be an important benefit. In this respect the instance of the china clay working at Lee Moor has been cited; although a 1 000 people are directly employed at the working, it has been estimated that half as many jobs again in the Plymouth area owe their existence to the operation. Whilst there clearly cannot be any studies of the employment created by a large open cast non-ferrous operation in Britain, since none at present exists, a theoretical study has been carried out by the Department of Economics at the University College of North Wales, Bangor, based on their model of the economy of Anglesey. This is, in essence, a working model of a representative rural economy, which would predict the net effect, in both incomes and total output, of each activity consequent upon a change in any other activity. A hypothetical working with an annual output of about 25 000 tonnes of copper per year and an operating life of 15 - 20 years was postulated. This was calculated to occupy 162 ha with a 324 ha waste and tailings area, 81 ha for a clear-water dam and 41 ha of buildings. The labour force for such a working was estimated to be 840 during the construction phase (60 from outside the area) and 375 during the stage of full production (90 from outside the area). During the construction phase it was shown that £6 000 000 of development of the type envisaged would raise the total output of the regional economy to £8 007 000 approximately, ie £2 007 000 of production had been called forth by the £6 000 000, when all the interacting increases had worked their way through the local economy. Total increases in incomes was £1 483 000. At the operating stage, the addition of output of £5 000 000 from the mine raised the total output of the island's economy to £6 016 244, ie approximately £1 016 244 of further production was created. The total increase in incomes at this stage was £452 173. The largest percentage increases in output by sector at the construction stage were for timber, quarrying and postal and telecommunications, and at the operating stage, road transport, water and electricity. This study unfortunately offers little guidance on the question of the impact of a large new mining development on tourism and recreational pursuits which are not of major importance in Anglesey, but are key activities in many upland areas.

Although no comparable work has been done on the economic effects of an increase in tourism and recreational activity, opponents of mineral development have tended to stress the superior economic effects of the former. They argue that money from tourism tends to remain in the local community and quickly be distributed to the advantage of hoteliers, guest house proprietors and numerous other service and retail outlets, while the profits from mining development, particularly those run by multi-nationals, would not all remain in either the local community or necessarily even in the country. Furthermore it has been argued that tourism gives rise to particularly labour-intensive forms of secondary employment such as the making of woollen goods or pottery. It is suggested that the economic value of land left in its wild state is infinitely greater than that under mineral exploitation, particularly in a country where the number of such places is very limited. Whilst these points merit very serious consideration, one cannot necessarily assume that tourism and large-scale mining developments are mutually exclusive. While certain kinds of mineral extraction, along with the traffic congestion they generate, are likely to deter tourists from their locality, other types are proving to be of undoubted interest to visitors. Not only has an upsurge of interest in industrial archaeology led to the profitable re-opening of a slate mine for visitors, but current operations such as china clay extraction in Devon are attracting a large number of sightseers. It is difficult to be precise about what specifically attracts visitors to, or deters them from, tourist areas, and what statistics are available with a bearing on this are out of date.

The authors of the Bangor study considered that, apart from the economic benefit to the local community from a mining project, there would be important social benefits; they assert that "even if in the short-run skills have to be imported into a region, the future opportunities for local youth are still widened, as vacancies occur due to staff turnover. The effect of this is to maintain a greater level of social cohesion". Furthermore, it is argued that the employment offered by opencast mining is nothing like as seasonal as that afforded by the tourist industry. One has, however, to bear in mind the more limited duration of such mineral developments, which could well do little to improve the long-term employment prospects for such areas. Nevertheless, there are those who appear to feel that mining or quarrying development is less intrinsically damaging to the character and social structure of remote areas than is a large influx of tourists, who may also make very heavy demands in environmental terms.

The economic benefits to the national as opposed to the local community are generally considered in terms of the balance of payments. It has been argued that the metals which would appear to offer prospects of the largest potential import savings are copper and nickel. At 1977 (February) prices, 50 000 tonnes of refined copper produced from UK sources would reduce the country's import bill by £42 millions a year, and 10 000 tonnes of refined nickel by £32 millions. (Against this would have to be set any possible losses to the balance of payments from a reduction in the inflow of foreign tourists or an increase in British holidays taken abroad.) However, bearing in mind the extremely volatile nature of the world's non-ferrous metal markets, and the high element of risk attached to any new development for extraction of such metals in Britain, predictions of this kind have to be treated with some caution.

SHORT AND LONGER TERM TRENDS

The range of minerals that is produced in upland Britain and those that have a production potential, the complexities of the supply and demand situation for each with some operating within the context of a home market whilst others are traded world-wide, and the fact that almost all are to be found in areas of scenic value where their extraction competes with other forms of land use, make any attempt to draw together a few concluding generalisations about the future difficult indeed. Suffice it to say that where internationally traded minerals are concerned, the future may be said to lie in the resolution of the equation which places on one side the value that should be put on their extraction in upland Britain because of their relatively low unit cost or their rarity value, or because a case can be made out for their working in terms of balance of payments, employment opportunities, etc, and on the other side the value that should be put on limited if not scarce resources of outstandingly attractive tracts of upland countryside (in some instances, even with the status of National Parks) which in themselves have economic importance as recreation and tourist areas. The equation is easy to state in these terms – the way it will be resolved more difficult to predict except in those instances where the mineral is worked underground and has little surface impact.

In the case of those minerals traded only on the home market (mainly aggregates), environmental constraints again will make themselves felt. Undoubtedly, if the working of materials in the most sensitive environments becomes more difficult, the substitution of one material for another where this is technically possible will occur providing any additional extractive costs and/or transport costs can be met. In this latter respect, experiments are now taking place into the possibility of using pipelines to carry aggregate materials. Although costs per tonne kilometre using this method could be 30% cheaper than by 32 tonne lorry between a quarry and a single point source in the market area, and experimental trials look promising, a full scale scheme has yet to be validated both economically and technically. Whether or not a cheaper transport mode is eventually introduced, the notion of material substitution is well exemplified by the possibility of the Rossendale sandstones replacing the limestone aggregate of the Peak Park in North Western markets.

However, against a general background of rising demand, new ways of meeting the needs of areas of high demand are now being considered which will have least environmental cost. The underground mining of the more valuable chemical limestones is a case in point since this technique could reduce landscape damage in sensitive areas yet supply markets close at hand. Unfortunately costs per tonne are generally 50% above open pit operations of equivalent output and even if the mines in question were close by points of demand (eg on the south-eastern edge of Brecon Beacons or the north-western side of the Peak Park) it is unlikely that reduced transport costs would totally offset the increased production expenditure. It is not beyond the bounds of possibility, of course, that the government might eventually accept that the additional costs involved in mining should be legitimately considered as a trade-off against the conservation of the environment in special areas. Nevertheless, it has to be said that the acceptance of such a notion with its concomitant financial implications still seems some way off as does the notion, so often postulated, of subsidising the transport of the waste quartz of Dartmoor to south-eastern markets where it is much needed.

A further possibility for the future involves the working of the high quality igneous roadstones of Northern Scotland to counter the increasing demands for aggregate for this purpose being made on the traditional upland sources close by the major urban markets. As will be obvious from what has been said in the third section of this chapter, the expense involved in transporting these materials over a very considerable distance to the major markets in the North-West, the Midlands or the South-East would in normal circumstances be prohibitive. However, a quarry working suitable stone could be located on the coast of Northern Scotland remote from centres of population and away from areas most used for recreation. If this were of suitably mammoth proportions, producing between 10 and 20 million tonnes per year, economies of scale might help offset transport charges. Undoubtedly, there is evidence to show that a quarry with an output of 10 million tonnes per year could produce aggregate as much as 21% cheaper than that working one million tonnes. Since the costs per tonne of material transported in ships of about 3000 tonnes can be as low as one tenth of those using 32 tonne lorries, the economic transport of materials over long distances by water looks at least a possibility in this instance. However, trans-shipment at ports to vehicles to carry the material to the final point of usage would be a further cost factor that has to be considered.

The concept of the remotely located mammoth quarry is clearly worth more research since it could eventually begin to make a marked impact on the traditional relationship between points of aggregate demand and their nearest least cost point of supply to the advantage of the environment. However, the implications of a decision to embrace such a notion are so considerable in terms of changing the present commercial structure of the aggregates industry that they are hardly likely to be countenanced in the near future.

NOTE
Figures 1 and 4-7 are partly based on *United Kingdom Mineral Statistics* and on production information known to the author. Since official statistics are normally grouped for publication purposes by new counties in England and Wales and by pre-local government reorganisation counties in Scotland, this arrangement has been retained here.

REFERENCES AND BIBLIOGRAPHY
Blunden, J R (1975)   *The mineral resources of Britain: a study in exploitation and planning.*   London: Hutchinson.
Ministry of Housing and Local Government (1960)   *The control of mineral workings.*   London: HMSO.
Institute of Geological Sciences (1975)   *United Kingdom mineral statistics.*   London: HMSO.
Mining Environmental Research Unit (1974)   *Surface minerals extraction.*   (Unpublished).
Mining Environmental Research Unit (1974)   *Concept of the 'super' quarry.*   (Unpublished).
Mining Environmental Research Unit (1974)   *Limestone mine prefeasibility study.*   (Unpublished).
Commission on Mining and the Environment (1972)   *Report.*   London: The Commission.

2 The encouragement of rural-based industry at the local level

D S CAMPBELL

The object of this paper is to help identify the characteristics and trends of rural-based industry in upland Britain and to set out how these are encouraged, with a view to helping to devise alternative strategies for these areas.

The move of population from agriculture and the countryside to manufacturing industry and the towns has been the most important continuing trend in British society for more than two hundred years. However, while agriculture has always been and will remain the predominant industry in country areas, it has never been the only means of livelihood for country people. Today, when economies of large scale production seem to yield much smaller dividends, and more sophisticated agriculture calls for more ancillary service provision, there are greater opportunities for manufacturing and service industries to expand in country areas than at any time since the 18th century.

Before more industry moves to rural locations, the deep seated tradition of an urban base for manufacture, the glamorous attraction which towns have always had for country people, and the environmental problems of the planners must be overcome. There is none the less a consensus of both government and people that a larger proportion of the population should live and work in country areas. The Development Commission was established as a result of the Development and Road Improvement Funds Act of 1909/10 with the object of combating rural depopulation, and there is no less need for its work today, but there are reasons to hope that after sixty years the tide is slowly beginning to turn in its favour.

The problems of creating a broader industrial base in upland areas of Britain do not differ in kind from the problems in all rural areas but there are differences in emphasis, some of which should be noted:

(i)   A decline in the number of people employed on the land balanced to some extent by a notable increase in the energy per caput required by farm workers in the form of tractors, land rovers, power saws, grass dryers etc., needing sophisticated maintenance services.

(ii)   The traditional outward migration of the indigenous population stimulated to some extent by better educational opportunities and the media, balanced by an immigration of second home owners, retired people, and an increasing number who prefer the life style and accept the lower standard of living which a sparsely populated area offers, creating, however, an unbalanced age structure.

(iii)   The progressive rundown of 19th century industries which came to upland areas to exploit water power and relatively low grade mineral deposits which may in due course be balanced by renewed industrial interest in unpolluted air and water, and even the possibility of small scale hydro-electricity.

(iv)   Major improvements of communications of all sorts which reduce the disadvantages of remoteness from markets, centres of innovation, and sources of components and raw materials, and improvements in the personal mobility of the lowland and urban population which allows the tourist trade to extend over the greater part of the year and helps to break down the psychological barrier which inhibits industrial managers and their wives from contemplating a move to a comparatively remote area.

(v)   Finally, one cannot overlook the modern preoccupation, particularly by the urban population, with the sun, preferably semi-tropical, leading to rejection of the winter cold and mists of upland areas as places to live and work.

In 1921 the Development Commission set up the Rural Industries Intelligence Bureau (later the Rural Industries Bureau) and from this, and pioneer work by Rural Community Councils, the organisation now known as the Council for Small Industries in Rural Areas (CoSIRA) has grown up, with Organisers in each county of England, and until recently Wales; an experienced staff of advisers, instructors and accountants, and, again until recently, organisations in Scotland and Northern Ireland.

Most small country based servicing and manufacturing businesses which request CoSIRA services can receive the continuing advice of an Organiser who, after five, ten or even twenty years experience of businesses employing less than twenty skilled men, will have acquired a considerable degree of expertise. Through the Organiser the firm may obtain either free, or on a fee basis, technical instruction in both basic industrial skills such as welding, wood and metal machining, agricultural machinery, etc., and in traditional rural skills such as farriery, wrought iron work, thatching and saddlery. Among the most valuable services are the advice of management accountants who have considerable experience of small businesses, whilst other experts in workshop layout, production management, adaption of buildings, marketing and publicity are available on CoSIRA's staff. Loans are available for buildings on a twenty year term, and for equipment and working capital on shorter terms up to a total of £30 000, at current interest rates, and on rather less security than commercial banks sometimes require. CoSIRA do, however, insist that before a loan is offered, the firm makes a careful feasibility study, in itself a valuable discipline. In addition to these special services, CoSIRA provides support for small trade groups, assists participation in exhibitions at home and overseas, and organises a variety of weekend business courses, study tours and training courses. However, perhaps the most valuable service of all which CoSIRA provides may be the interest and advice of an independent friend on a continuing basis over many years, in the huge variety of problems from planning applications, safety regulations, tax and accounting to the more direct industrial problems of the right product, the right means of production and the right method of selling.

CoSIRA keeps in close touch with the parallel organisations in Scotland, Wales and Northern Ireland and there are regular exchanges of ideas on new ways of helping small industries in country areas. Recently, the Development Commission has instituted a policy of focal point approach and throughout England areas of special need have been identified. In a number of these areas the Development Commission has financed the construction of advance factories of a size which will allow small businesses to start up and expand to create local employment. An increasing amount of Organisers' time and advisory services are now being concentrated in the areas around these advance factories, seeking out any way in which the local economy as a whole can be stimulated.

Cumbria has a number of sites in small country towns which have been approved by the Development Commission for the building of these small advance factories which the District and County Councils, in making their case to the Development Commission through the medium of a County Action Plan for the regeneration of the rural part of the County, expect to provide a focus for total regeneration. CoSIRA, Rural Community Councils/Councils of Voluntary Service and local (or parish) Councils are concerned with the selection of these sites and after approval the County Small Industries Committee, working through its attached Organiser/s defines an 'Area of Pull' in which the Development Commission, CoSIRA and the Rural Community Council will make maximum effort to increase and broaden the range of employment, and prevent further deterioration.

The allocation of the advance factories in the Assisted Areas is the responsibility of the Regional Director of the Department of Industry and the Development Commission, who seek mainly to encourage the expansion and development of indigenous firms, especially those with particular links to the rural community, but not those simply needing to rehouse without expansion and the creation of a reasonable number of new jobs. In the Assisted Areas applications from firms wishing to come into the area are welcomed.

The mix of CoSIRA services in any one area of England varies with local needs but throughout there is an undoubted element of 'horse to the water'. The vital and essential element in rural industries is the individual with enterprise, skills, management ability and drive and ideas. At best advisory and credit services can only act as a catalyst. There are some reasons to believe that in the remoter country districts the process of emigration to the towns, the Commonwealth and to the professions, generation after generation by the more enterprising and possibly more intelligent members of country families, has reduced the spark of enterprise among indigenous country men. Equally, modern society has undoubtedly reduced the rewards and increased the difficulties of individual initiative. How far an official organisation can and should attempt to stimulate enterprise and individual initiative is a subject which this symposium might well debate. It must be noted, however, that though there is a strong tradition that upland areas breed men of rugged individualism, one of the most deep rooted problems of these areas may well be a shortage of local men who are ready to go it alone in some new enterprise, at least in their own country. This shortage, real or apparent, makes it all the more important to give every possible assistance and encouragement to the individual with an idea and the drive to carry it through.

It must always be remembered that upland areas in England and in almost all parts of Britain are only relatively remote in comparison to one of the most thickly populated countries in the world. The barriers to economic and industrial development are more often psychological than real.

23 Opportunities for rural-based industries in upland Scotland

D A OGILVIE

INTRODUCTION

Rural depopulation has been a feature of Scottish life for 150 years. A process of enforced clearance was started at the beginning of the 19th century by landlords who were seeking sheep pastures among the sparse areas of land suitable for agriculture. The subsistence tenants who lived there were evicted, many of them leaving the country as emigrants to North America. Later, the discovery of coal and iron created large industries in the centre and west of Scotland and the drift of population from the countryside continued. More recently, great improvements in the efficiency of agriculture and forestry have diminished still further the job opportunities in rural areas. The extent of the depopulation in the countryside is shown by the decrease of the rural proportion from 45% in 1861 to only 14% in 1970 (Credland & Murray, 1969). Figure 1 gives the percentage changes in regional populations over the years 1961-1974.

Five regions in Scotland are predominantly upland and rural in character. These are the Highlands and Islands, Dumfries and Galloway, The Borders, Tayside and Grampian. Each area presents different problems and opportunities for small scale enterprises, and a brief outline of the main regional features will help to give some perspective to the rural industrial scene. The map of administrative areas of Scotland (Figure 2) shows the locations of the region concerned.

THE HIGHLANDS AND ISLANDS

The Highlands and Islands of Scotland cover about one-half of the area of the country (one-fifth of the whole of Great Britain), but support a population of only 300 000. Except for the regional centre of Inverness (population 50 000)

Figure 1
POPULATION CHANGES, SCOTLAND 1961-1974

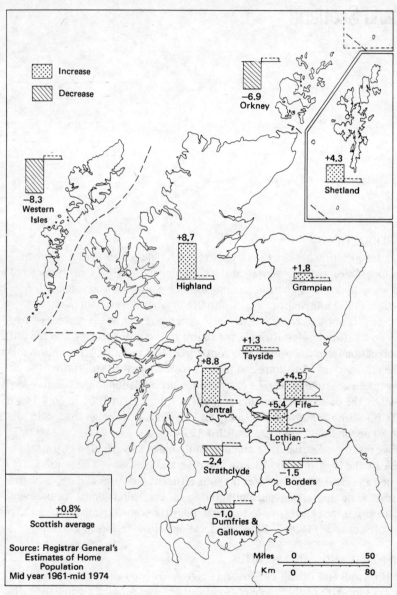

Courtesy HMSO

Figure 2
SCOTLAND'S REGIONS, 1975

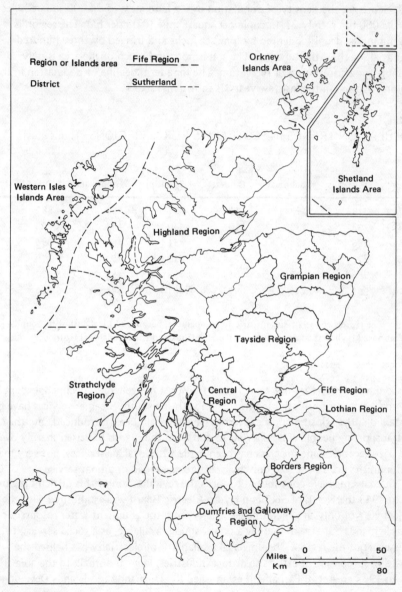

Region or Islands area — Fife Region — —
District — Sutherland — — —

Orkney Islands Area

Shetland Islands Area

Western Isles Islands Area

Highland Region

Grampian Region

Tayside Region

Strathclyde Region

Central Region

Fife Region

Lothian Region

Borders Region

Dumfries and Galloway Region

Miles 0 — 50
Km 0 — 80

Courtesy HMSO

the area is entirely rural and very thinly populated. Including Argyll District, now part of Strathclyde Region, but similar in character to much of the rest of north west Scotland, the density of population over a land mass of 14 000 square miles (3 620 000 ha) is only 21.4 people per square mile (0.08 per ha). The region is mountainous, deeply indented by long sea lochs and fringed by three hundred islands along the Atlantic coast. The soil is poor and much of the area is only suitable for afforestation or recreation. The long term decline of population in the region, reversed in the last few years, is shown in Table 1.

Table 1
POPULATION TRENDS IN SCOTLAND'S RURAL REGIONS (Thousands)

	Highlands & Islands	Dumfries & Galloway	Borders	Tayside	Grampian	Scotland
1921	328	159	111	437	450	4 882
1931	293	152	110	430	444	4 803
1951	286	154	112	451	462	5 096
1961	277	152	105	452	453	5 179
1971	283	150	101	453	452	5 227
1974	299	144	99	401	448	5 226

Note: The figures for 1974 are not strictly comparable, because of local authority boundary alterations. Argyll District is included in the Highlands and Islands regional figure.

Source: HMSO (1975a)

Communications are not easy. Public transport has generally declined, except for the main railway routes linking the region with the south. Steamer services have been curtailed, although some new car ferries have recently been introduced, and the cost of transporting people and materials to and from the islands has risen sharply over the past decade. Some progress has been made with local air services, but very many communities are still served only by a second class road or a boat service.

Three events have contributed towards the revitalisation of this difficult region: (i) In 1943 the North of Scotland Hydro-Electric Board was established with the objectives not only of generating electricity from the abundant water resources of the Highlands but also of making a power supply available, as a social service, to every part of the region. The universal availability of electricity has helped the Board in its consistent efforts to attract industries, large and small, to the area. (ii) In 1965 an Act of Parliament established the Highlands and Islands Development Board with wide powers to promote the economy of the region. In ten years the Board has invested £26.5 million in grants and loans to industrial, tourist and

agricultural projects, backed by large scale efforts in publicity, planning and research. The Board can claim credit for the expectation of 11 200 jobs which should arise from its investment (Highlands and Islands Development Board, 1976).
(iii) In 1971 the discovery of oil under the North Sea started an economic revival in the eastern Highlands and the northern isles which has rapidly eclipsed all previous efforts to help the region. Within two years unemployment has dropped from more than 8% towards zero, and land and skilled labour, in the coastal areas principally affected, are now at a premium. An influx of international construction companies, paying high wages and demanding modern skills and the effective use of labour, has galvanised the areas affected into activity. On the remoter western parts of the Highlands, however, oil has as yet made little impact, and the only source of regular employment remains the small scale industrial or craft-based enterprise.

DUMFRIES AND GALLOWAY
South West Scotland, like the Highlands, is a sparsely populated region with only 144 000 people in an area of 2 460 square miles (640 000 ha). The main activity of the region is agriculture, although there are also areas of forest and moorland. Excluding the regional centre of Dumfries (population 28 000) the density of rural population is 46.3 per square mile (0.18 per ha). It has suffered as heavily as anywhere in Scotland from a continued decline in rural job opportunities. Virtually all rail services have disappeared except for those serving the regional centre of Dumfries and for the tenuous link to the Irish rail ferry at Stranraer. Local bus services have also declined, although recent road improvements have made the area easy of access by car from the industrial north west of England.

While unemployment in the south west has for some years been at a high rate (7.3% in 1975) the actual numbers of people out of work are small. Throughout the whole rural area, excluding Dumfries, the unemployment in 1975 only amounted to 2 800 people. In such a widely scattered population this unemployment cannot be improved by the establishment of large industries. The south west is therefore well suited to the promotion of small-scale industries.

THE BORDERS
A compact area lying between Edinburgh and England, the Borders are predominantly agricultural in character, being world famed for sheep and for the woollen industry which grew up in the small towns along the rivers which intersect the region. The population of 99 000 is spread over an area of 1 780 square miles (462 000 ha) giving a density of 55.6 people per square mile (0.21 per ha).

Because the Borders have so long depended on agriculture the rural employment opportunities have declined in proportion with the progressive mechanisation of farms. Table 1 shows how in the 23 years from 1951 to 1974 the population had fallen from 112 700 to 99 000 (Registrar General for Scotland, 1975). The Borders are, however, an attractive and accessible part of Scotland, and considerable success has followed the efforts of the local authorities and of the Eastern Borders Development Association (disbanded in 1975) towards attracting small scale industries. The amenities of the area, the ready availability of factories and houses, the good climate and the pleasant environment have provided effective incentives to Borderers and to incomers alike to settle and establish their own enterprises in the region.

TAYSIDE

The rural problems of Tayside are eased by the nearness of the area to the main industrial centres of Scotland, by good road and rail communications and by the economic influence of the city of Dundee. The population of 401 000 (of which 207 000 live in the cities of Dundee and Perth) is fairly stable, and in the area of 3 500 square miles (900 000 ha) the rural part represents 55.4 people per square mile (0.22 per ha). Although the region's traditional industry, the processing of jute, has declined, the newer industries of offshore oil servicing, synthetic fibres and office machinery have begun to absorb much of the capacity of the region.

Small-scale rural industries in Tayside have tended to be either sub-contracting manufacturers working for major companies, or firms based on the natural resources of the area, principally soft fruit, farm produce and timber. Latterly the influence of North Sea oil has been strongly felt, and over the next decade there is likely to be a continued growth in servicing companies for oil rigs and in allied engineering concerns.

GRAMPIAN

The north east is a rural and upland region which has a strong focus in Aberdeen city. The two traditional activities of the region are fishing and agriculture. Of the population of 448 000 about 181 000 live in or immediately around Aberdeen and the density of the rural population in the area of 3 640 square miles (940 000 ha) is 73.3 per square mile (0.28 per ha).

Until 1972 the region presented the typical rural problem of unemployment and outward migration, both to other parts of Britain and overseas. For the five years from 1966-1971 unemployment ranged between 2.8% to 5%, about twice the national average for Britain as a whole.

Off-shore oil discoveries since 1971 have had a much more dramatic effect on the north east than on any other part of the country. There has been a rapid increase in constructional and servicing activity and Aberdeen has become the recognised off-shore oil centre not only of Scotland but for the whole of Western

Europe. The city's airport is now the busiest in the world for helicopter operations. Unemployment, at 3.1% in August 1975, is the lowest in Scotland.

This oil-borne boom has not come without its adverse effects on small-scale industries. The cost of houses and of small workshops has risen very rapidly. In and near Aberdeen houses have more than doubled in price in eighteen months and now approach London values. Wage rates in oil related activities pose a threat to small firms which may either lose their skilled labour or face a cost structure which they cannot afford. Thus although oil is bringing boom conditions to the north-east generally, for some small scale industry the present disadvantages outweigh the opportunities.

In 1970 the North-East of Scotland Development Authority was formed to bring the region's planning and infrastructural role under a single organisation. From 1971 the Authority was heavily engaged in meeting the problems of accommodation, factory space, labour and planning resulting from the great influx of oil exploration and off-shore servicing companies. Since 1975 it has formed the industrial development arm of the new Grampian Regional Authority.

THE SCOTTISH DEVELOPMENT AGENCY

In December 1975 a new statutory body, the Scottish Development Agency, was created with the objectives of "furthering economic development; the provision, maintenance or safeguarding of employment; the promotion of industrial efficiency and competitiveness; and furthering the improvement of the environment." (HMSO, 1975b). The Agency took over the staff and functions of the former Scottish Industrial Estates Corporation and the Small Industries Council for Rural Areas of Scotland. In the discussion papers which led to the drafting of the Agency's Bill the rural policy was outlined: "Although the major role of the Agency will lie in the promotion of industry and in environmental regeneration in urban or semi-urban areas, the Government intend that it should also be given a clear policy remit to encourage and assist rural development."

Substantial government funds are available to the Agency towards its task of regenerating Scotland's economy, £200 million for the first five years. The intended investment, however, by a single oil company in North Sea operations — £2 000 million over 10 years by British Petroleum — puts into perspective the relative contributions of government and the oil industry towards the country's future prosperity.

ADVANCE FACTORIES

In its advance factory programme the Agency has evolved, with each of the local authorities concerned, timetables of factory and workshop building which include a small, but significant proportion of rurally based units. In 1977, out of

147 projects totalling 273 455 m^2 of factory accommodation, 37 (11 912 m^2) are in or near rural and upland areas. The employment potential represented by these new rural factories and workshops is about 475 jobs. Table 2 gives the locations and sizes of the factories under the first phase of the programme.

Table 2
ADVANCE FACTORIES IN RURAL AREAS – SDA's PROGRAMME IN 1977

	Area (m^2)	Availability
Borders Region		
Coldstream	2 x 230	To be built
Eyemouth	951	November 1977
Hawick	2 x 230	To be built
Galashiels	2 x 230	To be built
Innerleithen	200	To be built
Dumfries & Galloway		
Dalbeattie	951	To be built
Gatehouse-of-Fleet	93	Ready
Gretna	2 x 465	To be built
Kirkconnel	951	Ready
Kirkcudbright	2 x 140	Ready
Langholm	185	To be built
Newton Stewart	465	To be built
Stranraer	2 x 230	To be built
	951	Ready
Grampian		
Alford	2 x 230	To be built
Ballater	150	To be built
Banff	2 x 230	To be built
Buckie	960	To be built
Dufftown	200	To be built
Huntly	2 x 230	To be built
Tayside		
Aberfeldy	5 x 100	Ready
Alyth	2 x 230	To be built
Blairgowrie	465	To be built

Source: Scottish Development Agency (1976).

It should be noted that in north and west Scotland the Highlands and Islands Development Board is promoting a similar but separate programme.

SERVICES TO RURAL FIRMS

As part of its programme of assistance to smaller companies the Scottish Development Agency's Small Business Division gives special services to firms based in rural areas. Regional Development Officers, working in the country districts can call for management advice, technical or marketing assistance and for loans at favourable rates to help in the development of promising enterprises. Training programmes can be arranged, in companies' own premises, to bring the workforce up to recognised standard of proficiency in welding, machine tool operation or woodworking. Additionally, for hand craftsmen specially favourable schemes of recruitment, finance and training are available.

The keynote of the Small Business Division's rural work is personal attention. In each of the services offered direct contact is made with the owner of the business by the Regional Development Officer and the specialist professional staff. The effectiveness of the service is demonstrated by a growth rate (in employment terms) of 55.9% over the two year period 1972-74 for small rural firms which were receiving such help as against 15.0% for small rural firms generally over the same period (Small Industries Council for Rural Areas of Scotland, 1974).

INDUSTRIAL OPPORTUNITIES IN THE UPLANDS

In rural Scotland three principal categories of small scale industry may be identified — traditional, advanced and craft. With a few obvious exceptions, such as industries which are based on coastal activities (fish processing and boat building, for example) the same categorisation may be applied to upland areas.

Traditional firms are those which serve a predominantly local market or are dependent on a local raw material. They are characterised by a low rate of growth, by modest investment in capital equipment and by labour intensive operations. Although unspectacular in economic terms they provide nevertheless a firm economic base for the small scale industrial sector in the countryside. Some examples of traditional industries are agricultural and motor engineering, building, whisky, the production of woven textiles and knitwear, and timber operations and conversion.

Table 3, derived from surveys conducted by the Small Industries Council for Rural Areas of Scotland, shows employment changes between 1972 and 1974 ranging from − 6.6% in textiles to + 4.4% in building and + 10.3% for timber operations.

Advanced industries provide much greater possibility of rapid growth. They are characterised by an element of technology and skill usually introduced by the

Table 3
SMALL RURAL FIRMS — EMPLOYMENT CHANGES

Industry Classification	Employment 1974	Percentage of Total	Percentage Change 1970-72	1972-74
Agricultural equipment	452	1.5	+ 4.2	+12.7
Blacksmiths	826	2.7	-- 2.1	+ 9.5
Builders	5653	18.2	− 0.3	+ 4.4
Cloth/Textiles/Weavers	2632	8.5	− 0.4	− 6.6
Coachbuilders	263	0.8	− 4.8	+ 1.5
Electronics/Scientific instruments	598	1.9	+ 59.9	+ 59.7
Engineering —				
Agricultural	2167	7.0	+ 1.4	+ 12.3
Electrical	201	0.6	+ 33.0	+ 22.6
Marine	1054	3.4	+ 3.6	+ 11.9
Precision	1197	3.8	0	+ 54.7
General	1556	5.0	− 0.5	+ 37.9
Food	1359	4.4	+ 90.0	+ 38.2
Foundries	205	0.7	+ 16.2	+ 17.8
Furniture	74	0.2	+ 64.1	−18.7
Garages	365	1.2	− 2.1	+ 21.3
Joiners	3665	11.8	− 3.0	+ 0.6
Jewellers	98	0.3	+ 47.0	+ 22.5
Knitwear	2563	8.2	+ 10.0	+ 14.9
Leather	178	0.6	+ 11.9	+ 40.2
Plastics	567	1.8	+ 52.6	+ 97.6
Pottery	278	0.9	+ 21.9	+ 39.6
Precast concrete/brick	886	2.8	−10.0	+ 8.4
Printing	380	1.2	+ 22.2	+ 26.2
Sawmillers/timber/ forestry	824	2.7	+ 1.5	+ 10.3
Sports Goods	402	1.3	+ 57.2	+ 68.2
Stonemasons	101	0.3	− 4.3	+ 16.1
Miscellaneous —				
Industrial	1871	6.0	+ 3.2	+ 71.6
Consumer	495	1.6	+ 35.6	+ 17.3
Crafts	199	0.6	+ 31.9	+ 15.0
Totals	31109	100.0	+ 6.0	+15.0

Source: Small Industries Council for Rural Areas of Scotland (1972 & 1974)

owner, by investment in machinery and plant, by high added values and by markets which may be regional, national or in some cases, international. The location of advanced industries in a rural or upland area may have come about either for environmental reasons (at the choice of the entrepreneur) by the availability of factory space and housing (through central or local government initiatives), or rarely by the availability of a pool of suitable labour. Examples of advanced industries, with their corresponding employment changes, are food processing (+38.2%), electronic and scientific instrument making (+59.7%), precision engineering (+54.7%) and plastics (+97.6%). The growth rates of advanced industrial activities appear capable of considerably exceeding the national or regional averages for business as a whole.

Craft activities can flourish in the remotest parts of the country. Provided that the design and quality of craft goods are of a sufficiently high standard it is no disadvantage for craftsmen to be working in isolation. Often, indeed, they may have chosen a remote location as a way of life to complement their artistic temperament. In some cases the environment has inspired their craft — a weaver reflecting the colours of spring and autumn in the Borders in his fashion fabrics or a glass engraver expressing the wild nature of a storm-swept rocky northern coastline in his designs.

Economically, crafts are not a major industry, being worth only £15 million annually at retail values and employing between 1500 and 2000 people in Scotland. They have, however, a secondary effect by providing social leaven and leadership in small communities and by contributing hand made items for the important tourist industry.

Schemes of subsidised apprenticeships, training grants and other financial and marketing assistance are available to craftsmen in Scotland from the Scottish Development Agency and the Highlands and Islands Development Board. The modest degree of help (£80 000 in 1977/78) can be justified in the words of the Bolton Committee of Inquiry into small firms. "We consider that support for the crafts is justifiable on social and cultural grounds. Respect and care for these values is in our view obligatory for any rich and civilized nation. Since a lively crafts sector may also produce substantial economic benefits, complementing the contribution of the arts to the promotion of tourism, we think that effective, if modest, financial support is well worth consideration" (Department of Trade and Industry, 1971).

CONCLUSIONS
Many factors of economics and geography act against the interests of industrial undertakings in upland areas of Scotland. Transport costs are high and access to materials and markets can be difficult. Suitable labour may be scarce and the

facilities for training inadequate. Accommodation both for working and living may be hard to find.

Nevertheless, for small scale enterprises these difficulties may be counter-balanced by the excellence of the working environment and the quality of the workforce. Drawn in many cases from predominantly agricultural communities the employees of small rural firms often show a strong identity with their employer and the enterprise; the divisive distractions of trade unionism are rare and industrial disputes are consequently exceptional.

Government intervention to support such undertakings can be provided on an appropriately modest scale. In the building of advance rural factories, the provision of a range of advisory and instructional services and in access to medium-term credit on favourable terms, institutions like the Highlands and Islands Development Board and the Scottish Development Agency can do much to provide a climate for the expansion and development of rural based industries.

In the final analysis, however, it is not government institutions which create employment, but employers. To ensure a steady growth in industrial job opportunities in upland areas of Scotland it is necessary to give encouragement and support to the man who really matters, the private entrepreneur who puts his own energy, skill and money into the undertaking.

REFERENCES

Credland, G & Murray, G (1969) *Scotland – a new look*. London: Scottish Television Ltd.

Department of Trade and Industry (1971) *Report of the Committee of Inquiry on Small Firms*. Bolton, J E (Chairman) Cmnd 4811 London: HMSO.

HMSO (1975a) *Scottish Abstract of Statistics, No. 5*. Edinburgh: HMSO.

HMSO (1975b) *Scottish Development Agency Act* Ch 69. London: HMSO.

Highlands and Islands Development Board (1976) *Tenth Report*. Inverness: HIDB.

Registrar General for Scotland (1975) *Annual estimates of the population of Scotland*. Edinburgh: HMSO.

Scottish Development Agency (1976) *Details of factories available*. Glasgow: SDA.

Small Industries Council for Rural Areas of Scotland (1972 & 1974) *Annual Reports*. Edinburgh: SICRAS.

4 Opportunities for rural-based industries in upland Wales

W I SKEWIS

INTRODUCTION

In this paper 'Upland Wales' has been interpreted as the area that has traditionally been referred to as Mid-Wales. The present population is 188 000, spread over 3238 square miles (8386 km^2) in the districts of Ceredigion, Meirionnydd, Montgomery, Radnor and Brecon. It is one of the most sparsely populated areas of Great Britain with 8% of the population of Wales in 40% of its area. From the turn of the century until this decade the population had steadily declined; indeed between 1951 and 1971 it fell from 197 600 to 183 500. However, since 1971 the tide has shown signs of turning and by 1975 the population had risen to 188 900. It is into this positive atmosphere that the Development Board for Rural Wales has been born.

RECENT DEVELOPMENTS

The Mid-Wales area has suffered from the usual range of interlinked rural problems of declining traditional industry, agricultural rationalisation, restricted job opportunities, falling population, and declining standards in social and public services.

These problems were bravely tackled by one of Britain's first regional development bodies, the Mid-Wales Industrial Development Association, which was founded in 1957 by the region's County Councils. The Association did not attempt to operate in all sectors of the economy. Its target was the attraction of new manufacturing industry to the region to create a range of attractive and well paid jobs that could retain part of the younger age group within the area. The Association also recognised that the successful development of new industry

277

in Mid-Wales could not be sustained by the sparse and scattered existing population. There had also to be a policy of attracting new population into the region along with the industry, by retaining more of the young people and by bringing in new population to repopulate the area.

In the first phase of the Association's life, from 1957 to 1964, it had to rely on persuading companies to commit themselves to the area and then build their own factories or have them built for them. Fourteen firms moved to the area in this phase. In 1964 the Association persuaded the Government and the Development Commission to begin building advance factories in Mid-Wales and two years later the region was given Development Area status and could then offer prospective industrialists both factories and attractive finance.

The effect of this work has been to create 4000 new jobs in the region in manufacturing industry, 55% for men, in 72 Government financed factories and 40 others from taking over existing premises or in factories that have been financed by the firms themselves. The figures exclude the work of the Mid-Wales Development Corporation in Newtown where another 42 factories have been built and over 1000 manufacturing jobs created.

THE DEVELOPMENT BOARD FOR RURAL WALES

The Mid-Wales Industrial Development Association, with modest resources, and Mid-Wales Development Corporation, with statutory backing, are two bodies that have achieved great success in their work, as have certain other organisations that have had responsibilities in rural Wales, but there was always a general feeling that some arrangement was required that brought greater resources to bear on the problem, although there was no general agreement on what sort of arrangement. The outcome has been the creation of the Development Board for Rural Wales as a statutory body with wide powers and responsibilities, though as yet modest resources. The discussion document that was circulated prior to the formation of the Board, after listing the various bodies who had been involved in rural Wales, said:

"While each of the above has made a vital contribution to dealing with the problems of rural Wales in the past, there has been the lack of one single minded agency with responsibility for co-ordinating the economic development of the area. Greater co-ordination is essential if full advantage is to be taken of the attractiveness of rural Wales as a place to live."

The Board has therefore been asked to try to co-ordinate and channel all the various efforts and initiatives towards set development targets and has also been given the powers to take action itself in many aspects of economic and social development.

In its early discussion the Board has made it clear that the creation of jobs in

278

manufacturing industry will continue to receive high priority and its first efforts are being aimed at finding occupants for the advance factories that are currently empty. The Board has also quickly endorsed the 'Growth Towns' policy, which was shaped by the Association 1965 and which was finalised with Government and became official policy in 1969. The Growth Towns were nominated as Aberystwyth, Bala, Brecon, Llandrindod Wells, Rhayader and Welshpool in addition to Newtown which had, at that time, been designated as a 'New Town' and the Mid-Wales Development Corporation had been founded. In 1974 Lampeter and Portmadoc/Penrhyndeudraeth were added to the list of growth towns, making nine in all, and at the same time a second tier of twelve centres were designated as 'Key Towns' which should be encouraged to grow through the normal processes of local government with such additional help as could be made available from central sources, without dilution of the Growth Towns priority. In fact advance factories have been built in several of these key towns.

The region is well aware of the difficulties that can arise from relying on incoming industry that leaves its roots elsewhere and, in times of difficulty, tends to retreat to its main plant where the management is based. This is doubly a problem in that it arises when the economy is low and any replacement firm is hard to find and for the workers alternative employment is scarce. Several of the advance factories that are currently empty in the Board area are victims of this process in the recent recession. That said, there is no doubt that the Board and the region will continue for some time to seek industry from outside and will often have to accept the branch factory operation, but will increasingly try to devise ways of bringing the whole plant and its management to Mid-Wales.

THE RESOURCES OF THE REGION

What can Mid-Wales offer the businessman and his business? How marketable a 'product' can the Board offer its customers who are interested in investing in the area?:

Industrial land and buildings:

(i)   Land is not expensive but zoned land is limited and serviced land is very restricted at present.

(ii) Most of the serviced land is in the public sector and normally has 'jobs created' criteria linked to it. There is a lack of private sector industrial land for service industry projects and for capital intensive projects that do not meet the job criteria.

(iii) Attractive advance factories of all sizes from 1500 sq ft (139 m^2) to 50 000 sq ft (4645 m^2) are available and rent free concessions are normally offered. Bespoke factories can be built if necessary.

Manpower:

(i)   At present unemployment percentages are high and there are sizeable pools of labour at several centres.

(ii) The labour almost always proves adaptable and effective when employed, but on paper it is largely unskilled and thus often unattractive when presented to customers.

(iii) The area's policies are geared to bringing workers into the area with the new industry. This is wholly accepted locally for key workers and is broadly accepted for other workers, though there is perhaps an increasing feeling that every effort should be made to encourage ex-patriots to return to the area.

(iv) The region, although well equipped educationally, lacks industrial training facilities.

(v) It is unusual, in that although it is a rural area, it has the services and facilities of two Universities available within its boundaries.

Housing:

(i) The Mid-Wales Industrial Development Association recognised that the policy of bringing population back to the area meant that houses had to be available in advance. In Newtown this has been achieved (with excellent results) but elsewhere the problems have been, and are still considerable.

(ii) Attempts to work through Housing Associations have so far been unsuccessful, but the Board are now trying to turn plans begun in 1974 into Housing Association houses by 1978 and 1979.

(iii) Local Authorities are struggling to meet their local needs, which has been increased by the region's happier population trends. They are willing to try to help but feel unable to keep houses empty awaiting incoming workers while they have a local waiting list. Their offers of priority for incoming key workers on house re-lets is not satisfactory for promotional purposes.

(iv) The Board in its Act, has been given housing powers, and must decide how these can best be used to achieve the end of having houses ready to match available factory space.

Finance:

(i) The region is a Development Area and there is a small area (Blaenau Ffestiniog) that is Special Development Area.

(ii) The area is therefore eligible for the full range of Regional Development Grants on buildings, plant and machinery plus all the facilities of the Selective Assistance and other schemes under the Industry Act 1972.

(iii) The Board has itself been given certain financing powers for helping the growth of industry and commerce. The details of these are being finalised but the powers will be as agents of the Welsh Development Agency though they will be promoted and operated directly by the Board.

(iv) The problem for the Board is to select from this the best possible deal for a customer from this range of financial assistance. To help customers, it is intended to offer advice on choosing and applying for finance as a part of the Board's overall development package.

Communications:

(i) Geographically the region is well located on the doorstep of several of Britain's main industrial areas.

(ii) Favourable geography is only of value however if it is made effective by suitable communications.

(iii) The executive in the area depends on his motor car for most business trips and to give him access to air services and to Inter City rail facilities (though there are limited railway services available in the region).

(iv) For the movement of goods, mileage is the important factor, and Britain's industry, its ports and its consumer markets are relatively accessible on that criteria.

Quality of life:

(i) There is no more attractive environment in Britain. The region offers the perfect answer to the increasing desire for non-urban living.

(ii) Educationally the region is excellent, both in schooling and by its ready access to Universities.

(iii) There is every opportunity for active sport and recreation though there is a lack of spectator sport. Social and cultural societies are extensively developed at local and regional level.

(iv) Several of the towns are well equipped with shopping but non can offer the highest grades of services (— there is no Marks & Spencer store in the area) and the region is therefore dependent, to some extent, on larger centres outside its boundaries, such as Shrewsbury, Wrexham, Chester, Hereford, Swansea and Cardiff.

FUTURE PROSPECTS

The Board believe that they can build an attractive package from the resources described. Of course the ability to influence 'product development' is a vital part of any marketing operation and the Board should, through its responsibility to co-ordinate development in its region and its powers to take direct action, be able to exert some influence on the 'product' it offers.

The Mid-Wales Industrial Development Association's work was, for very sound reasons, directed largely at incoming industry. Their success has led to there being a range of businesses within the region which are now firmly established and, with other successful local firms, offer a real source of potential growth if the Board's facilities can be made attractive for them.

In addition there seems every likelihood that within the region's population, there is a supply of embryo entrepreneurs who should be sought out and given the confidence, the resources and quite possibly the training, to found and run their businesses.

The Board already agreed that a substantial effort should be made to promote growth from within the region. It is likely that success will depend on the Board being able to make its Financial Scheme attractive to such projects and there is no doubt that some form of grant aid, to supplement the Board's loan funds, would be of great value. Apart from finance the Board will be offering a full range of technical advisory services similar to those formerly provided through CoSIRA, plus an expanded management and marketing advisory service. Particular attention will be paid to achieving growth by helping the company to develop its markets.

Traditionally the advance factory has been identified with incoming industry. It is hoped that the Board's future programme for industrial and commercial buildings will be widely based and will create space for both manufacturing and service industries and it may include buildings especially designed to service the needs of the embryo or expanding regional company. It may be possible for example to develop premises for businesses especially adapted to tap the £7 million spent annually by visitors to the area on gifts and souvenirs. This is expenditure that is currently supplied from goods that are mainly produced outside the region.

The Board believe that, in a World that is increasingly disenchanted with urban living, rural Wales offers sound opportunities that will prove more and more attractive to those from outside and that, if the Board can provide the means, there are many people at present within the region who will take the chance to establish themselves in business.

25 The future role of the Highlands and Islands Development Board in the encouragement of rural-based industries

J K FARQUHARSON

INTRODUCTION

I seem to recall once reading a book which purported to deal with the future of the Scottish Highlands. About 90% of it was in fact devoted to the past of the Scottish Highlands, and the remainder consisted of rather anaemic and somewhat politically slanted speculation about what might happen in the next few years. Perhaps it merely reflected that exaggerated concern — some might say obsession — about the past which, to my mind at least, serves as an unwelcome distraction in the task of building a healthier economic and social future for the Highlands and Islands. At all events, I hope to achieve a better balance in this paper.

First let me define my terms. The Highlands and Islands Development Board was set up in 1965 to assist the people of the Highlands and Islands to improve their economic and social conditions and to enable the Highlands and Islands to play a more effective part in the economic and social development of the nation; it is responsible to the Secretary of State for Scotland, and funded by grant-in-aid from the Treasury, with a current annual budget of about £11 million. The Highlands and Islands, in the context of the Board, covers about half the land-mass of Scotland (Figure 1) including all the significant islands except the Cumbraes in the Firth of Clyde, but containing a total population of only about 322 000. The Scottish Economic Planning Departmental defines 'rural factory building' as the provision of factories . . . "in rural areas or country towns having populations of not more than 15 000 inhabitants." Apart from Inverness (population 37 000), the largest towns in the Highlands and Islands have no more than 10 000 inhabitants — so only Inverness is excluded from my scope. 'Industry' I will take mainly to mean manufacturing and processing industry, together with

Figure 1
THE AREA OF THE HIGHLANDS AND ISLANDS DEVELOPMENT BOARD

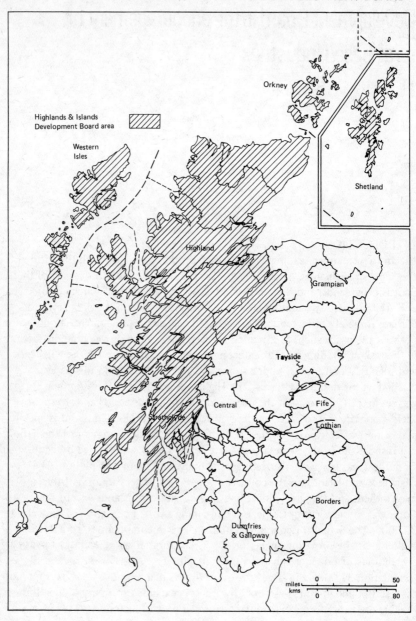

craft work. Agriculture and forestry, fishing and tourism each make a vital and major contribution to the economy of the area we cover, but they do not fall within my sphere of responsibility within the Board, and it would not be pertinent for me to discuss them in detail.

In tackling my theme, I shall distinguish three separate roles which I expect the Board to play in the foreseeable future. These may conveniently be described as the 'supportive role', the 'fostering role', and the 'research and lobbying role'. I will then go on to discuss various specific types of development in which we may be involved, and conclude with a brief general review of future prospects as I see them. To set the future scene in perspective, on the reasonable assumption that there will be no sudden radical change in the Board's direction, it will be necessary to refer to past and present policies. But I will do my best to be more forward-looking than those responsible for the book I mentioned above.

THE SUPPORTIVE ROLE

Our central task in encouraging rural-based industries, and the one for which we are best known, is to support commercial enterprises, both in helping to provide them with capital and in a variety of other ways. The Board offers direct assistance towards the capital funding of industrial, craft and selected commercial projects through grants, low-interest loans and/or subscription for shares. This assistance is individually tailored to the needs of each individual project, within certain constraints — in particular, we normally expect the private business to raise about 50% of the total capital required from commercial sources of funds (including bank overdraft facilities), and the absolute minimum requirement is a private sector contribution of 30%. Our vetting process requires the applicant to estimate the total capital required to fund his project — consisting usually of building costs, plant and equipment purchases, and working capital — and to demonstrate his ability to find the appropriate share of this sum from the private sector. In deciding whether to assist, we do our best to assess both the commercial viability of the project and the contribution it will make to the economic development of the area. Although we devote a good deal of effort to various kinds of industrial promotion, this type of assistance is largely responsive, in the sense that we are responding to someone else's plans rather than implementing our own. For this very reason, however, it enables us to stimulate a much higher volume of development than we could ever achieve by more direct measures, and represents an effective use of a large proportion of our total staff resources.

An important variation in the theme of straightforward financial assistance, and one which is rather more interventionist in character, is the construction by the Board of factories and workshops for leasing to light manufacturing or craft firms. These buildings may be either 'advance' — ie, built on a speculative basis in order to attract manufacturing projects to particular communities — or 'bespoke', custom-built for the needs of a particular business. Rents are fixed independently by the District Valuer, and are normally well below an economic level in relation to current building costs. In addition, the Board has discretion to waive rent for up to two years at the beginning of the tenancy, thus affording firms a modest relief from financial pressures during what can often be a difficult phase in their development. By choosing the locations for new factories and workshops, the Board is able, to a limited extent, to steer new projects to those areas which are in need of economic stimulation and are capable of providing the necessary labour for new enterprises. It is, of course, not our policy to try to inveigle firms to areas where their prospects of commercial success will be jeopardised by problems of inadequate labour supplies, insupportable transport difficulties or other features of some of our remoter communities. Development in these communities must generally be sought by means other than the attraction of 'footloose' manufacturing industry.

The third main strand in our supportive work is the provision of an extensive range of services for small firms throughout our area. Within our own staff we include specialists in finance and management services, production engineering, manpower questions, and marketing and transport services, as well as a number of people with first-hand experience of specific industries. When necessary, this expertise can be supplemented by the use of outside consultants to advise on specific problems. The methods whereby these resources are placed at the disposal of Highland firms are many and various. In the first place, we have built up a pretty comprehensive knowledge of manufacturing and crafts firms in our area during the past eleven years, so that we are fairly well able to assess their needs — whilst they too are increasingly aware of the Board as a source of help and advice. Through our financial staff, we keep in touch with firms who have received financial assistance, and this helps to identify specific problems where a Board specialist may be able to help — for example, in improving a budgetary control system or a workshop layout, in designing a training programme or a marketing policy. Another useful device is the organisation of business workshops or seminars in different centres where local businessmen can meet to discuss common problems, with benefit of guidance from outside specialists.

Perhaps the most widespread problem among Highland firms is that of marketing. Because of the distance which separates them from the country's main industrial areas and concentrations of population; small firms find it difficult to maintain adequate contacts with their markets and to keep abreast of competitive trends, whilst many lack the sophistication to conceive and pursue a positive marketing policy. We therefore give particular attention to direct support with marketing, notably by helping firms to show their products at appropriate trade exhibitions (including our own Highland Trade Fair held each October at Aviemore), and by the publication of an attractive regional product catalogue, the 'Buyer's Guide', which is widely circulated to commercial buyers at home and abroad.

Another field in which we are becoming increasingly involved is that of training. Many different forms of training are required if a rural population is to adapt successfully to the needs of new industries, and many smaller employers in rural areas need rather more help than can readily be made available from the Training Services Agency, the Industrial Training Boards or other bodies with nationwide responsibilities. Our object here is not to duplicate the functions of these national bodies, but to collaborate with them to complement the services which they can provide. Our help can take the form of financial support for specific training programmes, advice in the drawing up and monitoring of such programmes, or direct involvement in the organisation of suitable courses. We believe that this activity closely reflects the objectives of the European Social Fund, and are engaged in seeking their financial support.

THE FOSTERING ROLE

So much for the supportive approach. We recognise that something more is required if we are to fulfil the hopes of those responsible for establishing the Board, and if the full development potential of the Highlands and Islands is to be realised. We relish too the challenge to initiative and creativity which lies in seeking to devise or identify and realise new development opportunities. I call this the fostering approach because it involves us in taking some initiative to bring together an appropriate mix of people, a product or products, money, and probably several other factors, which can combine to form the basis of a business venture. And if experience has taught us anything, it is that the central resource in development is not money, not land, not ideas, not plans, but people. In devising or identifying new development opportunities, we must build and depend on people. I am talking, of course, about people outside our own staff resources — our own organisation and capacity is geared primarily to the supportive rather than the entrepreneurial role, and it is unrealistic to expect our staff to shoulder the main burden of responsibility for running a whole series of business ventures. So we attach great importance to finding the right people with whom to work — people with motivation and some ambition, combined with a sense of commercial realities and a decent modesty which permits them to recognise a problem when they see one.

Of course people must be matched with products which are appropriate to their experience or capacity, as well as being capable of finding a market at an economic price. It is of little use to find a product with a booming market if all the engineering skills of Birmingham are needed to make it, or to produce a simple article in penny-numbers when the market price is set by mass-production in some other industrial area. So, unless we are lucky enough to come across someone with a specialised talent, we tend to think of consumer products which require fairly simple skills and which perhaps command some slight cachet by virtue of their place of origin.

The fostering approach does not produce quick results, and we cannot claim any major successes for it yet. Nevertheless, we are experimenting now and will continue to experiment, particularly in the economically fragile parts of our area. Some examples may be mentioned:

(i) In Barra we have set up and financed a programme of training in hand-operated machine knitting — having first identified that there were a number of women in the island who were interested in working full-time at this activity, and that a knitwear marketing firm in London were prepared to offer advice on design and handle the marketing of production with a view to becoming commercially involved in the project after the labour force was adequately trained. This scheme has encountered various problems which we are still trying to resolve, and we are fortunate in having found an effective local manageress to supervise the operation on a day-to-day basis. However, without our willingness to meet the full cost of developing a trained work force, it is unlikely that any commercial interest could have been attracted.

(ii) In the Uists we have established that there are a number of experienced weavers who are not finding a suitable outlet for their capabilities. We are seeking to identify market openings for articles composed of or containing woven material, and may seek the assistance of design consultants to devise a new product range. This will then be put at the disposal of any organisation which is willing to employ the weavers. Alternatively, the weavers themselves may decide to set up a cooperative — a move in which we would give them every encouragement and help, provided that adequate local involvement and motivation were evident.

(iii) On the west coast of the island of Lewis, we are planning to finance the lion's share of major fish-drying and fish-meal projects, based on fishing resources to the west of the Outer Isles. The fish-drying venture will involve Norwegian interests and depend on their expertise and markets, but would have had no prospect of going ahead if the Board had restricted itself to its normal supportive role. So in this case we envisage a special kind of partnership to bring substantial development to a very remote and difficult area.

THE RESEARCH AND LOBBYING ROLE

The Board's powers of financial support are restricted by certain limits on the total amount of capital which can be invested in any one project at any one time.

Roughly speaking, this means that we have little or no financial leverage on industrial projects costing more than £1 million in total. It does not mean that we have no interest in encouraging such projects. The Board has always taken the view that the Highland economy would be strengthened by the establishment of a selected range of large-scale capital-intensive projects, particularly in the Moray Firth area. It is perhaps stretching a point to call these 'rural-based' but certainly they have a major impact on an extensive rural area.

If we are to have any hope of influencing such developments, we must first be able to talk intelligently about them, to understand what advantages the area may have for them, to know what the snags are. Hence the need for research. The Board has its own Policy Research Division, and beyond that is willing to spend quite substantial sums on specialised consultancy studies, often working in close consultation with the appropriate Regional or Island Council.

Armed with the results of our research, we are in a position to represent the economic interest of the area in a responsible way to both Central Government and commercial interests. This will continue to be an important part of our work, although passing largely unnoticed by the public at large. The outstanding current example is our work in connection with oil and/or gas processing, and petro-chemical production. The Board believes that this type of development should have a major contribution to make to the economy of the Inner Moray Firth area, and have supported the proposals to establish an oil refinery at Nigg Bay on the Cromarty Firth. We are now continually pressing the advantages of the Cromarty Firth for petrochemical developments based on North Sea hydrocarbons with both Central Government and with the oil and chemicals industries. Much here is likely to depend on whether the projected North Sea gas gathering pipeline system is built and — if it is — on the choice of landfall, and we are taking a very positive interest in the hope of exercising some influence in these matters.

NATURAL RESOURCE DEVELOPMENT

Let us turn now to consider some specific instances of rural-based industry which might be candidates for Board encouragement during the next twenty years or so. It would seem reasonable to start with an assessment of the potential for developing natural resources in our area. This general approach has already been fairly thoroughly explored by the Board, and I would not foresee a rapid burgeoning of new opportunities — the more obviously economic prospects are pretty fully exploited. However, if we allow a reasonable time-scale, there is scope for quite a number of new developments of this kind. Let me enumerate some of the possibilities:

(i) Food-processing: the scope here is limited by the availability of fish, sheep and cattle, and agricultural produce; however, fish-farming and the Board's new deer-farming experiment may open up new opportunities in due course.

(ii) Timber-processing: apart from individual large-scale projects which must await the maturing of a greatly enlarged crop of trees, we are seeking to encourage more modest and scattered forms of development, which could perhaps make use of scrub timber and contribute also to improvement in rural land use patterns in the Highlands and Islands.

(iii) New mineral projects: although we foresee no minerals 'bonanza' (and indeed, there is strong opposition to some minerals projects on environmental grounds), new techniques of exploration or exploitation and changing economic circumstances are likely to render viable the development and perhaps processing of some mineral resources which today lie fallow. Some of these could help to revitalise rural communities by providing steady local employment for men over a long period.

(iv) Production of peat coke: because of the relative abundance of competing sources of energy in the UK, we believe that large-scale development of peat for energy purposes is unlikely. Accordingly, we are trying to identify other uses for peat in which it would have a premium value. One such use could be the production of peat coke, which can in turn be used in the manufacture of silicon and ferro-silicon.

THE DOUBLE SIGNIFICANCE OF ENERGY

Perhaps the most exciting and challenging of all the natural resources of the Highlands is its potential as a fount of energy. I refer not so much to hydro-electricity, or even offshore oil and gas, which are already part of an evolving scene, as to nuclear energy, wave-power and (in a limited way) wind-power. At Dounreay, we have the Prototype Fast Reactor in service, and we believe that there are strong arguments for locating the first Commercial Fast Reactor there. This would keep the Commercial Fast Reactor well away from major centres of population — the people of nearby Thurso show little apprehension about the prospect. It would thus go some way to meeting the objections of its opponents, while retaining the benefit of all the work which has been devoted to this technology, and the option to expand our use of the technology at a later date should circumstances make this desirable. Harnessing of the power of the Atlantic waves to the west of the Outer Isles may well prove a partial alternative to nuclear power, and here too we are keeping in close touch with the progress of research sponsored by the Department of Energy. Should some of the present hopes for this form of energy be fulfilled, the implications for electro-intensive industrial developments in the Western Isles could transform the economic prospects of one of the least prosperous parts of the area which we cover. More generally, it is not entirely far-fetched to see the Highlands and Islands becoming a power-house for Britain, based primarily on oil and gas, nuclear energy and the power of the

Atlantic waves. If history develops this way — and we will keep trying to nudge it in that direction — there will be a strong tendency to locate at least one major industrial complex in the north.

But of course energy is even more significant in a different way. Contemporary patterns of rural development, which we blithely plan to extend and refine in the future, are utterly dependent on the availability of liberal supplies of energy at a tolerable cost. Who knows what the situation will be in this respect by the end of the century? It is all very well to depict the Highlands as a fount of energy: so they can be, but the resources available for our kind of rural development and the markets for our products depend on much wider considerations. If energy is scarce and expensive on a global basis, what will happen to our motor-borne tourist traffic, to the transport costs of our raw materials or finished products, to our energy-intensive agriculture and fishing? What indeed will happen to the international economy of which we are all part? Some might say we will have to develop an entirely different development strategy, emphasising greater self-sufficiency and simpler technology. Personally, I would prefer that we invest in developing as many new energy options as possible and for all their adaptability I doubt whether many Highlanders would relish emulating Mr and Mrs Good of Surbiton in their return to nature.

LIGHT INDUSTRY AND CRAFTS

Light industry is always in demand among development-hungry communities, and we shall continue to encourage its development in all the population centres of our area. Considering our extreme peripheral location within the UK, we have made reasonable progress in this respect, and this should be maintained if we can avoid a prolonged energy crisis. We have made particular efforts to encourage projects in the electronics field and there are small electronics manufacturing firms in such unlikely places as Sanday (Orkney Islands), Skye and Wick. But the term 'light industry' covers a very wide field, and we want as much diversity as we can get — the interesting point is that we have already succeeded in attracting some manufacturing activities which, on the face of it, sound very unlikely candidates for a Highland location. So we are not too convinced of the merits of a highly selective approach to industrial promotion.

What we call 'the crafts industry' has achieved a remarkable rate of expansion and diversification in recent years, and the industry has a unique role to play in Highland development. By its very nature, it is capable of extending its ramifications into many of the remotest parts of the area, where it is effectively impossible to attract or establish conventional manufacturing industry of any kind. This capacity for dispersal, which embraces both traditional and non-traditional crafts, is an invaluable attribute from our viewpoint, and we have every confidence in the further growth potential of the industry. Fields in which Highland craft producers have already achieved conspicuous success include glass, pottery and china; precious metals and jewellery; high quality knitwear; and soft toys. But the diversity of craft activity is already impressive, and we will build on this in the future. One other point is worth mentioning. The characteristic of dispersal, which is so valuable from a rural development viewpoint, gives rise to problems for the individual craft firms concerned. We have therefore formulated proposals for the establishment of 'Highlands Craftpoint', a new multi-functional project designed as an offshoot of the Board to stimulate and support the development of the crafts industry, primarily but not exclusively within 'our' area. These proposals are the outcome of a searching investigation of the needs of the crafts industry in the Highlands and Islands. Their central objective is to stimulate and support the development of the industry by providing a comprehensive range of services, including various forms of training; employment, technical and information services; marketing services; the improvement of design and quality standards; and the encouragement of new craft activities, particularly in the more remote parts of the Highlands and Islands.

FUTURE PROSPECTS – GENERAL REVIEW

Apart from the supreme issue of peace or war, it seems to me that the crucial factor overhanging decisions on strategy for rural development to the end of this century is that of progress in energy technology. Energy costs will have a decisive part to play in determining what is feasible in our work, through their impact on the markets we serve and on the technology we employ. There may be key roles for Dounreay and/or Hebridean wave power to play in this respect. The alternative of reverting to a simpler more self-sufficient way of life fills me with apprehension, not least because of the extreme social stresses it would entail. Provided we can solve the energy conundrum, the long term prospects are bright, and the Highlands and Islands can themselves contribute more than ever before to the national economy.

The Board has built up a formidable amount of experience as a foundation for its future work, and I am confident that it will have the confidence to respond to changing circumstances by pursuing a flexible approach. But the process is likely to be an evolutionary one rather than a series of radical shifts in direction; the main strands which I would discern include:

(i) The encouragement of a well balanced mix of small, medium and large-scale development according to various locational criteria, and using the various approaches I have described.

(ii) The encouragement of maximum diversity in the manufacturing and craft sectors of the economy to provide diversity of employment opportunities and to reduce the area's dependence on specific industries or markets.

(iii) Continuing efforts to exploit the existing natural resources of the area, including those relevant to the provision of energy, and to expand their potential with the object of increasing the supply of raw materials for an enlarged processing industry

(iv) The devotion of special attention to the more economically fragile areas within the Highlands and Islands, with a good deal of emphasis on grass roots development and use of the fostering approach.

Forecasting has always been a hazardous profession, and the visions we see before us may vanish like mirages as we approach. But we can only persevere, and then at least there is a chance that some of them may be realised. I count myself lucky to be involved in this endeavour.

26 Water resource development in upland Britain

D M SHEARER

INTRODUCTION

The area described as upland Britain has played a large part in the development of water resources in this country and it is possible that it will continue to do so in the future. This paper describes how water resources are expected to be further developed in England and Wales over the next twenty years and in particular the impact this is likely to have on the upland areas. It will also serve as a background to other papers which will deal in detail with particular aspects of water resource development and with development in Scotland.

The most recent and comprehensive work on water resource development in England and Wales was done by the former Water Resources Board (1973). Its report, it was disbanded in 1974, contained a recommended strategy which is still the basis for future planning. Since its publication, however, the industry has undergone a major re-organisation into the ten Regional Water Authorities shown in Figure 1. They have reviewed the Board's recommended strategy in the light of the opportunity which reorganisation has offered and with the benefit of a more recent prediction of the future population. Their comments and amendments are also described in this paper.

The problems of water resource development in Scotland are similar in some respects to those in England and Wales. The context in which they occur, however, merits a different treatment and they are dealt with separately.

To introduce the future strategy and how it will affect the upland areas, there is a brief discussion of water resources generally. A further section describes the various alternative ways in which these resources may be developed to provide a water supply to domestic and industrial consumers.

Figure 1
REGIONAL WATER AUTHORITIES

WATER RESOURCES

The single resource for the supply of water is rainfall. In particular it is that part of rainfall which is not lost by evaporation or by transpiration through plants but remains to replenish streams and underground water-bearing rocks. This residual rainfall is known as run-off and amounts to about half of the total rainfall.

Over the whole of England and Wales the average annual run-off is equivalent to a total flow of about 190 000 tcmd (thousands of cubic metres per day). As the present demand for public water supplies amounts to about 15 000 tcmd, there would appear to be an abundance of water available. While this comparison is interesting it represents only a small part of the total picture. Water supply is not the only use for streams and rivers and these other uses such as fisheries and general amenity use demand that only a portion of the total flow should be abstracted for supply purposes. Some of the residual flow left in the river can, of course, be made up of used water in the form of sewage and industrial effluents which have been returned. The transport and purification of these effluents is another legitimate use of a river but it is one which generally competes with other uses.

Probably the two major constraints on the use of water resources, however, are that rain does not fall where it is needed most nor does it fall whenever it is required. This was illustrated by Perret (1977) and Figures 2, 3 and 4 are derived from his work. Figure 2 shows the distribution of average rainfall over England and Wales and Figure 4 shows the distribution of population. It is immediately apparent that rainfall tends to concentrate upon the upland areas. These are also the areas which tend to be the least crowded. There is in fact almost an inverse relationship between areas which are wettest and those which have the highest demand for water.

This geographical distribution problem would be bad enough if the rain fell evenly throughout the year. Figure 3, which shows the rainfall in May 1976 as a percentage of the monthly average, shows that this is not the case. Across the country the range was from 250% to 25%.

The problems of water resource development are thus ones of storing sufficient water to provide a reliable steady output from a fluctuating supply of rain and transporting the water to the areas where it is needed.

TYPES OF WATER RESOURCE DEVELOPMENT

In upland Britain the most important form of resource development has been surface storage either in natural lakes or in man-made reservoirs. The water from the outlet works is either conveyed in a pipe or aqueduct directly to the place where it is needed or it is released back into the river to be abstracted later on downstream nearer the supply point.

The former use of surface storage is known as direct supply and most of the

Figure 2
AVERAGE ANNUAL RAINFALL IN ENGLAND AND WALES

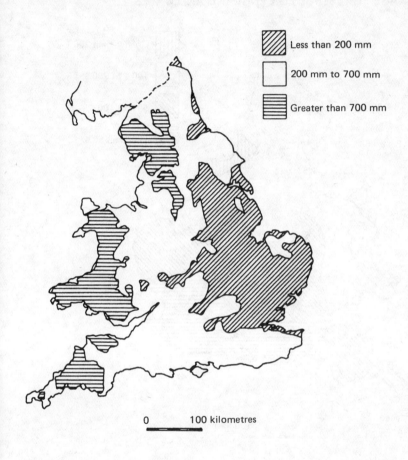

Less than 200 mm

200 mm to 700 mm

Greater than 700 mm

0   100 kilometres

Figure 3

RAINFALL IN MAY 1976 AS A PERCENTAGE OF THE MONTHLY
AVERAGE FOR 1916-50 FOR ENGLAND AND WALES

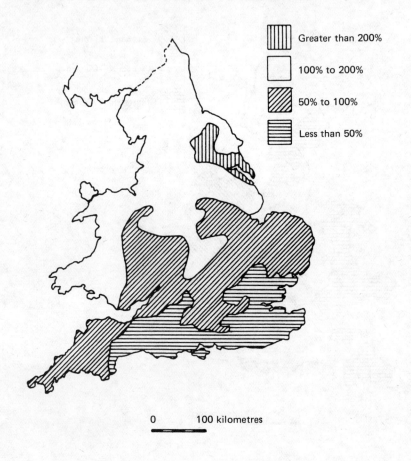

Greater than 200%

100% to 200%

50% to 100%

Less than 50%

0   100 kilometres

Figure 4
POPULATION DENSITIES IN ENGLAND AND WALES

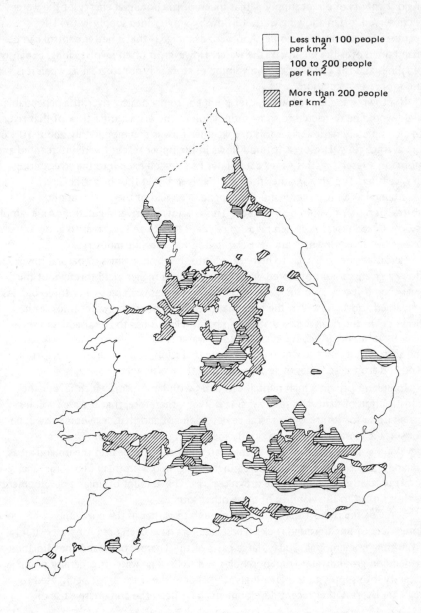

Less than 100 people per km^2

100 to 200 people per km^2

More than 200 people per km^2

developments up to about thirty years ago were of this type. Examples are Lake Vyrnwy supplying Liverpool and Thirlmere supplying Manchester. One of the major benefits of direct supply is that much of the potential energy of the water is conserved, often allowing water to flow by gravity into supply with little recourse to expensive pumping. Another advantage is that a better control can be maintained over the quality of the water. However, it often involves long, expensive pipelines and the yield for a given volume of storage is not so great as when it is used for river regulation.

If a town was supplied with water pumped from a nearby river, the dependable yield would be restricted to some proportion of the dry weather flow of that river. In a completely natural river this dry weather flow is commonly only about 10% of the average flow. However, if flood flows in the upper reaches were intercepted and stored in a reservoir, this water could later be released back into the river during dry weather. The 'dry weather flow' of the river would thus be artificially maintained at a higher level and the dependable yield of the water supply abstraction point would be increased. This is known as river regulation. An example is Cow Green reservoir which helps to regulate the River Tees so as to allow water to be abstracted downstream near Darlington for Teesside industry.

Because water only has to be released into the river at times of natural low flow, a given amount of stored water can support a higher yield throughout the year than if it was used for direct supply. The increase can be two or threefold. As explained above, however, the potential energy of the stored water is lost as it flows down the river to the abstraction point. Here it has to be raised from the river by pumping. Also, the quality of the water is usually lower when it reaches the abstraction point having received some pollution from natural run-off from the land and from discharges of sewage and industrial effluents.

In upland Britain a high rainfall coincides with land forms which favour the construction of dams and reservoirs. It is likely, therefore, that the area will be called upon for future water resource development and that development will be for surface storage. It is worth briefly mentioning other types of resource development, however. Although these are unlikely to appear in the upland areas, upland surface storage will be increasingly integrated with them in a comprehensive strategy to supply water to the urban centres. The amount of upland development : is thus linked to the viability of these other sources.

Some of the run-off soaks into the ground to gather in the pores and interstices of underground rocks. These aquifers have been used for water supply from time immemorial. Today, large parts of the Thames basin and the Midlands depend on groundwater from boreholes and wells. The water is generally pumped directly into supply but, increasingly, the underground storage is being used to regulate rivers. Other recent developments have been the conjunctive use of underground and surface sources together to produce a greater yield than the sum of the individual yields, and the artificial recharge of aquifers from surface sources.

The great estuaries of the Solway, the River Dee, Morecambe Bay and The Wash have all been considered as providing areas for surface storage. There is less loss of agricultural land involved and the storage can often be sited reasonably close to the centres of demand. However, the construction of these estuarial reservoirs raises many ecological and technical problems and the water for filling them has to be drawn from the more polluted downstream sources. All of this adds to their cost.

Desalination of sea water has often been suggested as a means of avoiding using land for reservoirs. Unfortunately, it is also very expensive. The Water Resources Board (1973) estimated that the unit cost of water from a desalination plant would between 2.5 to 15 times more expensive than water from a conventional source. Since then the rise in energy costs have widened the gap considerably. The environmental effects have often been under-estimated since a desalination plant is a large intrusion into the landscape comparable to a small electricity power station.

THE FUTURE DEMAND FOR WATER

Whilst it is impossible to estimate the future demand for water precisely, an attempt must be made. It is not unusual for a new project to take fifteen years to design, promote and build and a forecast must look at least that far ahead. A good forecaster will always say what assumptions his forecast is based upon and will also estimate how wrong he is likely to be. Unfortunately, these qualifications are often forgotten after the forecast has been quoted a few times. This is particularly true if it can be simplified to a phrase like 'the demand for water will double by the end of the century'.

Forecasting domestic water consumption depends upon estimating numbers of people and how much each of them will use. Industrial consumption is very much more complex depending as it does on the type of industry, the level of output of the product, the use to which water is put within the manufacturing process and the degree to which it is expedient to re-use water.

The Water Resources Board (1973) estimated that by 2001 demand on public water supplies would rise from 14 000 tcmd to between 26 000 tcmd and 28 000 tcmd. It would thus double. This estimate had to be made at a time when forecasts of population were undergoing significant changes. In 1965, the 2001 population had been predicted by the Office of Population, Censuses and Surveys (OPCS) at 66 million. In 1971 this was reduced to 58.5 million and to 55.5 million in 1972. The Board adopted for planning purposes the higher demand of 28 000 tcmd.

Allowing for the development of local sources in self-sufficient areas such as South-West England, they concluded that there would be an overall strategic deficit of 9 500 tcmd by the year 2001.

THE WATER RESOURCES BOARD'S PROPOSALS

The Board considered several ways in which this strategic deficit could be made up. Each alternative strategy was a mixture of the different types of development which have been described. Some relied heavily upon constructing new inland reservoirs in parts of upland Britain and elsewhere while others included estuarial storage and desalination plants. They attempted to weigh all of the implications of each alternative including cost, the use of land and the impact on the environment. They also considered the merits of local self- sufficiency compared with moving water from the wetter to the drier areas.

Their recommendations were inevitably a best compromise, but generally they favoured moving water to the drier areas. The proposals were divided into two parts, a short term programme for implementation by 1981 followed by a long term strategy.

Three new reservoirs were proposed for the short term, Brenig in North Wales; Kielder in Northumbria; and Carsington near the Peak District. Three existing reservoirs were to be enlarged, Stocks in Lancashire; Grimwith in Yorkshire; and Craig Goch in Mid-Wales. Four other existing reservoirs were to have their use changed from direct supply to include some degree of river regulation while further river regulation would be achieved by exploiting groundwater resources. The short term programme was completed by re-deploying the compensation water from the Elan, Ladybower and Vyrnwy reservoirs and by a tidal barrage scheme on the Yorkshire Ouse.

The Board's longer term strategy required the following major projects:
(i) Estuary storage in the Dee.
(ii) New reservoirs at Longdon Marsh near Tewksbury and Aston near Derby.
(iii) The enlargement of Hawsewater and Llyn Brianne.
(iv) The redeployment of Lake Vrynwy.
(v) Groundwater development in the Vale of York.

Other inland reservoir sites were also considered by the Board, but, for one reason or another, were not favoured. These included Irthing and Borrowbeck in Cumbria, Hellifield in Lancashire and Otmoor near Oxford.

LAND REQUIREMENTS

It is interesting to note that the Board rejected the least cost solution to the long term problem which depended heavily upon inland storage. This would have been about £100m cheaper at 1972 prices but would have taken 10 300 ha of land,

Figure 5

THE WATER RESOURCES BOARD PREFERRED STRATEGY OF RESOURCE DEVELOPMENT

303

almost twice as much as that for their preferred strategy. This and the impact on the environment was their principal reason for rejecting it.

A detailed look at the requirements by the water industry for land in upland Britain will be the subject of a separate paper. However, it is relevant to reproduce here the comments which were made to the Water Resources Board by various interests such as the Nature Conservancy, Countryside Commission and the NFU concerning two of the reservoirs situated in upland Britain which the Board recommended should be developed or enlarged. These were included as an Appendix to their 1973 report and illustrate the range of reactions which are encountered.

"Kielder (new): The site is on the river North Tyne in the Kielder Forest in Northumberland. The land is mainly owned by the Forestry Commission (who do not object to the proposal). The area is heavily wooded with conifer and the agricultural land is mainly low grade down to pasture. The proposed reservoir area of about 1 100 ha contains about 70 properties, of which about 45 belong to the Forestry Commission for occupation by their employees. The occupants would be re-housed nearby. The remaining properties include some farm buildings and several holiday cottages."

"The Countryside Commission would generally welcome the reservoir as an attractive landscape feature with considerable recreation potential; and because it would be large enough to reduce the need for other reservoirs, some of which might be proposed in national parks. The Nature Conservancy have no objection to the scheme. The MAFF say that the quality of the land and the type of holding is such that they are not able to suggest a reservoir site less damaging to agriculture: the NFU withdrew their objection at the Public Inquiry. The local planning authority are in favour of the scheme."

"Haweswater (enlargement): Manchester Corporation's Haweswater reservoir lies within the Lake District National Park on the headwaters of the river Lowther, a tributary of the Eden. . . ."

"The enlarged reservoir would require less than 200 ha of additional land. The existing hotel, road and footpaths would be submerged, but there would be little effect on agricultural land and other properties. A site of special scientific interest, Noddle Low Forest, would be affected and the Nature Conservancy would on this account object to the enlargement unless it were essential to save Morecambe Bay or Solway."

"The possibility of enlarging Haweswater has already aroused strong opposition. The Countryside Commission would regard raising the dam on the scale envisaged as a further serious intrusion on the landscape of the national park and suggest that the new higher dam and the greater water area would be out of scale with the surrounding hills; they would object to this enlargement."

CHANGES SINCE 1974

The Water Resources Board's report of 1973 is still the basis for forward planning in the industry. However, since its publication, two significant changes have occurred. The industry itself has been reorganised and the estimates of future population, and hence of future water demand, have continued to fall. There has also been in the short term an economic recession. The implications of this for the long term are not yet clear.

From about 200 separate water undertakings, nearly 2 000 bodies exercising sewerage and sewage disposal functions and 29 river authorities, the industry was reorganised in 1974 into ten multi-functional regional water authorities. Their boundaries are shown on Figure 1.

The Authorities have been charged with managing the whole water cycle. They have reviewed the resources which they inherited and in many cases have found that the new organisation will allow more scope for integrating supplies within their area. This will have the effect of deferring the need for new resources.

The Board's report had noted that the estimated year 2001 population of England and Wales had dropped from 66 million in 1965 to 55.5 million in 1972. This decline has continued. In 1976 the OPCS predicted a year 2001 population of 52.2 million. Unless the per capita demand for water increases faster than expected, this will also slow down the rate at which new resources will have to be developed.

Economic growth has also been less than expected. Between 1964 and 1970 it was hoped to increase national output by 3.8% compound per annum. In fact, national output increased by only 2.4% compound per annum between 1964 and 1974. The implications for the industrial demand for water are clear. The present economic recession has had an even more dramatic effect with the demand for water actually falling in some areas. Hopefully, this recession is only in the short term.

Such overall figures can, however, mask local shortages and particular areas, such as Teesside which is heavily dependent on the petro-chemical industry, are expected to show a rapid recovery of demand back to previous rates of increase.

The rapid relative rise in energy costs since 1974 also requires that some of the strategic proposals for the transfer of large quantities of water over watersheds between rivers should be reviewed. The costs of alternatives will also have risen, however.

CONCLUSIONS

Upland Britain will continue to be called upon to provide land for the supply of water which we, as an industrialised nation, demand. Over the next twenty years it is probable that new inland storage sites will be required as described in the

Water Resources Board's proposals. The rate at which these proposals will be implemented will probably be slower than suggested in their 1973 report. Notwithstanding this, there are parts of the country where local shortages are becoming acute and new sources are either under construction, such as at Kielder, or are being actively promoted such as at Carsington and Craig Goch. The 1976 drought was also a timely reminder of the meaning of reliable yield.

The Water Resources Board was aware of the rapidly changing environment in which they were making their plans and suggested a programme of reviewing proposals nearer the time of their implementation. These may alter the longer term strategies.

Any activity which attempts to predict the future has only a dubious claim to call itself a science. Water resource planning is certainly no exception. The days of firm plans have been over for many years and efforts are being directed increasingly to the difficult task of developing a flexible response to problems which does not demand a particular view of the future.

REFERENCES

Perret, M (1977)   Planning for water resources.   *Long Range Planning,* **10,** 65-72.

Water Resources Board (1973)   *Water resources in England and Wales.* London: HMSO.

7 Requirements by the Welsh National Water Development Authority for land in upland Wales and the problems of multiple use

J H T JAMES

INTRODUCTION

I would emphasise at the beginning of this paper that I am a Chartered Surveyor who came into the water industry upon re-organisation in 1974 and can in no way claim to be an expert in the field of water resources. I can however, claim to have some knowledge of the management of land. My experience of the water industry is limited to Wales and I shall therefore confine my remarks to the demands for land, and the associated problems of management, within Wales.

In Wales we do not suffer from quite the same pressure for recreational land use that is to be found in upland areas nearer to the great centres of population, but with that exception, I feel our problems and our requirements are reasonably typical of those to be found elsewhere in upland Britain.

In considering the future use of land by Water Authorities the problem falls into two quite distinct parts:
(i)   The requirement for additional land.
(ii) The efficient management of land owned by the Authority.

In the last category the expression 'land' also includes the efficient management of water/space.

LAND REQUIREMENTS

The fundamental principle of the regulation of river flows and the greater reliance on rivers as the immediate source of abstraction for public water supply is accepted. It is clear that the adoption of this principle will have a considerable effect upon the requirement for additional land. It will tend to reduce the numbers of small, purely local, reservoirs that might be needed and concentrate requirements into groups of much larger reservoirs in clearly defined areas. In the case of Wales these reservoirs already exist and all that is required is some enlargement.

The Report of the Water Resources Board indicated the following projects within upland Wales:

(i) Construction of Brenig Reservoir.

(ii) Enlargement of Craig Goch Reservoir.

(iii) Enlargement of Llyn Brianne.

Llyn Brenig has now been completed and is in the process of filling. The water surface of this lake has an area of 430 hectares. In addition to the water, the Authority owns an estate of 1020 hectares of which 375 hectares is forest, 565 hectares is open moorland and 80 hectares is pasture.

Llyn Brenig together with Alwen, Llyn Celyn and Llyn Tegid (Bala Lake) form the group of reservoirs used in the Dee Regulation system. The main abstraction of water, the majority of which goes to the North West Water Authority, occurs in the lower reaches of the Dee in the vicinity of Chester. The North West Water Authority have announced that they will not be seeking new sources of water within Wales and it is considered that the Dee System will be adequate to meet forseeable future demand.

The enlargement of Craig Goch is being actively considered at the present time by the Welsh National Water Development Authority (WNWDA) and the Severn-Trent Water Authority. If it is decided to proceed with the scheme the lake so created will have a surface area of 809 hectares and will be the largest man-made lake in Europe. The area of the existing Craig Goch reservoir is 88 hectares therefore the requirement for additional land will be 721 hectares. The land needed for this scheme is already owned by WNWDA.

Water from the present Elan Valley reservoir complex, which includes Craig Goch, is taken by aquaduct to the city of Birmingham. The enlarged reservoir would meet the foreseeable needs of the Severn-Trent and Welsh Water Authorities well into the next century. In addition to supplying Birmingham, Craig Goch would be used to regulate flows in the river Wye and the river Severn as well. By means of the proposed Wye/Usk transfer scheme Craig Goch water could be supplied to consumers in south east Wales.

The enlargement of Llyn Brianne is regarded as an alternative scheme to Craig Goch. It would supply the future needs of the WNWDA but would not be of use to the Severn-Trent Authority. Llyn Brianne lies in an extremely steep sided valley one half of which is devoted to forestry and the other to hill sheep farming. If it were decided to proceed with this scheme the requirement for land would not be great due to the conformation of the valley.

The areas in the west of Wales may currently be regarded as self sufficient and any future demands for water could be met by enlargements to existing systems.

It will be seen from the foregoing observations that the future demand for land in upland Wales for water purposes is so small as to be almost negligible.

LAND USE AND MANAGEMENT

The demand for additional land by Water Authorities may have very little effect upon the future of upland Britain but the use to which they put land already in their ownership will have considerable effect.

The main uses of upland areas can be summarised as follows:

(i)   Farming.
(ii) Forestry.
(iii) Water Catchment.
(iv) Recreation.
(v)   Nature Conservation.
(vi) Amenity/Landscape.

It is clear that the problem is not so much one of use, as one of the right use in the right place, and integration of apparently conflicting land uses.

The traditional use for hill land is farming, the raising of sheep and where the district permits, cattle. Superimposed upon this pattern in more recent years is forestry and the use of land for reservoirs. I am only concerned in this paper with the use of land by Water Authorities, but as all these functions can be found within one gathering ground they all merit consideration.

The prime requirement of any gathering ground is to provide water of an acceptable quality for the purpose for which it is intended. This must always be the first consideration of any Water Authority. This may place certain restrictions upon the use to which the gathering ground may be put, but with the advances in water treatment and the alterations in attitudes to the treatment of water, these need not be onerous.

It has always been accepted that sheep farming and forestry are suitable uses for water catchment areas. Cattle cause more problems but the very nature of most upland gathering grounds militates against their presence in large numbers. Although farming and forestry are regarded as inimical by many people I do not believe this to be so. I have always felt that it is not right to afforest good sheepwalk, but there are plenty of areas where it is clear that forestry is a more viable use. These are the two extremes of the scale. Most sheepwalks will benefit from the shelter afforded by trees and providing the planning of the area is done with care and with consideration the result will be a viable forest unit and a better sheepwalk — often provided with access roads and fencing used for both farming and forestry.

Recreational use of the countryside is on the increase and is likely to continue increasing in the future. As long as our towns continue to be unpleasant places in which to live, large numbers of people will seek recreation in the countryside. These people should not be ignored and cannot be kept out, therefore provision must be made for them. With a minimum of organisation a large number of recreational facilities can be made available and the disturbance to farming and forestry reduced to acceptable levels.

The main forms of upland recreation are:
(i)   Picnicking and sight seeing.
(ii) Walking.
(iii) Fishing.
(iv) Riding.
(v)   Wildlife Study.
(vi) Sailing.
(vii) Canoeing.
(viii) Water ski-ing.

Fishing and sailing make use of the water itself and cause relatively little disturbance to the farmer. All that is needed is suitable and agreed access. Sailing will also need a small area for unloading and launching boats and if the numbers are large enough, land for a club house. Both uses will need car parking space and toilets. Neither use causes any serious problem with regard to water quality.

Water ski-ing also makes use of the water but comes into a rather different category. Due to noise and the possibility of pollution by petrol and oil the areas that are suitable for water ski-ing are limited. Most conservationists are against this sport, because of the disturbance of peaceful areas caused by the noise of power boats and the numbers of people attracted to the site. Nevertheless, there is a considerable and legitimate demand for water ski-ing areas and Water Authorities are trying to make provision for this in their recreation plans, wherever access is good and conflicts with other interests can be reconciled, for instance, by planning, by time or space. Water ski-ing does not have very much effect upon farming or forestry carried out on adjoining areas.

Competitive canoeing, other types of canoeing do not really affect upland areas, takes place on rivers, frequently just below reservoir dams. The sport needs plenty of wild water and it is often possible to arrange water releases to suit a particular competition. There is a fine example of this on the Afon Tryweryn near Bala. Canoeing itself has little effect on farming or forestry but the sport attracts large numbers of spectators and may cause problems on land immediately adjoining the river. It is essential to arrange proper access, car parking, camping and toilet facilities. There may also be problems with fishing interests, though some anglers welcome releases of fresh water as a stimulant to fish activity.

Walking, riding and pony trekking affect land in catchment areas but are appropriate and do not cause serious problems with water quality. They cause very few problems in forestry areas, with the exception of some fire risk. On farm land they may lead to trespass and straying stock due to leaving gates open, but in hill areas much of the land is unfenced. Most of these troubles can be avoided by the planning of routes and adequate sign-posting. Most people will follow a footpath if they can easily see where it runs. The provision of good stiles at fence crossings will normally cure the problem of the open gate.

Large sheets of water in upland areas can be extremely beautiful, especially when combined with properly landscaped forestry. Add to this some sailing boats to give colour and movement and you have a major tourist attraction. The vast majority of people who use upland areas for the purposes of recreation are 'non participant'. They wish to watch, and to enjoy the beauty of the countryside without moving very far from their motor cars. Adequate provision must be made for these people. Gone are the days when a 'trespassers will be prosecuted' notice will make the problem quite literally go away. Car parks and picnic places must be provided, properly landscaped so that the intrusion of the motor car does not spoil the beauty which its owner has come to admire. Forest areas are particularly suitable for this, and can also be used to provide short 'nature trails'. Where you have a car park you will also need a toilet and provision for the collection of litter.

Where the details of car parking and picnic areas receive the attention they deserve, the loss of agricultural land and the annoyance to farmers is minimal. When this attention is skimped there will be permanent trouble. Indeed the provision of well located and designed 'honey pots' will attract and hold from straying the majority of visitors to the countryside.

The other main uses of upland areas that I have not yet dealt with are conservation and amenity. Conservation of its nature tends to be exclusive and relates normally to small areas of little agricultural value. One does not usually want unrestricted public access to these areas and I should have thought their effect upon strategy for upland Britain to be negligible, however important they may be in themselves.

Amenity is all embracing and starts with the landscape itself, developed by centuries of use by man. To preserve the landscape as we know it today depends upon the maintenance of a healthy agriculture in the hills and the judicious and careful use of forestry. All other uses must be fitted unobtrusively into this pattern. If all the bodies concerned with planning the activities in the hills work together with this object in mind the uncomparable heritage of upland Britain will be preserved for future generations and will continue to provide a livelihood for those who live there — even an improved livelihood for farmers if they are able to provide accommodation and meals, short stay camp/caravan sites, pony trekking and improved fisheries.

28 Recreational and amenity uses of reservoirs and other areas of water space in rural and upland areas

A BLENKHARN

INTRODUCTION

Reservoir construction made necessary by the growing demand for water has led to significant increases in the total areas of inland water resources in England and Wales. Often these reservoirs are associated with extensive areas of gathering grounds. As a result of the re-organisation of the water industry under the Water Act 1973, substantial areas of land and water are now under the control of ten water authorities, including the Welsh National Water Development Authority.

The Water Act 1973 gave the water authorities a clear duty to make the 'best use' of their land and water resources for recreational and amenity purposes. This means that the water industry now controls water resources which have considerable recreational potential and the water authorities have expressed a willingness to work with, and to become involved with the national park authorities and local authorities in the formulation of structure and local plans. It is clear that there are now better opportunities for the development of plans and policies with the creation of the new multi-functional water authorities. These new authorities with their considerable interests in land ownership or management are clearly in a well placed position on all aspects of planning as compared with their numerous predecessors. Where new reservoirs are being built or proposed, the initial planning includes consideration of all amenity aspects (including the provision of opportunities for participation by the general public as opposed to the past practice of limiting the use of the water to club membership only), consultation with recreational bodies, local authorities and government agencies.

The form of management of water and waterside lands will vary between the private and public sectors and this must have a direct bearing on the pattern of development. Some management policies and proposals can only be implemented if they are accepted and approved by local planning authorities. Close liaison with Planning Committees and planners is, therefore, vitally important at all stages. In deciding upon the pattern of development, it is essential to ensure that the physical constraints on water and on the land immediately alongside water, do not put intolerable burdens on the fabric of the resources, particularly if such burdens are sustained over long periods. Under these circumstances, the provision of facilities for quiet recreation such as picnic areas, viewing platforms, car parks, nature trails and the like can generally be provided without creating difficulties. On the other hand, the wider expanses of upland gathering grounds which, by their nature, are well away from the problems of intensive, localised use, might well be opened up by creating new footpaths for walking and rambling.

Given the support of central and local government, the water authorities can make a substantial contribution to the improvement of leisure facilities, both in national parks and in the countryside. In the present economic climate and because of the high cost of transport, the greatest contribution could be in urban fringe areas where facilities for leisure and recreation will relieve some of the pressures on national parks in particular and the countryside in general.

Because most of the water authorities' land and water resources are in rural areas, their plans for the recreational development of these resources may lead to conflict with those local planning authorities which are concerned with the prevention of the development of the countryside. Such problems are particularly acute in the national parks and other upland amenity areas where many of the reservoirs are located. This has two implications:

(i) that the statutory obligation placed on the water authority to make the 'best use' of their resources for recreational purposes, may conflict with the policies of local planning authorities; and

(ii) that reservoirs in lowland areas are likely to have greater recreational potential than those in the uplands.

The water authorities also have other functions which may affect recreational and amenity potential of water resources. Most important of these are land drainage and pollution control. In this respect there are no special problems, all that needs to be emphasised is that these functions, together with water conservation, are all elements in what is essentially a single task of managing river catchments, whether they be in upland, rural or urban settings, but there is some concern about the environmental aspects of river 'improvement' works, and of the relationships between conservation and land drainage.

The use for public enjoyment of any water space in the countryside must be compatible with the character and location of a particular site. There will be cases where the provision of facilities for water recreation will be just as appropriate in a national park or a country park and in some cases a good deal more economical to provide. The introduction of improved management techniques and especially zoning by time and space could be extremely valuable in dealing with local problems.

SIZE, LOCATION AND HEIGHT ABOVE SEA LEVEL OF RESERVOIRS
A total of 537 reservoirs in England and Wales of 5 acres (2 ha) or more are owned or managed by the water industry (see Table 1).   This figure includes 27

Table 1
NUMBER AND SIZE OF RESERVOIRS

Water Authority	Acreages					
	5-24.9	25-49.9	50-99.9	100-499.9	500+	TOTALS
Anglian	–	8	1	6	5	20
Northumbrian	4	4	5	11	2	26
North West	93	39	23	7	2	164
Severn Trent	17	4	4	10	5	40
Southern	–	1	1	4	–	6
South West	7	6	7	5	–	25
Thames	10	10	5	10	2	37
Wessex	7	3	3	4	1	18
Yorkshire	45	24	23	15	–	107
Wales	43	17	12	16	6	94
Totals	226	116	84	88	23	537

reservoirs controlled by 10 water companies, but these are not treated separately in the analysis but are included with the reservoirs of the appropriate water authority. Nearly 70% of these reservoirs are located within the areas of three water authorities, the North West, Yorkshire and Wales. The majority of these reservoirs are relatively small, 226 (42%) being less than 25 acres (10 ha) and another 116 (21%) below 50 acres (20 ha). Only 111 (21%) are larger than 100 acres (40ha), including 23 (4%) which exceed 500 acres (202 ha). Not only do the North West, Yorkshire and Welsh Water Authorities have the largest number of reservoirs, but they also have the highest proportion of smaller reservoirs. For example, 132 (80%) of the 164 reservoirs in the North West are below 50 acres (20 ha), while the comparable figures for Yorkshire and Wales are 64% and 65% respectively. The large reservoirs are more evenly distributed between water authorities. Of those between 100 and 500 acres (40 and 202 ha), 12 are in Northumbria, 10 in Severn Trent, 15 in Yorkshire and 16 in Wales, with only 7 in

North West. Similarly, the reservoirs above 500 acres (202 ha) are not concentrated into any particular area, although there are none within the areas of the Southern, South West or Yorkshire water authorities.

There is similar variation among these reservoirs in terms of their height above sea level (see Table 2).

Table 2
HEIGHT ABOVE SEA LEVEL OF RESERVOIRS

Water Authority	0-99	Height (in feet) 100-499	500-999	1 000+	TOTALS
Anglian	5	15	—	—	20
Northumbrian	—	6	13	7	26
North West	—	28	119	17	164
Severn Trent	—	20	13	7	40
Southern	4	2	—	—	6
South West	1	11	10	3	25
Thames	5	32	—	—	37
Wessex	2	13	3	—	18
Yorkshire	2	8	72	25	107
Wales	1	18	31	44	94
Totals	20	153	261	103	537

AREAS OF LAND AND WATER
The total area of these reservoirs at top water level is 22 883 ha (see Table 3). In terms of total water area, the highest proportions are included within the areas of Anglian (2 695 ha), North West (3 014 ha), Severn Trent (4 598 ha) and Wales (4 728 ha). Although more than half of all reservoirs were constructed before 1900, these represent only about one quarter of the total area of water. By contrast, the 54 reservoirs constructed since 1960 have a total area of 7,187 ha, nearly one third of the total. The remaining 181 reservoirs constructed between 1900 and 1959 represent just over 40% of the total area of water.

There are also important differences between water authorities. The 120 reservoirs in the North West built before 1900 comprise 61% of the total area of water, while the comparable figure for Yorkshire is 53%. By contrast, only about 10% of the total water area in both Thames and Wales was created before 1900. In several water authorities, a high proportion of the total area of water is contained within recently constructed reservoirs. For example, the 9 reservoirs

Table 3

AREAS OF LAND AND WATER OWNED BY WATER AUTHORITIES (hectares)

Water Authority	Water in Reservoirs	Gathering grounds and other lands	Total
Anglian	2 695	2 507	5 202
Northumbrian	1 751	5 555	7 306
North-West	3 014	48 304	51 318
Severn-Trent	4 598	20 039	24 637
Southern	381	1 335	1 736
South-West	872	4 030	4 902
Thames	1 782	2 127	3 909
Wessex	1 020	1 586	2 606
Yorkshire	2 042	20 327	22 369
Wales	4 728	26 126	30 853
Totals	22 883	131 956	154 838

built in Wales since 1960 represent 47% of the total area, while comparable figures for other water authorities are 53% in Northumbria, 46% in Southern and 50% in South West.

GATHERING GROUNDS

The water industry's land ownership is comparable to that of the National Trust. The largest areas of such land are owned by North West with 48 304 ha, Wales with 26 126 ha, Severn Trent with 20 039 ha and Yorkshire with 20 327 ha (see Table 3). Of the other water authorities, only Northumbrian and South West have more than 4 000 ha of land associated with their reservoirs.

Much of this total area of gathering grounds is made up of a small number of very large blocks of land, often associated with groups of reservoirs. The largest single block of land is the 17 806 ha associated with the Elan Valley reservoirs, while the Vyrnwy Estate, also in Wales, which acts as the gathering ground for Severn Trent's Lake Vyrnwy, has a total area of 9,017 ha. The North West water authority similarly owns a number of large gathering grounds associated with its reservoirs, including Wet Sleddale (9 962 ha), Haweswater (7 437 ha), the Longdendale·Group (5 484 ha), Thirlmere (4 098 ha), Anglezarke (3 962 ha) and Stocks (3 745 ha). In all, the water authorities own a total of 55 separate areas of 1 000 acres (405 ha) or more of land, including 11 above 5 000 acres (2 023 ha). Nearly all of these large blocks of land are in the uplands of the west and north;

316

22 of these above 1 000 acres (405 ha) are in the area of the North West water authority, 15 in Yorkshire and 9 in Wales.

The importance of this pattern of land ownership is not so much in its overall extent as in its location in relation to areas of high amenity value. In England, the water authorities own about 40 500 ha of land within the national parks. For example, about one sixth of the Peak District National Park is owned by three water authorities, while the North West water authority owns some 10% of the Lake District National Park. Comparable information is not available for Wales, although it appears that at least 15% of the Brecon Beacons National Park is in the ownership of the Welsh National Water Development Authority. Because of their nature, some upland gathering grounds are also important in some potential recreation areas closer to the major cities and conurbations along the flanks of the Pennines. For example, the North West water authority owns nearly 50% of the 23 310 ha included within the proposed Anglezarke Recreation Area, while about one sixth of the 38 850 ha of the proposed South Pennines Regional Recreation Area is included within gathering grounds.

RECREATION AND AMENITY USES
In all 344 reservoirs, nearly two-thirds of the total support some form of active recreation, either on the water surface or on the surrounding land areas (see Table 4). The most important single activity is fishing, which takes place at 327 reservoirs, including 30 used for both coarse and game fishing. At 228 of these there is no other form of active recreation. Apart from angling, only sailing has established itself as a major user of water supply reservoirs and is found at a total of 84, including 11 where it is the only activity.

Many of these reservoirs are used for more than one activity. For example, fishing and sailing are found together at 73 reservoirs, while only three of the reservoirs used for other active water sports are not also used for fishing. Individually, these other water-based activities are much less widespread than either fishing or sailing. Most common is sub-aqua diving which takes place at 22 reservoirs, while canoeing was reported at 19 reservoirs, rowing at 9, water skiing at 3 and swimming at 1.

RECREATIONAL USE AND HEIGHT ABOVE SEA LEVEL
The relationship between the pattern of recreational use and the height of reservoirs suggests that the main influence of height is on the distribution of coarse fishing. There are 80 reservoirs which provide coarse fishing, 48 of which are below 500 feet (152m), while only 2 of the other 32 are above 1 000 feet (305m). To a large extent this is probably the result of the water chemistry and other environmental conditions characteristic of reservoirs at the higher levels,

Table 4
ACTIVE RECREATION ON RESERVOIRS AND THEIR SURROUNDING AREAS

Water Authority	Coarse Fishing	Game Fishing	Sailing	Canoeing	Rowing	Sub-aqua Club/Police	Swimming	Water Skiing
Anglian	5	9	8	—	—	3	—	2
Northumbrian	2	23	3	2	2	5	—	1
North West	19	69	13	1	1	1	1	—
Severn Trent	8	23	11	1	1	2	—	—
Southern	—	6	2	1	—	—	—	—
South West	3	22	6	5	2	—	—	—
Thames	26	5	7	1	1	1	—	—
Wessex	2	12	5	—	—	15	—	—
Yorkshire	8	29	15	4	1	5	—	—
Wales	7	79	14	4	1	—	—	—
Totals	80	277	84	19	9	22	1	3

but it may also reflect the fact that many upland reservoirs are located in northern areas where coarse fish are reaching the limit of their distribution.

Height above sea level appears to have much less influence on the distribution of other activities. For example, there are 145 reservoirs between 500 and 1 000 feet (152-305m) which provide game fishing and another 50 above 1 000 feet (305m), 39 of which are in Wales. There are also a number of reservoirs which provide facilities for sailing at the higher levels. While 44 of the 84 reservoirs used for sailing are below 500 feet (152m), there are 28 between 500 and 1 000 feet (152-305m) and another 12 above 1 000 feet (305m). Similarly, 39 of the reservoirs over 1 000 feet (305m) provide opportunities for informal recreation, while only 12 of these in this category make no provision for recreation at all.

To some extent, this suggests that increasing height above sea level does not limit the potential of a reservoir for active recreation, with the notable exception of coarse fishing. At the same time, it is likely that this pattern also reflects the past policies of water undertakings in that recreational uses were normally first permitted at such reservoirs well away from the point of supply. There is also the point that the recreational potential of many upland reservoirs is reduced, not so much by their physical characteristics as by their inaccessibility and distance from the main centres of population.

INFORMAL RECREATION

The use of the land around reservoirs for informal recreation is more difficult to quantify for the main information available relates to the provision of basic facilities (see Table 5). These are provided at reservoirs by both water authorities

Table 5
RESERVOIRS WITH FACILITIES FOR INFORMAL RECREATION

Water Authority	Country Parks	Picnic Areas	Viewing Points	Car Parks	Bird Watching	Other Facilities
Anglian	—	3	1	9	12	—
Northumbrian	1	3	—	2	16	1
North-West	2	5	3	21	34	1
Severn-Trent	—	8	4	11	27	3
Southern	—	1	—	1	6	1
South-West	—	2	3	7	13	2
Thames	—	1	—	—	22	—
Wessex	—	2	2	3	12	1
Yorkshire	—	3	5	6	74	1
Wales	2	17	1	36	70	13
Totals	5	45	19	96	286	23

and other bodies. Water authorities provide a total of 71 car parks at their reservoirs, although occasionally these are restricted to sailors and fishermen. They also provide picnic areas at 21 reservoirs and viewing points at 13, but in only three cases are there refreshments facilities, while a children's play area is available at only two reservoirs. There appears to be little emphasis on the provision of interpretative facilities, for there are only three trails, one information board and one exhibition centre.

The other bodies which provide facilities for informal recreation are mainly in the public sector, primarily local authorities and the Forestry Commission. In some cases, the provision of facilities by such bodies has been grant aided by the Countryside Commission, especially where reservoirs are in national parks. Only occasionally have facilities been provided by private enterprise and there appears to be little use of concessionaires. Country parks have been established at five reservoirs and proposed at others, but elsewhere the facilities provided by other public bodies are similar to those provided by the water authorities, with the main emphasis on car parks, picnic areas, toilets and viewing points.

USE OF GATHERING GROUNDS

The recreational and amenity uses of gathering grounds are even more difficult to assess, partly because of the extensive areas of many upland catchments and partly because of the casual and informal nature of most of the activities they support. While there are some gathering grounds where no such use is recorded, generally it appears that these support the same range of activities as other upland areas. A high proportion of gathering grounds are used for birdwatching or nature study, but often it is not clear how far this is limited to the areas immediately surrounding the reservoir or whether any formal arrangements are made.

Similarly, many gathering grounds are described simply as being used for informal recreation or for walking, although sometimes this indicates only the existence of public rights of way or areas of moorland to which there is open access. For example, the Pennine Way crosses nine catchment areas, while access agreements have been made with the Peak Park Planning Board relating to four areas of land around reservoirs. In a few cases, nature or forest trails have been provided, while orienteering is practised over six areas of gathering grounds, and rock climbing at three. Some of these areas are also used for field sports, most notably for shooting, which sometimes means the public are excluded during the season. There is also horse riding or pony trekking in a few cases, while other more organised activities found on gathering grounds include clay pigeon shooting, motorcycle trials and hang gliding, but no detailed information is available about the extent and frequency of such uses.

CONCLUSIONS

A total of 537 water supply reservoirs are owned by the water authorities and water companies in England and Wales. More than half of these reservoirs were constructed during the nineteenth century and many are small or located in upland areas. Nevertheless, their total surface area amounts to more than 20 000 ha, a high proportion of which appears to have potential for the provision of opportunities for outdoor recreation. Some of the water authorities also own extensive areas of gathering grounds and other land associated with these reservoirs, much of it in the uplands. In terms of area, these upland catchments are far more important than the reservoirs themselves.

A high proportion of these reservoirs and gathering grounds are used for some form of active recreation. There are also indications of an increase in recent years, both in the number of reservoirs used for such purposes and in the range of activities permitted. At the same time, it remains remarkably difficult to quantify the extent of this use, except simply in terms of numbers of reservoirs and lists of activities. Very little information is available about the frequency and extent of participation, but it is clear that in many cases there is only a low intensity of use and that the number of people involved is small. Similarly, it appears that the majority of those who enjoy their outdoor recreation at reservoirs do so in an informal way on the adjacent land areas rather than on the water itself.

It must be recognised that the recreational development of more gathering grounds should be seen in the proper context of the social and economic problems of Britain's upland areas. Since 1945 a whole series of studies have been made of these problems, most recently by the Countryside Review Committee which endorses the principle of multiple use for such areas. While the water authorities appear willing to accept this principle, they are also conscious of their primary duty to ensure safe and adequate supplies of water. The water industry has not yet produced a Code of Practice for the management of catchment areas that relates to their use either for recreation or for agricultural purposes. Generally the view of the water authorities seems to be that the more intensive use of their upland gathering grounds will require careful consideration if the quality of the water supply is to be safe-guarded and in some cases can only be contemplated when major improvements have been made to treatment plant. There is also some acceptance of the view that it may be possible to extend recreational use within present operational constraints, although this would often require more intensive, costly management, including the introduction of a warden or ranger service.

29 Quality aspects of water in upland Britain

A B BALDWIN

INTRODUCTION
This paper considers quality aspects of water in upland Britain in a general fashion. It is, therefore, subject to the weaknesses of all generalisations. It considers quality as found today and how this bears on its uses for public supplies. It also makes some limited speculations about the way in which the activities of man may affect water quality in the future.

HISTORICAL ASPECTS
Streams and springs in upland Britain have been used for local supplies of water from time immemorial. As Britain's population exploded during the industrial revolution one of the consequences was the intolerable pollution of lowland rivers, forcing the townsfolk to seek sources further afield. The need for water grew inexorably and it became imperative to have reliable supplies. Water supply headworks with such attributes were created by building reservoirs in the uplands.

These sources of water were, and remain valuable, for a number of reasons. Until quite recently they were remote from man-made pollution. Access and land use on the gathering grounds could at one time be made subject to control by local pressures; later by private Acts of Parliament and advice from the Ministry of Health and now to a limited degree by Town and Country Planning Acts. Locations, such as we are discussing, lie in areas of high rainfall and as most of the uplands are of the older rocks, the geology is often suitable for reservoir construction at no great distance from the large conurbations.

The existence of limestone and chalk uplands are however the exception to the foregoing. Limestone country is quite unsuitable for building reservoirs and the chalk aquifers are best used as sources of water from underground. Studies of the limestone cap in the Peak District indicate that the fissuring is such that the flows from the limestone are but little modified compared to surface water streams. In the case of the Yorkshire Wolds however the release of water is more impeded so that spring flows can be classed as reliable and the release of underground water to the Rivers Derwent and Hull sustains substantial summer flows.

Existing impounding reservoirs with conventional draw-off towers and aqueducts to cities are seen today to have several disadvantages. A serious disadvantage is that the safe yield from using conservation works in this way is modest, compared with the using of storage facilities in summer, conjunctive with the flow of the river. Long lengths of expensive aqueduct are required to deliver the water. Few suitable sites remain and the environmental lobby fiercely resists the building of further reservoirs.

NATURAL QUALITY

In general upland water is soft, acidic and coloured. These qualities may be ascribed to the widespread presence of peat overlying grits and older rocks. Soft water is noteworthy for washing well with a minimum of soap. Acidic water is corrosive and gives rise to plumbo-solvency health problems, besides its effect on pipelines and plumbing. Colour, once grudgingly accepted, is now a source of complaint from households with washing machines.

It has been shown that there is a statistical correlation between the hardness of water and the occurrence of cardio-vascular disease. There would appear to be some disadvantage in living in an area enjoying soft water.

Quite commonly upland waters carry iron or manganese in solution and often a little of both. After treatment and neutralisation these metals may precipitate causing consumer problems.

Upland water is generally of good quality bacteriologically but sometimes, stored in impounding reservoirs of modest size, the habitual presence of seagulls is a cause for concern.

The EC has promulgated standards for raw water. In general the raw waters of this country comply with both chemical, physical and bacteriological standards but where this is not so it appears to the author to be quite impracticable to abandon any large source presently used which has given satisfaction for generations.

In earlier times water issuing from the uplands had potential energy which was then valuable. This was converted into useable power by water wheels and industry located in the foothills made use of this power. As the need for water power declined certain industries have continued to find advantage in upland water. For instance, its soft quality has been of considerable value to the textile industry but modern detergents and cleaning methods have reduced the significance of this advantage considerably.

A minority of upland water comes from limestone and chalk catchments. These waters are hard and slightly alkaline. They are generally of good bacteriological and organic quality, the latter depending on peat cover.

EXISTING FACTORS AFFECTING NATURAL QUALITY

The natural quality of upland water is affected by existing land use. This use is largely agricultural and problems can arise from sewerage pollution and the careless disposal of sheep dips. Silage pollution need not occur but does so with regrettable frequency. A more recent development is reclamation of bracken areas to grassland with herbicides. So far no difficulties have been reported from this operation.

The Forestry Commission strives continuously to increase afforestation of upland Britain. In the author's opinion this activity is wholly beneficial to water supplies interests. It has been argued that transpiration losses on afforested areas are greater than non-afforested areas. However, it has been shown that over a period of seventy years of increasing acreage of forest there is no statistically related increase in evaporation and transpiration losses on the catchment area of Lake Vyrnwy.

The use of chemicals on upland catchments should be approached with caution. Activities such as tree dipping with BHC, aerial spraying for pine looper moth, selective herbicides, phosphate rock application, etc. have all been subject to monitoring. These should continue with all developments for here complacency can be dangerous.

Quarrying in upland Britain can give rise to problems with turbidity and suspended matter in upland water. Quarries for building stone, limestone, gannister and refractory clay are common and all can cause serious problems.

The existence of old lead mines may sometimes but not always give rise to quality problems. There is risk that all forms of quarrying may give rise to loss of amenity in rivers. The consequences of quarrying can cause fish mortalities and be ruinous for game fisheries. The upland areas of Britain are being used increasingly for all forms of recreation, including the less formal ones of walking, angling, sailing, canoeing and similar activities. The custodians of stored water in the uplands are unaccustomed to the large numbers now visiting the areas and show signs of concern. They are concerned on four counts. Firstly, there are bacteriological problems arising from excretion. Secondly, visual quality of the environment, both small scale and large scale, suffers from the presence of litter — not long since quite unheard of. Thirdly, vandalism in the uplands is no less evident than in the cities.

Lastly, authorities are worried about possible liability for negligence when harm comes to unsupervised visitors or trespassers.

Generally, angling in upland Britain is limited because the quality of upland water will not generally support a food chain. The exception is the obvious one of limestone and chalk streams which will frequently support salmon and/or trout fisheries.

The natural quality of upland water could today be affected dramatically by spillages from road transport vehicles. Oil and chemicals of almost every conceivable kind can drain to watercourses following road accidents. One of the big worries of today is the presence of polynuclear aromatic hydrocarbons from internal combustion engines.

The Scammonden Dam, providing part of Huddersfield's water supply, is probably unique in the United Kingdom in that the water and highway engineers arranged to use the same embankment. The M62 motorway follows the line of the dam and a considerable stretch of the motorway is drained into the reservoir. In the event of a spillage on the motorway the drainage can be diverted (providing action is quick enough).

In normal circumstances the road drainage enters the dam and is a potential source of polynuclear aromatic hydrocarbons and lead. Analysis of the water shows that these two constituents are well below World Health Organisation limits. One now wonders if it would have been wiser to divert the drainage permanently in view of recent concern about these materials.

It is inevitable that an industrial society must dispose of industrial waste including potentially hazardous waste. The siting of tips is, therefore, an important aspect of community management.

Water supply has, for example, been seriously affected by phenolic wastes at Cowm Reservoir recently and not so long ago the Huddersfield supply from Wessenden Valley was similarly affected.

FUTURE TRENDS

As sites for new reservoirs are limited and objections so vigorous, opportunities to augment upland water resources in this way are rare. Another method is to enlarge existing reservoirs such as the examples at Winscar and Grimwith. Even where powers are obtained to raise a reservoir such as Grimwith there may be violent objection to using such a reservoir for direct supply. Amenity and fisheries interest can prove so powerful that their wishes can dominate the basis under which the scheme is designed. In the Grimwith case the reservoir must be used solely for river regulation with abstraction downstream. This arrangement requires more complex and more costly treatment. It involves risks using lower quality water and the opportunities for Bradford industry to enjoy soft water are reduced in time. It has been claimed that the additional water in the River Wharfe will be beneficial to the fisheries but the author is not aware of even a modest effort to quantify the benefit.

The possibility of inter-river transfers continues to draw nearer. Before deciding to make any such transfer careful appraisals will be needed of the chemical, physical and biological changes likely to occur. The chances of the unwitting transfer of fish disease and unwanted species of fish will have to be carefully weighed and all concerned will have to be constantly alert to recognise the unexpected.

In the past the liming of fields with MAFF grant appears to have had no noticeable effects on upland water. One can expect however that chemicals will be used in increasing quantity and of wider variety. The maintenance in good condition of increased upland pasture, the herbicide control of bracken and most particularly the addition of quantities of nitrates to the ground may all lead to undesirable concentrations of chemicals in upland water. From now on the monitoring of trends is a necessary precaution. This surveillance should be carried out in co-operation with MAFF and the Forestry Commission.

It has been said that afforestation is more profitable than sheep farming in upland Britain. Were the economics to be much the same in both cases, afforestation has advantages to those interested in upland water which do not obtain when the land is devoted to sheep. Whilst commonsense tells us that transpiration losses may well increase, evaporation losses may, over a year, be little different. Certainly soil erosion is reduced and if this increases the life of an impounding reservoir even modestly, it is a matter of considerable economic significance.

Studies indicate that apart from the occasion when just everywhere and just everything is saturated, the peak run-off is less from an afforested area than from other similar areas. This effect is obvious should one walk through a plantation days after snowfall and see the green fields clear of snow whilst it still lies at the foot of the trees.

The author would deprecate objections to afforestation on the tops of hills on amenity grounds. The sight of a substantial hill planted two-thirds of the way up with the top bare looks ridiculously like a bald-headed old man. This country is obliged to make use of such natural resources as we enjoy. The winning of minerals must go on in the future. The effect of quarrying and mining on upland water can be moderated by input into the planning procedures.

A large increase in the demand for recreation upon and access to land and water can be expected. The opening up of walks such as the Pennine Way and the Lyke Wake Walk can be seen to be a good thing as a matter of broad public policy. One may start off with the same attitude of mind towards meeting increased demand for sailing, swimming and playing on, in and about reservoirs. The increased public benefit must be weighed against the increased risk to the public. In the case of angling, whilst there are cases of pressure to open reservoirs quite unsuitable for fishing, it must be conceded that fish do exist in some reservoirs where fishing is not presently allowed. Experience would indicate that in today's conditions waters cannot be open for the exclusive use of one small section of the community; they must be open for use by the public at large for all the things they may enjoy, if they are to be open at all.

CONCLUSIONS

Those having the responsibility for managing upland water for public consumption plead that each case should be considered separately on its merits. Water is the important natural resource plentifully available in upland Britain. Its conservation and exploitation can be a source of work and wealth for the indigenous population.

In any particular catchment the water quality is fixed (within ranges) by nature. Changes in this quality occur only by man's actions. Not uncommonly his actions, whether they are to earn a living in agriculture, quarrying or mining or to enjoy life in any form of recreation, have a deleterious effect on the quality of upland water. Unfortunately, this result may also be accompanied by physical damage, disturbance to wild life and risk to flora. Some would have us preserve at least a sample of our heritage for future generations and some would wish to enjoy life unfettered while they can. The choice is a difficult one and in the present state of knowledge is straightforwardly a political decision.

30 Water supply in upland Scotland

W T DEVENAY

INTRODUCTION

From the map delineating the 'upland' areas of Britain, based on the EC Directive No 268/75, which in broad terms has been defined as identifying the less favoured areas, it is seen that by far the greatest proportion of such land is in Scotland and that practically all of Scotland can be regarded as 'upland'.

White certain areas of Scotland do not come within the classification of 'upland', for example the eastern coastal strip, the water supplies to these areas are, by and large, derived from sources in the upland areas and so, when one is considering water supply in upland areas, one is in effect considering the supply to the whole country.

HISTORICAL DEVELOPMENT OF WATER SUPPLY IN SCOTLAND

In early times, each dwelling or community established their water supply where it found it most convenient, generally from shallow wells sunk within the community or adjacent to the individual house but also from the local streams. As the settlements expanded, the arrangements for water supply were gradually taken over by the Local Authorities until water supply became accepted in Scotland as a Local Authority duty with the early absorption of any private water companies which had established themselves. Each authority tended to provide for its own needs and, though there were some exceptions, this led to a proliferation of small supplies.

Also, with the passage of time and because of the increasing pollution of the very local sources, new supplies tended to be sought in the upland areas adjacent to towns because of the obvious advantages accruing:

(i) They were relatively isolated with a minimum of human activity and so less liable to pollution.

(ii) Their elevation permitted cheap gravitational systems without involving the necessity for pumping.

(iii) The quality was such that little treatment was required.

Prior to 1968 there were about 199 Water Authorities in Scotland each making their own arrangements for and operating their own supplies. Since then, two reorganisations of the industry have taken place and while this has not materially reduced the number of sources currently in use, it should enable a radical examination of the present position, and a comprehensive assessment for the future to be made.

For example, in the Strathclyde Region alone, there are presently in use for a population of about 2½ million, some 264 separate sources ranging in scale from major impounding reservoirs such as Loch Katrine, the Glasgow supply, to the modest burn intakes which are prevalent in Argyll and Ayrshire. Practically all are in the 'upland' area. In the Grampian Region, population 400 000, there are 190 small sources in addition to abstractions on the Rivers Dee, Deveron, Dye and Ugie, and in the Highland Region there are 157 separate sources supplying 200 000 people. Again substantially all these sources are in the 'upland' area.

In Scotland at the present time, there are thirteen authorities responsible for the administration of the water supply function, nine first tier regional councils, three all purpose islands' councils and one bulk supply authority. It should be noted, however, that their responsibility does not cover river regulation and river pollution control. This lies with seven River Purification Boards.

UTILISATION – EXISTING SUPPLIES

(i) Public supplies. The population of Scotland, including the islands, is approximately 5 206 000. The bulk of this population, about 85%, is located in the area between in the west, the Firth of Clyde and in the east the Firths of Forth and Tay. Elsewhere the only sizeable concentrations of population are Aberdeen, Inverness and Dumfries. In the remainder of Scotland, which represents more than half the area, the population is only about 500 000. The bulk of water usage, therefore, takes place within a very limited part of the country.

Table 1 shows the consumption and yield of existing sources by Region. The figures given relate to the period May 1975 to March 1976, and are abstracted from data provided by the Scottish Development Department.

(ii) Private Supplies. There are some properties and farms in the country having their own private supplies which are not afforded by a statutory water authority. These supplies are usually derived from spring or burn intake but in total are of minor significance.

The principal private users are the Electricity Boards in respect of hydro-generation and thermal cooling water but their abstractions are returned to the rivers locally and represent only a use of the water, the overall net loss to the

Table 1
CONSUMPTION AND YIELD BY REGION FOR
PERIOD MAY 1975/MARCH 1976

Authority	Population Supplied (thousands)	Total Consumption Ml/d	Yield Ml/d	Balance Yield over Consumption ± Ml/d
Borders	99	31	53	+ 22
Central	356	212	338(1)	+126
Dumfries & Galloway	144	61	97	+ 36
Fife	342	118	123	+ 5
Grampian	449	137	159	+ 22
Highland	182	90	244	+154
Lothian	754	262	318(1)	+ 56
Orkney	18	7	12	+ 5
Shetland	18	8	19	+ 11
Strathclyde	2418	1140	1491(1)	+351
Tayside	396	136	201(1)	+ 65
Western Isles	30	10	18	+ 8
CSWDB (unallocated)	—	—	127	+127
Totals	5206	2212	3263	+1051

(1) Includes allocation from Central Scotland Water Development Board (CSWDB). The Board supplies only in bulk to relevant authorities.

Source: Scottish Development Department and Strathclyde Water Department.

rivers being nil. There is also some abstraction by power stations from the few remaining canals in the country not all of which is returned. In addition in industry generally there are some small abstractions. Details of private abstractions from surface sources are given in Table 2.

UTILISATION -- FUTURE DEMAND
Some years ago the Scottish Development Department (1973) carried out a survey of water supplies in Scotland. In this survey, data have been produced

predicting water consumption in Scotland up to the year 2001. Table 3 gives details of these estimates. In producing these estimates the prediction was based on the two main factors of changing population and changing rate of consumption

Table 2
PRIVATE ABSTRACTIONS BY TYPES OF SOURCES (Ml/d)

General Abstractions:	Gross	Net
Reservoirs	6.4	6.4
River Intakes	1080	86
Electricity Boards:		
Hydro-electric Reservoirs and River Intakes	8180	—
Thermal Cooling Water River Intakes	915	—
Canals:		
User Abstractions	240	20
Total Abstractions	10 421	112

Note: 'Net' usage is the amount of water which is abstracted and not returned locally to the source. 'Gross' usage is the total abstraction including water returned locally such as water circulated for cooling purposes.

Source: Scottish Development Department (1973)

Table 3
PUBLIC SUPPLIES – POPULATION AND CONSUMPTION TRENDS (HISTORICAL AND PROJECTED) FOR ALL SCOTLAND

1951		1961		1971		1981		1991		2001	
P	C	P	C	P	C	P	C	P	C	P	C
5098	1517	5180	1714	5228	2130	5350	2683	5599	3429	5900	4414

P = population (1000's)
C = total consumption (Ml/d)

Source: Scottish Development Department (1973)

331

per head of the population. At that time the Department had the benefit of a study on population projections which had been carried out by the Department's Central Planning Research Unit. In respect of consumption per head, a rate of increase of 2.0% per annum was taken, which was based on the historical trend.

Since the survey was published, recent evidence suggests that these predicted levels of consumption are likely to have been overstated. However, following the recent reorganisation of local government in Scotland, the Regional Councils have been looking closely at population changes, and discrepancies between the estimates of the different authorities are apparent, indeed the Strathclyde Regional Authority is predicting a fall in population at least until 1981. Some of this population loss will be a gain to other Scottish Regions but no doubt there will be some loss from Scotland as a whole. The most recent evidence too of the falling birth rate, will also lead to a slower rate of growth than would have been anticipated some years ago, unless there is a counter increase in the level of immigration.

In the years immediately following the war, the consumption of water in Scotland increased steadily. Industry was booming and house building was proceeding at a very high rate. However, over the last few years there has been a marked change in this situation. Indeed in the Strathclyde Region the year 1975/76 showed a net reduction in consumption in the Region as a whole compared with the year 1974/75. (Table 4).

Table 4
CONSUMPTION IN STRATHCLYDE REGION BY DIVISION

| | | Total Consumption (Ml/d) | |
		1974/5	1975/6
Argyll		28.7	30.1
Ayr		203.2	204.2
Lanark		211.2	212.3
Lower Clyde		710.9	700.8
	Totals	1154.0	1147.4

Source: Strathclyde Water Department.

It is suggested that the present economic situation is largely responsible for this drop in consumption, with the closing-down of factories and a considerable reduction in the volume of new house building in both the public and private sectors. It may be that in the future when the economy recovers, the rate of increase of consumption will revert to the previous pattern.

However, it is widely accepted that part of the present consumption is waste and in making a simple projection from the past to the future, no allowance is made for changing policies in respect of waste control. In the years to come, a big factor determining the rate of consumption must be the level, and effectiveness, of waste control activities. A recent examination of the position in the Strathclyde Region suggested that the consumption projected for the year 2001 could be overstated by more than 10% depending on the degree to which waste could be cut down. The prediction should, therefore, be regarded as a maximum.

POINTS OF CONFLICT
In the utilisation of water from 'upland' areas there has unavoidably been conflict between the water supply authorities and other users of these lands because the best interests of the competing parties do not have common direction.

There is conflict with farming in that substantial amounts of land are utilised for reservoirs, and often this is the better and more sheltered ground in the bottom of the valleys. The surrounding catchment draining to the reservoir is often subject to severe restriction in relation to the application of fertilisers and weedkillers and the water undertaking may obtain byelaws for the prevention of pollution. There is difficulty in relation to the consequent restriction of the discharge of effluent from byres, sheep dipping pens and the like to adjacent streams where these streams discharge directly to the reservoirs. Similar problems relate to catchments draining to direct intakes.

There is conflict with forestry because afforestation reduces run off which in turn adversely affects the water supplied by a given reservoir or intake.

These difficulties can sometimes be surmounted by the water authority acquiring all the catchment area, and indeed this has been done in many cases but with the increasing cost of land it is doubtful if it can be considered as a solution in the future.

There is conflict of interest between the water supply and many common leisure activities. Fishing interests become alarmed when the abstraction of water reduces the flow in stream and river. In an impounding scheme, any loss is often made good by the fishings provided in the reservoir itself, but in migratory rivers there can be problems. Sailing enthusiasts may disagree with Water Authorities who consider their reservoirs unsuitable because of size, location, method of treatment or the simple requirement of avoiding pollution at all costs. Additionally there are problems arising from public pressure for access generally to land forming the water catchment or to the waters edge, in the case of reservoirs, with the possibility of resulting pollution and even danger to the unwary. Here though the interests of water supply and agriculture sometimes find themselves on common ground.

In new schemes both of these aspects can possibly be taken account of and some compromise reached, but in many of the existing works this is not possible because of safety aspects or because the existing treatment processes would be unable to deal with the changed conditions.

FUTURE DEVELOPMENT

This limited paper has outlined the development of the Scottish water supply industry and given some indication of its size. Also an indication has been given of the problems to be faced in ensuring adequate supplies for the future. In assessing the amount of water to be provided, consideration must be given not only to anticipated consumption but also to the level to which reserves of supplies are to be maintained. This will obviously depend on such factors as: the interconnection of piping systems and the degree to which overall surpluses can be made available throughout the area; the time element involved in providing a new major source, which from first concept to completion easily could be 10 years or more; and the values placed on freedom from the effects of drought and the capacity to meet the demands of unexpected new industrial and urban development.

Unless there is a vast shift of population, the problems will be concentrated in the central belt of Scotland. There is, however, no lack of supply to meet the requirements; indeed it has been estimated that the average run off from the Scottish mainland surface is about 200 000 Ml per day compared with the present water supply level of about 2 000 Ml.

It is not intended here to discuss in detail possible schemes to achieve the target but merely to outline how the pattern of development might proceed.

From an economic point of view, it is certain that operationally the regional scheme will supersede small local sources wherever possible. As far as the central belt is concerned, this may apply to the extent that the very large interregional scheme will tend to supersede even regional development. Indeed the Central Scotland Water Development Board is already established for that purpose.

What is certain, however, is that in the foreseeable future Scotland will rely on surface water derived from the 'upland' areas. Underground sources will not be prominent in the planning of major schemes because of the lack of suitable geological formations.

What is not at this stage so clear is whether water authorities in Scotland will continue in their present role as supply authorities only or whether a system similar to that in England will eventually be adopted. This is one factor which, in the not too distant future, might make river regulation more common, with abstraction taking place in the lower reaches of the rivers adjacent to the points of demand. This may reduce opposition from fishery and amenity interests, keen to keep as much water in the rivers as possible. It may also reduce initial capital costs but it will raise operating costs of extra treatment — because of deterioration in quality with the passage downstream — and the pumping involved.

But direct supply or river regulating reservoirs are certain to be required and the consequent conflict with agriculture over loss of land will have to be resolved.

Fortunately, land in the 'upland' catchments, for direct supply, is not such as to be often a subject for the intensive use of fertilisers and manures, which will reduce problems due to nitrates and phosphates. There will be difficulties on these counts, however, when river regulating reservoirs and lowland abstraction are involved in water supply schemes.

REFERENCE

Scottish Development Department (1973)   *A measure of plenty — water resources in Scotland — a general survey.*   London: HMSO.

31 Potential power generation from large wind turbine generators sited in upland areas of Britain

D F WARNE & W E HARDY

INTRODUCTION

It is well known that the wind has been exploited as a source of energy for many centuries. It has often, however, been resorted to only when alternative sources of power or local circumstances are difficult. The lack of widespread acceptance and use can be attributed to three important factors:

(i)   air is of low density and relatively large and expensive devices are necessary to recover its kinetic energy;

(ii) wind is unreliable as a steady source of power (although in the longer term it is a fairly consistent source of energy);

(iii) the power in the wind is proportional to the cube of wind speed; since average wind speed can vary substantially, even within a particular locality, careful attention to siting is critically important.

The latter two points can be particularly restricting for small plant serving an autonomous system. The effect of wind intermittency is most serious, since storage capacity or diesel reserve must be installed to ensure security of supply, and the total cost of the system may be quite high. Also, siting options are limited, being usually tied to within a few hundred metres of the load to be supplied. This limits the wind speed available and therefore the potential energy output and economics of the system. Connection of large wind turbine generators to the network offers a solution to the problems of both storage and 'optimum' siting. The need for storage can be obviated using the plant in a 'fuel saver' mode; that is treating it as a high merit power source, displacing the output from least efficient thermal stations whenever the power is available. Optimum siting is also made possible by the widespread existence in the UK of 11 000 V and 33 000 V transmission and distribution networks.

It is for these reasons that much of the Electrical Research Association's (ERA) attention during its thirty year involvement in wind power has been directed towards the problems and benefits of large network connected machines. Many of the possible sites for these machines fall within upland Britain and this paper outlines the gross potential for energy production from these sites and the factors affecting economic viability.

GEOGRAPHICAL SCOPE FOR LARGE MACHINES

Although mean wind speed is one of the factors that critically influences the economics of large machines, it is difficult to provide accurate guidance for any particular location without on-site anemometry.

Possibly the best guidance in the UK at present is provided by Caton (1976) who proposes a series of percentile isovent or isopleth maps showing wind speeds exceeded for seven durations, from 0.1% of the time to 75% of the time. Factors to be applied for individual site location and characteristics are also suggested, so that a complete velocity-duration curve can be drawn up for any location. An isovent map derived from Caton for annual mean wind speed (AMWS) including correction factors for coastal areas, is shown in Figure 1.

Whilst Caton's maps (taken in conjunction with the correction factors suggested for various classifications of site) are useful, they are limited (as regional surface isovent maps probably always will be) in their validity when applied to specific locations. A comparison, for instance, with the results of ERA's anemometry of hill sites (Tagg, 1957) reveals discrepancies with predictions using Caton's method. The various factors to be accounted for in assessing AMWS on coastal hills are outlined in the following section.

Attention to reasonably accurate prediction of mean wind speed is not purely from academic interest. The simple momentum theory of the wind turbine indicates power output (W) is given by:

$$W = \tfrac{1}{2}p \; C_p \; A \; V^3$$

where p is air density, A is turbine swept area and V is wind speed. C_p is called the power coefficient, and for large machines may be up to about 0.47. This would indicate over 70% more power in a 12 m/s wind than a 10 m/s wind, but the argument does not strictly apply to mean wind speed levels; since C_p varies with wind speed, the variation of annual energy output with mean wind speed has to be calculated from individual machine characteristics. As an example, the annual output of a 40 m diameter machine at 10 m/s and 12 m/s mean wind speed might typically be 3.6 GWh and 5.0 GWh respectively. The necessity for accurate prediction of mean wind speed within 5 to 10% is clear when attempting to justify installation of equipment.

Figure 1
LINES OF CONSTANT AMWS (ISOPLETHS) RELATING TO UPLAND
BRITAIN (m/s)

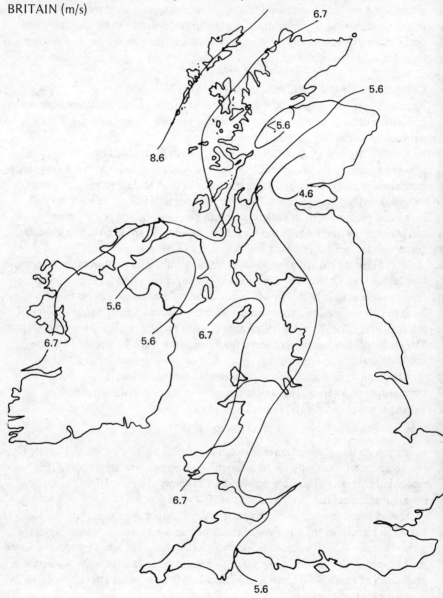

Recent design and cost studies indicate that the economics of large wind turbine generators are likely to be 'marginal'. This means that only the highest mean wind speed sites should be considered as potentially viable at this stage. The significance of this for upland Britain is that the most promising areas are on the west coast of Scotland, where AMWS exceeding 12 m/s have been measured by ERA on the more exposed hill sites.

SELECTION OF INDIVIDUAL HILL SITES

The criteria which are important when assessing economic viability of siting large machines can be broadly divided into two groups:
(i) factors determining cost of plant erection and connection to the local power network;
(ii) factors influencing annual mean wind speed and hence the energy potentially available.

The importance of the first can be considerably under-estimated. The hill approach gradient and surface condition generally affect site support costs, and more specifically they have important bearing on the cost of providing site access. Local main roads must enable large items of plant to be transported to the site. The suitability of the local network (particularly the fault capacity at the nearest substations) will determine the length of connection required, which can substantially affect costs.

Although much effort has been made in the field of wind regime prediction, further advances must be made before adequate practical techniques are available; complementary to this theoretical work, certain empirical methods are undergoing development at present. ERA's hill site anemometry programme has identified certain topographical features as indicative of AMWS.

In particular, the shape of a hill exerts significant influence on wind flow. Fairly steeply graded, smoothly profiled hills exhibit higher AMWS than hills of irregular shape with many sharp changes of gradient. There appears no obvious limit on approach gradient provided levelling at the summit is sufficiently gradual to avoid detachment of the boundary layer and attendant turbulence.

The exposure of a hill relative to surrounding terrain has important bearing on the selection of large numbers of coastal sites. It is obvious that a hill foreshadowed in the prevalent directions will produce a consistently lower AMWS. It is perhaps less obvious that this local screening can considerably modify prevalent directions. The local wind direction may be one in which the profile is less attractive. Clearly shape and exposure have a complex interactive effect on wind flow and may not be judged in isolation.

A third feature indicative of high AMWS of relatively consistent direction is the condition of vegetation. This depends upon climate, but hills which support a healthy growth of trees or bushes are unlikely to experience appreciable wind speeds. Alternatively, if a hill is covered by clipped scrub and trees sparse, stunted and showing marked 'flagging', relatively high AMWS may be expected.

It is evident that no single group of factors may be scrutinised in isolation with reliable result, and when all factors are considered in combination with many plant design variants, substantial analytical effort is required. ERA is presently exploring possible applications for computer modelling techniques in this field.

Depending upon the weighting given to each of the factors, the number of hill sites which are suitable in upland Britain varies between about 1000 and 2000, with a hill-top AMWS in the region of 8 to 12 m/s (at 10 m height above the hill).

Table 1
A PROJECTION OF NUMBER OF SITES AND INSTALLATIONS POSSIBLE FOR UPLAND BRITAIN OF DIFFERING AMWS (m/s)

	AMWS				
	8	9	11	12	Total
Number of sites	580	330	150	40	1100
Number of installations	1200	670	310	80	2260

A sample projection representing 1100 sites in upland Britain is shown in Table 1; the number of machines installable and the distribution with AMWS is indicated. (The number of machines per site is based upon a minimum spacing of 10 turbine diameters to avoid wake effects and interference).

GROSS ENERGY POTENTIAL

In order to estimate the annual energy production from an installation, it is necessary to know, in addition to AMWS, the frequency of occurrence of different wind speeds throughout the year. This information is usually presented as a velocity-duration curve (see Figure 2). ERA has found the shape of this curve to be relatively invariant for large numbers of sites.

Combining the velocity-duration curve with the plant power-wind speed characteristic (Figure 3) results in the power duration curve (Figure 4) for an installation. The area beneath this curve represents annual energy output.

A report published recently by the Department of Energy (Bird & Allen, 1977) admits to the uncertainty of 'optimum' machine size and hence large scale installation cost. Increasing the size of a machine raises the annual energy output, but attendant upon this are certain cost penalties. Of particular importance are potential increases in haulage, site access and support costs associated with larger

Figure 2
TYPICAL PROFILE OF A VELOCITY DURATION CURVE

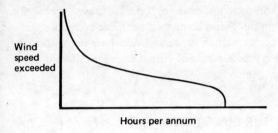

Figure 3
POWER-WIND SPEED CHARACTERISTIC FOR TYPICAL PLANT

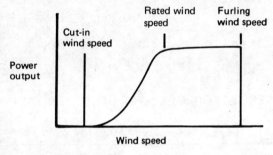

Figure 4
POWER DURATION CURVE

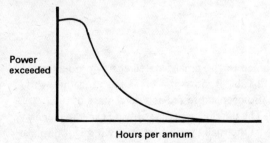

components and material quantities. Such cost penalties may escalate considerably in areas of particularly poor amenity.

Consequently it can be misleading to undertake estimates of energy production for large regions based on one machine size. Using methods described above, annual energy outputs for different machine sizes and AMWS have been estimated, and are presented in Table 2. Very wide ranges of output both for different machine sizes and AMWS are evident.

Table 2
ANNUAL ENERGY OUTPUT FOR DIFFERENT MACHINE SIZES AT EACH AMWS

AMWS (m/s)	Annual energy output (GWh)		
	40 m diameter	60 m diameter	80 m diameter
8	2.1	4.7	8.3
9	2.9	6.4	11.4
11	4.4	9.8	17.4
12	5.0	11.3	20.1

Table 3
BREAKDOWN OF TOTAL ENERGY PRODUCTION FOR UPLAND BRITAIN

AMWS (m/s)	Energy produced at each AMWS (GWh)		
	40 m diameter	60 m diameter	80 m diameter
8	2520	5640	9960
9	1943	4288	7638
11	1364	3038	5394
12	400	904	1608
Total	6227	13 870	24 600
Proportion of national electricity generation (%)	2	5	9

Tables 1 and 2 may be combined to give amalgamated energy production estimates for upland Britain, and Table 3 shows this breakdown together with national totals; the totals have also been expressed as a percentage of total national electricity production. The unreliable nature of wind generated energy limits the amount of conventional thermally generated energy it might displace on the supply network; it is presently thought that about 10% of electrical energy production could be met by large wind turbine generators without creating difficult control and stability problems.

TARGET COSTS FOR LARGE MACHINES

Since wind turbine installations may not be classified as 'firm' generating capacity, their cost effectiveness must be judged simply by the worth of energy produced. This is dependent on the cost and amount of fuel displaced in lower efficiency thermal generating stations and the uncertainty of these quantities, which exhibit both daily and seasonal fluctuation, has already been indicated. Consequently, it is at this stage possible only to bound a range of energy values.

Table 4
ESTIMATED ANNUAL VALUE OF ENERGY PRODUCED BY MACHINES OF DIFFERENT SIZES

AMWS (m/s)	Annual value of energy produced (£1000)					
	40 m diameter		60 m diameter		80 m diameter	
	1.1p/kWh	1.25p/kWh	1.1p/kWh	1.25p/kWh	1.1p/kWh	1.25p/kWh
8	23.1	26.2	51.7	58.7	91.3	103.7
9	31.9	36.2	70.4	80.0	125.4	142.5
11	48.4	55.0	107.8	122.5	191.4	217.5
12	55.0	62.5	124.3	141.2	221.1	251.2

The annual worth of energy production shown in Table 2 has been estimated at 1.1 and 1.25p/kWh. Table 4 gives this information, each figure representing the annual return on investment for its respective installation. The simplest of accounting techniques would produce target installation costs by multiplying each annual energy worth by the plant life. However, this practice takes no account of the decreasing worth of capital with time.

The discounted cash flow method facilitates such adjustments. A constant discount rate of 10% has been applied to each annual energy worth figure in Table 4, over an assumed plant life of 20 years. The resulting target capital costs for each installation are presented in Table 5. It is apparent that wide cost variations are afforded by the ranges of AMWS and machine size.

First taking energy produced at a value of 1.1p/kWh; a 40 m machine installed at an 8 m/s site should not exceed a capital cost of £216 000. An 80 m machine installed at a 12 m/s site might justify a cost of £2.1 million. At the higher energy value of 1.25p/kWh these target costs rise to £240 000 and £2.3 million respectively.

343

Table 5

APPROXIMATE TARGET CAPITAL COSTS FOR MACHINES OF DIFFERENT SIZES

AMWS (m/s)	Target capital costs (£1000)					
	40 m diameter		60 m diameter		80 m diameter	
	1.1p/kWh	1.25p/kWh	1.1p/kWh	1.25p/kWh	1.1p/kWh	1.25p/kWh
8	216	245	484	550	855	971
9	299	339	659	749	1174	1334
11	453	515	1009	1147	1792	2037
12	515	585	1164	1322	2071	2352

Note: The above costs were produced using the discounted cash flow method assuming a 20 year life and 10% discount rate.

CONCLUSION

While the target costs for a 40 m machine (see Table 5) are unlikely to be achieved, recent design and cost studies for larger machines (particularly 60 m diameter) indicate that there is a distinct possibility that the target costs are fairly realistic.

Two important problems need to be resolved if upland Britain is to be used to any extent for the generation of electricity from the wind. The first problem concerns the uncertainty of public reaction regarding the effect on the environment. This is a highly subjective and sometimes emotive issue; reactions will probably not be significant until a substantial number of machines are proposed; the full nature of public objection or support will only be gauged at the planning application stage and it is not appropriate at this stage to speculate. The second uncertainty is technical feasibility and reliability of large network connected machines; many large machines have been built and operated on a network, but only one has demonstrated adequate robustness and reliability over a prolonged period. It is to be hoped that increasing pressure for conservation of fuels will result in modern prototypes and a persistent programme of development to demonstrate adequate reliability.

ACKNOWLEDGEMENTS

The authors are grateful to the directors of ERA Limited for permission to publish this paper, and to colleagues for help in preparing data on which the paper is based.

REFERENCES

Bird, R A & Allen, J (1977)   *The prospects for generation of electricity from wind energy in the United Kingdom.*   Energy Paper No 21. London: Department of Energy.

Caton, P G F (1976)   *Maps of hourly mean wind speed over the United Kingdom, 1965-1973.*   Climatological Memorandum No 79. Bracknell: Meteorological Office.

Tagg, J R (1957)   *Wind data related to the generation of electricity by wind power.*   ERA Report C/T 115. Leatherhead: ERA.

32 The future of windmills for local use

J R C ARMSTRONG

INTRODUCTION

Whatever the conservationist merits of wind power, a domestic windmill is in general an item of capital expenditure that must be justified by returns in the form of energy costs saved over the life of the machine. There are few people who would opt for wind power, knowing that interest on the capital outlay would exceed the fuel bills saved.

'Alternative' energy sources become particularly attractive:

(i) When conventional energy costs rise relative to other costs (if a doubling in oil price leads to a doubling in manufacturing costs there is no advantage since the ratio of outlay to cost savings stays the same);

(ii) When inflation rate exceeds interest rate, since the cost of conventional power then increases faster than the cost of servicing the capital outlay.

Both of these conditions hold at the moment, and there has been a strong revival of interest in windmills and other renewable energy sources. This revival is rather different from the 1930's period in America, when thousands of home generators were installed simply because of the lack of rural electrification. Then, reliability was more important than price. Today, reliability is still important, but cost effectiveness is the overall criterion.

There are several factors which contribute to the cost effectiveness of an installation:

(i) Size. Table 1 lists some of the more popular electricity-producing windmills available in this country. The cost per installed kW decreases markedly with size, as would be expected. Efficiency, both of the rotor and of the electrics, also increases with size, making the power actually recovered at a given wind speed even more size dependent. Obviously, the limit to size is governed by the power demand of the building being served.

Table 1
COST OF DOMESTIC ELECTRICITY PRODUCING WINDMILLS

Make	Rotor Diameter (m)	Installed Capacity (W)	Approximate Basic Cost (£)	Price per[1] Installed kW (£)
WINCO	1.8	200	350	1 750
ELECTRO	2.5	600	1 100	1 833
QUIRKS	3.6	2 000	2 800	1 400
KEDCO	3.6	1 200	1 300	1 083
ELECTRO	3.6	2 200	2 100	954
KEDCO	3.6	2 000	1 500	750
ELECTRO	5.0	5 000	3 000	600
ELECTRO	7.0	10 000	5 000	500

1 The installed capacity is only reached in 8-12 m/s winds, depending on the machine. Price per unit of swept area can be misleading, since machine efficiencies differ greatly.

(ii) Storage. For most domestic applications 'real time' power (for lights, television etc.) is required as well as directly storable energy such as heat. All small windmill rotors are variable speed, so that direct connection of the generator to lights would result in dimming and brightening as the wind gusts and falls. For this reason, a battery storage interface is nearly always used, and most of the windmills in Table 1 have low voltage DC outputs. To supply 240 volt AC appliances, an inverter is also necessary. Batteries plus inverter can add two thirds to the cost of the basic machine. A standby generator is a possible alternative, but the cost is again high. (Mains electricity cannot be used for standby power since the Electricity Boards forbid, at the moment, the sharing of mains installed wiring with domestically generated power.)

(iii) Location and siting. These are perhaps the most important factors in the cost effectiveness equation. The difference in mean annual wind power (proportional to the mean of the cube of wind speeds) between a sheltered inland site and an exposed site, say, in the Western Isles, can be as much as 1000 times. For a given location, the advantages of good siting (including height) are considerable but must be set off against the costs of longer power transmission and a higher tower. Much of upland Britain has higher than average wind speeds and is well suited to the exploitation of wind power.

(iv) Cost of conventional energy supply. The type and cost of fuel displaced tend to accentuate the location effects described above. For instance, the London area has a low mean annual wind speed (5 m/s or less) but is well supplied with cheap North Sea gas. On the other hand, the Western Isles, with 8 m/s or more average wind speeds, have to pay much more than mainland Britain for locally generated electricity. For most of the country, however, the cost of energy supply is more or less constant, and the main difference lies between the types of supply used, with electricity being the most expensive and heating oil probably the cheapest.

The most convenient way to express the cost effectiveness of a machine at a particular site is in terms of its payback period — the time taken to recover the cost of the unit from the savings in fuel. Electro claim that their 5 kW machine, when used for direct heating in 8 m/s average winds, will pay for itself in eight years. On the other hand, a 200 W unit in the London area could have an infinite payback period.

WORK AT THE WIND ENERGY SUPPLY COMPANY (WESCO)
Studies carried out at WESCO have indicated four broad conclusions:
(i) It should be possible to design and build for unattended operation significantly larger machines than those currently available. Sixty feet (18.3 m) was chosen as a reasonable rotor diameter.
(ii) Such a machine would be too large for domestic use, but could be used commercially to heat glasshouses, factories, etc.
(iii) A low solidity two-bladed rotor based on helicopter technology could be both efficient and cheap to build.
(iv) A choked hydraulic circuit is particularly interesting for generating and transmitting heat to where it is required, since load matching can be maintained at all wind and rotor speeds.

Backing was obtained from NRDC for a prototype machine and design work was carried out during 1975-6. The site chosen was the MAFF's Experimental Horticulture Station at Efford in Hampshire. This has reasonable winds and the advantage that its many glasshouses have a particularly high heat requirement when the wind blows. Heat storage can therefore be dispensed with, and the windmill used solely to pre-heat water for the central heating system already in place. The prototype was built and installed in early 1977 with the help of Taylor Woodrow Construction Ltd., and is at present undergoing proving trials. Figure 1 shows the layout of the system. The main features are as follows:
(i) Rotor. Two-bladed, in fibreglass sections with steel backing. Automatic furling at high speeds by bearingless flexures which allow pitch-changing by the action of furling weights. Inboard cuffs to assist starting. The rotor carries strain

348

Figure 1
EFFORD PROTOTYPE WINDMILL

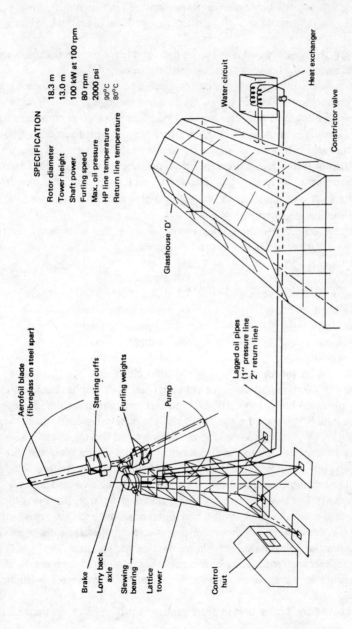

SPECIFICATION

Rotor diameter	18.3 m
Tower height	13.0 m
Shaft power	100 kW at 100 rpm
Furling speed	80 rpm
Max. oil pressure	2000 psi
HP line temperature	90°C
Return line temperature	80°C

Aerofoil blade (fibreglass on steel spar)

Starting cuffs

Furling weights

Pump

Brake

Lorry back axle

Slewing bearing

Lattice tower

Control hut

Lagged oil pipes
(1″ pressure line
2″ return line)

Glasshouse 'D'

Water circuit

Heat exchanger

Constrictor valve

349

gauge instrumentation for monitoring stress levels.

(ii) Head. Rotor carried by modified lorry back axle in which differential is locked to give 7:1 step up gear. Axle brake retained and operated by electric motor.

(iii) Slewing. Heavy duty ball race carries head and rotor. Slewing gear driven by hydraulic motor which also acts as orientation damper.

(iv) Hydraulic Circuit. Axle drive shaft connected to 600 cc displacement triple stage hydraulic pump fixed to tower. Oil pumped through 75 m high pressure line under glasshouse to calorifier house. 75% of pump pressure converted to heat in this line by friction. A further 20% pressure drop obtained across an adjustable constrictor valve before the oil passes through a heat exchanger and gives up its heat to the hot water circuit. Remaining 5% pressure drop occurs along large bore return line. Lines heavily lagged to limit heat losses to 10-20%.

(v) Controls. Manual controls for loading and off-loading hydraulic circuit, remote bleeding, dis-orienting rotor.

Electrical controls with hydraulic reservoir for eventual autmotaic operation of rotor off-load, rotor disorientation and mechanical brake.

(vi) Instrumentation.

Rotor	Wind speed
Rotor speed	Wind direction
Blade pitch change	Hydraulic oil pressure
Slewing rate	Oil temperature (high)
Tower stresses	Oil temperature (low)
Tower vibration	Oil level
Rotor shaft torque	Oil filter clogging

Whilst the instrumentation is not yet complete, the rotor has been run at modest speeds (at up to about 16 kW), and certain points have already become apparent. The first is that the control of slewing on a two-bladed rotor is very important. Apart from gyroscopic forces during rapid slewing, there is also a tendency to jerkiness due to the difference in angular inertia when the rotor is vertical and when it is horizontal. Almost all small windmills are three-bladed for this reason, and all large windmills (which tend to be two-bladed) have rigorous control of slewing rate. Another problem with large, flexible rotors is that the blades tend to droop in the horizontal position, and this opposes the starting torque of the rotor, though once it is turning, the effect disappears. These and other points have fairly simple engineering solutions.

On the positive side, rotor and pump noise are less than had been expected, and hydraulic load control appears to be particularly effective in controlling the rotor.

The cost of the 18.3m unit in production will probably be less than £20 000 installed, giving a cost per installed kW of £200-250. For a production unit on the Efford site, with prevailing oil, interest and inflation rates and allowances for maintenance etc., the payback period is about 11 years. If the displaced heating source were electricity, this period would shorten to about 5 years. Again, in higher wind regimes the payback period is much reduced (Table 2).

Table 2
PAYBACK PERIODS OF 18.3M HEATING WINDMILL

Mean Annual Wind Speed	Area[1]	Payback Period (Years)	
		vs Oil	vs Electricity
5 m/s	Sheltered upland Britain	17	9
6 m/s	S, W England coastal areas	10	4
	Exposed upland Britain		
7 m/s	W Scotland, W Ireland	7	2
8 m/s	W Isles, W Irish coast	4	1

[1] Higher than average wind speeds exist over smooth, convex hills, and machines can be sited to take advantage of this.

THE FUTURE

Whilst there will always be an interest in small (5m or less) windmills, their limited cost effectiveness will tend to confine them to the windier areas of Britain or to situations where economics is not the prime concern. Larger machines should be applicable to a wider area of the country as soon as quantity production can keep reliability up and cost down.

Application will be heating in the first instance. Addition of a small generator with a constant speed device will be fairly simple, so that a small priority electrical demand can be satisfied with the balance going to heating. Providing the electrical demand is small and can be foregone or met in other ways in a dead calm, no DC/AC conversion or buffer storage should be necessary.

One of the most perfect of all windmill applications is desalination. Storage is not a problem, and fresh water tends to be required on islands where wind power is abundant and fossil fuels are expensive. The Channel Islands, where fresh water is a particular problem, have some of the highest winds in Europe.

The danger in Britain is that a fall in inflation rate (coupled with high interest rates) and the abundance of North Sea oil and gas will make 'alternative' energy sources unattractive again. We would like to be able to contribute to the revival in wind power in particular so that momentum is maintained until the scarcity in fossil fuels becomes really serious.

33 The potential of small-scale waterpower for local use in upland Britain

D G WOOLSTON

LARGE-SCALE WATERPOWER

Large-scale dams do not present such ecological options in power generation as their advocates often imply (Lagler, 1971; Woolston, 1973). The 'amenity' controversy of the 1890's-1950's in Scotland (Lea, 1968) was the aesthetic-emotional beginning of awareness that hydroelectric power generation can be a cause of serious environmental damage. Large dams have also been used as a political tool for disposal of inconvenient populations, eg US Indians, and people at Cunene, Cabora Bassa, and in the Mekong Delta. Flooding and other farming difficulties often result from large dams. The greater disasters of fatal disease and dam-induced earthquakes are not impossible in Britain.

ESTIMATING QUANTITATIVE SMALL-SCALE POTENTIAL

Net output hydroelectricity in Britain is estimated as 16×10^9 kWh/year (Department of Trade and Industry, 1971). This is generally claimed to be a very high proportion of potential, but all plant opportunities under about 250 kW served by catchment areas of less than 50 km² are omitted thus distorting the value of the natural distribution of sites. By tapping all the potential of smaller streams total hydroelectric output could probably be raised to more than 40×10^9 kWh/year (MacKillop, 1972 & 1973). This amount could, for example, supply over 80% of housing energy consumption need. Complete utilisation of streams for the sole use of waterpower or of electricity generation is of course not recommended. Law and commercial interests also unduly favour large-scale exploitation of rivers. Thus the Water Resources Act (HMSO, 1963) penalised the small user with standard charges for water which seem much less crippling to large companies and public authorities. Since mean annual runoff for 50 km^2 would normally be expected to yield minimum flow 0.5 m^3/sec, some quite sizeable power opportunities are being omitted from surveys.

To consider a very modest typical old mill site:

| average head | 4 m | |
| minimum flow | 1 m^3/sec | (from 100 km^2 catchment) |

Then gross power $= \dfrac{40}{3}$ x flow x head $\quad = \quad$ 53.3 metric hp

Or net electrical power $= 6.4 \times 4 \qquad = \quad$ 25.6 kW

These calculations have been made by the closely agreeing formulae of Hamm (1971) and Agnew (1975) respectively. Assumed overall translation in the second case is 65%.

Theoretical estimates as to the available potential should redefine what is considered a 'utilisable' site, and by whom it is utilisable.

(i) Streamflow gauging. The difficulty is that surveying and assessment of potential have always been made for single specific sites (either large or small). When whole areas or river basins are surveyed, assessment is for large-scale potential only. The author knows of no survey of an extensive area for small-scale potential. The most obvious means of estimating this would be widespread streamflow gauging. However, long period runoff records for small streams are extremely rare, usually the work of enthusiasts. It might be suggested that a network of 'people's researchers' should undertake this task, as it clearly will not be done otherwise. Surveys of prevailing states of water ecology in streams could perhaps give a reading of flow and regime most economically. From these surveys a suitably devised ecological yardstick would indicate stream history. An analogous method has been successfully used by Griggs for assessment of sites for windpower (Putnam, 1948).

River flow measurement stations are located only on large streamflows, and are in any case so few as to make proper assessment near impossible. Gauged flow records are now computerised and summarised in the *Surface Water Yearbook* (Water Data Unit, 1974) but only 59% of England and Wales and 48% of Scotland is gauged even once. To supplement these inadequate data, turbines are used as meters.

Where there are large rivers there are also smaller tributaries, and thus flow at measurement stations can be assumed to consist of the sum of all tributaries' flow, minus evaporation and utilisation losses (if known). Ground-water gains to the streambed, depending upon local geology should be included in the calculation. Thus we might have a method for flow calculation for a group of tributaries. Total head is much easier to assess — from a map. Total energy content might be calculated from this information, assuming a certain scale of project on average.

(ii) The historical record. In extreme cases of full power utilisation the tailrace of one plant forms the same watercourse as the headrace of the plant next below. This kind of utilisation is characteristic of the peak of 18th-19th century water-power, and might provide another means of assessing potential. Reconstruction of the historical record has been pioneered by the Society for the Preservation of Ancient Buildings (SPAB), Windmills and Watermills section, and by the International Symposia on Molinology (ISM); but unfortunately their work is from the aspect of industrial archaeology, and corn-milling is heavily emphasised at the expense of other applications. Societies such as the SPAB, and ISM could provide considerable information towards re-instatement of small waterpower, but are not presently so orientated. For example, a survey estimating distribution and capacities of historical plant within an area of intensive utilisation might be generalised over a wider area.

Figure 1 prepared for ISM, gives an indication of areas of greatest historical small waterpower use. The major concentrations are in southern Snowdonia; in Northumberland south of the Cheviot hills; to the south of the Cleveland hills; and over the whole of south and south-east England. The last major concentration is in an area neglected by modern large-scale exploitation, which is unable to make use of smaller heads, and is too land-hungry for a densely populated area. Minor concentrations of old mill sites occur on Dartmoor, Exmoor, Isle of Man and in East Anglia. Upland, not unexpectedly, predominates, since head is more significant to power than flow and thus upland slopes have greater potential than sites of similar flow in lowland areas. Upland runoff may easily be three times as great as lowland.

(iii) Precipitation and evaporation as an indicator. A last method of estimating quantitative potential is to try to use precipitation and evaporation records to indicate runoff. Runoff is a residual of precipitation, once evaporation and transpiration have been allowed for. Once again the network of rainfall and evaporation stations is quite inadequate, and estimates for upland areas are particularly unreliable (Water Data Unit, 1974). Precipitation and evaporation records are neither widespread enough nor of long enough period generally to be of use.

354

Figure 1
CORN WATERMILL SITE DENSITY

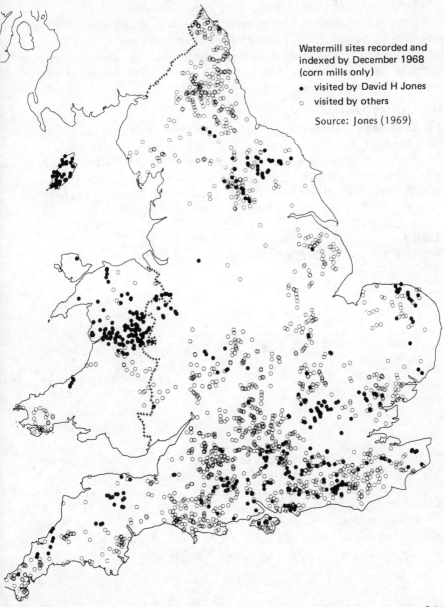

Watermill sites recorded and
indexed by December 1968
(corn mills only)

●   visited by David H Jones

○   visited by others

Source: Jones (1969)

Rather than attempting the almost impossible task of full quantitative assessment, perhaps it would be more constructive to build a few new small waterpower projects in typical locations, regarding the exercise as tapping the free power of the hydrological cycle, rather than another exercise in extracting the last drop of efficiency — a concept more appropriate to fossil fuel energy.

Calculations of available waterpower potential, large- or small-scale, will in any case probably be outdated by climate modifications in the near future. These may occur naturally, may be 'inadvertently' man-made, or be engineered. An era of interstate 'cloud-rustling' has just begun in the USA, and international weather warefare is already practised (Shapley, 1974).

UPLAND HYDROLOGY

The outstanding characteristics of natural upland hydrology are that rainfall exceeds evaporation in every month of the year on average; and that whilst rainfall increases with elevation, evaporation decreases. Both these factors provide a very high runoff favourable to waterpower, but cause waterlogging of land to damage agricultural possibilities. In addition, peat moors have great ability to store and slowly release water, thus stabilising stream regimen.

Table 1

MONTHLY EVAPORATION AND RAINFALL AT DONCASTER AND WOODHEAD (mm)

	MONTHS											
	I	II	III	IV	V	VI	VII	VIII	IX	X	XI	XII
Evaporation	2.5	10	23	46	71	84	74	56	46	23	7.5	5
Doncaster: rainfall	46	41	41	48	68.5	58.5	68.5	79	46	91.5	50	73.5
Woodhead: rainfall	104	89	94	79	86	94	107	112	117	148	130	117

Relatively high head is characteristic of upland streams, and in the steeper and less pervious watersheds flow is unfortunately extremely flashy and prone to flooding. Catastrophic upland thunderstorms, in which local falls of rain of 150-200 mm have occured, must be taken into account.

Whereas impounding reservoirs for large-scale projects nearly always submerges the most fertile lower parts of an upland valley, land submerged by smaller projects is likely to be higher and of less agricultural value. In addition, if fertile land is

356

to be submerged, small-scale projects can more easily be made productive of fish as well as power.

SMALL WATERPOWER APPLICATIONS

Power supply servicing of remote communities is essentially autonomous. The current inflation-dominated arguments for renewable energy sources are strong. Even more pressing non-economic arguments for small waterpower include conservation of the environment; growing desire for local independence; and re-organisation of control of industrial work and produce. Small waterpower has a high potential for a variety of socially useful and environmentally-suited small industries to be worked off upland streams. Technical appearances could resemble certain feudal, ancient Chinese, or industrial revolution practices as discussed below; but the new mills would be operated under an informal system of co-operative self-management.

The use of waterpower for electricity generation is not so favourable on a small scale. When heat or mechanical energy are locally required, electricity is a wasteful intermediate stage, with a total translation of about 50%. Unless standard domestic, industrial and farm machinery is to be converted from the normal alternating current by replacement of motors, then the flow of water must be controlled by a governor — as a cybernetic device, this is characteristically expensive, often more than turbine and generator costs together. Alternatively, electrical machinery should be specially manufactured to suit autonomous direct current generation; this might be an appropriate product for small upland industrial workshops, along with manufacture of small turbines.

It is not generally realised to what an extent the historical watermill, and its close relative the windmill were automated by the peak of their development (Reynolds, 1970). Automatic tentering of millstones ensured even grinding. There were safety and warning devices for exhaustion of grain supply, exhaustion of water, and rise in head-water level. Flow was regulated by means of a servo-mechanism to the sluice-gate. As late as 1924 the Dutch Government Aeronautical Service tested 'Dekkerising' of windmills, a streamlining process which tripled output and allowed operation on 364 out of 365 days. Even in 1950 in the south of Scotland there were many water-powered textile mills, corn mills, saw mills and engineering workshops driven by traditional wheels of the type to which the last major improvements were made by Fairburn in the 1740's. If there had not been a general shift towards centralised electrical generation of power, such mills might not have been neglected, and improvement of their design might have continued. Now that centralised servicing is being re-examined on both economic and environmental grounds, perhaps the interrupted development may continue, and lead to a technology with a stronger feel for both natural and human scale.

357

A water-powered metal works is kept in working order at Abbeydale, Sheffield. The production of scythes and other agricultural implements ceased there in 1933 but during 1939/1945 the plant again became 'economic', and was worked to produce steel helmets for the Army. Carpentry workshops might be driven off turbines linked to saws, drills, lathes and sanders. The Tula Arms Factory is also a fine example of a dynamic and inventive people's technology of small water-power (Britkin, 1967).

Low power availability does not need to be a serious limitation in small work-shops, since all machines are not required simultaneously, and demand can, to a large extent, be adjusted to suit available pondage. Such adjustment ought to be more easily made under more highly motivated self-managed working conditions. Thus the occasionally erratic availability of power could mean that workers would simply leave the plant when the dam runs dry, leaving the pond to refill overnight.

Table 2
APPLICATIONS OF SMALL-SCALE WATERPOWER

Cornmills	—	threshing, grinding, flour milling.
Textile manufacture	—	weaving, fulling cloth.
Water pumping	—	drainage, irrigation, cleaning and cooling.
Sawmills	—	timber reduction, shingle and planing mills.
Blast furnace	—	bellows, in eg steel or glass works.
Lathes	—	metal and wooden pipes.
Dynamo	—	electricity for home, farm, village, industry.
Trip hammer	—	forges, crushing gravel and ores.
Power shears	—	metal farm- and hand-tool manufacture.
Tumbling	—	mixing concrete, soils, animal feeds.
Rolling mills	—	paper, metals.
Grinding	—	metal farm- and hand-tool manufacture.
Winding and drawing	—	wire and rope making.
Mortar mill	—	grinding powders.

not via wheel :

intermittent counterpoise	—	tilt-hammer forge, crushing, pumping.

Source: Needham (1965)

The main mechanical applications of small waterpower were in farm, craft workshop, and light industrial use. Stationary farm machinery is suitable, such as grinding and pumping. Plunger-pumps, traditionally wind-powered, are simple and reliable for irrigation purposes; but larger capacity centrifugal pumps can also be used. Two types of typically intermediate technology machinery are suitable in farming:

(i)   where absence of operating troubles is important, solid long-life machines are best;

(ii) where cheapness in first cost is essential, simple self-built low technology or scrap re-cycling devices are underused at present.

A kind of low technology automation is found in such machines as the Persian or Chinese noria, or wheel-of-pots (Needham, 1965). From a noria, pumping in the streamflow by which it is itself driven, a flume leads to storage and a gravity-feed irrigation system. A ship-mill, which is like a permanently moored free-wheeling paddle-steamer, can be operated as a small 'run-of-river' power unit. There will be little maintenance, very low initial cost, and little or no disturbance to other users or to natural streamflow and ecology, since there is no necessity for a dam. Colladon's current wheel (on the River Rhone in 1865) and Ombredane's electric generating set mounted on a raft are similar floating projects, requiring no dam. Cheap and relocatable small dams have been used recently in Russia, and these are made from tensioned, reinforced tarpaulins, anchored to the banks and streambed. A revival of the crafts of timber and crib dam building would not be out of place, either environmentally or aesthetically.

A RE-CYCLING WATER ECONOMY

Self-contained monastic communities, with characteristic economy, made maximum use of available streamflow (Luckhurst, undated). Water taken in a leat from the river backed-up behind the dam to form a pond used for fish-farming. The flow was next used to drive a cornmill and sieve grain. Thence to the vats for brewing, and to the kitchens, from whence to the laundry to drive fullers' hammers. Leaving here it was used in the tannery, and finally to flush away refuse. With modern knowledge of intensive aquaculture without poisons, and sensible application of hygiene, it ought to be possible to improve further on this monastic model of water economy. Particularly, fish-farming by small-scale ecosystem polyculture has been favourably investigated by McLarney et al (1976) at the New Alchemy Institute, Mass., USA. The rich possibilities for a new kind of autonomous rural-based community are alluring to all concerned with developing the full natural and human potential of the land. Unfortunately, despite recent appearances to the contrary, there is no basic change of heart by those who control the present systems of production of food and energy. The easy social justification of their work by such as the New Alchemy Institute in terms of increased world protein production is of absolutely no avail, so long as control remains in the present hands.

Figure 2
HOME-CONSTRUCTED PLANT

— on a Welsh farm (above) — old binder wheel and
axle shaft and gearing from old mowing machine
— on a Scottish farm (below) — old cart wheels and a
car dynamo.

  Source: Sczelcun (undated)

corn mill

corn mill

forge

rolling mill

tannery

grinding

snuff mill

corn mill

corn mill

Figure 3
WATERMILLS ON RIVER PORTER, SHEFFIELD
Source: Miller (1936)

Figure 4
COLLADON'S CURRENT WHEEL
(after an exhibit in the Science Museum)

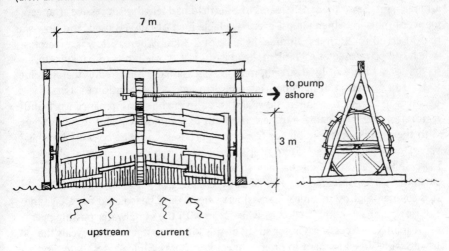

upstream   current

Figure 5
OMBREDANE'S FLOATING HYDROELECTRIC PLANT
(after inventor's drawing)

INTERCONNECTED PLANT

An integrated water economy between different plant is also possible. Thus watercourses between plant on the same stream can be successive or parallel in arrangement. Several of the streams of Sheffield had lengthy successive arrangements of mills, in which almost every available inch of fall was used, and flow was re-utilised up to 20 times within a distance of 2-3 km. Whereas flow is a factor which can be re-used at each plant, head is subject to the limits of backing-up, so that on a highly utilised stream, mills are occasionally rendered inoperable due to the full operation of neighbouring mills' storage. An association of users becomes necessary to regulate flow, and this also enables maintenance work and restoration of storm damage to be carried out in common. Upland stream valleys, with their many sites suitable for few other purposes, could be colonised in this way. Developers of large waterpower sources have used interconnected plant to increase firm, and for load-sharing between plant. Complexes of interconnected small mills were operated (eg at Blae Beck, Grassington, in the Yorkshire Dales). It is claimed that by this means any single wheel could be isolated to receive the full flow, and any combination of wheels run with the same water passing over all of them in succession. Closer study of this kind of arrangement reveals the usual savings in equipment in inter-connected systems. Sluice-gates, dams and watercourses are fewer, although aqueducts may be necessary where watercourses must intersect due to topographical or topological restrictions. Further, to increase firm, the principle of pumped storage may be introduced into the layout. This will be cheaper and simpler if turbines of reversible type are used.

To the shared economy of power supplies could be joined an exchange economy of product, between communities operating plant.

RIGHTS AND INTERESTS IN STREAMS AND RIVERS

A clear distinction should be made between consumptive, potentially pollutive uses of water (such as irrigation and industry, which decrease quantity and/or quality of flow) and non-consumptive uses (such as navigation and small waterpower). The Water Resources Act (HMSO, 1963) makes no such distinction, but imposes a kind of indiscriminate 'window tax' on all users of water from streams and rivers. There is a case to be made for categorising large-scale waterpower as a partially consumptive use, and perhaps for banning it completely.

Interest in streams and rivers is essentially pandemic. Current usage however places minority industrial interests as custodians of water, attempting to 'supply' and exploit a resource which, without their intervention would be a natural dependence, as free as the air. As the natural limits to industrial growth become more and more obvious, comparative evaluation of 'rights' of access to water becomes more difficult for governments to undertake. In the context of a large-

Figure 6
'BACKING-UP' ARRANGEMENT

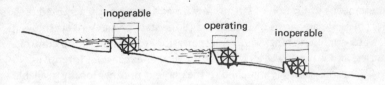

Figure 7
INTERCONNECTED PLANT ARRANGEMENTS

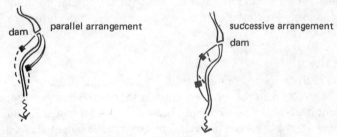

Figure 8
ARRANGEMENT OF MULTIPLY-INTERCONNECTED PLANT

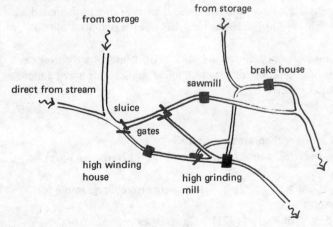

scale industrial base, all interests can no longer be satisfied. Bureaucratic delay in settlement of disputes typically causes uncertainty among local people, and resultant blighting of an area.

Full simultaneous utilisation of streamflow for all the presently accepted uses has been reached in many areas of Britain — and the state of many rivers shows it. Irrigation, water-supply, fishing, water transportation, navigation, flood control, recreation uses, and waterpower all clamour for further expansion. Intensive small-scale utilisation, carefully matched to the context of other locally available renewable energy and food resources, could turn a precarious water situation into a sustainable future.

Waterpower has inherent potential but its utilisation in practice is severely limited by the current social and political system. Any modern attempt to restore and possibly improve upon earlier small waterpower practice must expect to encounter the jealousy of greater forces, such as state authorities and hydroelectric companies. These forces must bear the responsibility for having, in the past, broken up many syndicates of users and are unlikely, in the future, to favour their re-establishment.

SUMMARY

The qualitative potential of many small waterpower plants on upland streams would be greater than that of a few much larger ones. Primary evidence for this statement is the historical record of watermilling, and recent environmental testimony against large dam projects. The quantitative potential of small-scale products, though difficult to assess, is by no means insignificant. Control and continued development of small waterpower projects must be passed into the hands of the only people qualified to understand their ambience: the immediate local population. By this means the full natural and human potential will be realised.

Without the necessity for matching the National Grid, and where power can be used at the point of generation, direct mechanical applications may be more efficient than electricity generation.

REFERENCES

Agnew, P W (1975)   Personal communication.

Bennett, R & Elton, J (1898)   *History of cornmilling.*   Liverpool: Simpkin Marshall.

Britkin, A S (1967)   *Craftsmen of Tula.*   Jerusalem: Israel Programme for Scientific Translation.

Department of Trade and Industry (1971)   *Digest of Energy Statistics.* London: HMSO.

Grover, N C & Harrington, A W (1949)   *Stream flow.*   New York: Dover.
HMSO (1963)   *Water Resources Act.*   London: HMSO.
Hamm, H W (1971)   *Low-cost development of small waterpower sites.*
New York: Volunteers in Technical Assistance.
Jones, D H (1969)   Water-powered cornmills of England, Wales and Isle of Man.
In: Jespersen, D H (Ed).   *Transactions of the 2nd International Symposium
on Molinology.*   Lyngby, Denmark: ISM.
Lagler, K F (1971)   Ecological effects of hydroelectric dams. In: Berkowitz, D A
& Squires, A M (Eds.)   *Power generation and environmental change:
Symposium of the Committee on Environmental Alteration, American
Association for Advancement of Science.*   Boston: MIT Press.
Luckhurst, D (undated)   *Monastic watermills.*   London: Society for Preservation
of Ancient Buildings.
Lea, K J (1968)   Hydroelectric power developments and landscape in the highlands
of Scotland.   *Scottish Geographical Magazine,*   **84**, 239-255.
MacKillop, A (1972)   Low energy housing.   *The Ecologist,*   **2**, (12), 4-10.
MacKillop, A (1973)   Personal communication.
McLarney, W O et al (1976)   Aquaculture.   In: Merrill, R (Ed.)   *Radical
agriculture.*   New York: Harper & Row.
Miller, W T (1936)   *Watermills of Sheffield.*   (unpublished).
Needham, J (1965)   *Science and civilisation in China.*   Cambridge University
Press.
Pearsall, W H (1950)   *Mountains and moorlands.*   London: Collins.
Putnam, P C (1948)   *Power from the wind.*   New York: Van Nostrand.
Reynolds (1970)   *Windmills and watermills.*   London: Hugh Evelyn.
Sczelcun, S (undated)   *Survival Scrapbook 5: Energy.*   Brighton: Unicorn.
Shapley, D (1974)   Weather warfare: Pentagon concedes 7-year Vietnam effort.
Science,   **184**, 1059-61.
Water Data Unit (1974)   *Surface Water Yearbook, 1966-1970.*   London: HMSO.
Woolston, D G (1973)   Big dams cast long shadows.   *Undercurrents,* **5**.
Revised and rewritten as *Unsolicited advice to the International Commission
on Large Dams.*   (unpublished).
Woolston, D G (1974)   Water running wild: people's waterpower.   *Undercurrents,*
6.
Woolston, D G (1976)   Waterpower: essentially co-operative energy. In:
Harper, P & Boyle, G (Eds.).   *Radical technology.*   London: Wildwood.

34 Future possibilities for fuel cropping in upland Britain

D I THOMAS & J E G GOOD

INTRODUCTION

Without exception all governments see the solution to perceived energy problems principally in highly capital intensive developments of coal, nuclear power and lower quality reservoirs of oil, not only to replace existing supplies, but also to provide for planned growth in demand. The capital intensity of these projected developments is orders of magnitude higher per delivered unit of energy than traditional direct fuel technologies (Lovins, 1976; Carosso, 1975), and of such a scale that many observers, such as the strategic planners of the Shell Group in London (Lovins, 1976), have concluded that no major countries outside the Persian Gulf can afford these centralised high technologies on a scale large enough to run a country.

A general acceptance of this fact of life would rapidly induce an ethos for the very careful use of remaining energy resources and the conservation of capital and materials. Parsimony would not be a formula for translating finite energy resources into inexhaustible energy supplies and ultimately all fossil-reservoirs of hydrocarbon would be phased out as energy sources. There would be mounting pressure to devise technologies for the capture of the various manifestations of natural energy flow ie the tides, the wind, hydropower and the sun. Fuel cropping is a potential energy source deserving conscientious research.

FUEL CROPPING

Wood growing is one of the most energy efficient means of capturing energy. Although agriculture offers gross annual yields equal to or in excess of those which may reasonably be anticipated from silviculture, due to agriculture's requirement for annual management and harvesting it is energetically inferior. In present-day forestry employing relatively intensive silvicultural programmes, approximately 5% of the harvested energy is consumed in harvesting and management (Jaatinen, 1976; Nilsson, 1976; Smith & Johnson, 1977); this compares favourably with other present-day energy technologies. Aside from harvesting the biggest potential energy consumer in silviculture is nitrogen fertilisation; the second is mechanical site preparation (Smith & Johnson, 1977).

On a dry weight basis, the heat values of wood range from 18.5 to 21 MJ/kg compared with 42 MJ/kg for No 6 fuel oil, 31.5 MJ/kg for bituminous coal and 43 MJ/kg for natural gas (Sarkanen, 1976). Resinous conifers and woods with significant oil content, such as cedars, give higher heating values such as 21 MJ/kg for Ponderosa Pine and 22.5 MJ/kg for Western Red Cedar (National Academy of Sciences, 1976). Freshly cut wood has a high moisture content (40 to 50% on a dry weight basis) which reduces the heat value by as much as 70%; a kilogram of wood with a calorific value of 20 MJ/kg would yield 14 MJ at 15% moisture content (National Academy of Sciences, 1976). The net heat value of freshly cut wood is usually about 7 MJ/kg and it would be very highly desirable to refine seasoning techniques for the parsimonious removal of moisture close to the point of harvest.

Although wood has a lower calorific value than coal and petroleum, it is nevertheless fairly attractive as an energy source which can be economically shipped a considerable distance (Table 1). A 5 000 mile (3 107 km) sea journey with road and rail links at each end would consume less than 10% of the delivered energy.

Table 1
TRANSPORTATION COSTS FOR WOOD

Rail	(1)	0.43 MJ/tonne-km
Road	(1)	1.80 MJ/tonne-km
Waterway	(1)	0.44 MJ/tonne-km
Marine	(2)	0.16 MJ/tonne-km

1 tonne dry wood $\equiv 19.5 \times 10^3$ MJ

Sources: 1 Hirst & Moyers (1976)
         2 Leach & Slesser (1976)

Should fuel cropping in Britain prove a viable practice, then due to a continuing pressure for good quality agricultural land, it would be obliged to exploit the less productive land area, which in general means the uplands. It is quite possible that limited forestry developments may be introduced into lowland areas, possibly to the mutual benefit of silviculture and agriculture, but the contribution to a national energy supply would be small compared with that emanating from the uplands; agricultural waste and organic waste in general may provide a significantly larger contribution than lowland forestry (Moorcroft, 1974) *Spartina anglica* grown on Britain's intertidal mud-flats has been proposed as a fuel crop (Heslop-Harrison, 1975). Unfortunately the area is limited at 12 000 ha (Ranwell, 1967) and there are the energy costs of annual cropping to contend with.

Forestry in Britain currently provides pulp and structural material, and at present there are large importations of these commodities. In some future semi steady-state economy there may be considerable scope for moderating this demand, particularly in an economic system converted to conservation and recycling practices. The energy costs of producing timber are low compared with steel and aluminium (1.5 GJ/tonne compared with 9.6 GJ/tonne for steel and 60 GJ/tonne for aluminium (Zerbe, 1971)) making it an attractive structural material, although demand for fuel crops is not automatically at variance with this demand for structural timber and pulp; the scope for recycling pulp and timber is large and ultimately discarded pulp and timber could contribute to fuel stocks.

SILVICULTURE AND TREE IMPROVEMENT

Britain is well placed to consider the potential for growing trees for fuel. We have one of the most favourable climates in the temperate regions for tree growth and many years of experience in overcoming the problems posed by our exposed upland planting sites with their often degraded soils. However, while land available for afforestation remains largely restricted to the uplands the possibilities for exploiting the systems of intensive culture based on broadleaved tree species of the type devised recently in the US (McAlpine *et al*, 1967; Szego *et al*, 1972; De Bell, 1972; Rose, 1977) will be small. Such systems, involving coppicing, short rotations and frequent routine management require sheltered sites on good to medium soils and with good access if the returns are to justify the costs (although these constraints may relax in a different economic climate). Of course if better land became available for afforestation then there is every reason to believe that similar increases in yield over those obtained by conventional forestry methods could be achieved here as in the US trials. Even on the poorer sites it might be worth considering trial plantations of species such as red alder *(Alnus rubra)* which has been found to produce exceptional yields (average in British Columbia 38 dry tonnes/ha/year) under widely varying site conditions elsewhere.

Improvements in yields of conifer crops, which are likely to remain the major forest type in most of upland Britain, could be substantial as a result of existing and predicted research advances in tree physiology and tree breeding. Until recently tree breeders have been severely handicapped in their aims by the long life-cycle of forest trees and the frequency of juvenile periods which may extend for the first 10-30 years of life and during which flowering may be scarce or totally absent. It has often been necessary to graft scions of older trees on to seedling rootstocks in order to bring selections together for crossing. A further complication is that many mature trees or grafts do not flower annually.

Considerable progress has been made recently in identifying factors affecting flowering, and in some cases techniques are now being developed for reliable stimulation of heavy flowering under field conditions so that controlled fertilisation and seed production can be effected on a regular basis (Longman, 1975). In some species rooted cuttings have been induced to flower in glasshouses and growth chambers soon after potting up, thus allowing precise control by the tree breeder. Early flower induction in birches is being used in Finland for large scale crossing to produce improved seed (Lepistö, 1973) and it is estimated that by 1985 birch cultivars will be producing 100% more timber than the unimproved species. There is no reason to doubt that similar improvements can and will be achieved in other forest tree species.

At a more controlled level than those already described, tissue culture offers the possibilities of even greater advances. It is already possible to raise plantlets of a number of broadleaved and coniferous species from young embryos and from bud primordia and nodal stem cuttings on defined artificial media (Winton, 1970; Sommer et al, 1974, 1975; Brown & Sommer, 1975). It should soon also be possible to raise plantlets from single somatic cells in liquid culture so that within a few years we will be able to clone or reproduce vegetatively many of our forest trees en masse. This opens up the possibility for producing any number of the best of these species as and when required. Of course such developments must be used carefully and adequate precautions taken to ensure reasonable genetic variability in our forests if the pest and disease problems associated with monocultures in other crop plants are to be avoided. However, similar risks have been an acceptable part of fruit production for many years.

Tissue culture offers additional advantages to those of rapid cloning just discussed. The genetic base can be broadened by: selecting for advantageous mutations in cultured cells; and by controlled artificial hybridization (Winton et al, 1974; Brown, 1976). If reliable methods could be developed for screening gametic (haploid) plantlets for vigor, disease and pest resistance and other desirable traits, much of the need for expensive and time-consuming field trials of the conventional type might be removed. Promising genotypes could be recovered from cultures and used in subsequent breeding programmes to obtain hybrid vigor. Such hybrids could then be mass produced by cloning. Again, it will soon be possible to hybridize cells from different species and even perhaps from different genera together followed by plantlet production and screening for desirable traits.

It will be seen that the future for fuel cropping in the uplands looks brighter than some present analyses may suggest. The potential for increased yields as a result of tree selection, tree breeding and modified management procedures are considerable, doubling of present yields being quite conceivable in the short term for some species with the possibility of considerably greater improvements.

ENERGY CONVERSION

In general all techniques for upgrading fuel quality into more portable and more convenient forms incur energy penalties (Maugh, 1972; Goldstein, 1975) of about 50% or more eg conversion to methanol and ethanol or oil by pyrolisis. Conversion to electricity incurs a 70% penalty for remote power stations where the improved efficiency of combined heat and power cycles cannot be exploited. It will therefore be advantageous wherever possible to use wood in its original form eg wood-burning stoves, boilers and power-stations.

YIELD AND ENERGY BUDGET

The general yield class of Sitka spruce grows at about 11 tonnes/ha/year (Busby, 1974) if suitable allowance is made for complete tree utilisation (Keays, 1974). Let us, for the sake of demonstration in the following exploratory arithmetic, estimate that the silvicultural and tree improvements mentioned above will double this yield to 22 tonnes/ha/year.

Let us make the following assumptions about potential forest area so that the maximum yield from tree fuel cropping can be ascertained. Suppose that a combination of population decline and enhanced agricultural husbandry will, in say 100 years, permit all land between the 120 m and 600 m contours to be occupied by forests. The very approximate area of this land is about 6 000 000 ha (based on a computer summation for England and Wales (Ball & Williams, 1977) and visual assessment of the relative contribution of Scotland and Northern Ireland).

Table 2 indicates the magnitude of energy capture for potential renewable energy sources.

Ryle (1977) has hypothesised that a British economy could function on an annual energy budget (electrical equivalent) of 2.1×10^9 GJ, albeit by introducing quite radical changes in the manner in which society is organised, particularly in the sphere of eliminating wasteful practices. Although 2.1×10^9 GJ is only about 20% of existing gross consumption, when used carefully in association with heat pumps, combined heat and power converters and superior

Table 2
CAPTURE OF RENEWABLE ENERGY SOURCES

Hydropower	(1)	0.13×10^9 GJ (electrical)
Windpower	(2)	0.96×10^9 GJ (electrical)
Solar collectors	(2)	0.3×10^9 GJ (electrical)
Fuel cropping		2.5×10^9 GJ (thermal)
Organic waste	(3)	0.3×10^9 GJ (thermal)
Total		1.39×10^9 GJ (electrical)
		2.8×10^9 GJ (thermal)

Sources: 1 Mackillop (1972)
2 Ryle (1977)
3 Author's estimate of all organic waste at 50% conversion efficiency.

insulation, it is equivalent to a large fraction of present-day energy consumption. Furthermore fuel crops could make a major contribution.

It may be generally believed that there is little urgency to perfect silviculture for fuel cropping, because our reserves of coal are expected to last some hundreds of years at existing extraction rates. Public acceptance of the notion that land is one of our most valuable long-term resources, may, however, produce pressures which discourage the despoiling of remaining productive land, especially if there are practicable and demonstrated, sustainable alternatives. Perhaps it is not too soon to explore the potential of fuel cropping in the uplands.

REFERENCES

Ball, D F & Williams, W M (1977)   *The Uplands of England and Wales — Land characteristics and classification.*   Bangor: Institute of Terrestrial Ecology.
De Bell, D S (1972)   Potential productivity of dense young thickets of red alder. *Forestry Research Note, Crown Zellerbach,* No 2.
Brown, C L (1976)   Forests as energy sources in the year 2000.   *Journal of Forestry,* **74,** 7-12.
Brown, C L & Sommer, H (1975)   *An atlas of gymnosperms cultured in vitro: 1924-1974.*   Macon: Gainesville Forestry Research Council.
Busby, R J N (1974)   *Forest site yield guide to upland Britain.*   Forestry Commission Forest Record, 97. Edinburgh: Forestry Commission.
Carosso, M et al (1975)   *The energy supply planning model, PB-245 382 and PB-245 383.*   Springfield, Va: National Technical Information Service, Bechtel Corporation.

Goldstein, I S (1975)   Potential for converting wood into plastics.   *Science,* **189,** 847-852.

Heslop-Harrison, J (1975)   Reforming the cellulose economy.   *New Scientist,* **266.**

Hirst, E & Moyers, J C (1973)   Efficiency of energy use in the United States. *Science,* **179,** 1299-1304.

Jaatimen, E (1976)   Energy accounting in forestry. In: C O Tamm (Ed.) Ecological Bulletins No 21, *Man and the Boreal Forest.*   Copenhagen: Swedish National Science Research Council.

Keays, J L (1974)   Full-tree and complete-tree utilisation for pulp and paper. *Forest Products Journal,* **24,** 11.

Leach, G & Slesser, M (1973)   *Energy equivalents of network inputs to food producing processes.*   University of Strathclyde.

Lepisto, M (1973)   Accelerated birch breeding in plastic greenhouses. *Forestry Chronicle,* **49,** 172-3.

Longman, K A (1975)   Tree biology research and plant propagation. *Proceedings of the International Plant Propagation Society,* **25,** 219-236.

Lovins, A B (1976)   Energy strategy: the road not taken?   *Foreign Affairs,* **55,** 65-96.

MacKillop, A (1972)   Low energy housing. *The Ecologist,* **2,** No 12, 4-10.

Maugh, H T (1972)   Fuel from wastes: a minor energy source.   *Science:* **178,** 599-602.

McAlpine, R L, Brown, C L, Herrick, A M & Ruark, H E (1967)   'Silage' sycamore. *Forest farmer,* **26,** 6-7.

Moorcroft, C (1974)   Plant power.   *Architectural Design,* **44,** 18-29.

National Academy of Sciences (1976)   Fuel from biomass. In: *Renewable Resources for Industrial Materials.* Washington: National Academy of Sciences.

Nilsson, P O (1976)   The energy balance in Swedish forestry. In: C O Tamm (Ed.) Ecological Bulletins No 21,   *Man and the Boreal Forest.*   Copenhagen: Swedish National Science Research Council.

Ranwell, D S (1967)   World resources of *spartina townsendii (sensulato):* economic use of *spartina* marshland.   *Journal of Applied Ecology,* **4,** 239-256.

Rose, D W (1977)   Cost of producing energy from wood in intensive cultures. *Journal of Environmental Management,* **5,** 23-35.

Ryle, Sir Martin (1977)   Economics of alternative energy sources.   *Nature,* **267,** 111-117.

Sarkanen, K V (1976)   Renewable resources for the production of fuels and chemicals.   *Science,* **191,** 773-776.

Smith, D W & Johnson, E W (1977)   Silviculture: highly energy efficient. *Journal of Forestry,* **75,** 208-210.

Sommer, H & Brown, C L (1974)   Plantlet format in pine tissue cultures. *American Journal of Botany*, **61,** supplement 5, 11.

Sommer, H, Brown, C L & Kormanik, P P (1975)   Differentiation of plantlets in longleaf pine (*pinus palustris* Mill.) tissue culture in vitro.   *Botanical Gazette*, **136,** 196-200.

Szego, G C, Fox, J A & Eaton, D R (1972)   *The energy plantation.* Intersociety Energy Conversion Engineering Conference. Seventh Conference Proceedings, Paper 729168.   San Diego, California.

Winton, L (1974)   Shoot and tree production from aspen tissue cultures. *American Journal of Botany*, **57,** 904-909.

Winton, L, Parham, R A, Johnson, M A & Einspahr, D W (1974)   Tree improvement by callus, cell and protoplast culture.   *Journal of the Technical Association of the Pulp and Paper Industry*, **57,** 151-152.

Zerbe, J (1971)   *Forest Products Journal*, **21,** 16.

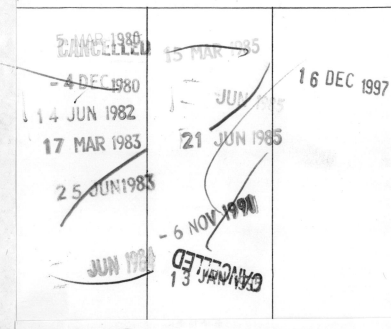